# The Role of Consent in Human Trafficking

Human trafficking is consistently featured on the global political agenda. This book examines the trafficking of adult female victims for sexual exploitation, and specifically the understanding of consent and its influence in establishing the identity and treatment of trafficking victims.

Jessica Elliott argues that when applied to situations of human trafficking, migration and sexual exploitation, the notion of consent presents problems which current international laws are unable to address. Establishing the presence of 'coercion' and a lack of consent can be highly problematic, particularly in situations of human trafficking and illegal prostitution, activities which may be deemed inherently coercive and problematically clandestine.

By examining legal definitions of human trafficking in international instruments and their domestic implementation in different countries, the book explores victimhood in the context of exploitative migration, and argues that no clear line can be drawn between those who have been smuggled, trafficked or 'consensually trafficked' into a situation of exploitation. The book will be of great use and interest to students and researchers of migration law, transnational criminal law and gender studies.

**Jessica Elliott** is a Senior lecturer in law at the University of the West of England, UK.

# The Role of Consent in Human Trafficking

Jessica Elliott

Routledge
Taylor & Francis Group
LONDON AND NEW YORK

First published 2015
by Routledge
2 Park Square, Milton Park, Abingdon, Oxon, OX14 4RN

and by Routledge
711 Third Avenue, New York, NY 10017

*Routledge is an imprint of the Taylor & Francis Group, an informa business*



*British Library Cataloguing in Publication Data*
A catalogue record for this book is available from the British Library

*Library of Congress Cataloging-in-Publication Data*
Elliott, Jessica, author.
The role of consent in human trafficking / Jessica Elliott.
pages cm
Includes bibliographical references and index.
ISBN 978-0-415-81611-3 (hardback) -- ISBN 978-0-203-59481-0 (ebk)
1. Human trafficking--Law and legislation. 2. Consent (Law) 3. Sexual consent. 4. Prostitution--Law and legislation. I. Title.
K5297.E43 2014
345'.025--dc23
2014016357

ISBN: 978-0-415-81611-3 (hbk)
ISBN: 978-0-203-59481-0 (ebk)

Typeset in 10/12 Baskerville MT Pro by
Servis Filmsetting Ltd, Stockport Cheshire

Printed and bound in the United States of America by Publishers Graphics, LLC on sustainably sourced paper.

# Contents

# 1 Introduction

## 1.1 Introduction

Human trafficking has, since the turn of the century, consistently featured on the global political agenda,[1] and recognition of the growing dimensions of this criminal activity has been the catalyst for a host of legal and policy responses aimed at the prevention of trafficking, the prosecution and punishment of traffickers and, more recently, for making provisions for identifying, assisting, supporting and protecting the victims of this phenomenon.

The trade in human beings has flourished as a result of increased economic and social integration, and has been facilitated by the ease of movement of workers, capital and goods, all of which are aided by increasingly sophisticated global networks of communication and transport. One consequence has been the globalisation of certain criminal activities, which has generated its own reaction: 'We are compelled by the globalization of crime to globalize law and law enforcement'.[2] Under this umbrella of globalised law and law enforcement we find the anti-trafficking regime, in the forms of international criminal law and international human rights law, which form part of a global campaign against modern slavery-related practices.

The body of persons engaging in transnational movement includes economic migrants – regular and irregular – students, visitors and asylum seekers. Those entitled to enter for non-economic purposes may abuse their status, or those with economic objectives may present themselves as being in one or another of the categories. Such persons may be subject to deportation and/or criminal proceedings for breach of immigration law or engagement in unlawful activities in the destination state, and will have access to, for example, procedural rights as regards deportation or criminal trial.

This body of persons involved in transnational movement also includes adult

1 Particularly, although not exclusively, over the past decade or so. This is evident through discussion throughout the book of the central anti-trafficking instruments adopted at a United Nations (UN), Council of Europe (CoE) and European Union (EU) level, within that time period.

2 US Senator John Kerry, cited in P Andreas and E Nadelmann *Policing the Globe: Criminalization and Crime Control in International Relations* (Oxford University Press, New York, 2006).

female victims of human trafficking for the purpose of sexual exploitation, the latter being the chief concern of this body of work. As a system of bespoke rights for trafficked victims has been increasingly brought into the anti-trafficking regime,[3] the role of consent – or lack thereof – in human trafficking has become increasingly important in traffick-related debate, and it has become apparent that this element has a significant role to play in terms of establishing who the victims are, and how they should be treated.

The economic attractions of destination states are a significant motivating factor behind the global movement of persons and the individual choice to migrate (through regular or irregular channels). Consequently, the facilitation of illicit, clandestine entry into destination states presents a lucrative opportunity for those who can organise it, and the varying estimates[4] as to the magnitude of this phenomenon and its victims indicate that it is a significant international problem which requires an international response.

## 1.2 Defining trafficking and smuggling

As with all transnational criminal projects, it is necessary to begin with the definition of the prohibited conduct which states are obliged to criminalise in their national legal systems.[5] In order to launch a coherent and cohesive multi-pronged attack on human trafficking, particularly one invoking the criminal law, there is need to reach consensus as to what human trafficking actually is in a legal sense, so that there is clarity as regards both the meaning of 'trafficking in persons', and the obligations placed on state parties to the various agreements and legislation which form the anti-trafficking regime. The most recent international legal definition of 'trafficking in humans' is provided within Article 3 of the United Nations Protocol to Prevent, Suppress and Punish Trafficking in Persons, Especially Women and Children (Trafficking Protocol),[6] and is replicated verbatim in Article 4 of the Council of Europe Convention on Action Against Trafficking in Human Beings (CoE Trafficking Convention).[7] More recently, this definition has been for the

3 See ch 6 for discussion of state obligations as to the identification, assistance, support and protection of victims.

4 See ch 2, Introduction, for estimates as to the magnitude of this clandestine activity.

5 It may also be necessary to recognise that, although the central instruments comprising the international legal anti-trafficking regime for the most part appear to provide for situations of purely 'internal' trafficking as well as those which involve the crossing of international borders, destination states may view the identification of conduct taking place wholly within their territory as a matter exclusively for them to regulate. This may mean that sex trade activities and conditions which are deemed to amount to 'exploitation' may vary between jurisdictions.

6 Article 3 of Protocol to Prevent, Suppress and Punish Trafficking in Persons, Especially Women and Children, Supplementing the United Nations Convention Against Transnational Organized Crime (adopted November 2000 by United Nations General Assembly Resolution A/RES/55/25, entered into force 25 December 2003) (Trafficking Protocol).

7 Article 4 of Council of Europe Convention on Action against Trafficking in Human Beings and its Explanatory Report (adopted 3 May 2005, entered into force 1 February 2008) Warsaw, 16.V.2005, Council of Europe Treaty Series No 197 (CoE Trafficking Convention).

most part replicated verbatim in Article 2 of the Directive 2011/36/EU of the European Parliament and of the Council of 5 April 2011 on preventing and combating trafficking in human beings and protecting its victims[8] with the additional aspect of specifically including begging as a form of 'forced labour or services'. These instruments form the legal 'anti-trafficking regime' as discussed throughout this book, and their respective provisions define human trafficking in the following way:

> 'Trafficking in persons' shall mean the recruitment, transportation, transfer, harbouring or receipt of persons, by means of the threat or use of force or other forms of coercion, of abduction, of fraud, of deception, of the abuse of power or of a position of vulnerability or of the giving or receiving of payments or benefits to achieve the consent of a person having control over another person, for the purpose of exploitation.
>
> Exploitation shall include, at a minimum, the exploitation of the prostitution of others or other forms of sexual exploitation, forced labour or services,[9] slavery or practices similar to slavery, servitude or the removal of organs.

This definition has taken significant and at times controversial steps in clarifying what human trafficking is in a legal sense. The definition is comprised of three elements – the 'action', the 'means' and the 'purpose' (of exploitation), all of which must be present in order for the activity in question to constitute human trafficking. The 'action' element is characterised by the 'recruitment, transportation, transfer, harbouring or receipt of persons'. The 'means' is 'threat or use of force or other forms of coercion, of abduction, of fraud, of deception, of the abuse of power or of a position of vulnerability or of the giving or receiving of payments or benefits to achieve the consent of a person having control over another person', and the 'purpose' is 'exploitation', the meaning of which is expanded upon within the provision above. These terms of 'action', 'means' and 'purpose' will be used henceforth to refer to each component element of the tripartite trafficking process. When referring to the definition of human trafficking throughout the book, this will always be taken to refer to the above-mentioned definition unless explicitly stated otherwise.

From the outset, trafficking must be distinguished from smuggling. There can be a tendency to view trafficking through a lens of immigration offences, thereby effectively treating it as something closer to smuggling than trafficking, which is an incorrect approach.[10] Smuggling is defined by the Protocol against the Smuggling of Migrants by Land, Sea and Air (the Smuggling Protocol) as:

8 Article 2 of Directive 2011/36/EU of the European Parliament and of the Council of 5 April 2011 on preventing and combating trafficking in human beings and protecting its victims, and replacing Council Framework Decision 2002/629/JHA [2001] OJ L101/1 (EU 2011 Directive).

9 Here, the EU 2011 Directive includes the words 'including begging'.

10 Home Affairs Committee 'Sixth Report: The trade in human beings: human trafficking in the UK' (2009) para 86.

> … the procurement, in order to obtain, directly or indirectly, a financial or other material benefit, of the illegal entry of a person into a State Party of which the person is not a national or a permanent resident.[11]

The trafficking/smuggling divide is dealt with in Chapter 2 and is material to the understanding of how we classify 'victims' in the context of forced and voluntary migration. Where a person has been smuggled, there is no formally recognised 'victim'. Smuggling is viewed as a consensual process (correctly or otherwise) and so the classification of a putative victim as trafficked, smuggled or otherwise plays a pivotal role in determining what happens to that person on discovery in the destination state, or in transit. This book will argue that the perceived 'neat' legal divide between the two categories is in fact anything but, and that instead there is a spectrum of persons on the voluntary/involuntary smuggled/trafficked scale, a body of whom are being failed by the current system(s) in place.

## 1.3 The role of consent

The current international legal definition of human trafficking adds the following specific caveat that:

> The consent of a victim of trafficking in persons to the intended exploitation set forth in subparagraph (a) of this article shall be irrelevant where any of the means set forth in subparagraph (a) have been used.[12]

No such qualification was included in early traffick-specific instruments, which tended toward defining 'trafficking in persons' as transportation of women for the purpose of exploitation of prostitution, regardless of any consideration of consent.[13] The inclusion of a 'lack of consent' element in current accepted international legal definition has been the subject of some debate,[14] and has been the catalyst for this book.

We can see therefore that the trafficking definition makes it clear that some form of 'means' is necessary to vitiate consent or deem it irrelevant where adult victims are concerned. Lee asserts that:

11 Article 3 of Protocol against the Smuggling of Migrants by Land, Sea and Air, Supplementing the United Nations Convention against Transnational Organised Crime (adopted November 2000 by United Nations General Assembly Resolution A/RES/55/25, entered into force 28 January 2004) (Smuggling Protocol).

12 UN Trafficking Protocol art 3(b); CoE Trafficking Convention art 4(b); EU 2011 Directive art 2(4).

13 Early anti-trafficking legislation is considered at various points in ch 3, but see, in particular, section 3.2 ff.

14 See, for example, K Abramson 'Beyond consent, toward safeguarding human rights: implementing the United Nations Trafficking Protocol' (2003) 44 *Harvard International Law Journal* 473; B Balos 'The wrong way to equality: privileging consent in the trafficking of Women for sexual exploitation' (2004) 27 *Harvard Women's Law Journal* 137; J Doezma 'Who gets to choose? Coercion, consent and the UN Trafficking Protocol' (March 2002) 10(1) *Gender and Development* 20–27.

> … dichotomies of 'legal' vs 'illegal' migration, 'trafficking' vs 'smuggling', and consent vs use of force and deception within the trafficking debate may be artificial and unhelpful; they draw attention away from the broader context of exploitation, patterns and processes of exclusion, and complex conditions of migratory movements within and beyond borders.[15]

Potentially, then, a recasting of consent and victimhood in a trafficking and exploitative migration context is needed. As will be seen, lack of consent plays a pivotal role in the determination of who is and who is not a victim of human trafficking, and consequently what rights and protections they are or are not entitled to. Consent is an elastic concept, which can be perceived in a variety of ways. In stating that consent to exploitation is irrelevant where the 'means' have been employed, the wording of the definition clearly recognises the potential for consensual exploitation to take place. It is submitted at this point that this book recognises that an individual can consent to being exploited, and essentially argues that the 'lack of consent' requirement creates a false dichotomy between consent and coercion and that this, along with the effect of economic coercion,[16] creates a 'grey area' category of persons who fall somewhere on the spectrum between trafficked and smuggled.

When referring to a 'spectrum' of trafficking/smuggling or consent/coercion in this body of work, it should be noted at this point that this is a descriptive device to help elucidate the range of considerations that might go toward determining whether or not any particular decision (of the victim) might be said to be autonomous but that, in making legal determinations – for example – 'Is X a trafficker? Is Y a victim?', it will always be necessary to come down on one side of the line or the other. Has the prosecution shown that there was no consent? Can it be shown that the woman did not, in fact, consent? There can be no spectrum of convictions, only guilty or not guilty but the issue for consideration here is that there might be (and indeed it is argued that there is) a range of victims, of whom the most favoured are victims of trafficking, the next, 'victims' in a 'grey area' and those who are perhaps not victims at all, i.e. smuggled migrant workers.

The current terminology used in defining human trafficking places great emphasis, then, on lack of consent and the presence of some form of coercion, or other 'means'. The 'lack of consent' element is therefore a condition precedent to identifying a victim of human trafficking, and it is here that the difficulty lies. If it is to be accepted that consent (or lack thereof) is relevant in the context of human trafficking – and therefore the trade in women for sold sex – then this renders it difficult to determine who are, and who are not, victims of human trafficking, and leaves those who may have consented (or for whom there is no objective evidence of coercion) in a state of limbo; they have been more than smuggled (at least in a moral, if not in a legal sense), but less than trafficked.

15 M Lee *Trafficking and Global Crime Control* (Sage 2011) 10.

16 See ch 7 for discussion of the role of 'economic coercion of circumstances' in the making – by a migrant – of the decision to migrate, and what this might mean for the migrant.

'Lack of consent' and 'coercion' are central to the anti-trafficking regimes but they are inherently elusive of definition and difficult in terms of application. Consideration of both (consent/coercion) will be a central concern of this book, including the taxing matter of the effect of severe and pressing economic circumstances.[17] A proportion of those whose movement is facilitated by people smugglers or 'migration facilitators' will travel in a fully informed and voluntary manner. They may have formed their own expectations about what to expect in the destination state. The facilitators may have presented an utterly false view of what the prospects will be in the destination state, the typical example being a promise of work in, say, the catering trade when in reality the person involved is destined for the sex trade. In even more extreme cases, the person will have been taken abroad against her will, invariably to severe conditions, typically some form of exploitation.

Apart from direct coercion of the individual by a trafficker, there may be 'coercion by circumstances', particularly economic disadvantage. It is necessary to consider whether or not this contextual coercion may amount to pressure of the kind which makes any subsequent transportation trafficking, rather than mere smuggling into better economic conditions. In the latter case, the economic coercion will have been central to the transaction but, in the former, whether or not there is lack of consent (amounting to coercion) may be problematic. The distinction is vital. If there is no ostensible coercion (or lack of consent on the part of the person transported) then the person is simply an economic migrant without access to the bespoke rights which are available under international arrangements applicable to formally trafficked persons.

Since people smuggling is frequently viewed as being of a voluntary nature, smuggled individuals will be liable to removal from the destination state owing to the voluntary commission of immigration offences, although they may not be liable simply for working there. However, a substantial proportion of those transported across national and international boundaries will have been transported so that (knowingly or not, willingly or not) they may engage in activities in the destination state which may be both exploitative and unlawful, such as working in illegal conditions (for example, for less than minimum wage, for excessive hours, or in severe or dangerous conditions) or to work in the sex trade.

Such people are often described as having been trafficked for the purpose of exploitation – an example of criminal activity which is defined by reference to lack of consent, or at least the presence of 'coercion' in some form. This is not without its difficulties, particularly with respect to some instances of engagement in the sex trade where, as is the case in the UK for example, mere participation in sex work is not unlawful, and may be seen by some of those engaged in it as comparable with the lawful activities of those who have been smuggled for economic ends (and will be seen as such by the authorities in the destination state). Yet, as will be explained in this body of work, it is in practice very difficult to maintain the

17 Addressed in ch 7.

distinction between prostitution as mere economic activity and prostitution as exploitation (consensual or otherwise) of the women involved.

The difficulties inherent in maintaining this distinction have particular significance in the context of human trafficking, where identifying lack of consent (of the women involved) – to being moved, for what purpose, and in what conditions – is no easy task. Furthermore, such is the nature of exploitation of women in the sex trade (whether or not the women have been transported in order to engage in it) that the conditions in which 'smuggled prostitutes' may find themselves may be little different from those encountered by 'trafficked prostitutes'. Formally, the first category would, on the face of it, be seen as acting voluntarily – and would therefore be subject to such legal sanctions as any illicit economic migrant – whereas the latter would be seen to have been subject to some form of force or coercion and therefore not acting in a fully voluntary manner.

Treating such women differently may give the appearance of unfairness, save, perhaps, from the perspective of a state wanting to maintain border integrity by removing those encountered by the authorities. The appearance of unfairness derives from the recognition of women who can properly be described as 'trafficked prostitutes' or victims; persons with human rights and access to specific, bespoke protections under the anti-trafficking regime(s), which will in some cases – amongst other things – interfere with the right of the destination state to peremptory removal of the women unlawfully present in its territory.

Even the woman who is willingly smuggled into a country knowing that she will take part in the sex trade may not have anticipated how awful her conditions would be. It is here that the unfairness of treating such women differently from those who have been formally trafficked may be most apparent and most questionable. The question is explored as to whether this category of persons – those who may be tentatively referred to as 'consensually trafficked' – is to be offered protection beyond the ambit of ordinary human rights law.

## 1.4 The identification and treatment of victims

As observed by Jones, '... perhaps the most perplexing obstacle to prevention of human trafficking lies in the inability of governments and nongovernmental organizations to properly identify victims of human trafficking and quantify their numbers'.[18] Misconceptions about trafficking, smuggling and consensual economic migration, coupled with a lack of understanding about trafficking and exploitative migration, lead to the misidentification of victims. The ramifications of misidentification include, amongst other things, the potential criminalisation of victims for offences committed as a result of trafficking-related compulsion.[19]

18 S V Jones 'Human trafficking victim identification: should consent matter?' (2012) 45 *Indiana Law Review* 483, 484.

19 See ch 6.

Lee refers to the 'criminalisation of migrants', stating that:

> … 'unwanted' migrants and a range of non-citizens are regarded as problem populations and subjected to an 'amplified process of penalization.' In this context, illegal migrants, bogus asylum seekers, border crossers who have been smuggled and trafficked, are the archetypal 'unwanted' migrants of the twenty-first century.[20]

Within these categories, we find those who are considered to be 'deserving' of some form of assistance, and those who are not. The difficulty lies in that '… the people moving in irregular ways often do not fit neatly into the category of either 'refugee' or 'voluntary economic migrant'.[21] The 'crimmigration'[22] approach, whereby the central focus would be on the immigration status of putatively trafficked persons, leads to the misidentification of those trafficked persons, i.e. genuine victims are, for some reason or other, determined to be 'not trafficked'.

As to consent and the identification of victims, '… the term draws upon certain embedded structures of political liberalism …'.[23] Jones prefers a liberalist approach and rejects a more paternalistic stance.[24] He states that the latter, in deeming consent irrelevant, '… stands in sharp contrast to respect for the actors' human dignity'.[25] The focus within this book is not intended to ignore the validity of genuine consent, or to attempt to mirror the 'false consciousness'[26] argument historically levelled at prostitutes. Instead, the approach is to recognise that the 'lack of consent' requirement introduced to the international legal definition of trafficking leads to a series of problems affecting the identification of victims, which need to be addressed. There will, therefore, be a focus in this work on the exploitation and its effects and an attempt to find a way to mitigate genuine 'hard' cases, as simply returning trafficked and/or exploited migrants home may serve to put them back into the same conditions, economic or otherwise, that led to them leaving in the first place.[27]

Since isolating real instances of consent or coercion will in some cases be very difficult, mistakes and misidentifications will be made. The 'consensually trafficked' or 'smuggled' (yet exploited) woman will have such human rights protections as apply to her, such as the right to a fair trial,[28] and protection from removal

20 M Lee *Trafficking and Global Crime Control* (Sage, 2011) 6.

21 Alexander Betts 'Towards a "soft law" framework for the protection of vulnerable migrants' in Research Paper No 162 'New issues in refugee research' UNHCR 1.

22 J P Stumpf 'The crimmigration crisis: immigrants, crime and sovereign power' (2006) *ExpressO* 367.

23 Judith Butler 'Sexual consent: some thoughts on psychoanalysis and law' (2011–2013) 21 *Columbia Journal of Gender and Law* 216–17.

24 Which he refers to as the 'gendered' approach.

25 Jones (n 18) 503.

26 S Schulhofer *Unwanted Sex: The Culture of Intimidation and the Failure of Law* (Harvard University Press, 1998).

27 C Hoyle, M Bosworth and M Dempsey 'Labelling the victims of sex trafficking: exploring the borderland between rhetoric and reality' (2011) 20(3) *Social and Legal Studies* 313–92, 321.

28 Article 6 of Convention for the Protection of Human Rights and Fundamental Freedoms (opened for signature 4 November 1950, entered into force 3 September 1953) (ECHR).

to a place where a real risk of ill-treatment exists,[29] but she will not have the specific protections conferred upon victims by the anti-trafficking regime, such as protection from peremptory removal, or a right to assistance and support etc. A state would be able to rely upon its rights to deny the extension of these benefits of trafficked women to smuggled ones and it would of course be in the state's interests to classify as many trafficked women as 'smuggled' as it could.

There may be an analogy to be drawn here with the situation of refugee applicants. Those who satisfy the criteria of the Convention Relating to the Status of Refugees 1951 (Refugee Convention)[30] have access to the protections which it confers, as well as to any human rights provisions which are relevant to them. Such is the difficulty in establishing formal refugee status, so pressing may be the circumstances of some of those who cannot do so, that states have been willing to allow a number of such people a variety of discretionary remedial concessions on humanitarian grounds, such as exceptional rights to remain in their territories. These concessions do not make their beneficiaries 'refugees' but are an acknowledgement that the mechanical, standardised application of complex criteria combined with great evidential obstacles can result in genuine 'hard cases', which discretionary measures can to a degree mitigate without undermining the integrity of the refugee regime.

A similar humanitarian response to marginal cases of trafficked women, even of women who have not formally been trafficked might be appropriate, given the circumstances in which women are recruited into the transportation of and trade in humans and the severity of the exploitative conditions in which they find themselves in the destination states. It is therefore suggested that governments may be able to adopt a policy parallel to a humanitarian right to remain as a response to this transnational criminal activity, which must be seen in its proper context and addressed from a perspective which not only aims to criminalise the traffickers, but also to protect their victims.

Primarily, owing to the problematic nature of correctly determining the presence of coercion and lack of consent and, secondly, owing to the fact that there may at times be little difference between the conditions experienced by women falling into either category, a proposal will be made in this book as to how the impact of the reluctance of states to concede too much as regards 'merely' smuggled, exploited prostitutes may be mitigated, without undermining significantly the purposes of the anti-trafficking regimes.

## 1.5 Structure and chapter outlines

This research set out to investigate the legal nature of the trafficking of women for sexual exploitation. However, it soon became apparent that consent (or lack thereof) had an important part to play in determining who the victims are and how they should be treated, and that there are ramifications of inclusion of this

29 Article 3 of the ECHR, and art 33(1) of the Convention Relating to the Status of Refugees (adopted 28 July 1951, entered into force 22 April 1954) 189 UNTS 137.

30 ibid.

controversial element for putative victims of trafficking or smuggling for the purpose of exploitation. This is what the book aims to explore. A chapter-by-chapter breakdown of structure and content is provided below.

### *1.5.1 Chapter 2: The contextual and legal background*

Chapter 2 primarily provides analysis of the 'push' and 'pull' factors that lead individuals to make the decision to migrate, as it is accepted that many trafficking situations may at least begin on a voluntary and consensual footing. This includes, inter alia, poverty, discrimination, and the influence of organized crime groups.

Secondly, this chapter provides an analysis of the vexed nature of the trafficking/smuggling divide, correct determination of which is essential in order for victims to be identified as such.

Finally, the relevant obligations on states to address the trafficking phenomenon in terms of prevention, prosecution, punishment and the support and protection of victims are outlined, so that those most central to the arguments advanced in this book (i.e. those relating to the treatment of victims) may be dealt with in more depth at a later point, in Chapter 6.

### *1.5.2 Chapter 3: Defining trafficking: the evolution of an international legal definition*

The scope of the legal definition of human trafficking is analysed in Chapter 2 with reference to the main anti-trafficking instruments, which form 'the anti-trafficking regime'. Unless stated otherwise, this will always refer to the UN Trafficking Protocol, the CoE Trafficking Convention and the EU 2011 Directive. The analysis in this chapter primarily includes discussion of the 'action' element of 'recruitment, transportation …' etc of the victim, and considers matters such as the requirement and legitimacy of border crossing.

This is followed by analysis of the more controversial and problematic 'means' element of trafficking – that of 'coercion, force …' etc. Examples and anecdotal excerpts are used to elucidate each element of the 'means', which are not clearly separable. This part of the chapter also tests the ambit and scope of the 'means' element, particularly the limits of 'coercion'.

As regards the 'purpose' elements of trafficking (i.e. the manifestations of 'exploitation' as provided for within the definition), human rights law is drawn upon to elucidate the meaning of some of the terms used within these instruments. Justification for this cross-treaty interpretation is discussed in terms of Articles 31 and 32 of the Vienna Convention on the Law of Treaties,[31] and the meaning of terms such as 'slavery', 'forced labour' and 'sexual exploitation' are discussed. The determination that human trafficking is a tripartite process defined by reference

31 Vienna Convention on the Law of Treaties (done at Vienna on 23 May 1969, entered into force on 27 January 1980, in accordance with Article 84(1)) United Nations, Treaty Series, vol 1155 (Vienna Convention). See ch 3 at section 3.3 for discussion of this issue.

to lack of consent leads into the specific discussion of consent to exploitation in Chapter 4.

### *1.5.3 Chapter 4: Consent in the law, and consent to sexual exploitation*

The basic conditions for a valid consent are analysed, drawing upon and discussing various areas of the law where such a notion is employed and thereby paving a pathway for analysis of the specific role of consent in the context of human trafficking, undertaken in Chapter 5.

Furthermore, this chapter considers the autonomy/liberalist *v* paternalist approaches taken to prostitution and exploitative prostitution. This includes specific discussion of sex work as a legitimate form of labour, what constitutes 'exploitative' labour and also whether prostitution/sex work is inherently exploitative.

Competing feminist perspectives are drawn upon, as is conflicting evidence as to consent in the context of prostitution and sexual exploitation (which are not conflated here). The argument is explored as to whether we might ask for a high standard of consent in such contexts, where so much is at stake, and bearing in mind the evidence that points to a proportion (perhaps significant) of prostitution clearly being forced, but in some cases appearing to be uncoerced.

### *1.5.4 Chapter 5: The effect of consent in human trafficking*

As has been noted above, this body of work has particular focus on the meaning and effects of 'consent' within and without of a trafficking context, juxtaposed against the meaning of 'coercion' and other 'means'-related aspects of the legal definition of human trafficking, although the approach taken here does not consider these two elements to be the only situations. As the detailed analysis undertaken in Chapter 5 will indicate, consent/coercion is treated here as a spectrum, as opposed to a dichotomous approach, which would have the putative trafficked person being deemed either to have consented or to have been coerced, as the latter would represent too simplistic a view of this complex phenomenon.

The intricacies of a valid consent in a trafficking context are considered, as are the realities of consent in a trafficking context. The final parts of the chapter address the effects of the inclusion of a consent element in the trafficking definition, and closes with discussion of possible alternatives to the current situation which has created a 'grey area' between the trafficked and the smuggled sex worker. This leads into Chapter 6, which addresses the treatment of victims and the effect that the 'lack of consent' requirement has here.

### *1.5.5 Chapter 6: The 'victim-centred' approach to tackling trafficking: determining who the victims are, and how they should be treated*

The ramifications of positive or negative identification of an individual as a victim of human trafficking are considered in Chapter 6, which evaluates the legal and policy issues surrounding the current framework applicable to the identification and treatment of victims once discovered in the destination state. The UK is used as a central example, following implementation of the requirements of the relevant international legal instruments with respect to the treatment of trafficked victims. The victim-specific provisions of the legal anti-trafficking regime are analysed, as is the implementation and success or otherwise of these requirements within the domestic legislative framework. This chapter essentially explores the bespoke regime applicable to victims of human trafficking, and argues that the threshold for the identification of victims is currently being set too high and that genuine victims of trafficking are being misidentified as a result.

### *1.5.6 Chapter 7: Less than trafficked, more than smuggled: dealing with the 'consensually trafficked'*

This chapter explores the issues surrounding those who fall short of the formal trafficking threshold, as well as those who might be deemed 'consensually trafficked'. Traditional liberalist perspectives are drawn upon and considered, as to their suitability as a lens through which to view consensual exploitive migration.

Human trafficking is contextual, as the frequent flow of victims from poorer origin states to richer destination states indicates, and following consideration in Chapter 2 of the 'push' factors leading to global migration (and therefore a proportion of all instances of human trafficking), the effect of 'economic coercion of circumstances' (on what might otherwise be deemed consent) is considered.

From an immigration perspective, this form of coercion does not negate the commission of an immigration offence for which the state has a legitimate interest in prosecuting the putative victim. It is recognised that states have a legitimate interest in immigration control and therefore may be reluctant to adopt an approach which is too broad and encompassing. Nonetheless, the argument is made that in the sole context of human trafficking, severe pressing economic need may render consent less valid or less freely given than otherwise and may, in fact, amount to coercion, particularly where traffickers knowingly take advantage of the pressing economic need of putative victims in order to recruit them. The tentative nature of such an ambitious argument is acknowledged and discussed.

The latter part of this chapter focuses on the justifications for offering more favourable treatment to the consensually trafficked, and considers what those concessions might be. This body of work explores victimhood in the context of exploitative migration, and argues that there is no clear line which can be drawn between those who have been merely smuggled, those who have been trafficked or those who have been 'consensually trafficked' into a situation of exploitation.

# 2 The contextual and legal background

## 2.1 Introduction

In many instances, human trafficking illustrates the link between migration outflow from impoverished regions, and subsequent exploitation of the migrant by those involved in the trafficking process. Trafficking is contextual, and frequently takes place against a backdrop of poverty and lack of opportunity in the origin state. The role of 'push' factors – such as economic hardship – in the global trade in human beings clearly have a part to play in the continuance of trafficking and exploitative migration-related activity. The trafficking of women for sexual exploitation constitutes criminal activity which goes far beyond smuggling, to a point where victims are deprived of their autonomy and basic rights such as liberty and freedom of movement. However, the line between trafficking and smuggling is blurred, and the difference turns largely on consent.

As noted in the Introduction to this body of work, it is essential from the outset to make the distinction between individuals who play no voluntary part in becoming part of the global trafficking network, and individuals who elect to enter trafficking networks as a method of facilitated migration. There exists a spectrum, along which lie those who did not consent to any part of the trafficking process, those whose consent was vitiated by deception or some other relevant factor and those who fully consent to facilitated migration for the purpose of working in the sex industry, albeit in exploitative conditions.[1] For completeness, there will also be those who fully consent to the facilitated migration process for the purpose of working in the sex industry in conditions which cannot be deemed to be 'exploitative'.[2]

Aronowitz observes that: 'Often both smuggled and trafficked individuals leave a country of origin willingly'.[3] The services of trafficking networks are actually in

1 It is accepted here that consent to prostitution – even where it is to be undertaken in exploitative conditions – can in some circumstances be valid. This is further discussed throughout ch 4.

2 There is disagreement as to whether or not prostitution is inherently exploitative. The position of this author is that it is not always exploitative per se, but that many conditions surrounding it may render it so.

3 A Aronowitz 'Smuggling and trafficking in human beings: the phenomenon, the markets that drive it and the organisations that promote it' (2001) 9 *European Journal of Criminal Policy and Research* 163, 164.

demand by potential migrants and putative trafficking victims;[4] not every trafficked person 'falls' into the hands of traffickers. Potential migrants may see traffickers as 'migration brokers',[5] or facilitators – agents who aid them in their quest to migrate.

Industrialisation, technological advances and globalisation are an advantage to traffickers, as new mediums of transportation and communication exist which they can draw upon to maintain and expand trafficking networks. Cooperation and communication among the international community and affected states is imperative in order for a multi-pronged attack on trafficking to be successfully made. Harmonised criminal law and human rights responses must take account of the need to prevent trafficking, prosecute and punish the trafficker, and to protect and provide for the victim. In order for trafficking to be tackled effectively, both supply and demand factors need to be addressed, as it is these push and pull factors which underpin and facilitate the trade in humans. Criminalisation, monitoring mechanisms and law and policy which addresses prevention, prosecution and punishment (of traffickers) as well as that providing for support and assistance to victims are all imperative to a successful anti-trafficking regime.

The aim of this chapter is to provide an overview of the legal and contextual background to migration and trafficking-related activity. Section 2 will address the contextual factors acting on the would-be trafficked which serve to facilitate the continuance of human trafficking, with a view to emphasising the role of certain factors such as economic hardship (on the part of the migrant) in illicit migration and human trafficking. Even if one were attainable, this section does not set out to provide a fully comprehensive account of the trafficking phenomenon, the clandestine nature of which precludes such a thing. Section 2.3 addresses the vexed delineation between trafficking and smuggling. In a legal and moral sense, these activities are seen as distinct, but in reality the line is blurred. The matter largely turns on consent, and the identification of an individual as whether 'trafficked' or 'smuggled' plays a central role in how that individual is to be treated. Section 2.4 will specifically address the central state obligations imposed by the international legal anti-trafficking regime, which include the prosecution and punishment of traffickers, prevention of trafficking, and (briefly) the treatment of victims.[6] This sketch represents only a part of trafficking activity; it is sufficient to explain the legal regime, yet the whole picture might indicate that aspects of anti-trafficking law may be inadequate as Chapters 6 and 7 will discuss as regards specifically the treatment of victims. Other aspects of the international legal regime are not at all considered irrelevant here, yet they go beyond the ambit of the focus of this book

4 Europol 'Trafficking of women and children for sexual exploitation in the EU: the involvement of Western Balkans organised crime' (public version) Crimes Against the Person Unit, 18 http://www.europol.europa.eu/publications/Serious_Crime_Overviews/Western_Balkans_THB_Threat_Assessment.PDF (last accessed 1 August 2007, link no longer live).

5 A Phizacklea 'Migration theories and migratory realities: a gendered perspective' in Danielle Joly *International Migration in the New Millennium: Global and Regional Perspectives* (Ashgate, 2004) 152.

6 The treatment of victims is considered in more depth in chs 6 and 7.

and so will not be considered further. The corresponding UK legislative framework will also be considered.

## 2.2 Contextual factors underlying the continuance of human trafficking

### *2.2.1 The scale of human trafficking*

Human trafficking is large-scale and lucrative. The United Nations (UN) estimates that, globally, human trafficking annually nets about US$12 billion.[7] The International Organization for Migration (IOM) estimates the figure to be closer to US$31 billion.[8] We are left in no doubt about the lucrative nature of this activity, which is described as 'one of the most lucrative organised crime activities generating a global multibillion dollar a year income'.[9] Estimates as to the magnitude of the human trafficking phenomenon range from 700,000[10] women and children victims of trafficking for sexual exploitation, to several million[11] victims being trafficked worldwide annually, the latter figure including other forms of exploitation.

It has been estimated that 120,000 women and children are trafficked specifically into Western Europe each year.[12] Specific research conducted in 1998 led to an estimate that trafficked women both into and within the UK amounted to between 142 and 1420 per year.[13] In 2003, government estimates envisaged around 4000 sex trafficking victims being present in the UK at any one time.[14] These victims will originate from all over the world.

The underlying causes of this activity are manifold, and tend to work together to ensure its continuance. These factors can be analysed within a framework of

7 V Malarek *The Natashas: Inside the New Global Sex Trade* (Arcade Publishing, New York, 2004) 5.

8 Some discrepancy between these figures can be explained by the fact that the IOM and the UN do not necessarily use the same definitions of 'trafficking in humans'. See ch 2 for discussion of the legal definition of trafficking in humans.

9 Europol (n 4) 4.

10 European Commission, Justice and Home Affairs 'Trafficking in women: the misery behind the fantasy: from poverty to sex slavery – a comprehensive European strategy' Brussels (6 March 2001).

11 International Organisation for Migration – however, IOM uses a broad definition for human trafficking and so its statistics may not be the most reliable. See http://www.iom.int/jahia/Jahia/pid/1 (last accessed 1 March 2010).

12 See International Organization for Migration 'Consequences of trafficking and policy responses' http://www.iom.int/jahia/Jahia/about-migration/managing-migration/managing-migration-irregular-migration/consequences-of-trafficking-and-policy-responses (last accessed 1 July 2011), and Frank Laczko (International Organization for Migration) 'Human trafficking: the need for better data' (November 2002) http://www.migrationinformation.org/Feature/display.cfm?ID=66 (last accessed 1 July 2011).

13 L Kelly and L Regan 'Stopping traffic: exploring the extent of, and responses to, trafficking in women for sexual exploitation in the UK' (Imprint London, Home Office, 2000) 22.

14 Joint Committee on Human Rights Twenty-Sixth Report (Session 2005–6) [78/205] http://www.publications.parliament.uk/pa/jt200506/jtselect/jtrights/245/24507.htm#n109 (last accessed 1 July 2011).

economic and social influences, which shape the market forces of supply and demand, which arguably lead to some or all instances of global human trafficking today.

The UK is predominantly a destination state. Europol reports that: '[m]ost trafficked prostitutes come from the Balkans and former Soviet Union, or from the Far East, especially China or Thailand'.[15] This tallies with the findings of the 2010 Project Acumen Report,[16] which found that, in the UK, of the 2600 women identified by the investigation as 'trafficked', 1300 were from China and the remainder were predominantly from Eastern Europe and Thailand. Statistics from 2010–2011 in the UK revealed the top 10 countries of origin of putative victims[17] discovered in the UK, with the highest number originating from Nigeria, with Romania and China also featuring significantly.[18] Other notable source countries include Africa, Asia, Latin America and the Caribbean, and the Middle East, indicating the scale of the trafficking phenomenon and the wide geographical variety of origin countries.[19] Notwithstanding the fact that the same country names come up again and again, the difficulty in capturing reliable data with regard to a clandestine activity such as trafficking means that a realistic picture is not easily achievable.

Transit countries will be those that are most amenable to traffickers on the move at the time. Although frequented trafficking routes may be identified at times, they are not static. Ultimately, it can be said that:

> … it would be simpler and far more accurate to identify that traffickers will seek to use whatever routes offer the best chances of a risk-free passage and this will obviously change according to many circumstances, not least of which is the law enforcement with regards counter trafficking tactics & action.[20]

Most typically, one might assume that women are trafficked from poorer states to richer western states. To a large extent this is true, yet it is not always the

15 Europol (n 4) 15.

16 Project Acumen: ACPO Migration and Associated Matters 'Setting the record: the trafficking of migrant women in the England and Wales off-street prostitution sector' (August 2010) 5 http://www.acpo.police.uk/documents/crime/2010/201008CRITMW01.pdf (last accessed 20 December 2010).

17 That is, victims who have been referred into the national referral mechanism (NRM) – the process used in the UK in order to determine whether or not an individual is, in fact, a victim of trafficking. The NRM is discussed in ch 6.

18 Other notable source countries included Albania, Czech Republic, Ghana, Hungary, Lithuania, Slovakia, Uganda and Vietnam. See 'It happens here: equipping the UK to fight modern slavery' Policy Report by the Slavery Working Group, Centre for Social Justice (March 2013) available at http://www.centreforsocialjustice.org.uk/UserStorage/pdf/Pdf%20reports/CSJ_Slavery_Full_Report_WEB(5).pdf (last accessed 23 January 2014).

19 These include Africa, Asia, Latin America and the Caribbean, and the Middle East – in a broad sense, then, many of the countries of the world have been identified as sources countries. See First Report of the Dutch National Rapporteur: 'Trafficking in human beings' Table 4.1. *Registration data relating to reports of (possible) victims of THB over the period 1992–2000* (2000) 49.

20 Europol (n 4) 17.

case. Countries where there is a demand for an active sex trade, and where the sale of sex is most lucrative for traffickers, are most likely to be destination countries. Brussa[21] identifies consumer demand as a central underlying factor affecting the continuance of the sex trade, and also the knock-on effect that this demand has upon the traffickers, who see and exploit the opportunity for economic gain.

This demand can be created by the residents of the host country,[22] seasonal visitors or international presence. Traffickers are led by market forces, which may include 'seasonal' markets, driven largely by tourism, or major events such as the 2012 Olympics in London.[23] In Bosnia and Herzegovina, it is estimated that 70 per cent of all profits from prostitution come from internationals.[24] This can be contrasted with the situation in southern Asia, where the clientele has been reported to be largely of domestic origin.[25] Accordingly, it can be seen that traffickers draw from the resources in the origin states and use these resources to supply the demand, wherever it happens to be at the time.[26]

### *2.2.2 'Push' and 'pull' factors*

Potentially, migration can be seen as 'an individual, spontaneous, and voluntary act, which rests on the comparison between the present situation of the actor and the expected net gain of moving, and results from a cost-benefit calculus'.[27] According to this statement, a potential migrant makes a rational, individual decision to migrate for material purposes, with the material rewards being higher than the cost of the migration activity itself. Mill states that:

> He who chooses his plan for himself, employs all his faculties. He must use observation to see, reasoning and judgment to foresee, activity to gather materials for decision, discrimination to decide, and when he has decided, firmness and self-control to hold to his deliberate decision.[28]

21 See L Brussa 'Survey of prostitution, migration and traffic in women: history and current situation' (European Union, EG/PROST (91) 2) 43.

22 Brown identifies that in Thailand, Thai men comprise a significant proportion of consumers in the sex sector. See L Brown *Sex Slaves: The Trafficking of Women in Asia* (Virago Press, 2001).

23 See, for example, Stewart Tendler 'Sex trafficking and illegal workers threaten Olympics' *The Times* (24 March 2007).

24 UNICEF, UNOHCHR, OSCE, ODIHR 'Trafficking in human beings in South Eastern Europe' (2004) 65 http://www.iom.md/materials/1_traff_human_beings_se.pdf (last accessed 14 January 2014); Organization for Security and Co-operation in Europe 'Minutes from October 18 Trafficking Round Table Meeting' (OSCE, Priãtina, 22 October 2001).

25 See Brown (n 22).

26 Furthermore, residents of developed states may travel to developing states for the purpose of purchasing sexual services.

27 J Arango 'Theories of international migration' in Danielle Joly *International Migration in the New Millennium: Global and Regional Perspectives* (Ashgate, 2004) 18.

28 J S Mill *On Liberty and Other Essays* (Oxford University Press, Oxford, 1991) 65.

A liberal perspective privileges the autonomy of the individual in weighing up her options and determining for herself her future,[29] and takes the view that free will is the embodiment of autonomy.[30] The migrant, smuggled person or trafficked victim who voluntarily leaves home in order to seek a better future therefore does so having assessed the merits of staying or leaving.

Outshoorn states that: 'The dynamics of trafficking are best explained by migration theory'.[31] Theories of migration are frequently based upon, inter alia, factors such as wage disparities,[32] and the same 'push' factors can be identified in the context of trafficking. Migration is complex and diverse and it varies in forms, motivations and contexts. It is a dynamic process, and cannot easily be explained by any one static theoretical framework. Empirical research can likely tell us much more than theory can about why people migrate.[33]

As Lee observes: 'For many trapped in dire poverty or displaced by political turmoil, migration through irregular means has become their only way of escape'.[34] Furthermore, '… the governments of Western capitalist states see this 'torrent of people in flight' as a serious threat to their stability'.[35] The backdrop of push factors such as economic difficulty call into question somewhat the true level of autonomy exercised by the migrant who, to use an extreme example, is on the brink of starvation.

The same factors influencing the decision to migrate – and therefore having an effect on trafficking patterns – are frequently cited by various sources,[36] indicating that several main themes can be identified. These largely centre on socio-economic problems, such as poverty, economic difficulty and lack of opportunity in the origin state, arising as a result of, for example, underdevelopment,[37]

29 ibid.

30 I Jones 'A beastly provision: why the offence of "intercourse with an animal" must be butchered' (2011) 75(6) *Journal of Criminal Law* 528–44, 530.

31 J Outshoorn 'The political debates on prostitution and trafficking of women' (2005) 12(1) *Social Politics: International Studies in Gender, State and Society* 141–55, 143.

32 See J Arango and A Phizacklea 'Migration theories and migratory realities: a gendered perspective' in Danielle Joly *International Migration in the New Millennium: Global and Regional Perspectives* (Ashgate, 2004), where various migration theories are discussed.

33 See, for example, J Mertus 'Human rights of women in central and eastern Europe' (Spring 1998) 6 *American University Journal of Gender Social Policy & Law* 369; GfK Ukraine 'Human trafficking survey: Belarus, Bulgaria, Moldova, Romania, and Ukraine', Kyiv, Ukraine (December 2006), prepared by GfK Ukraine for the International Organization for Migration http://www.childcentre.info/projects/traffickin/dbaFile13968.pdf (last accessed 1 February 2007); UNICEF and others (n 24).

34 M Lee 'Human trade and the criminalization of irregular migration' 33 (2005) 1(15) *International Journal of the Sociology of Law* 1.

35 P Cole *Philosophies of Exclusion: Liberal Political Theory and Immigration* (Edinburgh University Press, 2000) 1.

36 ibid; also see UNICEF and others (n 24), OSCE (n 24), Arango (n 27), Brown (n 22).

37 'Addressing the human rights challenges underlying the criminalisation of irregular migrants and national minorities in Europe'. Keynote speech by Nils Muižnieks, Council of Europe Commissioner for Human Rights, Centre for European Policy Studies Seminar, Brussels (22 February 2013) 3 https://wcd.coe.int/ViewDoc.jsp?id=2037599 (last accessed 30 February 2014).

regional conflict, political unrest or economic transition. Gender discrimination[38] and gender-based violence often go hand-in-hand with this:[39] 'The movement of women within countries and across frontiers is usually a result of their unequal bargaining power and vulnerability to exploitation'.[40] These underlying factors work together to render women in some origin countries particularly vulnerable to human trafficking, and the demand for sexual services for sale creates the potential for them to be sexually exploited in the destination state.

The context in which human trafficking takes place has not gone unnoticed in law and policy responses to the phenomenon; for example, the UN General Assembly in 1994 recognised that that '[Trafficking is the] illicit and clandestine movement of persons … largely from developing countries with economies in transition …',[41] thereby specifically recognising the impact of economic factors on trafficking patterns. The decision to migrate can lead to women falling into the hands of traffickers, and there exist certain influencing factors in countries of origin which are specific to women and therefore have the effect of rendering them particularly vulnerable to trafficking and exploitative facilitated migration.

Konrad provides the following analysis as regards the prevalence of trafficking for sexual exploitation:

> … the unequal economic development of different countries; mass unemployment in many countries of origin, but also inequality, discrimination and gender-based violence in our societies, the prevailing market mechanisms; the patriarchal structures in the source and destination countries; the demand side including the promotion of sex tourism in many countries of the world, the mindsets of men, etc. – the primary root-cause is poverty, most particularly among women.[42]

Organised crime plays a significant role in the continuance of human trafficking.[43] Kalaitzidis asserts that transnational organised crime groups (OCGs)[44] are wholly

38 K Mahoney 'Theoretical perspectives on women's rights and strategies for their implementation' (1996) 21(3) *Brooklyn Journal of International Law* 799–856, 799.

39 See Mertus (n 33); GfK Ukraine (n 33); T Obokata 'Trafficking of human beings as a crime against humanity: some implications for the international legal system' (2005) 54 *International and Comparative Law Quarterly* 445–58; H Konrad 'Trafficking in human beings – the ugly face of Europe' (2002) 13 *Helsinki Monitor* 260; Europol (n 4) 4; Lee (n 34).

40 Report of the Special Rapporteur on Violence Against Women, its Causes and Consequences (1994) UN ESCOR E/CN.4/1997/47/Add.4 Commission on Human Rights, 53rd Session, Provisional Agenda Item 9(a) at 19 http://www.awf.or.jp/pdf/h0010.pdf (last accessed 11 January 2007).

41 UN General Assembly 'Traffic in women and girls' UN Doc A/RES/49/166 (23 December 1994) http://www.un.org/documents/ga/res/49/a49r166.htm (last accessed 18 June 2014).

42 Konrad (n 39) 263.

43 See Europol (n 4) 13; S Warnath 'Trafficking of women and children: the future direction of United States policy: Report of the US-EU Trafficking in Women Seminar' (L'viv, 9–10 July, 1998, 63–66, L'viv, Ukraine, 1998) 63; Brussa (n 21) 42.

44 OCGs are defined by art 3 of the Organized Crime Convention as: 'For the purposes of this Convention: (a) "Organized crime group" shall mean a structured group of three or more persons,

responsible for the huge growth in irregular migration.[45] OCGs exploit social vulnerability in order to fuel the trade in humans. [46] Such organisations have been subject to considerable international scrutiny since before the turn of the century, as the United Nations Convention against Transnational Organized Crime (Organized Crime Convention)[47] indicates. The Organized Crime Convention is a reaction to an already exiting and rapidly growing and evolving problem; OCGs have been described as potentially being 'more organised than the law enforcement agencies themselves'.[48]

The myriad issues considered above confirm that the motivations of female migrants, who potentially become victims of human trafficking, are based upon more than simply material hardship, although this is undeniably a central factor. The combined factors considered make them vulnerable to 'migration brokers' and traffickers. Social and economic marginalisation, often in a society which permits discrimination or even violence against women, cultivates a climate which encourages and facilitates human trafficking. These oppressive conditions also contribute to making it harder to isolate exactly what part consent (or lack of it) has played in the decision to migrate.

The 'push' factors identified, which are largely – but not exclusively – economic in nature, contribute to the decision to leave a place or country in order to seek economic gain. As has been identified, many trafficking situations may begin on a voluntary (and therefore consensual) basis, so far as the person being transported is concerned at least. This serves to blur even further the line between trafficking and smuggling. The following section will engage in an analysis of the difficulties inherent in distinguishing trafficking from smuggling; an essential determination for the purposes of the consent debate.

## 2.3 Distinguishing trafficking from smuggling

From the outset, it is necessary to distinguish 'trafficking' from 'smuggling'. The 'conceptual confusion' between 'trafficked persons' and 'smuggled migrants' has not gone unnoted.[49] The House of Commons Home Affairs Committee inquiry into human trafficking in 2009 noted in that: '[w]e are concerned about the

existing for a period of time and acting in concert with the aim of committing one or more serious crimes or offences established in accordance with this Convention, in order to obtain, directly or indirectly, a financial or other material benefit …'.

45 A Kalaitzidis 'Human smuggling and trafficking in the Balkans: is it Fortress Europe?' (2005) 5 *Journal of the Institute of Justice and International Studies* 1.

46 Explanatory Memorandum to the Proposal for a Directive of the European Parliament and of the Council on preventing and combating trafficking in human beings, and protecting victims, repealing Framework Decision 2002/629/JHA (COM(2010) 95 final) 1.2.

47 United Nations Convention against Transnational Organized Crime (adopted November 2000 by United Nations General Assembly Resolution A/RES/55/25, entered into force on 29 September 2003) (Organized Crime Convention).

48 Europol (n 4) 25.

49 On the Inter-Agency submission regarding the draft Trafficking Protocol, see A Gallagher, *The International Law on Human Trafficking* (Cambridge, 2010) 94.

continuing tendency to view trafficking as an immigration crime, coupling it with facilitation or people smuggling, which is completely different'.[50] Both as more typically understood concern the movement of goods rather than people. The terms are used at times without consistency but, for the most part, trafficking refers to the movement of goods across borders – goods which it is unlawful to possess in the destination state, such as guns or drugs. People 'move' or 'migrate' – legally or otherwise – across international borders. Sometimes, however, they are 'transported', in the same way that 'goods' are. If the action taken goes no further than simply 'movement' of these people, even the act of transportation may not necessarily be unlawful. More usually, transportation is to avoid restrictions upon movement, such as immigration barriers, which can affect refugee applicants, economic migrants, and those who have been subject to coercion as to cross-border transportation and exploitation. This distinction (between trafficking and smuggling) is important as it underpins the crux of the consent 'problem' and determines what, if anything, the migrant is entitled to on discovery in the destination country.

Smuggling is typically characterised by transportation of goods while avoiding import charges. 'Goods' in this context refers to items which would otherwise lawfully be allowed to circulate in the destination state, such as cigarettes or alcoholic drinks. The cross-border movement of people cannot be categorised so simply. Where possession of these 'goods' is unlawful, it is more usual to term the activity 'trafficking', but the terms are not scientific or necessarily mechanically applied and there will always be exceptions in the way that they are used. Those who may require assistance to be smuggled – refugee applicants, economic migrants – face the obstacle of immigration laws, which may include criminal prosecution for breach or attempted breach of these laws. Such persons, therefore, need the 'help' of smugglers and may then on arrival safely present themselves to the authorities if they are refugee applicants, or 'disappear' in the destination state if they are in the latter category of illicit economic migrants seeking work. These people have been willingly transported. Those who have been taken without consent or whose consent has been obtained through coercion, deception or fraud etc have been trafficked.

The conditions of the transportation of the two groups may not differ greatly, but the conditions in the destination state may. The interests of those involved in the transnational trade in humans may go no further than:

> … the procurement, in order to obtain, directly or indirectly, a financial or other material benefit, of the illegal entry of a person into a State Party of which the person is not a national or a permanent resident.[51]

50 House of Commons Home Affairs Committee: Sixth Report 'The trade in human beings: human trafficking in the UK' (2009) para 86.

51 Protocol against the Smuggling of Migrants by Land, Sea and Air, Supplementing the United Nations Convention against Transnational Organised Crime (adopted 15 November 2000 by United Nations General Assembly Resolution A/RES/55/25, entered into force 28 January 2004) (Smuggling Protocol) art 3.

Those who engage in such activity engage, by definition, in the smuggling of humans. When compared with the analysis of the tripartite trafficking definition which is discussed in Chapter 4, it can be seen that smuggling is comprised solely of an 'action' – the illicit movement of a person from one location to another. The definition of smuggling leaves no room for a 'means' of, say, coercion, or a 'purpose' of exploitation. The Smuggling Protocol focuses squarely on the smuggler, as opposed to mere illegality of entry (of the smuggled person). It takes a neutral standpoint as to how those who illegally migrate through the services of a smuggler should be treated by the law – the ultimate decision as to how to proceed here is left to the receiving country.[52] Increased border control and regulation is seen as a central facet of combating smuggling.

Those engaging in the illicit movement of persons may, however, have further economic interests than those arising from transport alone. They may have a stake in the exploitation of the economic activities of the persons whose entry they have facilitated – either as a means of recouping the (typically inflated) transportation fare, or as a means of additional, sustainable profit, from a human commodity which can be used, and sold, many times over.

It is usual to talk about the 'exploitation' of trafficked persons, meaning something beyond mere regulatory irregularity (such as payment below the minimum wage) but also to degrading conditions and serious limitations on personal freedom, in extreme cases reaching slavery-like practices or servitude.[53] Prominent among such conditions are those taken to work in the sex industry, where the evidence is that many (almost always women, sometimes children) are held in subjugation and compelled to engage in humiliating and injurious practices at the instigation of those who have trafficked them or into whose custody they have been trafficked.[54] The traffickers, like the smugglers, are driven by the search for profit but the traffickers are motivated by the prospect of high profits at relatively low risk. The risk is diminished by the transnational nature of the business, which makes the investigation and prosecution of trafficking crimes especially difficult and requires international cooperation to provide the framework of an effective response.

### *2.3.1 Where trafficking and smuggling meet: a false divide?*

Piotrowicz and Redpath-Cross state that: '... smuggling involves the consent of the individual ...', whereas '[t]here is no real consent from the trafficked person';[55] further, that 'The individual may believe that he or she is being smuggled, when in reality he or she is being trafficked'. This sums up many of the issues

52 ibid art 5.

53 See S Scarpa *Trafficking in Human Beings: Modern Slavery* (Oxford, 2008); Brown (n 22).

54 See, for example, *R v O* [2008] EWCA Crim 2835; *Rantsev v Cyprus and Russia* [2010] (Application no 25965/04).

55 R Piotrowicz and J Redpath-Cross 'Human trafficking and smuggling' in B Opeskin, R Perruchoud, J Redpath-Cross (eds) *Foundations of International Migration Law* (Cambridge University Press, Cambridge, 2012) 234–59, 234.

associated with defining and understanding trafficking and smuggling. The first two statements underpin one of the central differences between trafficking and smuggling – the issue of lack of consent. The latter statement indicates how easily the line between these two perceived distinct practices can become blurred. There is the tendency to oversimplify the trafficking/smuggling divide: 'In practice, the relationship between the smuggler and the client is far from straightforward'.[56] The power disparity between the smuggler and the smuggled leaves the latter open to abuse and exploitation.

The Smuggling Protocol's emphasis is on strengthening border controls; it is less concerned with protection of the migrant:

> In contrast to trafficking, smuggling of migrants across borders is seen as a violation of state sovereignty and essentially a crime against states. Notwithstanding restrictions imposed by major human rights instruments, states' power to refuse entry and to expel aliens has been seen as an integral part of their territorial sovereign power since the late nineteenth century.[57]

This statement itself begs the question as to who is the target for criminalisation where smuggled persons are concerned – is it the smuggler, or the smuggled?

The sometime involvement of illicit border crossing in trafficking may well contribute to the confusion between the two offences. On this basis, third country nationals are put in a particularly difficult position in terms of potential 'victimhood', because a determination that they have been smuggled rather than trafficked has a significant effect on what happens to them next. The words 'irregular migrant' carry undertones of a voluntary act/nature – they have a stigmatic effect. However, rather than having a simple intent to subvert immigration regimes and laws, it may simply be that structural inequalities, civil conflict etc have driven this person to move. The effects of economic instability increase the dependence of those affected on traffickers and 'migration brokers': '… irregular migrants have become the new "problem populations" in need of control'.[58] Poor victim identification rates may be a by-product of this, that is, the presumption of some of those coming into contact with victims may be one of 'not trafficked' or 'complicit smuggled prostitute'.[59]

Lee opines that the distinction between trafficking and smuggling is 'artificial and unhelpful':[60]

> … smugglers may subject migrants to much worse conditions than they anticipated at the time of the agreement. There are many harrowing accounts

56 Lee (n 34) 7.

57 ibid.

58 ibid 8.

59 See S V Jones 'Human trafficking victim identification: should consent matter?' (2012) 45 *Indiana Law Review* 483, where a range of persons who 'may' constitute a victim of human trafficking are contemplated and discussed.

60 Lee (n 34) 7.

> of irregular migrants being misled or lied to, abandoned at various transit points, physically or sexually abused or raped, and beaten up by smugglers or their 'enforcers' for failure to pay their debts.[61]

Physical violence and psychological and sexual abuse of smuggled persons during the smuggling process is well documented.[62] This artificial distinction (between trafficking and smuggling) influences the treatment of the 'victims' by the state, that is, it reinforces that belief that there are 'deserving' victims (i.e. trafficked) and 'undeserving' individuals to whom no victim status should be attributed. Lee states that: 'I would go a step further and suggest that not all trafficked persons are seen as equally "deserving".[63] That is to say, they may be seen as complicit in their trafficking and exploitation. The distinction between victims who are 'innocent' and those who are 'blameworthy' or underserving is made clear by Jones, who identifies different categories of putatively trafficked victim.[64] He considers that a liberal perspective precludes treatment of consenting parties as victims, even where coercion of circumstances (say, economic) is strong and where exploitation has taken place.[65] The appearance of consent, however, or lack of evidence as to its absence, render determination of someone as either trafficked or smuggled difficult. As noted by Lee, assumptions about how a 'victim' should behave often lead to misinterpretations by the authorities and 'victim blaming'.[66] Examples from the UK indicate that where circumstances show that victims seem to have a level of autonomy through, for example, possessing a mobile phone or some money, this contributes – sometimes incorrectly – to a determination that they have not been trafficked.[67] An expectation of a 'perfect' victim,[68] who for example shows ostensible signs of physical struggle, can be damaging.

Conversely, the smuggling/trafficking distinction is still useful, as 'pure' cases of one or the other are barely comparable in terms of the moral and legal culpability of the 'agent' (that is, the trafficker or smuggler) and the 'complicity' of the 'victim'. This, however, does not mean that the significant grey area between the two 'pure' cases need not and should not be provided for. A reconceptualisation of consent and victimhood is needed to suit situations where lack of consent can be difficult to establish, yet – as will be seen throughout this body of work – the presence or otherwise of which makes a radical difference in terms of victim

61 ibid (n 34), referring to P Kwong *Forbidden Workers. Illegal Chinese Immigrants and American Labour* (New Press, New York, 1997). Also see K L Chin *Smuggled Chines – Clandestine Immigration to the United States* (Temple University Press, Philadelphia, 1999).

62 Piotrowicz and Redpath-Cross (n 55) 248–49.

63 Lee (n 34) 7.

64 See Jones (n 59).

65 ibid 510.

66 Lee (n 34) 8.

67 See *R v N and LE* [2012] EWCA Crim 189; J Elliott and K McCartan 'The reality of trafficked peoples access to technology' (2013) 77(3) *Journal of Criminal Law* 255.

68 See R Uy 'Blinded by red lights: why trafficking discourse should shift away from sex and the "perfect victim" paradigm' (2011) 204 *Berkeley Journal of Gender, Law and Justice* 204–219.

identification and treatment. Ill-treatment and exploitation of migrants in terms of smuggling and trafficking is not as clear-cut as one might think:

> [I]t is recognized that women often consent to migrate within their country or abroad for various reasons, including prostitution. They, however, do not agree to work or live under slave-like conditions. In this way, GAATW and STW criticize the terminological distinction between voluntary and involuntary migration for the purpose of sex work, usually understood by law enforcement agencies and policy makers as the only proper form of trafficking.[69]

### *2.3.2 Treatment of trafficked and smuggled persons*

Both trafficking and smuggling pose significant challenges to affected states. They may also possess common features. The central aspect of the global trade in human beings is clearly economic gain. This lucrative business provides ample incentive for traffickers and smugglers to obtain persons to transport, exploit, and profit from the exploitation thereof. Humans are transported for a variety of purposes, and unlike the inanimate objects noted above, the 'commodity' here, that is the transported humans, are entitled to certain rights and protections. Affected states may, as a result, principally have an interest in combating the trade on the basis that cheap labour may distort national labour markets, for instance, and also for the purpose of maintaining border integrity. Beyond this is the humanitarian objective of combating sexual exploitation of those trafficked or smuggled for that purpose: '… in many States, migration management is viewed from a law enforcement perspective'.[70] Piotrowicz and Redpath-Cross recognise that: '… trafficking and smuggling are treated primarily as matters of criminal law, yet there is a clear human rights dimension in relation to the treatment of victims'.[71]

Those who are transported by coercion and exploited, that is, those who are trafficked as opposed to smuggled, are correctly seen as victims, who ought to be entitled to specific treatment and protections that are not accorded to ordinary irregular economic migrants. In order for anti-trafficking regimes to be legitimate and adequate, it is necessary for them to take into account the needs and interests of victims and not be content with simply establishing arrangements for more effective prosecution of traffickers.

Smuggled persons, on the other hand, are not readily seen as, or attributed any 'victim' status. Cole recognises that, from a liberalist perspective: 'Where we can judge that a person's situation is due to their voluntary actions, then we can hold them responsible for that situation, and they have no claims against us'. On this basis, the state – in the interests of controlling immigration and maintaining border integrity – distinguishes between voluntary and involuntary migrants, and

69 N Piper 'Labour migration, trafficking and international marriage: female cross-border movements into Japan' (1999) 5 *Asian Journal of Women's Studies* 69–99, 78.

70 Piotrowicz and Redpath-Cross (n 55) 247.

71 ibid 234.

accords them different treatment. As Ravenstein asserts: 'none … can compare in volume with that which arises from the desire inherent in most men to "better" themselves in material respects'.[72] However, despite the 'self-generated character of much of the migration'[73] of today, this does not negate the fact that traffickers are taking advantage of those potential migrants. To adhere to a liberalist perspective, all exploited migrants who fall short of the formal trafficking definition (which defines trafficking of adults as a non-consensual process) should have no access to any nuanced regime or system of rights or assistance. However, as will be argued later (in Chapters 5–7), the intricacies of consent, coercion and exploitation mean that uniform application of an either/or approach to attributing victim status in situations of both trafficking and smuggling into exploitation, is inappropriate and overly simplistic.

The voluntary nature (perceived or actual) of smuggling on the part of the victim precludes victimhood. Consequently, there is no bespoke regime of rights provided for with respect to smuggled persons. There is little in terms of specific protection or assistance offered by the Smuggling Protocol. There is no reference to physical and psychological recovery or assistance, neither is there any requirement of assistance in legal proceedings. There is, however, some consideration of the treatment of smuggled persons, by smugglers, in the Smuggling Protocol. Primarily, there is the potential for imposition of harsher penalties on smugglers where particularly dangerous or degrading circumstances are involved.[74] The Protocol accepts that smuggling can harm or endanger the lives of migrants.[75] There is no obligation or encouragement that state parties consider allowing smuggled persons to remain temporarily or permanently on their territories. Because there is no perceived victim here, the corollary is that there is no need to consider attributing bespoke rights and assistance. Repatriation of smuggled migrants is poorly dealt with,[76] as there is no duty incumbent upon either the sending or receiving state to take account of migrant safety in the repatriation process – the *travaux préparatoires* make it apparent that the mention of migrant safety in this context[77] solely has procedural reach and does not extend to consideration of the ultimate fate of the returnee. The risk here is that smuggled persons will fall foul of OCGs and may end up being trafficked by the same, which in turn defeats the purpose of the aim to combat organised crime which the two Protocols and the Organised Crime Convention[78] to which they are annexed are intended to have. There is reference in Article 16(4) of the Smuggling Protocol to the particular needs of women and children, but little beyond that. However the

72 E G Ravenstein 'The laws of migration: second paper' (1889) 52(2) *Journal of the Royal Statistical Society* 286.

73 A Wright *Organised Crime* (Willan Publishing, 2006) 94.

74 Smuggling Protocol art 6(3).

75 ibid preamble.

76 Gallagher (n 49) 92.

77 Smuggling Protocol art 18(5).

78 United Nations Convention against Transnational Organised Crime (adopted by General Assembly resolution 55/25 of 15 November 2000, entered into force on 29 September 2003).

Smuggling Protocol does include provisions aimed at preventing the worst forms of exploitation of migrants in Article 6(3). *Refoulement* is also at issue, with respect to the conditions to which the individual will be returned. Smuggled migrants are, in some states, detained on arrival, and prior to removal. This has ramifications for those who may have in fact been trafficked and it warns of the dangers of making rapid assessments as to the status of any given individual as trafficked or smuggled. Essentially, the smuggled migrant has recourse to ordinary human rights law and humanitarian law, as would any citizen present on the soil of a state subject to such regimes.

Trafficked persons have access to certain assistance and protections. These vary depending upon the stage of identification, that is, whether the individual in question has conclusively been determined to have been trafficked, or whether there are – as the earlier stage of the identification process – warrants 'reasonable grounds' to consider that the person may be a victim of trafficking, yet the conclusive decision has not yet been reached. The treatment of trafficked victims is dealt with thoroughly in Chapter 6. The difference in treatment received by trafficked victims and smuggled persons '... is based on the perception of the drafters that the two groups can be neatly categorised and contrasted'.[79]

### *2.3.3 Criminality of trafficked and smuggled persons*

Nils Muižnieks, Council of Europe Commissioner for Human Rights, states that:

> '... persons who have been smuggled into a country should not be seen as having committed a crime. This is an established principle of international law. There are also agreed international standards to protect persons who have been victims of human trafficking from any criminal liability'.[80]

Although in principle this is true, in practice the criminalisation of irregular migrants for immigration-related offences is not an infrequent occurrence. Both of the UN Protocols stress that criminality should not follow as a result of having been smuggled or trafficked,[81] yet this does not preclude the imposition of criminal sanctions for immigration offences by individual states. The Council of Europe Convention on Action Against Trafficking[82] specifically provides for a 'non-punishment principle',[83] as does Directive 2011/36/EU on preventing and combating trafficking in human beings and protecting its victims,[84] whereby

79 Piotrowicz and Redpath-Cross (n 55) 253.

80 Keynote speech by Nils Muižnieks (n 37).

81 See art 5 of the Smuggling Protocol, and art 26 of the Trafficking Protocol.

82 Council of Europe Convention on Action against Trafficking in Human Beings and its Explanatory Report (adopted 3 May 2005, entered into force 1 February 2008) Warsaw, 16.V.2005, Council of Europe Treaty Series – No 197 (CoE Trafficking Convention).

83 ibid art 26.

84 Directive 2011/36/EU of the European Parliament and of the Council of 5 April 2011 on preventing and combating trafficking in human beings and protecting its victims, and replacing Council Framework Decision 2002/629/JHA [2001] OJ L101/1 (EU 2011 Directive) art 8.

prosecutors must exercise discretion in deciding whether or not to pursue a criminal prosecution for any offences committed as a result of compulsion (falling sort of duress) arising from the trafficking situation. This provision potentially has wide reach, but is not drafted in binding terms and therefore should not be interpreted as conclusively meaning that trafficked persons will never be prosecuted for compulsion-related offences.[85] This principle has been implemented into domestic policy and practice in the UK through the Crown Prosecution Service Guidelines,[86] which provide for prosecutorial discretion where trafficked victims have been compelled to commit offences as a result of the trafficking situation, including consideration of whether prosecution is in the public interest. Various case law examples have indicated that this guidance is not frequently and uniformly adhered to, and furthermore that the existence of the guidelines is not as widely known about as it should be.[87] This provision exists in order to address the potential for revictimisation of trafficked persons.

Unsurprisingly, no such equivalent exists with respect to smuggled persons either at UN, CoE or EU level; nor does such provision exist domestically. Whilst simply being a smuggled person is not criminalised by domestic law, a plethora of associated offences exist which target, for example, the possession of false identity documents.[88] Once again, the lack of perceived victim status of smuggled persons breeds a lack of incentive to consider whether or not criminalisation of these persons is in the public interest.

The focus on border control, which inevitably accompanies anti-smuggling measures in particular, means that the smuggled persons are really not the central focus. Muižnieks states that:

> … criminalization is a disproportionate measure which exceeds a state's legitimate interest in controlling its borders. To criminalize irregular migrants, in effect, equates them with the smugglers or employers who, in many cases, exploit them. Such a policy causes further stigmatization and marginalization, even though the majority of migrants contribute to the development of European states and their societies. Immigration offences should remain *administrative* in nature.[89]

There is clearly a tension in policy and practice that straddles the line between treating smuggled persons as just another irregular migrant who should be criminalised for any relevant immigration offences, or taking a more humanitarian

85 See *R v O* (n 54); Re *LM* [2010] EWCA Crim 2327, [2011] 1 Cr App R 12, [2011] Crim LR 425; *R v N and LE* [2012] EWCA Crim 189.

86 Crown Prosecution Service 'Prosecution of defendants charged with offences who might be trafficked victims' 4 at http://www.cps.gov.uk/legal/h_to_k/human_trafficking_and_smuggling/ (last accessed 25 February 2009).

87 See *R v O* (n 54); *R v LM and Others* (n 85) *R v N and LE* (n 85).

88 See *R v O* (n 54), for an illustration of criminalisation of a trafficked person for her use of false identity documents in an attempt to escape the country in order to flee from her trafficker.

89 Keynote speech by Nils Muižnieks (n 37).

view, which takes full account of the position and the needs of the same irregular migrant.

The root causes of smuggling and trafficking are no doubt the same in many cases. The Smuggling Protocol pays little attention to this issue. Brief mention of measures to target 'the root socio-economic causes of the smuggling of migrants, such as poverty and underdevelopment' and to recognise the 'the socio-economic realities of migration' is made in Article 15(3), and the preamble refers to international cooperation to address the 'root causes of migration, especially those related to poverty'.

Criminalisation in the context of irregular migration can be argued to be:

> … first a political and then a legal construct. Putting the stigma of a criminal on a person who migrates irregularly, in the hope of attaining better living conditions or being provided with international protection, is contrary to established principles in international law and ethics. Moreover, and above all, it is utterly superficial and counter-productive given that it leaves untouched the root causes of migration.[90]

Owing to the transnational nature of smuggling and many instances of trafficking, an inherent feature is that both involve more than one, or even several, jurisdictions. Furthermore, organised criminal gangs control much of the activity, so that the use of criminal law to counteract these activities is highly desirable, whilst the obstacles to dealing with transnational organised crime are substantial. Nonetheless, cooperation and agreement between states as to the identification and seriousness of the wrongs and an acceptance of cooperative obligations to respond to the transnational criminal activity may mean that these obstacles and difficulties can be reduced. It is this approach which forms the core of the normative structures presented in this monograph.

This distinction between trafficking and smuggling is of huge importance for the trafficked or smuggled migrant, as it opens or closes the door to assistance and protection that is otherwise unavailable. The difficulties arising from the trafficking/smuggling divide will become more apparent as this monograph unfolds. This chapter now turns to consideration of the relationship between transnational law criminal law and human rights in section 2.4, and will go on to outline and provide an overview of the obligations placed upon states by the international legal anti-trafficking regime.

## 2.4 Transnational criminal law and human rights

As is the case with respect to many transnational criminal activities, states have found that recourse to criminal sanctions, however desirable, is extremely difficult without modifications to the substantive criminal law, including the creation of extraterritorial offences, and elaborate cooperation between national investigatory and prosecution authorities of states. Establishing each of these transnational

90 ibid.

regimes has to take into account its particular characteristics but they have factors in common. One of those features, which of course applies to all criminal law and procedure, not simply transnational law, is the relevance of human rights law – both as imposing certain specific duties on states, even with respect to private action (such as the activities of organised crime) and for the protection of victims, on the one hand, and for providing the framework for criminal investigation and fair trials for those suspected of offences under the transnational regime on the other hand.

The aim of anti-trafficking legislation is to combat trafficking through imposing criminal responsibility on the traffickers and obligations on the state, both to prevent and punish traffickers as well as to provide protection and support to victims with respect to their human rights. One element in the response of states to trafficking is to criminalise the activities of those who engage in trafficking, partly as a mark of the seriousness of the impact of trafficking on the women caught up in it,[91] and partly owing to the transnational nature of trafficking activity. With respect to the latter, the prospects of a wholly national, effective, criminal response may be remote as a result of jurisdictional restrictions and the need for criminal cooperation between affected states.[92] Where there is conduct wholly within one state (that is, where 'internal' trafficking occurs) and defendants are found, it may be possible to proceed against them under the 'ordinary' criminal law,[93] without needing to go into the complications of trafficking prosecutions.

Provided that an adequate anti-trafficking regime is in place, the state in question has fulfilled its human rights obligations up until the point where the putative victim is discovered in the destination state. Consequently, another element of the response to trafficking has been explicit recognition of the 'special position' of the victims of human trafficking. What this means is that due to the non-consensual nature of human trafficking, these women should not be treated as mere illegal immigrants, subject to peremptory removal processes and/or criminal proceedings for immigration[94] (or some other[95]) offences committed as a result of having been trafficked.

This may have a purely humanitarian basis but can be reinforced by the ordinary human rights obligations of the destinations states – the trafficked women may have suffered inhuman treatment or have been subjected to slavery-like practices or forced labour,[96] which might include protection against return to a

91 It is recognised here that trafficking is not restricted to the exploitation of women for paid for sex. However, this provides the framework of enquiry for this book.

92 Although the EU 2011 Directive could go some way toward resolving some of these issues, as it refers to jurisdictional matters.

93 In the UK, for example, provisions exist which target activity which can take place either as part of or independently from human trafficking – one such example being the criminalisation of 'controlling prostitution for gain', contrary to the Sexual Offences Act 2003 s 53.

94 See *R v O* [2008] (n 54) and J Elliott '(Mis)Identification of victims of human trafficking: the case of *R v O*' (2009) 21(4) *International Journal of Refugee Law* 727–41.

95 See *R v LM* (n 85).

96 See ch 3 for elucidation of the meaning of these terms as aspects of 'exploitation' as a 'purpose' element of human trafficking.

jurisdiction where there is a real risk that the same thing could happen to them again. The obligations of states under the anti-trafficking regime include positive actions, such as effective criminal prosecution of the individuals involved, the engagement of the victims in the criminal process etc. Where criminal proceedings may properly be taken against the victims, their vulnerability must be taken into account in determining what constitutes a fair trial.

The interrelation between international criminal law and human rights law is central to the anti-trafficking regime. The following sections will set out the international legal regime outlining the obligations placed upon states. The relevant legal provisions of the relevant UN, CoE, and EU instruments will be considered. Aspects of the legal regime which are central to the enquiry made in this book – namely the definition of human trafficking,[97] the role of consent,[98] and the treatment of 'victims'[99] – are considered in greater detail in subsequent chapters.

### *2.4.1 The international criminal regime: state obligations*

This section serves to outline the principal features of the main international instruments which deal with trafficking as a transnational criminal matter. The object is not to produce a comprehensive account of these provisions, but to indicate and outline the structure of the regimes, the main obligations placed upon states by these regimes, and to identify those issues which will be treated in some detail later in this body of work.

#### *2.4.1.1 Criminalisation, prosecution and punishment of traffickers*

The legal and policy responses to human trafficking are paramount to making destination states into hostile environments for traffickers and organised criminal networks to operate. The transnational nature of human trafficking demands an international response. This has come notably from the UN, the CoE, and the EU, all of which have recently produced instruments aimed at strengthening measures to prevent and combat human trafficking.

In 2000, the UN Trafficking Protocol was adopted. Article 3 provides the definition of human trafficking, which is reproduced in the Introduction to this book and is explored in Chapter 3. More recently, the CoE drafted the Convention on Action against Trafficking in Human Beings.[100] The CoE Trafficking Convention replicates verbatim the definition of human trafficking and many of the obligations

97 See ch 3 for full discussion of the international legal definition of human trafficking.

98 See ch 5 for full discussion of the role of consent in human trafficking.

99 See ch 6 for full discussion of provisions and practice relating to assistance to and support of victims.

100 CoE Trafficking Convention (n 82).

contained within the UN Trafficking Protocol – but it goes further in some respects.[101]

In order to effectively combat trafficking, criminalisation of trafficking activity is needed. State parties are called upon by the Trafficking Protocol to criminalise human trafficking where: perpetrators acted with intent; acted as accomplice; or played an organisational or directorial role in the commission of the trafficking offence.[102]

Article 18 of the CoE Trafficking Convention provides a solid obligation as regards measures to establish trafficking activity as criminal conduct at a domestic level. Unlike the Trafficking Protocol, which remains silent on the issue of criminal sanctions beyond actual criminalisation of human trafficking, the CoE Trafficking Convention makes specific mention of sanction in Article 23(1),[103] and recognises that aggravating circumstances may lead to harsher sanctions.[104] The European Convention on Extradition[105] and the European Arrest Warrant[106] use potential sentencing as part of the definition of extradition offences and it is, then, necessary that trafficking and associated offences be at least so punishable in order to use the criminal cooperation mechanisms of the European systems.[107]

Combating human trafficking has also consistently featured high on the EU

101 Most notably in terms of the provisions concerning the treatment of victims – see ch 6 for fuller discussion of this issue. The CoE Trafficking Convention also has broader scope of application than the UN Trafficking Protocol as the former only applies (unless stated otherwise) 'where those offences are transnational in nature and involve an organized criminal group', art 4. The CoE Trafficking Convention, however, applies 'to all forms of trafficking in human beings, whether national or transnational, whether or not connected with organised crime', art 2.

102 ibid art 5.

103 This Article states that: 'Each Party shall adopt such legislative and other measures as may be necessary to ensure that (trafficking offences) are punishable by effective, proportionate and dissuasive sanctions. These sanctions shall include, for criminal offences established in accordance with Article 18 when committed by natural persons, penalties involving deprivation of liberty which can give rise to extradition'.

104 Aggravating circumstances are addressed in art 24 which identifies these as where: '… the offence deliberately or by gross negligence endangered the life of the victim; the offence was committed against a child; the offence was committed by a public official in the performance of her/his duties; the offence was committed within the framework of a criminal organisation'. The Article does not specify the sanction or consequences of aggravated offences, beyond stating that the above-mentioned offences shall be 'regarded as aggravating circumstances in the determination of the penalty', thereby calling for more severe penalties where such offences are committed.

105 European Convention on Extradition (signed 13 December 1957, entered into force 18 April 1960).

106 See Council Framework Decision 2002/584/JHA of 13 June 2002 on the European arrest warrant and the surrender procedures between Member States [2002] OJ L190/1.

107 Article 2 of the European Convention on Extradition envisages sentencing of at least 12 months, and the European Arrest Warrant applies 'where a final sentence of imprisonment or a detention order has been imposed for a period of at least four months' and 'for offences punishable by imprisonment or a detention order for a maximum period of at least one year'. See Summary to Council Framework Decision 2002/584/JHA, ibid. The summary goes on to state that: 'If they are punishable in the issuing Member State by a custodial sentence of at least three years, the following offences, among others, may give rise to surrender without verification of the double criminality of the act: terrorism, trafficking in human beings …'.

agenda in recent years, with law and policy adopted over the past decade indicating a clear intention to do just that.[108] Article 5(3) of the EU Charter of Fundamental Rights[109] even provides for explicit prohibition of trafficking in human beings.[110] The most recent EU legislation comes in the form of the 2011 Directive.[111] The initial UK response demonstrated a reluctance to opt in to this directive, claiming that there would be 'No benefits for the UK'.[112] Unsurprisingly, this decision was criticised.[113] Subsequent to the text of the directive being finalised, the UK Government indicated an intention to opt in[114] – an intention which was carried out.

The 2011 Directive reconciles discrepancies between Member State law in terms of prevention and prosecution (of trafficking and traffickers) as well as protection and treatment of victims of trafficking. Substantive criminal law provisions include prohibiting and making punishable the acts provided within the definition of human trafficking, provided in Article 2 (which is phrased in almost exactly the same terms as the UN Trafficking Protocol and CoE Trafficking Convention[115]) by a maximum of at least five years custodial sentence.[116] The 2011 Directive also provides for aggravating circumstances on the part of the trafficker which are

108 See European Commission website: 'Together against trafficking in human beings' http://ec.europa.eu/anti-trafficking/index.action (last accessed 1 January 2014).

109 See Charter of Fundamental Rights of the European Union [2000] OJ C364/01, reprinted [2010] OJ C83/389 http://www.europarl.europa.eu/charter/pdf/text_en.pdf (last accessed 12 January 2014), implemented by the Treaty of Lisbon amending the Treaty on European Union and the Treaty establishing the European Community, signed at Lisbon, 13 December 2007 (2007/C 306/01).

110 ibid art 5.

111 EU 2011 Directive (n 84).

112 Home Office 'Home Office defends position on human trafficking' (31 August 2010) http://www.homeoffice.gov.uk/media-centre/news/trafficking-directive (last accessed 1 July 2011).

113 See, for example, CARE 'EU Directive on Human Trafficking: why the Government should opt in' http://www.care.org.uk/wp-content/uploads/2011/02/EU-Directive-on-Human-Trafficking-Why-the-UK-should-opt-in-7-Feb-2011.pdf (last accessed 25 March 2011).

114 See Parliamentary Business 'MPs debate EU Directive on Human Trafficking' UK Parliament website 10 May 2011 http://www.parliament.uk/business/news/2011/may/trafficking-in-human-beings/ (last accessed 11 May 2011, where it was stated that the European Scrutiny Committee recommended in a report that the UK Government should opt in, and Damian Green stated that: '... the [European Scrutiny] Committee acknowledged that the objective of preventing and combating trafficking cannot be sufficiently achieved by member states alone and can, by reason of both its scale and effects, be better achieved by action at EU level. Our intention to opt in is consistent with that view.' See Home Office (Minister of State of Immigration, Damian Green) 'EU Directive on Human Trafficking – Written Ministerial Statement' (22 March 2011) http://www.homeoffice.gov.uk/publications/about-us/parliamentary-business/written-ministerial-statement/eu-direct-human-trafficking-wms/ (last accessed 22 March 2011), and European Scrutiny Committee report 'Trafficking in human beings' (9 March 2011) http://www.publications.parliament.uk/pa/cm201011/cmselect/cmeuleg/428-xxii/42805.htm (last accessed 24 March 2011).

115 The definition provided within the EU 2011 Directive replicates almost verbatim the UN Trafficking Protocol definition, yet goes further with regard to the 'purpose' element in that it includes 'begging' as an example of forced labour or services.

116 As required by EU 2011 Directive art 4.

punishable by a maximum of at least 10 years custodial sentence.[117] A welcome move under the directive is the establishment of jurisdiction over Member State nationals or residents who commit trafficking offences outside their country of nationality or residence.[118]

The UK response has been to criminalise human trafficking and related activity with a veritable plethora of offences, so that the elements of the internationally accepted definition of human trafficking are fragmented across different provisions. Various provisions were enacted and repealed[119] so that at present many of the central provisions relating to sex trafficking are found in the Sexual Offences Act 2003 (SOA 2003).

Trafficking into, within and out of the UK are criminalised by section 59A of the SOA 2003. According to this provision, A commits an offence if he facilitates the entry, travel within, or departure from the UK of B, and A intends to or believes that another is likely to do something which would constitute a 'relevant offence', the latter being primarily (although not exclusively)[120] an offence under Part 1 of the SOA 2003.[121] Part 1 has broad reach, including offences ranging from rape[122] to controlling prostitution for gain,[123] and due to the sheer magnitude of 'relevant offences' contained within that Part, it seems that simplified, consolidatory legislative measures would not be unwelcome. The Modern Slavery Bill may help to achieve this.[124] A further trafficking offence is provided within section 4 of the Asylum and Immigration (Treatment of Claimants, etc.) Act 2004, which addresses facilitation of entry or arrival into the UK of an individual, coupled with non-consensual exploitation of said individual. All of the aforementioned offences include a lack of consent element, save in the case of minors. The penalty for a

117 Article 4 covers aggravating factors, which are where: the offence was committed against a victim who was particularly vulnerable, which, in the context of this directive, shall include at least child victims; the offence was committed within the framework of a criminal organisation within the meaning of Council Framework Decision 2008/841/JHA of 24 October 2008 on the fight against organised crime [2008] L300/42; the offence deliberately or by gross negligence endangered the life of the victim; the offence was committed by use of serious violence or has caused particularly serious harm to the victim. Inchoate offences are also punishable – art 3 requires 'Inciting, aiding, abetting and attempting' to be made punishable by states.

118 ibid art 10.

119 Such as the offence of 'Trafficking in prostitution', found in s 145 of the Nationality, Immigration and Asylum Act 2002 and repealed by the Sexual Offences Act 2003 (SOA 2003) (Schedule 7) as of as of 1 May 2004 (SI 2004/874).

120 SOA 2003 s 60 also includes as 'relevant offences': 'an offence under section 1(1)(a) of the Protection of Children Act 1978 (c 37); an offence listed in Schedule 1 to the Criminal Justice (Children) (Northern Ireland) Order 1998 (SI 1998/1504 (NI 9)); an offence under art 3(1)(a) of the Protection of Children (Northern Ireland) Order 1978 (SI 1978/1047 (NI 17)), or anything done outside England and Wales and Northern Ireland which is not an offence within any of paragraphs (a) to (d) but would be if done in England and Wales or Northern Ireland'.

121 SOA 2003 s 60.

122 ibid s 1.

123 ibid s 53.

124 Draft Modern Slavery Bill https://www.gov.uk/government/publications/draft-modern-slavery-bill (last accessed 29 March 2014).

trafficking offence under national law ranges from a fine not exceeding the statutory maximum, to a custodial sentence not exceeding 14 years.[125]

People smuggling offences are dealt with elsewhere in the UK legislative framework,[126] and are characterised by illicit facilitation of movement of an individual. The maximum penalty for smuggling offences is a 14-year custodial sentence. Consequently, there is on the face of it potentially no difference as to the sanction to be applied to traffickers and smugglers prosecuted in the UK, although severity sentencing may vary to reflect the severity of the offence in individual cases. Further to this, the ultimate sanction in a trafficking case will vary according to whether (and which of) any of the 'relevant offences' is also committed. The criminal law anti-trafficking provisions in the UK clearly have had some reach in terms of prosecution and punishment for trafficking offences, as decided cases indicate.[127]

Prohibition and prosecution are, of course, only part of the picture. Preventative measures and effective monitoring mechanisms are undoubtedly a valuable aspect of the anti-trafficking regime. The following section will consider such measures as are envisaged by the main anti-trafficking instruments.

#### *2.4.1.2 Prevention and monitoring*

The UN Trafficking Protocol requires that states take measures to prevent human trafficking and re-victimisation, such as 'research, information and mass media campaigns and social and economic initiatives'.[128] Cooperation with non-governmental organisations and other relevant bodies is called for in implementing such measures.

The Trafficking Protocol also calls for action by origin states to 'alleviate the factors that make persons, especially women and children, vulnerable to trafficking, such as poverty, underdevelopment and lack of equal opportunity'.[129] Noll[130]

125 SOA 2003 s 59A.

126 Immigration Act 1971 s 25 (substituted by the Nationality, Immigration and Asylum Act 2002 s 143) creates an offence of assisting unlawful immigration (known as facilitation) and also covers acts previously dealt with under the old offence of 'harbouring'. Immigration Act 1971 s 25A (also substituted by the Nationality, Immigration and Asylum Act 2002 s 143) creates an offence of knowingly facilitating the arrival or entry of another into the UK for gain, coupled with knowledge or reasonable cause to believe that the individual is an asylum seeker. Immigration Act 1971 s 25B(1) (also substituted by the Nationality, Immigration and Asylum Act 2002 s 143) addresses assisting entry into the UK in breach of deportation of exclusion order. Immigration Act 1971 s 25B(3) provides for assisting entry/remaining of an excluded person.

127 See, for example, *Re Attorney General's Reference (Nos 37, 38 and 65 of 2010)* [2010] EWCA Crim 2880; [2011] Crim LR 336, (2010) 108(2) LSG 18; *The Times* (24 February 2011); *R v Maka (Shaban)* [2005] EWCA Crim 3365; [2006] 2 Cr App R (S) 14; *Re Attorney General's Reference (No 6 of 2004)*, also known as *R v Plakici (Luan)* [2004] EWCA Crim 1275, [2005] 1 Cr App R (S) 19, (2004) 148 SJLB 541.

128 UN Trafficking Protocol art 9(2).

129 ibid art 9(4).

130 G Noll 'The insecurity of trafficking in international law' in Vincent Chetail (ed) *Globalization, Migration and Human Rights: International Law Under Review* (Bruylant, Bruxelles, 2007) 343, 353.

asserts that the relevant factors such as poverty and lack of education which exacerbate the risk of human trafficking are in fact themselves human rights violations. However, Piotrowicz recognises that:

> … it nevertheless remains the case that the state has not done the trafficking. The fear of having one's social and economic rights violated might also suffice to make someone vulnerable to other threats but it is a big leap from there to the point where the state is responsible for the criminal acts of another. To make a tort analogy, is not the damage too remote?[131]

Further to these requirements, the Trafficking Protocol addresses the issue of cooperation and training of law enforcement and immigration officials, as well as other relevant authorities, in terms of the exchange of information to help determine whether individuals attempting to cross international borders are either traffickers or victims of trafficking. The Protocol states that '[t]he training should also take into account the need to consider human rights and child-and gender-sensitive issues'.[132] Information exchange regarding the types of travel documents used by traffickers and trafficked persons, and the methods and means used by OCGs to recruit and transport victims such as the routes used etc, is also envisaged.[133]

Similarly, the CoE Trafficking Convention goes beyond prosecution and punishment of traffickers, and also has a provision relating to origin state action regarding the reduction of vulnerability of the putative victim.[134] Measures to prevent human trafficking envisaged in the Convention are very similar to those envisaged by the Trafficking Protocol. A monitoring mechanism is provided for within Article 36 of the Convention, whereby a Group of Experts against trafficking in human beings (GRETA)[135] and the Committee of the Parties[136] will help to ensure effective implementation through the provision of periodic reports relating

131 R Piotrowicz 'The legal nature of trafficking in human beings' (2009) 4 *Intercultural Human Rights Law Review* 179, 184–85.

132 UN Trafficking Protocol art 10(2).

133 ibid art 10(1).

134 Article 5(2) states that: 'Each Party shall establish and/or strengthen effective policies and programmes to prevent trafficking in human beings, by such means as: research, information, awareness raising and education campaigns, social and economic initiatives and training programmes, in particular for persons vulnerable to trafficking and for professionals concerned with trafficking in human beings.'

135 Described in the Explanatory Report to the CoE Trafficking Convention as 'a technical body, composed of independent and highly qualified experts in the area of Human Rights, assistance and protection to victims and the fight against trafficking in human beings, with the task of adopting a report and conclusions on each Party's implementation of the Convention'. See Explanatory Report to the CoE Trafficking Convention para 354 http://conventions.coe.int/Treaty/EN/Reports/Html/197.htm (last accessed 1 July 2011).

136 Described as 'a more political body, the Committee of the Parties, composed of the representatives in the Committee of Ministers of the Parties to the Convention and of representatives of Parties non-members of the CoE, which may adopt recommendations, on the basis of the report and conclusions of GRETA, addressed to a Party concerning the measures to be taken to follow up GRETA's conclusions'. See Explanatory Report to the CoE Trafficking Convention para 354, ibid.

to the implementation measures adopted by each party and the adoption of non-binding recommendations with respect to the implementation measures taken or yet to be taken.

The EU 2011 Directive includes similar prevention-based provisions,[137] calling for information campaigns and social and economic initiatives. Establishment of national monitoring mechanisms such as National Rapporteurs[138] (or 'equivalent mechanisms') by Member States is required by Article 19 of the Directive. The 'equivalent mechanism' in the UK is the Inter-Departmental Ministerial Group on Trafficking, whose duties have included monitoring progress on the UK Action Plan on Tackling Human Trafficking,[139] and the implementation of the CoE Trafficking Convention.

Measures to discourage the demand for the product of exploitation of trafficked persons are encouraged – Article 6 of the CoE Trafficking Convention suggests that demand sanctions may be considered by states, by requesting that:

> To discourage the demand that fosters all forms of exploitation of persons, especially women and children, that leads to trafficking, each Party shall adopt or strengthen legislative, administrative, educational, social, cultural or other measures ...[140]

The UN Trafficking Protocol has a similar provision,[141] as does the EU 2011 Directive.[142] The inclusion of demand sanction measures was not uncontroversial.[143] Accordingly, the provision is not binding. This continues the theme of

137 EU 2011 Directive art 18.

138 Article 19 provides that the role of the Rapporteur would include carrying out assessments of trends in trafficking in human beings, gathering statistics, and measuring the results of anti-trafficking actions, and produce regular reports.

139 See Home Office and Scottish Executive 'UK Action Plan on tackling human trafficking' (March 2007) http://www.ungift.org/doc/knowledgehub/resource-centre/Governments/UK_Action_Plan_to_Combat_Human_Trafficking_en.pdf (last accessed 4 January 2014).

140 CoE Trafficking Convention art 6. Article 9 of the CoE Convention also specifically calls for consideration by Parties of the criminalisation of use of the services provided by the object of exploitation (i.e. the trafficked person) where there is knowledge of the individual's status as trafficked.

141 Article 9(5) targets the demand aspect, and requires that: 'States Parties shall adopt or strengthen legislative or other measures, such as educational, social or cultural measures, including through bilateral and multilateral cooperation, to discourage the demand that fosters all forms of exploitation of persons, especially women and children, that leads to trafficking'.

142 Article 18(1) states that: 'Member States shall take appropriate measures, such as education and training, to discourage and reduce the demand that fosters all forms of exploitation related to trafficking in human beings'. The directive also specifically calls for consideration by Member States of the criminalisation of use of the services of the trafficked person where there is knowledge of her status as trafficked – art 18(4).

143 The Explanatory Memorandum to the Proposal for the EU 2011 Directive highlights the potentially controversial nature of such measures in stating that: 'The issue of introducing a specific obligation to criminalise clients who knowingly use sexual services from a trafficked person was controversial among stakeholders. Several MS [Member States] pointed out that in any case such a provision should not be binding'. See Explanatory Memorandum to the Proposal for the 2011 Directive, 2.1.2.

addressing prostitution in a trafficking context without prejudice as to how individual countries or Member States choose to address it.[144]

Legislation aimed at reducing the demand for sold sexual services has been enacted in several countries over the last decade or so, including the UK. The UK response is reflected in section 53A of the SOA 2003, inserted by the Policing and Crime Act 2009, section 14. The provision contains a strict liability offence which criminalises the purchase of sexual services from an individual who is forced, coerced, or deceived into providing them.[145] The proposed use of demand sanctions such as these, although part of a larger overarching UK action plan to combat human trafficking,[146] was at least initially based upon a Swedish model, where the purchase of sold sex has been criminalised since 1999.[147] The Swedish model does not require the existence of force, coercion etc – it constitutes an outright prohibition in any circumstances. The evidence as to the success or otherwise of the Swedish provision is contradictory, to say the least.[148]

The following section will outline both the human rights and bespoke anti-trafficking legislative framework applicable to victims of trafficking.

144 The terms 'sexual exploitation' and 'exploitation of prostitution' are not defined within the trafficking definition, as discussed in ch 3.

145 SOA 2003 s 53A, inserted by the Policing and Crime Act 2009 s 14.

146 Home Office and Scottish Executive 'UK Action Plan on tackling human trafficking' (n 139).

147 The Swedish Law Prohibiting the Purchase of Sexual Services 1998: Law (1998:408) Prohibition of the Purchase of Sexual Services; *Lag ou förbund mot köp av sexuella tjänster* (1998): *Dem som mot ersattning skaffar sig en tillfällig sexuell förbindelse, doms – om inte gärningen är belagd med straff enligt Brottsbalken – för köp av sexuella tjänster till böter eller fängelse i högst sex månader. För försök döms till ansvar enligt 23 kap. Brottsbalken*, now enshrined in the Swedish Penal Code.

148 Some sources report a positive effect. In the 2003 and 2004 reports, the Swedish National Rapporteur for Trafficking in Women at the National Criminal Investigation Department noted that the Swedish Law has had positive effects as regards combating trafficking. See *Justis- og Politidepartementet* (Ministry of Justice and the Police) 'Purchasing sexual services in Sweden and the Netherlands: legal regulation and experiences, an abbreviated English version, a Report by a Working Group on the legal regulation of the purchase of sexual services' (issued on 8 October 2004) http://www.regjeringen.no/upload/kilde/jd/rap/2004/0034/ddd/pdfv/232216-purchasing_sexual_services_in_sweden_and_the_nederlands.pdf (last accessed 1 July 2011); see also G Ekberg 'The Swedish law that prohibits the purchase of sexual services: best practices for prevention of prostitution and trafficking in human beings' (October 2004) 10(10) *Violence against Women* 1187–218, 1199. Conversely, others refer to the lack of empirical evidence on which the enactment of the law was founded, as well as the adverse side effects for prostitutes. See J Elliott 'Criminalising the purchase of sexual services: the use of strict liability as a form of risk management?' in J Child, K Doolin, A Beech, J Rain *Whose Criminal Justice: Regulatory State or Empowered Communities?* (Waterside Press 2011); J Levy 'Swedish abolitionism as violence against women' Paper presented at the Sex Worker Open University Sex Workers' Rights Festival, Glasgow (6 April 2013); and V Clausen 'An Assessment of Gunilla Ekberg's account of Swedish prostitution policy' (January 2007) http://www.sexworkeurope.org/sites/default/files/resource-pdfs/ekberg_kritik.pdf (last accessed 18 January 2014).

### *2.4.2 The international human rights regime and the treatment of victims – state obligations*

In this book, the term 'human rights' in the main refers to the law and practice under the European Convention on Human Rights (ECHR)[149] (which is binding on all the states concerned). In some cases, it is necessary to take into account other human rights agreements, such as the International Covenant on Civil and Political Rights (ICCPR);[150] therefore, other such instruments will be referred to at times.

#### *2.4.2.1 Human rights obligations*

Although human trafficking is sometimes referred to as a breach of the human rights of the trafficked person, it is worth noting from the outset that trafficking does not necessarily involve such a breach.[151] A conviction for trafficking would not depend upon demonstrating any such breach.

Human rights obligations are addressed to states, whereas trafficking per se involves criminal acts carried out by private actors. The state has obligations under human rights law to have in place adequate measures – legislative or otherwise – to ensure that individuals are protected from human rights abuses which may occur as a result of being or having been trafficked, such as being subjected to inhuman or degrading treatment[152] or slavery and its related practices or forced labour.[153] Consequently, violations where the immediate cause of the damage is the act of a private person (and therefore a non-state actor) arise from the failure of the state to act – to prevent the violation, to provide an effective remedy for the violation, or in some cases, to provide for the criminalisation of the private conduct of traffickers and effective investigations into suspected trafficking offences. Further to this, human rights obligations may arise with respect to how victims must be treated once they are discovered in the host state and have escaped the control of their traffickers.[154]

The human rights framework relating to victims of human trafficking is simply that which is applicable to any human being in need of certain types of protection, and includes, for example, protection of those who – if returned to the origin state – face a real risk of ill-treatment amounting to human rights violations. These

149 Convention for the Protection of Human Rights and Fundamental Freedoms (opened for signature 4 November 1950, entered into force 3 September 1953) (ECHR).

150 International Covenant on Civil and Political Rights (adopted 16 December 1966, entered into force 23 March 1976) 999 UNTS 171 (ICCPR).

151 See Piotrowicz (n 131) 184–85.

152 Provided within art 3 ECHR and discussed in depth in ch 6.

153 See, for example, *Siliadin v France* (Application no 73316/01) [2005] ECHR 545; *R v Tang* [2008] HCA 39 (28 August 2008) 142; *Rantsev v Cyprus and Russia* [2010] (Application no 25965/04) ; *Hadijatou Mani Koraou v Republic of Niger* [2008] ECW/CCJ/JUD/06/08; *OOO et al v Commissioner of Metropolitan Police* [2011] EWHC 1246 (QB). The applicable human rights provisions with respect to slavery, forced labour and practices related to slavery are discussed in depth in ch 3.

154 See ch 6 for discussion of this issue.

human rights obligations overlap with the requirements of the trafficking instruments (discussed below and in Chapter 4) but are further protected by the possibility of national and international legal action to challenge state action or inaction. Trafficked persons may therefore have recourse to protections under Article 3 of the ECHR or Article 33(1) of the Refugee Convention.[155] As discussed in Chapter 6,[156] the applicable standard here is that laid down in *Soering*,[157] namely 'where substantial grounds have been shown for believing that the person concerned, if extradited, faces a real risk of being subjected to torture or to inhuman or degrading treatment or punishment in the requesting country'.[158] It has been established that application of this principle now extends beyond extradition.[159]

Such obligations arise in the context of victims of human trafficking because of the context of some cases which arise in practice. These include the possibility of threats and reprisals (from traffickers) on return (of the victim) to the origin state, the potential for re-trafficking, or even serious ill-treatment due to social ostracism from the individual's community as a result of the woman having worked in prostitution.[160]

Aside from the rights and protections conferred by ordinary human rights law, there are specific aspects of the anti-trafficking regime which offer nuanced and bespoke rights and protection to victims of human trafficking. These will be outlined in the following section, and discussed in greater depth in Chapter 6.

### *2.4.2.2 The treatment of victims*

The applicable framework regarding the provision of support, assistance and protection to victims of human trafficking includes adoption of measures to identify, protect and rehabilitate victims once discovered in the destination state, and provide for victims to remain in the territory of that state where necessary and appropriate, as well as relevant provisions relating to repatriation.

The Trafficking Protocol offered very little by way of obligations to provide any specific rights or protections to victims of human trafficking, in stating that parties may '*consider* implementing measures to provide for the physical, psychological and social recovery of victims of trafficking in persons'[161] (emphasis added). Such measures could, according to the Protocol, include access to accommodation and counselling. States are asked to consider issuing temporary residence permits[162] while giving consideration to humanitarian and compassionate factors.[163]

155 Convention Relating to the Status of Refugees (adopted 28 July 1951, entered into force 22 April 1954) 189 UNTS 137 (Refugee Convention).
156 See ch 6.
157 See *Soering v UK* (1989) 11 EHRR 439.
158 ibid para 91.
159 See, for example, *Cruz-Varas v Sweden* (1992) 14 EHRR 1.
160 See ch 6.
161 UN Trafficking Protocol art 6(3).
162 ibid art 7(1).
163 ibid art 7(2).

Consequently, the Protocol imposes no solid obligation on parties to adopt any measures which are favourable in terms of victim protection.

The CoE Trafficking Convention, however, requires more, primarily calling for the provision of a recovery and reflection period of at least 30 days in situations where there are 'reasonable grounds' to believe that an individual is a victim of trafficking.[164] The UK currently provides a period of 45 days, which could be extended in certain circumstances.[165] When this period has passed and an individual has been positively identified as a victim of human trafficking, a residence permit should be granted either where a victim is cooperating in criminal proceedings or an investigation, and/or, where provision of the permit is deemed necessary owing to the 'personal situation' of the trafficked victim.[166]

A lack of clear implementing legislation as regards this matter in the UK is apparently attributable to the fact that domestic policies such as that of discretionary leave are already considered sufficient to meet this requirement.[167] The matter is arguably not so clear cut, as the discussion in Chapter 6 will indicate.[168] Where a residence permit is granted in the UK, it will be for a minimum of one year.[169]

States are required to protect the identity and private life of victims,[170] and to provide assistance in terms of providing accommodation and medical treatment, and access to counselling and interpreters etc.[171] Further obligations include providing access to legal assistance and free legal aid, as well as to compensation from the perpetrators.[172] The 'possibility' of states 'not imposing penalties on victims for their involvement in unlawful activities, to the extent that they have been compelled to do so' is addressed in Article 26, but it is not framed in terms of a solid obligation for any state to do so.[173]

Paramount to securing access to the above-mentioned benefits is correct and timely identification of victims. Article 10 of the CoE Trafficking Convention provides for the development of identification procedures and the training of relevant officials to execute these procedures. Previous UK victim support efforts were minimal, and include the Poppy Project.[174] Following ratification of the CoE

164 ibid art 13.

165 Home Office 'Impact assessment of ratification of the Council of Europe Convention on action against trafficking in human beings' (6 October 2008) 5 http://www.ialibrary.berr.gov.uk/ImpactAssessment/?IAID=da0f3cecd6214381bef9e9514cb46afd (last accessed 10 May 2010, link no longer live).

166 UN Trafficking Protocol art 14.

167 Home Office (n 165) 6.

168 See ch 6.

169 Home Office (n 165) 6.

170 UN Trafficking Protocol art 11.

171 ibid art 12.

172 ibid art 15.

173 See ch 6 for further discussion of this issue.

174 The Poppy Project is funded by the Office for Criminal Justice Reform (reporting to the Ministry of Justice) and offers accommodation and support to female victims of trafficking. This project has played a valuable role in identifying and supporting victims of human trafficking. See the Poppy Project http://www.eaves4women.co.uk/POPPY_Project/POPPY_Project.php (last accessed 21 March 2014).

Trafficking Convention, the UK has in place a 'National Referral Mechanism' (NRM). Under this mechanism, indicators are used by front-line professionals to help identify putative victims, before referring their details on to a designated Competent Authority[175] who are charged with making a decision as to whether there are 'reasonable grounds' to believe that the individual has indeed been trafficked.[176] The Anti-Trafficking Monitoring Group has concluded that the UK NRM has thus far been somewhat problematic.[177] This merits further discussion, which will take place in Chapter 6.

The EU 2011 Directive makes some provision for the support, assistance and protection of victims, and states that more rigorous protection of victims' rights is one of its major objectives.[178] Assistance must be given before, during and for an appropriate time after criminal proceedings have concluded (which can continue in any case without involvement of the victim[179]) so that victims may have access to the rights laid down in the 2011 Directive and Framework Decision 2001/220/JHA, the latter of which relates to the standing of victims in criminal proceedings.[180]

Access to assistance under the 2011 Directive depends upon a 'reasonable-grounds indication'[181] that the individual in question is a victim of trafficking. As with the CoE Convention, a mechanism for victim identification must be established,[182] and 'assistance and support' is to include comparable measures to those required under the CoE Convention – accommodation, counselling etc.[183] Victims are to have access to legal counselling and representation,[184] and are to be subject to a risk assessment to determine the level of protection needed and whether, say, a witness protection programme or similar is necessary.[185]

Rather than including specific provisions regarding residence permits – temporary or otherwise – the 2011 Directive instead points to Council Directive 2004/81/EC April 2004 on the residence permit issued to third-country nationals who are victims of trafficking in human beings or who have been the subject of an action to facilitate illegal immigration, who cooperate with the competent authorities,[186] and Council Directive 2004/83/EC of 29 April 2004 on minimum

175 In the case of the UK, these are the Home Office Immigration and Visas (previously UK Border Agency) and the UK Human Trafficking Centre.

176 Home Office (n 165) 5.

177 See the Anti-Trafficking Monitoring Group 'Wrong kind of victim? One year on: an analysis of UK measures to protect trafficked persons' (June 2010) http://www.antislavery.org/includes/documents/cm_docs/2010/a/1_atmg_report_for_web.pdf (last accessed 1 January 2014).

178 EU 2011 Directive preamble para 7.

179 ibid art 9.

180 Council Framework Decision 2001/220/JHA of 15 March 2001 on the standing of victims in criminal proceedings [2001] OJ L82/1.

181 EU 2011 Directive art 11.

182 ibid art 11(4).

183 ibid art 11(5).

184 ibid art 12(2).

185 ibid art 12(3).

186 Council Directive 2004/81/EC of 29 April 2004 on the residence permit issued to third-country

standards for the qualification and status of third country nationals or stateless persons as refugees or as persons who otherwise need international protection and the content of the protection granted.[187] Consequently, the issuance of residence permits becomes a possibility either where the victim is cooperating in criminal proceedings where the state is trying to obtain a prosecution against the traffickers, or where there is need for such a permit on the basis of refuge or subsidiary protection.

Article 8 of the 2011 Directive also provides for non-application of penalties to victims who have committed criminal acts as a result of having been trafficked, although this is not a clear obligation as tentative language is used in that the Article states that Member States are asked to take '... necessary measures to ensure that competent national authorities are *entitled* not to prosecute ...' (emphasis added). The UK currently has in place two Crown Prosecution Service (CPS) Protocols which provide for prosecutorial discretion as regards offences committed by victims as a result of having been trafficked.[188]

The provisions of the various instruments comprising the legal anti-trafficking regime clearly aim for a multi-faceted attack on trafficking and illicit facilitated migration. Those most central to the inquiry made by the monograph are the definition of 'human trafficking', which raises the issue of 'coercion' or 'lack of consent' of the person transported and, secondly, the consequent provisions relating to the assistance and support to be offered to victims, the correct identification of whom depends upon their having being coerced, forced, and therefore 'lack of consent' etc. The question arises about the relationship between coercion and the lack of consent of any potential victim. It has been/will be submitted that 'coercion' ought not to be understood solely as the forcible overriding of any wish of the woman (amounting to kidnapping into exploitation in another country). However, identifying the circumstances when the treatment of the woman and the context in which she makes any decision such that we may say that she has been 'coerced' is problematic.

It is useful here to reiterate the dual aspect of the definition of human trafficking – it may be used as a basis of criminal liability but it may also be used for collateral purposes, such as indicating when the various cooperation obligations apply or for identifying who is a victim. One's first reaction would likely be in favour of identical interpretations (of the definition of trafficking) whenever a question of interpretation arose, especially where all or any of them had been given domestic

nationals who are victims of trafficking in human beings or who have been the subject of an action to facilitate illegal immigration, who cooperate with the competent authorities [2004] OJ L261/19.

187 Council Directive 2004/83/EC of 29 April 2004 on minimum standards for the qualification and status of third country nationals or stateless persons as refugees or as persons who otherwise need international protection and the content of the protection granted [2004] OJ L304/12.

188 Crown Prosecution Service 'Prosecution of defendants charged With offences Who might be trafficked victims' and 'Prosecution of Young defendants charged With offences Who might be trafficked victims' http://www.cps.gov.uk/legal/h_to_k/human_trafficking_and_smuggling/ (last accessed 1 January 2014).

effect in those terms, but that would be to concede, for instance, that the stricter requirements of the criminal law would prevail over the broader humanitarian objectives of identifying victims.

To elaborate upon this point – in practice, we know that it is very unlikely that any question of interpretation will arise other than in a domestic forum (or by a domestic body). These days, national courts often (though not always) use the Articles on interpretation of the Vienna Convention on the Law of Treaties,[189] which they regard as being customary international law, whenever they are faced with the interpretation of a treaty. They are also, of course, bound by domestic law, not just principles of interpretation but other principles and rules, one of which, is the principle of legality – that a criminal defendant is entitled to have the law setting out the offence with which he is charged interpreted strictly in his favour.

One can easily imagine that a defendant to a criminal charge of trafficking will allege that the women consented to being transferred and exploited and so there was no trafficking offence. He would argue that 'consent' covered all circumstances other than direct coercion (of which, he would say, there had been none). A transported woman would want to argue that she had been trafficked in the widest range of circumstances and that she was a trafficked victim. She would want to say (and she would not have any presumptions in her favour as a criminal defendant would) that she had not consented – that she had been deceived, driven by press of economic circumstances, could not have consented to the appalling conditions amounting to a slavery like practice etc.

There is a conflict between the standards of the criminal law and the humanitarian objective of identifying victims who are to be protected. One solution would be to adopt the same understanding in both sets of cases, which would have to be the criminal standard, at the expense of some possible 'victims'. Another would be to say that, even for criminal purposes, the definition of trafficking clearly envisages an absence of consent in a wider range of circumstances than direct coercion and, even for establishing criminality, it is for a court to examine whether or not there was consent by the women in this case, and where there was not there would be the criminal offence of trafficking and the transported women would be victims. The latter may be the preferable solution. The third possibility is that we use a different test to determine who is a trafficker and who is a victim. This might serve both criminal and humanitarian purposes but could easily lead to confusion and might not be too popular with destination states, which would have both to prosecute more traffickers and protect more victims.

Where women are smuggled but not trafficked because of difficulties – legal and evidential – about establishing that there was not consent, then – as will be argued in Chapter 7 – states should, even if they are not obliged to, consider treating women who have endured oppressive, exploitative conditions short of

189 Vienna Convention on the Law of Treaties (done at Vienna on 23 May 1969, entered into force on 27 January 1980, in accordance with art 84(1)) United Nations Treaty Series 1155 (Vienna Convention) arts 31 and 32.

slavery-like practices as 'victims', in the same way that discretionary powers are sometimes used with respect to failed refugee applicants. Clearly, the variety of interests covered by the trafficking definitions do not lead to simple interpretative solutions.

Consideration of the consent/coercion spectrum in this body of work approaches the question through consideration of the 'lack of consent' of the woman, making it clear that no automatic conclusions are to be drawn that lack of consent equates with coercion.

## 2.5 Conclusion

Human trafficking continues as a result of a melting pot of factors which link supply and demand. It is clear that the factors underlying the continuance of this activity in Europe – and worldwide – are many, and rest largely, although not exclusively, on poverty and lack of opportunity. The supply side is maintained through factors which are largely economic and gender-based; the economic marginalisation of women in impoverished regions, and the discrimination and lack of access to basic rights suffered by the same women. These various factors serve to ensure that a continual source of migrants is available to be smuggled, trafficked, or 'consensually' trafficked for the purpose of exploitation. Whether the individuals involved have in fact been smuggled, trafficked, or something in between the two, it seems clear that as long as these 'push' factors exist, and as long as the demand for sold sex exists, there will be a global business in sex trafficking and facilitated migration for the purposes of working in the sex trade.

These 'push' factors, however, do not work alone to perpetuate exploitative illicit migration. The economic and social factors underpinning this activity are exacerbated by the presence of OCGs who see an opportunity for financial gain caused by the demand for sold sex in certain countries. The demand ensures a continuous search for more potential victims, whether these victims are recruited through kidnap, deception, or other means. Corruption within law enforcement institutions also plays a significant part, as does border control, and increased ease of travel and communication as a result of globalisation. The evidence indicates that although routes and transit countries can be identified at given times, the routes will continually change in response to their discovery and any subsequent interruption of trafficking activities.

A comprehensive strategy to combat human trafficking needs to come from all angles. These many and varied factors require a variety of legal and non-legal responses, ranging from a legislative response which criminalises the traffickers, to measures geared toward prevention in countries of origin, transit, and destination. It is clear that a multi-pronged attack is necessary, which involves not only the criminalisation of traffickers and protection of victims, but international cooperation and coordination on what action to take. The legal anti-trafficking regime outlined earlier in this chapter indicates an increasing willingness by affected states to take part in a coordinated and effective international (and national) response to the trafficking phenomenon; thereby strengthening the anti-trafficking regime and moving ever closer to as unified a system as possible – a system which not only provides for prosecution and punishment of traffickers, but also prevention of trafficking activity and the provision of support, assistance and protection to victims.

Sex trafficking is an example of serious non-consensual exploitation, which sees the perpetrators taking advantage of some of the most economically marginalised sections of society. Either way, the empirical evidence considered throughout this chapter suggests that many of the individual migrants concerned at least embark upon their journey on a consensual basis; consenting to work in the sex trade, consenting to migrate and work in the sex trade, or initially consenting to the trafficking process with consent being rendered ineffective by deception or some other form of 'means'.

The concept of consent is clearly central to determinations of who is, and who is not, a victim of human trafficking. These issues, therefore, are central to the inquiry made by this body of work and justify the focus on consent and victims of trafficking for exploitative facilitated migration. Although state obligations beyond solely those relating to victims are an integral part of the anti-trafficking regime, they are not central to this book and therefore will not be covered any further than they have been in this chapter.

Now we know what states must do, it becomes necessary to examine what trafficking is in a legal sense,[190] which will in turn pave the way for discussion of why the issue of consent in the context of sexual exploitation[191] and trafficking for that purpose[192] is so fundamentally important if adequate protection of vulnerable parties and victims is to be successfully achieved.[193] For criminal cooperation and human rights compliant measures to be possible, it has been necessary to reach legal consensus as to exactly what human trafficking consists of. This transnational activity requires transnational response, the starting point for which is an internationally agreed definition of what constitutes 'trafficking in humans'. This will now be discussed in Chapter 3.

This chapter has examined the contextual and legal background to human trafficking, including consideration of the 'push' factors underlying the continuance of human trafficking, and the influence of organised crime. The international anti-trafficking regime has been outlined, as have the obligations placed upon states by said regime, as well as the elements of the regime which are persuasive rather than obligatory.[194] The notion of consent – in the wider legal context and also specifically in the context of sold sex – is integral to the enquiry made by this book and will be introduced and defined, and considered in a variety of legal contexts in Chapter 4.

190 Discussed in ch 3.

191 Discussed in ch 4.

192 Discussed in ch 5.

193 Discussed in chs 6 and 7.

194 For example, art 6(3) of the UN Trafficking Protocol asks that parties '*consider* implementing measures to provide for the physical, psychological and social recovery of victims of trafficking in persons' (emphasis added).

# 3 Defining trafficking: the evolution of an international legal definition

## 3.1 Introduction

Trafficking activity has prompted a variety of concerns and a variety of responses on international and national levels. For the purposes of the enquiry made within this body of work, it is necessary to establish what trafficking is in a legal sense. The definition of human trafficking has evolved over time, and the current internationally accepted position is represented in the various instruments outlined in previous chapters.

As has been explained, at the beginning of this century, the UN Trafficking Protocol provided us with a comprehensive definition of trafficking, which has been adopted in subsequent anti-trafficking instruments. Following two years of negotiations at the UN Centre for International Crime Prevention in Vienna, the Protocol was signed by more than 80 countries in December 2000. This represents the first globally accepted definition of 'trafficking in persons', with the same definition reproduced verbatim in the recent CoE Trafficking Convention,[1] and almost the same in the recent EU 2011 Directive[2] (which varies only through the explicit inclusion of 'begging' as a form of exploitation – specifically under the umbrella of 'forced labour' – sufficient to make transportation for this purpose 'trafficking').

The definition provided by these instruments is of a more detailed and technical nature than those previously offered, extending the 'purpose' element of human trafficking and raising the matter of the relevance of consent (or lack thereof) of the victim. Because it is central to the discussion in this chapter, it is useful to replicate the definition here, with the minor variation provided within the EU 2011 Directive being included in brackets. Accordingly, 'Trafficking in persons' is:

1 Council of Europe Convention on Action against Trafficking in Human Beings and its Explanatory Report (adopted 3 May 2005, entered into force 1 February 2008) Warsaw (16.V.2005), Council of Europe Treaty Series – No 197 (CoE Trafficking Convention) art 4.

2 Directive 2011/36/EU of the European Parliament and of the Council of 5 April 2011 on preventing and combating trafficking in human beings and protecting its victims, and replacing Council Framework Decision 2002/629/JHA [2001] OJ L101/1 (EU 2011 Directive) art 2.

> The recruitment, transportation, transfer, harbouring or receipt of persons, by means of the threat or use of force or other forms of coercion, of abduction, of fraud, of deception, of the abuse of power or of a position of vulnerability or of the giving or receiving of payments or benefits to achieve the consent of a person having control over another person, for the purpose of exploitation.
>
> Exploitation shall include, at a minimum, the exploitation of the prostitution of others or other forms of sexual exploitation, forced labour or services, (including begging) slavery or practices similar to slavery, servitude or the removal of organs ...

The definition goes on to state that consent (to the exploitation) is irrelevant where any of the means set out in the above paragraph are employed, and that it is not necessary to prove that any of those means were employed where a child is concerned, a child being any person under 18 years of age.[3]

Human trafficking can therefore be broken down into three elements: the 'action' of recruitment, transportation etc, the 'means' of coercion of force etc, and the 'purpose' – that of 'exploitation' – which is expanded upon by a non-exhaustive list of what may constitute 'exploitation'. Therefore, trafficking is, by definition, a tripartite process, and all the elements of the definition must be present in order for activity to come within the scope of the definition.

The aim of this chapter is to analyse exactly what trafficking is according to current internationally accepted legal definition. This will be achieved through tracing the development of legal definitions of trafficking and evaluating these definitions in terms of the three elements outlined above; the 'action', 'means' and 'purpose'. Section 3.2 serves to give a very brief overview of the development of the relevant instruments addressing trafficking and slavery over the past 100 years, to show how we have reached the definition in use today. Section 3.3 discusses the first element mentioned above: the 'action' and its component parts. In section 3.4, the 'means' element of trafficking will be analysed. Section 3.5 will deal with the final element of the process: the 'purpose' of 'exploitation'.

## 3.2 Frameworks of understanding: the changing face of 'trafficking'

Human trafficking has, for the most part, been dealt with by instruments and/or provisions specifically targeting trafficking, allowing for wider and less technical notions of 'exploitation' to be caught by the anti-trafficking instruments, rather than being subsumed by anti-slavery legislation. Some of these anti-trafficking

3 The notion of consent in the specific context of human trafficking raises a multitude of problems and issues which merit in-depth discussion; consequently the role of consent in human trafficking will be dealt with in depth in a later chapter – ch 5.

instruments merely contain prohibitions;[4] others contain a specific definition of 'trafficking in persons'.[5]

This is without doubt the correct approach, for simply to equate trafficking and slavery is incorrect and provides an incomplete picture of the scope of trafficking. In any case, the slave trade is the correct analogy, as opposed to slavery. For the purposes of this discussion, it must be accepted that slavery goes beyond formal slavery (that is, a status – one person being owned as property by another – identified and permitted by law) to include de facto slavery, the treatment of one person by another, private person which, while being illegal in national law, does not have the effect of altering the legal status of the victim, simply creating conditions analogous to those of one who is held as a slave.

Secondly, trafficking, and the slave trade, are both processes, but the elements of these processes differ at points. Slavery may be a 'purpose' element of either process – that is to say, it can occur as an end result of each (and clearly must be for anti-slave trade instruments). The definition of trafficking, however, goes much further than anti-slavery legislation in that it envisages a broad spectrum of activities which constitute the 'exploitation' which can occur as an end result (or 'purpose') of the trafficking process, such as slavery-like practices and forced labour. This kind of exploitation, combined with elements of movement of people and their control through 'means' such as coercion, constitutes human trafficking as currently understood.

The purpose of this discussion for the book is to establish as far as is possible the scope and parameters of trafficking activity. This will be done in order to provide a broader framework of understanding of the existence and evolution of the different types of human exploitation (consensual and non-consensual) which have become increasingly prevalent in recent years as a result of the recognition of trafficking activity, and the development of a definition of human trafficking. This will in turn facilitate detailed analysis of the role of consent within that framework, to be discussed in Chapter 5.

The earliest trafficking-specific instruments preceded the League of Nations Convention to Suppress the Slave Trade and Slavery 1926.[6] The move to address sex trafficking began with the International Agreement for the Suppression of the

4 Such as the Convention on the Elimination of All forms of Discrimination Against Women (CEDAW) (1980) December 18, 1979, 1249 UNTS 14 (opened for signature in 1980, entry into force in September 1981) art 6, and the Convention on the Rights of the Child (adopted and opened for signature, ratification and accession by General Assembly resolution 44/25 of 20 November 1989, entered into force 2 September 1990) art 35.

5 Such as the three main instruments which form the anti-trafficking regime which is discussed throughout this body of work: Protocol to Prevent, Suppress and Punish Trafficking in Persons, Especially Women and Children, Supplementing the United Nations Convention Against Transnational Organized Crime (adopted November 2000 by United Nations General Assembly Resolution A/RES/55/25, entered into force 25 December 2003) (Trafficking Protocol); CoE Trafficking Convention (n 1); EU 2011 Directive.

6 League of Nations Convention to Suppress the Slave Trade and Slavery (signed at Geneva on 25 September 1926, into force 9 March 1927, in accordance with art 12) 60 LNTS 253, Registered No 1414 (1926 Slavery Convention).

White Slave Traffic of 18 May 1904,[7] which was primarily concerned with governmental coordination of information concerning 'the procuring of women or girls for immoral purposes abroad'. Subsequently, the International Convention for the Suppression of the White Slave Traffic[8] was signed on 4 May 1910. The preamble speaks of suppression of the activity known as 'white slave traffic' – the application of these early instruments merely to the 'slave traffick' of white people reflected the concern at the time over European women being recruited and exported for work in brothels.[9]

A lack of definitional clarity in early instruments means that the term 'trafficking' was to an extent used without discrimination; the meaning of the term was complicated by use of the terminology 'white slave traffic' in the 1904 Agreement and the 1910 Trafficking Convention, which heavily implies a cross-over between the slave trade and the process of trafficking. Notably, the 1910 Trafficking Convention explicitly uses the word 'slave' in the Convention's title, yet does not refer to 'slave', 'slavery' or 'slave trade' in the definition provided in Article 1,[10] thereby raising somewhat of a question mark as to the suitability of the use of 'slave' in the title.

Further trafficking-specific legislation came into existence in 1933, when the International Convention on the Suppression of the Traffic in Women of Full Age[11] was signed. The instrument had the effect of extending pre-existing treaties to women of full age who had been trafficked, even with their consent. This Convention, drafted after the Slavery Convention, moved away from that employed in earlier trafficking Conventions, and avoided terminology such as 'slave' and 'slavery'.[12]

7 International Agreement for the Suppression of the White Slave Traffic (18 May 1904, entered in to force 18 July 1905) 35 Stat. 1979, 1 LNTS 83 (1904 Agreement).

8 International Convention for the Suppression of the White Slave Traffic (4 May 1910) 211 Consol TS 45, 1912 GR Brit TS No 20 (1910 Trafficking Convention), as amended by Protocol Amending the International Agreement for the Suppression of the White Slave Traffic, and Amending the International Convention for the Suppression of the White Slave Traffic (4 May 1949) 2 UST 1999, 30 UNTS 23 (entered into force 21 June 1951).

9 C H Hauge 'Prostitution of women and international human rights law: transforming exploitation into equality' (1995) 8 *New York International Law Review* 23, 34.

10 Article 1 of the 1910 Trafficking Convention (n 8) provides the following definition: 'Whoever, in order to gratify the passions of another person, has procured, enticed, or led away, even with her consent, a woman or girl under age, for immoral purposes, shall be punished, notwithstanding that the various acts constituting the offence may have been committed in different countries'. Article 2 replicates the definition to an extent, but takes it further by doing away with the statement 'even with her consent' and instead including a list of 'means' which must be proven to have been employed by the trafficker: 'by fraud, or by means of violence, threats, abuse of authority, or any other method of compulsion'.

11 International Convention on the Suppression of the Traffic in Women of Full Age (11 October 1933, entered into force 24 August 1934) 150 LTR 431 (1933 Trafficking Convention).

12 Article 1 of the 1933 Trafficking Convention (n 11) provides the following definition: 'Whoever, in order to gratify the passions of another person, has procured, enticed or led away even with her consent, a woman or girl of full age for immoral purposes to be carried out in another country, shall be punished, notwithstanding that the various acts constituting the offence may have been committed in different countries'.

The above-mentioned traffick-specific treaties were consolidated in 1949 with the enactment of the Convention for the Suppression of the Traffic in Persons and of the Exploitation of Prostitution of Others 1949[13] (1949 Trafficking Convention) which drew upon the language used in the 1910 Trafficking Convention.[14] Prostitution was considered legal under the 1949 Convention, and thus the emphasis was taken away from the perceived immorality of prostitution and prostitutes, and placed upon punishment of those responsible for the trafficking.

Ordinary dictionary definitions give a representation of how the term 'trafficking' was/is viewed in a non-legal sense, according to popular understanding. In the narrowest sense, trafficking is defined as 'the transportation of merchandise for the purpose of trade',[15] with the object of trafficking being 'saleable commodities'.[16] The key, with regard to human trafficking, is in the word 'commodities', that is, trade being done in objects or products which could be bought and sold, and ultimately disposed of, at the will of those involved in the commerce. Some non-legal definitions go further, referring to trafficking as '[to] deal or trade in something illegal',[17] thereby implying exchanges of a covert and clandestine nature, a form of trade which could be applied equally to drugs, arms, humans or other relevant subjects.

The term has historically been applied to the buying and selling of humans. Writings from the early 17th century refer to '[t]hose which made it a trafficke to buy and sell slaves',[18] thus making a link between the trade in slaves and use of the term 'trafficking'. Historical use of the word also demonstrates a link between trafficking and migrant prostitutes: 'These traffickes, these common truls I mean, walke abroad'.[19] This perceived link follows the same route as early traffick-specific legal instruments, which assumed that the paradigmatic trafficked victim would be a female who was kidnapped, transported across the globe and forced into prostitution or sex work.

Since the drafting of early legal instruments, the word 'traffick' has, in legal fora, consistently been applied to the movement of a person from one location to another for the purpose of some form of exploitation. Early traffick-specific instruments limited their application to situations of sexual exploitation, or specifically, the exploitation of prostitution of another. It may be this perceived link with

13 Convention for the Suppression of the Traffick in Persons and of the Exploitation of Prostitution of Others (approved by General Assembly Resolution 317(IV) of 2 December 1949, entered into force 25 July 1951) (1949 Trafficking Convention).

14 Article 1 of the 1949 Trafficking Convention (n 13) contains the following definition: 'The Parties to the present Convention agree to punish any person who, to gratify the passions of another: (1) Procures, entices or leads away, for purposes of prostitution, another person, even with the consent of that person; (2) Exploits the prostitution of another person, even with the consent of that person'.

15 *Oxford English Dictionary Online*, Additions Series http://www.oed.com/ (last accessed 1 September 2006).

16 ibid.

17 ibid.

18 ibid.

19 ibid.

prostitution and sexual exploitation which has led to trafficking law developing separately from that which specifically addresses the slave trade and labour law. The legal definition of today supersedes early examples. For example, various different 'means' of acquiring the victim are envisaged, ranging from outright kidnapping to more covert means, such as the use of deception or other forms of coercion.[20] The scope of the 'purpose' element of human trafficking has been developed to include many more forms of 'exploitation' than solely that of a sexual nature.[21]

The justification for drawing comparisons between trafficking and slave trade provisions throughout this chapter is based upon the fact that both are clearly linked, in that they provide examples of non-consensual movement of persons coupled with human exploitation and control. Some commentators refer to human trafficking as contemporary slavery, or the new slave trade.[22] This is resisted here as a comprehensive proposition on the basis that 'exploitation' sufficient for trafficking does not always amount to slavery (even in extended understandings of it), although it certainly can do in certain circumstances.

The point is that trafficking may, either in a philosophical sense or in popular understanding, represent a modern form of slavery and those engaged in the process be regarded as slave traders, but that in a legal sense it also goes further because it includes different types of exploitation (including slavery, *sensu stricto*) between which distinctions can be made (albeit not always easily[23]). Trafficking can be said to be 'based' upon slavery, but trafficking in not synonymous with the slave trade, the only 'purpose' of which was slavery. Non-consensual exploitation is clearly a central defining characteristic of trafficking activity; the 'purpose' is always exploitation of some form, and this element breaks down into the non-exhaustive forms outlined within the definition, which seems to envisage a spectrum of exploitative activities; the condition of slavery being the most serious.

The remainder of this chapter will examine in detail the component parts of the trafficking definition; those of the 'action', 'means' and 'purpose'.

20 Discussed in section 3.4 below.

21 See section 3.5 below.

22 See *Prosecutor v Kunarac, Kovac & Vukovic*, Case No IT-96-23-T & IT-96-23/1-A, Judgment 118 (12 June 2002) 536; S Scarpa *Trafficking in Human Beings: Modern Slavery* (Oxford University Press, Oxford, 2008) 4; F Gold 'Redefining the slave trade: current trends in the international trafficking of women' (2003) 11 *University of Miami International & Comparative Law Review* 99, who refers to human trafficking as 'the twenty-first century's slave trade' 100; L Kelly and L Regan 'Stopping traffic: exploring the extent of, and responses to, trafficking in women for sexual exploitation in the UK' (Imprint London, Home Office 2000); and the 'Miami Declaration of Principles on Human Trafficking' (2006) 1 *Intercultural Human Rights Law Review* 11, which states that human trafficking is 'a human rights violation that constitutes a contemporary form of slavery'.

23 See, for example, Allain, who is critical of the European Court of Human Rights (ECtHR) in *Rantsev* for not adequately engaging with the distinction between different types of human exploitation such as slavery and servitude. See J Allain '*Rantsev v Cyprus and Russia*: the European Court of Human Rights and trafficking as slavery' (2010) 10(3) *Human Rights Law Review* 546–57.

## 3.3 The 'action'

### *3.3.1 Evolution of the 'action' element*

The three elements of 'action', 'means' and 'purpose' have become more clearly defined as the legal definition of trafficking in humans has evolved. The first part of the process, the 'action', is evident both in the current definition of the slave trade contained in the 1926 Slavery Convention – in that instrument, the 'action' is constituted by 'capture, acquisition or disposal'[24] – and in the 1910 Trafficking Convention, where the 'action' element remains the same for women over or under age, and can be identified as 'procured, enticed, or led away …'. This terminology is of a different nature to that used in the 1926 definition of the slave trade. The language of the Slavery Convention is more in keeping with the characteristic of ownership, which is central to slavery as a 'purpose' element of the slave trade, and accordingly implies a more solid degree of permanence through use of terms such as 'disposal'.

The terms 'procurement', 'enticement' and 'led away', as used in the 1910 Trafficking Convention, carry implications of a more tentative and coercive nature; the use of persuasion and trickery, which will be examined further at a later point as regards the 'means' element of the trafficking process.[25] Although trafficked victims may frequently be viewed as possessions or commodities by the trafficker(s) or at least the ultimate recipient of the victim, this does not necessarily always constitute 'ownership' in the sense that slavery and the slave trade implies.[26] The terminology is used for both definitions, but that of the slave trade in particular, implies a restriction upon movement and therefore a deprivation of liberty. The terminology used by the 1910 Trafficking Convention is more in keeping with old-fashioned ideology, which saw 'innocent' women being led astray and introduced into prostitution.

The language of the 1910 Trafficking Convention was replicated in Article 1 of the Convention for the Suppression of the 1949 Trafficking Convention. The definition and the instrument were subject to some criticism[27] and it has now been

24 Article 1(2) of the 1926 Slavery Convention (n 6) states that: 'The slave trade includes all acts involved in the capture, acquisition or disposal of a person with intent to reduce him to slavery; all acts involved in the acquisition of a slave with a view to selling or exchanging him; all acts of disposal by sale or exchange of a slave acquired with a view to being sold or exchanged, and, in general, every act of trade or transport in slaves'.

25 See section 3.4 of this chapter.

26 See Jean Allain, 'The Parameters of "Enslavement" in International Criminal Law' (paper presented at an International Symposium at the Research Centre for International Criminal Law and International Humanitarian Law, China University of Political Science and Law, 25–26 April 2009), 14–20; J Allain 'The definition of slavery in international law' (2009) 2(2) *Harvard Law Journal*; J Allain '*R v Tang*: clarifying the definition of "slavery" in international law' (2009) *Melbourne Journal of International Law* 246; Allain '*Rantsev v Cyprus and Russia*' (n 23) 546–57.

27 The European Parliament labelled the 1949 Trafficking Convention 'obsolete and ineffective' as a result of the lack of emphasis on coercion and deception: see Resolution on Trafficking in Human Beings [1996] OJ C032, P. 0088, A4-0326/95.

superseded by the definition contained within the three main legal instruments considered throughout this work.[28]

The 'action', 'means' and 'purpose' elements of trafficking are clearly visible in the definition featuring in the more recent instruments, i.e. the UN Trafficking Protocol etc. The definition appears to be based on definitions of the slave trade but is tailored and expanded specifically to address human trafficking. The 'action' element in the current definition can be identified as 'recruitment, transportation, transfer, harbouring or receipt of persons'.

### 3.3.2 *The 'recruitment, transportation, transfer, harbouring or receipt of persons'*

Lee recognises that: 'Smugglers and traffickers may use a combination of deceptive, clandestine or even legal modes of migration, switching strategies at different stages of the journey'.[29] The adaptability of traffickers is such that any means of obtaining or keeping a victim that can be used, will be used.

'Recruitment' can be elaborated upon, but mainly with direct reference to the 'means' aspect of trafficking, as the subjects of trafficking are frequently recruited through, for example, a fraudulent job advertisement or a false promise from someone they trust – this 'means' element is considered further at a later point in this chapter.

'Transportation' and 'transfer' can take many forms, from legitimate border crossing to the use of totally covert means; an account provided by one particular trafficked victim describes the use of a type of canoe that is undetectable by radar.[30]

The inclusion of 'harbouring' illustrates that those retaining the subject in any way play just as guilty a part in the process as those who acquired the subject in the first place, as do those who 'receive' the subject. Once again, the terminology of the trafficking definition implies that action of a less forceful nature than that intimated within the Slavery Convention may suffice, illustrating the potential differences of degree between the different 'purpose' elements of trafficking envisaged by the trafficking definition, also to be discussed later.[31]

Along a similar line, the language of the current internationally recognised trafficking definition seems to be more supportive of a perspective that privileges autonomy than that used in early traffick-specific or slavery-specific instruments.

28 See the UN Trafficking Protocol (n 5), the CoE Trafficking Convention (n 1) and the EU 2011 Directive (n 2).

29 M Lee 'Human trade and the criminalization of irregular migration' (2005) 33(1–15) *International Journal of the Sociology of Law* 4.

30 Francis Loncle 'Eastern Europe exports flesh to the EU: the "Natasha" trade' *Le Monde Diplomatique* (December 2001).

31 The terminology used in the trafficking definition makes it clear that that it is possible to consent to exploitative activity, but that any instance of the 'means' shall render the consent irrelevant. The 'autonomy v paternalism' perspectives (as to consent to prostitution and sexual exploitation) are discussed in ch 4.

This, coupled with the inclusion of a 'means'/lack of consent element, indicates changing frameworks of understanding of human trafficking, and may also (speculatively) indicate recognition of increased consensual economic migration[32] to, say, work in the sex trade.

### *3.3.2.1 The requirement of border crossing*

Modern disputes over trafficking definitions include the issue of whether international borders must be crossed in order for the activity to constitute trafficking.[33] This part of the process constitutes part of the 'action' element. The definition of 'slave trade' in the 1926 Slavery Convention did not make explicit mention of the necessity to cross international frontiers; thus one might assume that a slave might be acquired and sold within the same country, and that such activity might still constitute 'trade' within the meaning of the Convention. Restricting the Convention to purely cross-border situations would not be in the interests of effectiveness of eliminating slavery.

Regarding trafficking, the instruments drafted within the early 20th century appeared to incorporate an element of international border crossing. The 1904 Agreement relates to the 'procuring of women or girls for immoral purposes abroad'. Article 3 of the agreement specifically refers to repatriation, which indicates that cross-border activity was envisaged when the agreement was drafted. The 1910 Trafficking Convention does not specifically state that borders must be crossed, although it does state that perpetrators 'shall ... be punished, notwithstanding that the various acts constituting the offence may have been committed in different countries',[34] and it also envisages extradition of perpetrators.[35]

The ambit of the 1933 Trafficking Convention was confined solely to international trafficking of women of full age, even with their consent, from one country to another, thereby establishing a need to cross international borders in order for the crime to constitute trafficking. The 1949 Trafficking Convention does not openly further this trend of requiring a cross-border element. No explicit or implicit mention is made of the need for international borders to be crossed in order for the activity to qualify as trafficking. Subsequent proposed definitions took this further; a coalition of non-governmental organisations (NGOs) named the Human Rights Caucus[36] referred to the 'action' element within its definition as: '[The] recruitment, transportation within or across borders, purchase, sale, transfer, harbouring

32 Potentially through illicit channels, thereby engaging the legitimate interests of the state as regards protecting border integrity.

33 Gold (n 22) 103.

34 1910 Trafficking Convention art 2.

35 ibid art 5.

36 Members of the Human Rights Caucus include: International Human Rights Law Group, Foundation Against Trafficking in Women, Global Alliance Against Traffic in Women, Asian Women's Human Rights Council, La Strada, Ban-Ying, Fundacion Esperanza, Foundation for Women, KOK-NGO Network Against Trafficking in Women, Women's Consortium of Nigeria, Women, Law & Development in Africa (Nigeria).

or receipt of persons'. Similarly, the International Organisation for Migration (IOM) defines the 'action' element of trafficking as when: 'A migrant is illicitly engaged (recruited, kidnapped, sold etc) and/or moved, either within national or across international borders'.[37]

Article 4 of the UN Trafficking Protocol states that the offences must be 'transnational in nature'. The transnational nature of the Trafficking Protocol illustrates the international dimension of trafficking, and recognises the potential for the trafficking process to take place through a chain of people across international borders and, therefore, to involve transnational organised crime.

Article 2 of the CoE Trafficking Convention explicitly states that both national and transnational trafficking is caught by the definition, and goes further in stating that no connection with organised crime is necessary, which may be a deliberate attempt to distance itself from the more restrictive terms of the Trafficking Protocol. The involvement of international organised crime groups features as a central concern of the Trafficking Protocol, the transnational element of which renders it inapplicable to purely internal situations. To do so is to render it less effective, as both purely internal situations and situations where an already trafficked person was recruited again and moved on within one country, would fall outside this definition, and thus be left to be addressed only by national law.

The EU 2011 Directive makes specific provision as regards Member States establishing jurisdiction over trafficking offences where 'the offence is committed in whole or in part within their territory',[38] thereby indicating that even wholly internal trafficking falls within the scope of the directive. Similarly, UK domestic legislation enacted to address human trafficking – the Sexual Offences Act 2003 (SOA) – contains provisions that specifically refer to trafficking for sexual exploitation into, within and out of the UK.[39]

Instances of 'internal' trafficking are reported.[40] However, that which may be termed 'intra-state' or 'internal' trafficking/non-consensual exploitation may frequently result in a remedy which lies in the hands of the state in question applying its national criminal law. That the state may deal with such cases according to national law may well have been (and still be) the usual situation. It is the attractiveness of foreign markets, the resulting profits, the disparity between economic conditions between states and the ease of transportation which have facilitated and even encouraged the transnational trade. However, states have seldom agreed on the need to deal with 'intra-national' or 'internal' trafficking/non-consensual exploitation, save where the activity reaches the standards of serious human rights violations, such as slavery and its related practices.

37 International Organization for Migration 'Trafficking in migrants, IOM policy and responses' Working Paper (March 1999).

38 EU 2011 Directive art 10(1)(a).

39 Sexual Offences Act 2003 (SOA 2003) s 59A.

40 UNICEF, UNOHCHR, OSCE, ODIHR 'Trafficking in human beings in south eastern Europe' (2004) 65 http://www.iom.md/materials/1_traff_human_beings_se.pdf (last accessed 14 January 2014) 116.

#### *3.3.2.2 Legality of border crossing*

It is made clear in the Explanatory Report to the Council of Europe Trafficking Convention that entry of trafficked persons into a state's territory need not specifically be illicit.[41] Legal border crossing and lawful presence on national territory therefore do not negate a finding of human trafficking under the CoE Trafficking Convention. The UN Trafficking Protocol is silent as to whether lawful entry would be outside the offence of trafficking, and the *travaux préparatoires* do not elaborate upon this point. The EU 2011 Directive makes no mention of limitations regarding the legality of border crossings – this is logical as requiring illicit entry into a state would render the directive inapplicable to any EU nationals or residents who were then trafficked within the EU.

The issue of the legality of border crossing is one of the elements of this activity, which distinguishes trafficking from smuggling of humans. The terminology used within the Smuggling Protocol[42] clearly requires international border crossing, and illegal entry into the host state. Smuggling is, therefore, a matter of facilitation of illegal migration. It is simply constituted by an 'action' element.

The inclusion of lawful border-crossings within the concept of trafficking has practical advantages, as it includes the trafficking of those who have lawfully entered a state. These differences between trafficking and smuggling underpin the purposes of the separate regimes – one is aimed at combating the facilitation of illicit border crossings, the other is aimed at combating exploitation, and accordingly recognises that even those legally present on the soil of a destination state may have been brought there to be subjected to exploitation.

### *3.3.3 The 'action': some conclusions*

In establishing what trafficking actually is according to legal definition, it is made apparent by the trafficking definition that legality or otherwise of border crossing is not a problematic issue here. The inclusion of a transnational aspect in the Trafficking Protocol illustrates the recognition of the international dimension of this phenomenon. The trafficking of humans is an activity that frequently involves the crossing of international borders, and the Trafficking Protocol exists to supplement a Convention that targets transnational organised crime; activity which is, by definition, cross-border in nature. The inclusion of activity that does not cross international borders makes trafficking law more applicable and effective, to address many situations of exploitative coercive movement of persons. This ensures that 'human trafficking' includes those bought and sold within a state,

41 See Explanatory Report to the CoE Trafficking Convention (n 1) para 80 http://conventions.coe.int/Treaty/EN/Reports/Html/197.htm (last accessed 14 January 2014).

42 Protocol against the Smuggling of Migrants by Land, Sea and Air, Supplementing the United Nations Convention against Transnational Organised Crime (adopted November 2000 by United Nations General Assembly Resolution A/RES/55/25, entered into force 28 January 2004) (Smuggling Protocol).

although in reality cases of 'internal' trafficking may be dealt with according to national law.

The 'action' element of trafficking, although of a broader nature than its slave-trade counterpart, has not been subject to extensive change as the definition has evolved, predominantly as a result of its being the least problematic element of the trafficking process in definitional terms. The language 'recruitment, transportation ...' etc is sufficiently drafted to cover any acquisition of a person. The broader language used when compared with that of slave trade provisions suggests an 'action' of a potentially less immediately forceful nature and therefore wider reach. The 'action' element of trafficking carries implications of what is to come; the underhandedness and trickery employed by the trafficker, which comprises the second element of the process: the 'means', which in turn qualifies the action and makes it part of human trafficking as distinguishable from the slave trade per se. This element will now be discussed.

## 3.4 The 'means'

### *3.4.1 Evolution of the 'means' element*

The 'means' follows on from the 'action', and refers to the manner in which the action is executed – for example, a person is 'recruited' (action) through 'force' (means) for 'exploitation' (purpose). Both international trafficking and slavery legislation provide respective definitions which contain a 'means' element, although they differ somewhat in nature. The 'means' element of the slave trade, as contained in the 1926 Slavery Convention, is constituted by 'all acts involved' in the 'capture, acquisition or disposal' of the subject. Through the inclusion of 'every act of trade and transport in slaves', the definition covers the reduction of free men into slaves, and the movement, transportation, or sale etc of those already enslaved.

As regards human trafficking, the 'means' element is more specific and is the most controversial element. Trafficking instruments have at times embraced and at times shied away from the inclusion of specific means within their definitions. The 1910 Trafficking Convention imposed a requirement for various 'means' to have been employed where the woman in question is over age[43] – these means were 'by fraud, or by means of violence, threats, abuse of authority, or any other method of compulsion'.[44]

This differential treatment, dependent on age, is largely in keeping with the habitual distinction between those who were perceived to be immoral women – prostitutes – and pure and innocent women who were involuntarily brought into this market, the aim of the relevant legislation being to police the prostitutes rather than the traffickers. The terminology used, that is, 'any other method of

43 'Over age' refers to women over 20 completed years of age, as stated in the 1910 Trafficking Convention (n 8)).

44 ibid art 1.

compulsion', has the potential for wide construction, and would have reached a whole variety of ways of bringing pressure onto the victims. Unquestionably, it would be unreasonable to allow consent from those under age – minors should not be deemed capable of consenting to such activity – yet, by requiring that something extra in the case of adult females, this instrument impliedly introduced the issue of consent, or lack thereof.

The 'means' element entirely disappeared with the introduction of the 1949 Trafficking Convention, which was, until fairly recently, the main instrument to combat sex trafficking as it was perceived at the time. The 1949 Convention was criticised for its lack of a 'means' element and it was evidently felt that the drafting of a future instrument should focus on coercion. Since then, almost every suggested definition after the 1949 Convention has included a list of means, such as those provided within the definition of trafficking contained in the UN Trafficking Protocol, the CoE Trafficking Convention and the EU 2011 Directive. To reiterate, these are:

> … by means of the threat or use of force or other forms of coercion, of abduction, of fraud, of deception, of the abuse of power or of a position of vulnerability or of the giving or receiving of payments or benefits to achieve the consent of a person having control over another person …[45]

Some of the terms used within the provision are ambiguous, and are open to differing interpretations. Jordan argues that that the definition would be problematic if incorporated into domestic law in its current state.[46] Notably, the UK implementing legislation of anti-trafficking measures looks very little like the international definition, as the different offences potentially comprising human trafficking are dealt with by a series of different provisions which ultimately do the same job.[47]

In its (unofficial) Annotated Guide to the Complete UN Trafficking Protocol (the Guide), the International Human Rights Law Group suggested a definition which it deemed suitable for inclusion in domestic legislation as it avoids confusing

45 UN Trafficking Protocol (n 5) art 3; CoE Trafficking Convention (n 1) art 4; EU 2011 Directive (n 2) art 2.

46 See A D Jordan 'Annotated guide to the complete UN Trafficking Protocol' (May 2002, updated August 2002); Ann D Jordan 'Initiative against trafficking in persons' International Human Rights Law Group 9.

47 Trafficking into, within and out of the UK are criminalised by SOA 2003 s 59A. According to these provisions, A commits an offence if he facilitates the entry, travel within, or departure from the UK of B, and A intends to or believes that another is likely to do something which would constitute a 'relevant offence', the latter being primarily (although not exclusively) an offence under Part 1 of the SOA 2003, such as, for example, controlling prostitution for gain (s 53). SOA s 60 also includes as 'relevant offences': 'an offence under section 1(1)(a) of the Protection of Children Act 1978 (c 37); an offence listed in Schedule 1 to the Criminal Justice (Children) (Northern Ireland) Order 1998 (SI 1998/1504 (NI 9)); an offence under art 3(1)(a) of the Protection of Children (Northern Ireland) Order 1978 (SI 1978/1047 (NI 17)), or anything done outside England and Wales and Northern Ireland which is not an offence within any of paragraphs (a) to (d) but would be if done in England and Wales or Northern Ireland'.

and ambiguous language: 'Trafficking in persons shall mean the recruitment, transportation, transfer, harbouring or receipt of persons, by any means, for forced labour or services, slavery or practices similar to slavery, servitude or the removal of organs'.[48] The terms 'forced labour or services' are intended to include prostitution in this context.[49]

The Guide goes on to state that the 'means' aspect of the trafficking is not important; the process of moving the person (action) and the subsequent exploitation (purpose) are the key aspects. The drafters of the UN Trafficking Protocol – and those of the instruments replicating the definition – evidently did not share this view, as the inclusion of an extensive list of means demonstrates. It is this aspect which differs so greatly in comparison with the 1926 Slavery Convention definition of the slave trade.

It is evident from the wording of the latter that particular means of 'capture, acquisition or disposal'[50] were not envisaged; the requisite means was constituted by 'all acts involved'[51] in capturing, acquiring or disposing of the subject. This statement is comparable with 'by any means', as contained in the above-mentioned trafficking definition proposed by the International Human Rights Law Group. The inclusion of a specific list of 'means' in the current definition muddies the waters from the perspective of identifying victims, as in a technical sense a specific 'means' may have to be identified to have been used against the victim in order for the putative victim to be deemed to have been trafficked. Where no such objective proof (of, say, coercion) is evident, this renders correct victim identification inherently problematic.[52]

Each element of the 'means' aspect as included within the UN Trafficking Protocol will now be considered in more depth.

### *3.4.2 'By means of the threat or use of force or other forms of coercion, of abduction, of fraud, of deception, of the abuse of power or of a position of vulnerability'*

#### *3.4.2.1 Threat, force, coercion and abduction*

Although deceptive means such as false advertisements for employment (discussed below) are frequent methods of recruitment used by traffickers, less subtle ways of recruitment are also identified.[53] These include kidnap or abduction, the use of force or coercion in the form of actual violence or the threat of violence, the involvement of family members in recruiting the victim, and drug and alcohol addiction. Some women and girls report being kidnapped.[54]

48 Jordan (n 46) 7.
49 ibid.
50 1926 Slavery Convention (n 6) art 1(2).
51 ibid.
52 See ch 6 for discussion of the mechanism for victim identification.
53 UNICEF, UNOHCHR, OSCE, ODIR (n 40) 7.
54 ibid 52.

Coercion is envisaged as a prospective 'means'. To coerce is to 'persuade (an unwilling person) to do something by using force or threats; to obtain (something) by such means'.[55] According to the ordinary meaning of the word, factors which lead to a state of duress or compulsion could be included. Logical construction of the term would mean that coercion in the context of trafficking would solely include methods directly employed by the trafficker(s). A recent domestic human trafficking case recognised coercion where there was 'some evidence of threats and inhuman treatment and restriction of the women's liberties and confiscation of their passports'.[56] There is clearly the potential for broad scope and construction here.

It seems that psychological coercion is to be included within the scope of the term,[57] which could potentially come about through threats, intimidation or bullying. Invisible chains exist by way of psychological coercion and are as effective as physical means in holding a person in slavery.[58] The scope of this term, however, may be ambiguous and legally uncertain.[59] Psychological coercion, and exactly what it amounts to, suggests a potentially broad spectrum of tactics ranging from 'strong' to 'weak' pressure. The more easily dealt with cases will concern 'strong' forms of psychological coercion, which may also be 'threats' and therefore be caught by the trafficking definition in any case. However, there will be cases of a weaker nature where the degree of psychological coercion is less severe.[60]

Accounts provided by trafficking victims further illustrate this method (i.e. of psychological coercion): '(A) man came to the house and I refused to entertain him. My friend said that if I did not do it she would tell my family that I was a prostitute and that our family would be shamed in the village'.[61]

Coercion of this form – through threats to reveal the nature of the employment to the family or community – can be a powerful tool because in some societies a prostitute may be considered unfit to marry or to reintegrate with the community. This has the effect of alienating victims from their place of origin, which keeps them under the control of the traffickers.

Physical force is a tool commonly employed by the traffickers.[62] Empirical

55 *Oxford English Dictionary* (2nd edn, Oxford University Press, 2003).

56 *Regina v Lorenc Roci, Vullnet Ismailaj* [2005] EWCA Crim 3404.

57 See *RE's Application for Judicial Review, Re Queen's Bench Division (Northern Ireland)* [2014] NIQB 15, para 56 of which refers specifically to less ostensible signs of coercion and, for example, Stockholm Syndrome in trafficked victims. Also illustrative is a US case where threats were used in *United States v Jimenez-Calderon*, 135 Fed. Appx. 562 (3d Cir. 2005) *Indicted* 9/26/02, *Sentenced* 8/7/03 and 5/4/04, D. New Jersey.

58 Centre for Social Justice Report: 'It happens here: equipping the United Kingdom to fight modern slavery' (March 2013) 12.

59 See K Kim 'The coercion of trafficked workers' Paper presented at the annual meeting of the Law and Society Association, Renaissance Chicago Hotel, Chicago IL (27 May 2010).

60 For example if the threats/coercion are of an economic nature.

61 L Brown *Sex Slaves: The Trafficking of Women in Asia* (Virago Press, 2001) 110.

62 See Brown (n 61), which includes many different examples of the experiences of trafficked persons. Also see *United States v Rojas*, 356 F.3d 876, 879 (8th Cir. 2004) *Indicted* 1/28/04, *Convicted* 4/2004 & 8/27/04, *Sentenced* 11/23/04, N.D. Georgia, where physical force was used.

research conducted by Brown provides many examples, such as the following, which demonstrates the use of physical force: 'My husband let his friends use me and they gave him money. At first I refused but then he would beat me. He was pleased with me when I earned money for him'.[63]

Clearly, the use of direct or indirect force and varying types of violent and non-violent coercion all feature as elements of human trafficking. The following section will consider some of the more non-violent types of 'means' – those of deception and fraud.

#### *3.4.2.2 Deception and fraud*

Many accounts provided by trafficked victims include details about the promise of a legitimate border crossing and employment of a specified nature upon arrival in the destination state, yet in reality the victim may be subject to illicit entry into the destination state and forced to work as a sex worker or some other form of labourer – a reality far from that which was promised. Such deception can render a situation of smuggling or facilitated migration one of human trafficking.

Europol states that:

> The majority of identified trafficking cases involve women and girls who had no idea that they would be forced to work in the sex industry. Those females that are aware or have some suspicion that they will be prostituted also suffer in that the conditions they work in probably bear no relation to what was explained to them by the trafficker or pimp, with the amount of money they are allowed to keep being the main issue.[64]

There are ample anecdotal instances of such deceptive practice.[65] Brown provides an account of a 15-year-old Cambodian girl who came from an extremely poor family. She met a woman who appeared to be very rich and who promised her employment, yet she was deceived about the nature of her employment:

> There was woman who sometimes came to our village. She was rich with jewels and beautiful clothes and she said she could find good jobs in the city for some of us girls. I wanted to go with her so when she came back I went for an interview with some others. There were two men with her and they asked us lots of questions. I was really happy because they chose me and two others to get jobs. We left the next day in a taxi and we went to Phnom Penh.

63 Brown (n 61) 74.

64 Europol 'Trafficking of women and children for sexual exploitation in the EU: the involvement of Western Balkans organised crime', public version, Crimes Against the Person Unit 18 http://www.europol.europa.eu/publications/Serious_Crime_Overviews/Western_Balkans_THB_Threat_Assessment.PDF (last accessed 1 August 2007, link no longer live) 33.

65 See Brown (n 61).

> We thought we were going to work in a shop but instead they sold all of us to different brothels.[66]

Ample examples and similar stories can be found in the literature.[67] Kelly[68] draws upon examples from an IOM study, which indicate the difficult technical nature of determining certain aspects of trafficking, and uses 'deception' as an example. The following case study is cited:

> A young woman was studying in Tashkent and living in a hostel. A woman she did not know said that she was recruiting girls for summer jobs in the Israeli sex industry. When the young woman arrived she worked for several months and received no payment. When she raised this, her pimp ("balobay") said she had been earning a percentage all along, but that he had been saving it for her. After eight months, she was picked up by the police for overstaying her visa. Her pimp promised to bring the money she was owed (9,000 Euros) to the jail. He never came and she wants to return to claim her money, but has been told by the Israeli authorities that if they pick her up again they will prosecute her.[69]

This account indicates initial consent, invalidated by deception. If the intention not to pay was always present, the consent was never valid as it could not be considered to have been informed[70] – one of the central requirements for a valid consent. As regards the above-mentioned case study, Kelly notes that whether or not trafficking has occurred depends upon whether one can infer that there was deceit about earnings and the intention to pay, as there is no deception with respect to the nature of the 'work'.[71] Therefore, it is necessary to determine what the individual must consent to, and at what point consent must be given in order for it to be valid. This is further discussed in Chapter 5.

The *travaux préparatoires* to the UN Trafficking Protocol[72] remain silent on the issue of deception. The Explanatory Report to the CoE Trafficking Convention

66 ibid 90.

67 International Organization for Migration 'Trafficking in women and children from the Kyrgyz Republic' (Irina, Case Study 6) (November 2000) 26 http://iom.ramdisk.net/iom/images/uploads/Kyrgyzstan_Report%20on%20Trafficking_2000_En_1071070736.pdf (last accessed 30 November 2008).

68 See International Organization for Migration 'Fertile fields: trafficking in persons in Central Asia' (A report prepared by Liz Kelly, Child and Woman Abuse Studies Unit, London Metropolitan University April 2005).

69 ibid 67–68.

70 Informed consent is discussed in chs 4 and 5.

71 See Liz Kelly, International Organization for Migration (n 68) 68.

72 United Nations General Assembly 'Report of the Ad Hoc Committee on the Elaboration of a Convention against Transnational Organized Crime on the work of its first to eleventh sessions, Addendum, Interpretative notes for the official records (*travaux préparatoires*) of the negotiation of the United Nations Convention against Transnational Organized Crime and the Protocols thereto' (2000) UN Doc A/55/383/Add.1.

provides little elaboration, stating that '[f]raud and deception are frequently used by traffickers, as when victims are led to believe that an attractive job awaits them rather than the intended exploitation'.[73] As the Explanatory Report to that Convention indicates, the clearest form of deception occurs in relation to the nature of the work to be undertaken.[74] Once passports have been handed over, victims will find themselves in a very difficult position. The IOM documents numerous examples of passports and travel documents being confiscated, which is a method of control employed by many traffickers.[75]

The UN Special Rapporteur on Violence against Women, its Causes and Consequences identifies two main patterns of trafficking for the purpose of prostitution. These are the 'two step' and 'one step' methods.[76] The 'two-step' pattern has in the past been more common, and targets those women already working in prostitution, in order to recruit them so that they may be trafficked abroad. The 'one-step' pattern targets women and girls in their homes and villages to be trafficked for prostitution. This method frequently involves someone approaching the victim or her family, and deceiving them, for example, as to the nature of employment which they are offering the girl/woman in question (although in some cases, daughters may be sold by their families[77]). The 'one-step' method is more aggressive, and becoming prevalent as the demand for younger women increases as a result of, for example, fear of AIDS.[78]

Traffickers react to law enforcement measures. As new markets are identified, recruitment methods are adapted accordingly. Varying methods of recruitment are reported by victims of trafficking, who may not always perceive the risk. Common themes emerge from these, almost always involving deception of some sort. Europol identifies the following recruitment methods:[79] false offer of employment; false representation of declared sex work; false promise of marriage or some other form of approach by a 'lover boy'; and false allegation of criminal conduct and subsequent debt bondage. A recent domestic case involving a Romanian father and son trafficking team provides a clear example of deception being used to recruit the women, who, like many before them, believed that the job offers of 'waitress' or 'entertainer' were legitimate.[80]

73 Explanatory Report to the CoE Trafficking Convention (n 41) para 82.

74 ibid.

75 Liz Kelly, International Organization for Migration (n 68) 24.

76 See Report of the Special Rapporteur on Violence Against Women, its Causes and Consequences (1994) United Nations Economic and Social Council E/CN.4/1997/47/Add.4 Commission on Human Rights, 53rd Session, Provisional Agenda Item 9(a) http://www.unhchr.ch/Huridocda/Huridoca.nsf/0/043c76f98a706362802566b1005e9219?Opendocument (last accessed 1 July 2011).

77 UNICEF, UNOHCHR, OSCE, ODIR (n 40) 52.

78 International Organization for Migration 'Slavic women trafficked into slavery' *Trafficking in Migrants Quarterly Bulletin* (Geneva, Switzerland, May 1995) http://www.iom.ch/IOM/Publications/books_studies_surveys/MIP_traff_women_eng.htm (last accessed 1 September 2005).

79 Europol (n 64) 19.

80 *BBC News* 'Romanian father and son found guilty of sex trafficking' (18 January 2011) http://www.bbc.co.uk/news/uk-12221632 (last accessed 18 January 2011).

A worrying and growing trend is that women are increasingly being used in the recruitment process in source countries.[81] Some of these women will have become involved as a result of prior participation in organised crime, and others will have previously been trafficked themselves. The problems arising from the use of females in the recruitment process are clear, as potential female migrants may be more likely to trust another woman. Statistics from the Dutch National Rapporteur suggest that, of those suspects arrested in 2002–2003, one quarter were female.[82] Bosnia-Herzegovina in particular has a bad track record in this respect – Europol reports that in 2004, almost 60 per cent of identified recruiters were women.[83] They were all of Bosnian nationality and the victims described them as friends. It has also been reported that in Serbia and Montenegro, couples have been used in the recruitment process.[84] These worrying accounts and trends all indicate that deception and abuse of trust all feature heavily in the trafficking phenomenon.

#### *3.4.2.3 Other forms of coercion*

Although not explicitly mentioned within the trafficking definition, it is commonly accepted that debt bondage is another means of retaining control over the trafficked person.[85] It features heavily in many accounts provided by victims, which indicates that this method is frequently employed by those involved in the trafficking process.[86]

This practice is defined by the Supplementary Convention on the Abolition of Slavery, the Slave Trade, and Institutions and Practices similar to Slavery 1956[87] as:

> … the status or condition arising from a pledge by a debtor of his personal services or of those of a person under his control as security for a debt, if the value of those services as reasonably assessed is not applied towards the liquidation of the debt of the length and nature of those services are not respectively limited and defined.[88]

81 United Nations Office on Drugs and Crime 'Global report on trafficking in persons' (February 2009) 6 http://www.unodc.org/documents/Global_Report_on_TIP.pdf (last accessed 1 July 2011).

82 Europol (n 64) 19.

83 ibid 30.

84 ibid.

85 See Brown (n 61) *passim*, which provides many accounts of trafficked victims who have been subjected to exploitation and control through debt bondage.

86 ibid.

87 Supplementary Convention on the Abolition of Slavery, the Slave Trade, and Institutions and Practices Similar to Slavery (Adopted by a Conference of Plenipotentiaries convened by Economic and Social Council resolution 608(XXI) of 30 April 1956 and done at Geneva on 7 September 1956, entered into force 30 April 1957) (Supplementary Slavery Convention).

88 ibid art 1.

This relatively commonplace strategy is illustrated by the following account, provided by a Filipina woman:

> We were sent into a big compound surrounded by high fences and it was very heavily guarded. There were three houses in the compound and all were filled with other Filipina who looked at us. We were told that we had to work in a club so that we could pay back our airfare and the money that the club owner had paid for us. We had to entertain the client because how else could we pay back the debt?[89]

The notion of 'economic coercion' (i.e. economic coercion of circumstances) is considered by some commentators to be a viable 'means' element of human trafficking.[90] The mainstream interpretations of 'coercion', however, leave little room for such a notion and it therefore sits outside trafficking as traditionally understood. Bearing in mind the central 'push factor' of poverty considered in Chapter 2, however, it is clear that economic coercion of circumstances is a significant driver in terms of the decision to migrate into a situation of exploitation. Accordingly, this matter will be discussed in Chapter 7, in the context of the discussion of what concessions we might consider for the 'consenting' trafficked migrant who may be 'merely' economically coerced.

#### *3.4.2.4 Abuse of a position of vulnerability*

As has been established, the current trafficking definition 'extends beyond conventional criminal law notions of coercion and duress, or even of fraud and deception, to include exploitation by abuse of social or cultural authority or of a position of vulnerability'.[91] It seems clear – from the above discussion and from the wording 'force or other forms of coercion' within the trafficking definition – that trafficking can occur without the means of any actual physical force, that is, psychological coercion may well suffice. The UN Trafficking Protocol requires signatory states to try to alleviate factors that make persons, especially women and children, vulnerable to trafficking, such as poverty, underdevelopment and lack of equal opportunity,[92] thereby envisaging a wide range of factors which could render someone vulnerable to trafficking. The terminology 'position of vulnerability' in the definition is uncertain, because a situation amounting to just that could be brought about by a variety of factors and circumstances. Perhaps the most obvious example would be where a member of a certain family or community is told what to do by a family member or an influential member of the community.

89 Brown (n 61) 115.

90 K Hyland 'Protecting human victims of trafficking: an American framework' (2001) *16 Berkeley Women's Law Journal* 29, 49; J Bhabha 'Reforming immigration policy: start by protecting rights, not borders' (2005) *Boston Review*.

91 B E Hernandez-Truyol and J E Larson, 'Sexual labour and human rights' (2006) 37 *Columbia Human Rights Law Review* 391–445, 432.

92 UN Trafficking Protocol (n 5) art 9.

If it is culturally unacceptable for the subject to do otherwise, the result is that they are effectively compelled to obey.

Abuse of a position of vulnerability requires a counterpart position of power or authority on the part of the abuser. This can be illustrated by reference to the case of *Larissis and Others v Greece*,[93] where a military officer was accused of proselytising those who were his subordinates. The thrust of the case against him was that 'the accused took advantage of the trust inherent in the relationship between a subordinate and a superior'.[94] Accordingly, his conviction for proselytising was not an unjustified interference with his right to practise his religion under Article 9 of the ECHR. It is not inconceivable that a putative trafficking victim could be subject to pressure in a similar way.

With respect to those victims already in another country than that of their origin – perhaps as a result of already having been trafficked or having been moved part way along the trafficking chain, abuse of a position of vulnerability may include various factors to be taken into account. These factors include the victim being far from home, potentially on the wrong side of the immigration law in the destination state, not being a native speaker of the language of that state and being reliant upon economic gain for survival just as any person might be.

The potential for broad construction of this term means that it may be capable of encompassing situations where an otherwise 'smuggled prostitute' becomes a 'trafficked prostitute' where the traffickers abuse her vulnerability while *in situ*. An example of UK domestic case law is useful here to illustrate the application (by an agent) of external pressure of an economic nature in order to coerce sex workers to take on more work than they were happy to do. In *R v Moir (Sharon Carol)*[95] the defendant had run an escort agency primarily from her home. She had approximately 350 women on her books, and on any given day there were 10 to 12 women working. The agency retained one-third of the sum paid by customers. Moir continued to maintain that she was unaware that the women were having sex with customers and said they were merely being paid for their time. She argued that there was no evidence of force or coercion of the women, and maintained that those involved in the use of the brothel had done so voluntarily.

While there was no evidence of physical force or coercion, in passing sentence the judge had emphasised the economic coercion used by Moir to force the women to work, by denying them future work if they refused a customer at the end of a shift. Therefore, Moir used the threat of withholding money in order indirectly to coerce the girls to work, thereby abusing their economic vulnerability. If a person feasibly has no other options, then the exploitative situation becomes coercive.[96]

An example of abuse of a position of vulnerability can be found when examining the mail-order bride industry. It has been suggested that the position of

93 *Larissis and Others v Greece* (App nos 23372/94, 26377/95, 26378/94) [1998] ECHR 13.

94 ibid para 15.

95 *R v Moir (Sharon Carol)* [2007] EWCA Crim 3317.

96 J Bhabha 'Trafficking, smuggling and human rights' (March 2005) *Migration Information Source: Special Issue on Migration and Human Rights* http://www.migrationinformation.org/Feature/display.cfm?id=294 (last accessed 21 August 2007).

mail-order brides has come to 'strongly resemble the international trafficking of women'.[97] This industry promotes the commodification of women through offering catalogues of potential brides who can be 'purchased'. These women will frequently have joined such agencies as a result of social pressure to marry, or financial hardship through lack of opportunity for economic gain.[98] Once the opportunity to marry has been bought by the consumer, the women will be transported from their country of origin – frequently an economically impoverished country – and subjected to conditions which in some circumstances amount to sexual exploitation or involuntary servitude.[99]

On strict application of the terms of the trafficking definition, one can conclude that the 'action' of 'recruitment, transportation ...' has been satisfied. One could argue that the women or girls consented through joining the agency. This could be counteracted through asserting abuse of a position of vulnerability, if taking advantage of her economic hardship is to be so deemed. If the bride is effectively used as a domestic servant, does this then amount to trafficking? The answer to this question is 'possibly', as there is evidence[100] to suggest that some mail-order brides do indeed experience levels of exploitation by their 'husbands' once in the destination state, which may reach the trafficking threshold, and furthermore it could be argued that some of these brides may not be truly informed as to what they are consenting to.[101]

Nonetheless, not all such brides will experience situations which could be classed as sufficiently coercive or exploitative for the purpose of the trafficking definition. Consequently, although the mail-order bride industry may objectively be seen as inherently exploitative, this industry per se will not be caught by the technical trafficking definition,[102] although individual cases may be.[103]

### 3.4.3 The 'means': some conclusions

The development of the 'means' aspect of the trafficking process has been far from smooth. The introduction of this element in the earliest trafficking instruments,

97 D R Lee 'Mail fantasy: global sexual exploitation in the mail-order bride industry and proposed legal solutions' (1998) 5 *Asian Law Journal* 139, 141.

98 ibid 143.

99 ibid 140.

100 See 'Bride trafficking unveiled' Current TV (9 May 2011).

101 ibid.

102 Similarly, mail-order brides may not fall within the scope of art 1(c)(i) of the Supplementary Slavery Convention, which relates to a woman being promised for marriage by a third party in return for some form of payment of consideration, as the Article states that the woman must be 'without the right to refuse'. Although women who join mail-order bride agencies may have done so because they feel backed into a corner as a result of lack of opportunity for economic gain in their home states, in the sense of the definition provided by the Supplementary Slavery Convention they theoretically retain the right to refuse any particular offer. Theory may not translate easily into practice here, however.

103 On this topic, see J Jones 'Trafficking internet brides' (March 2011) 20(1) *Information & Communications Technology Law* 19–33.

and the subsequent disappearance of it with the 1949 Trafficking Convention, demonstrated a lack of consensus as to what trafficking actually is in a legal sense. The fact that the 1949 Convention was so strongly criticised for its lack of 'means' rendered inevitable the reintroduction of this element in future international standards.

The main point of tension with the 'means' element as it stands today is that the separate 'means' or forms of coercion are yet to all be fully interpreted. A wide range of 'means' is contemplated, which 'reflect differences of degree rather than ... nature'.[104] The 'means' identifies the deceptive and at times purely brutal methods of recruiting and retaining control over the victim employed by the trafficker. The coercion element is what distinguishes human trafficking from exploitative migration of a lesser form, that is, where one consents to migrate into a situation of exploitative employment.

The (unofficial) Annotated Guide to the Complete UN Trafficking Protocol[105] is misplaced in making the assertion that the 'means' element is not important, for without the 'means', there is no trafficking. One who trafficks a human being who is deemed capable of choice cannot be treated in the same fashion as one who trafficks an inanimate object.[106] The distinction must be made between the agent who kidnaps his victim, and the agent who aids a person in his migration into exploitative circumstances. This illustrates the fact that, where human beings are concerned, responsibility must be apportioned accordingly. If no physical force or other relevant form of coercion is employed, then the 'agent' who would otherwise be labelled a trafficker is perhaps no more than a facilitator in the exploitative migration process, or perhaps a perpetrator of serious exploitation which, owing to the presence of or appearance of consent, falls below the formal standard of human trafficking.

## 3.5 The 'purpose'

### *3.5.1 Evolution of the 'purpose' element of trafficking*

The 'purpose' element of slave trade provisions was ultimately to reduce the victim to, and to hold the victim in, a state of slavery as defined in the 1926 Slavery Convention. The explicit scope of the 'purpose' element of the trafficking definition is much wider in comparison, as humans are trafficked for 'exploitation'.

Contemporary definitions of human trafficking include forced labour and even slavery as a 'purpose' element of trafficking, as well as sexual exploitation and the

104 Explanatory Report to the CoE Trafficking Convention (n 41) 84.

105 A D Jordan (n 46) 7.

106 See for example the Protocol against the Illicit Manufacturing of and Trafficking in Firearms, Their Parts and Components and Ammunition, supplementing the United Nations Convention against Transnational Organized Crime (adopted June 2001 by United Nations General Assembly Resolution A/RES/55/255), which defines illicit trafficking as: 'the import, export, acquisition, sale delivery, movement or transfer of firearms ...', thus demonstrating only an 'action' element.

exploitation of prostitution. These were the sole 'purpose' elements envisaged by earlier traffick-specific instruments. Until the 1949 Trafficking Convention, the subject of trafficking was specified as involving either a woman or a child. That Convention altered the terminology so that the terminology was gender neutral and the subject was a trafficked 'person'. The current internationally accepted definition of 'trafficking in persons' extends the 'purpose' element, so that it may be much more encompassing in terms of the potential subjects of trafficking and the types of exploitation experienced. According to the definition, a person is trafficked through the relevant 'action' and 'means':

> … for the purpose of exploitation. Exploitation shall include, at a minimum, the exploitation of the prostitution of others or other forms of sexual exploitation, forced labour or services, slavery or practices similar to slavery, servitude or the removal of organs.[107]

The Explanatory Report to the CoE Trafficking Convention states that: '[n]ational legislation may therefore target other forms of exploitation but must at least cover the types of exploitation mentioned as constituents of trafficking in human beings'.[108] The Explanatory Report observes that the types of exploitation included in the definition are broad because 'criminal activity is increasingly diversifying in order to supply people for exploitation in any sector where demand emerges'.[109] Evidently, the 'purpose' element hinges on 'exploitation' or at least the intention to exploit. Consequently, a broad interpretation – and therefore a broad scope of the reach of the trafficking definition – may be possible.

### *3.5.2 The interrelation of treaty obligations: interpretation of the 'purpose'*

The wording of the trafficking definition used within the main instruments discussed throughout this book raises some issues with regard to interpretation of the 'purpose' element, which is broadly 'exploitation', with the definition going to give an inexhaustive list of what this may comprise. Aust states that: 'treaties … are the product of negotiations leading to compromises to reconcile, often wide, differences'.[110] Accordingly, unclear or undefined wording may be the product of concessions made in order to secure signatures and ratifications.

As will be discussed, some terms of the trafficking definition have been deliberately left undefined.[111] Others, however, directly reproduce the wording used in

107 The trafficking of human organs goes beyond the ambit of this book and therefore will not be considered here.

108 Explanatory Report to the CoE Trafficking Convention (n 41) 85.

109 ibid 86.

110 A Aust *Modern Treaty Law and Practice* (2nd edn, Cambridge University Press, 2007) 184.

111 For example, specificities regarding the defining of prostitution and the exploitation thereof, and 'sexual exploitation', were deliberately avoided, owing to a lack of uniform approach to addressing prostitution between states. These terms are, therefore, 'without prejudice' as to how the domestic law in different states deals with prostitution.

various international human rights treaties – forced labour or services, slavery or practices similar to slavery, and servitude.[112] These terms are not defined within the instruments comprising the international anti-trafficking regime, and so we must look elsewhere. As a point of common sense, since both the UN and CoE have drafted human rights treaties which predate their respective anti-trafficking instruments and use the same terms (such as 'slavery' etc), it would seem logical on the face of it that these terms would be intended to have the same meaning. However, whether these terms and concepts are so readily interchangeable so that they might have the same meaning in both criminal and human rights law instruments, is not a matter so simplistically disposed of and therefore merits further discussion.

To the very greatest extent, judicial interpretation of the relevant texts will be carried out by national courts (although it should not be overlooked that interpretation by officials will be a necessary step before any proceedings begin – their conclusions may or may not be upheld by the courts). The Explanatory Report to the CoE Trafficking Convention explicitly states that:

> It was understood by the drafters that, under the Convention, Parties would not be obliged to copy *verbatim* into their domestic law the concepts in Article 4, provided that domestic law covered the concepts in a manner consistent with the principles of the Convention and offered an equivalent framework for implementing it.[113]

Consequently, the terms used to elucidate the minimum standards of 'exploitation' envisaged by the legal anti-trafficking regime may vary between contracting parties, particularly where sexual exploitation is concerned. However, some concepts such as slavery and servitude may have more settled (or conversely, more disputed[114]) meanings owing to their definition in legal instruments, as well as their interpretation and application through case law. These meanings and definitions will be brought out throughout the discussion in the latter part of this chapter.

The legal anti-trafficking regime raises the issue of the interrelation between treaty obligations arising under different instruments – those which address criminal law, and those which address human rights law. Although the terminology for parts of the 'purpose' element of human trafficking and the forms of 'exploitation' provided therein are clearly borrowed from international human rights law, this would mean that, in principle, one could not be binding as to the meaning of the other. State criminal law – be it of national or international origin – must, in its interpretation, take into account the human rights obligations of the state. To do anything less is to run the risk of discordance and lack of harmony between

112 The various human instruments addressing these specific rights will be discussed at a later point in this chapter.

113 At para 70.

114 See, for example, the various writings of J Allain, who is at times critical of the interpretation and application of the specificities of 'slavery' or 'servitude' in case law. See Allain 'The parameters of "'enslavement'" in international criminal law' (n 26).

national law and human rights obligations. For example, failure by a state to criminalise torture could lead to that state being unable to impose punishment for conduct by private actors, while itself being subject to obligations relating to non-torture under its human rights obligations. Such a situation would be incomprehensible and ineffective in combating the very problems identified.

It is increasingly the case that the interpretation of international treaties is done with regard to other international obligations of the parties concerned. The quest for coherence in a decentralised international system is a strong motivating factor, as such an approach both provides a means of reducing the chances of states facing incompatible obligations, and also increased likelihood of coordinated and coherent strategies to combat international problems such as human trafficking. In the fields of international criminal law and human rights, the impact of other obligations – explicit or implied – is undeniable. There is, however, a principle of treaty interpretation which is of increasing importance, and is located in Part III,[115] section 3[116] of the Vienna Convention,[117] specifically in Articles 31 and 32. The principles embodied in those two articles have been held by the International Court of Justice to reflect customary international law.[118]

Article 31 of the Vienna Convention states as a general rule of interpretation that: '[a] treaty shall be interpreted in good faith in accordance with the ordinary meaning to be given to the terms of the treaty in their context and in the light of its object and purpose'. Interpreting a treaty according to its object and purpose encapsulates 'the duty of giving effect to the expressed intention of the parties, that is, their intention as *expressed in the words used by them in the light of the surrounding circumstances*'[119] (emphasis in the original). The object and purpose of one of the main anti-trafficking instruments – the CoE Trafficking Convention – is stated as the following:

> … to prevent and combat trafficking in human beings, while guaranteeing gender equality; to protect the human rights of the victims of trafficking, design a comprehensive framework for the protection and assistance of victims and witnesses, while guaranteeing gender equality, as well as to ensure effective investigation and prosecution; to promote international cooperation on action against trafficking in human beings.[120]

The text of the EU 2011 Directive (although not a treaty, yet a relevant instrument to the discussion since it uses almost entirely the same definition of trafficking)

115 Part III of the Vienna Convention deals with 'Observance, Application and Interpretation of Treaties' – Vienna Convention on the Law of Treaties (done at Vienna on 23 May 1969, entered into force on 27 January 1980, in accordance with art 84(1)) United Nations Treaty Series vol 1155 (Vienna Convention).

116 Part III, s 3 of the Vienna Convention deals specifically with 'Interpretation of Treaties'.

117 Vienna Convention (n 115).

118 *Libya v Chad* [1994] ICJ Reports 6 para 4.

119 A McNair *Law of Treaties* (Clarendon Press, Oxford, 1961) 365.

120 CoE Trafficking Convention art 1.

makes it clear that it shares the above-mentioned objectives,[121] thus clearly pointing to human rights standards by referring specifically to them.

The 'context' referred to in Article 31(1) of the Vienna Convention is elaborated upon in subsection (2), and includes preamble and annexes, as well as 'any agreement relating to the treaty which was made between all the parties in connection with the conclusion of the treaty'[122] and 'any instrument which was made by one or more parties in connection with the conclusion of the treaty and accepted by the other parties as an instrument related to the treaty'.[123] The scope of these provisions may include, for example, 'primary criteria'[124] to interpretation such as explanatory reports.[125] To interpret and elucidate the terms used within the CoE Trafficking Convention, for example, the Explanatory Report to that Convention refers specifically to the main international human rights instruments for the purposes of defining certain terms used within that Convention, such as forced labour,[126] slavery[127] and servitude.[128] This indicates that these terms are intended

121 See EU 2011 Directive (n 2).

122 Vienna Convention art 31(2)(a).

123 ibid art 2(b).

124 Aust (n 110) 187.

125 ibid 191.

126 Paragraph 89 of the Explanatory Report to the CoE Trafficking Convention (n 41) states that, although the Convention does not define 'forced labour', nonetheless 'there are several relevant international instruments, such as the *Universal Declaration of Human Rights* (art 4), the *International Covenant on Civil and Political Rights* (art 8), the ILO *Convention concerning Forced or Compulsory Labour* (Convention No 29), and the 1957 ILO *Convention concerning the Abolition of Forced Labour* (Convention No 105)'. Paragraph 90 of the Explanatory Report goes on to state that: 'Article 4 ECHR prohibits forced labour without defining it. The drafters of the ECHR took as their model the ILO Convention concerning Forced or Compulsory Labour (No 29) of 29 June 1930, which describes as forced or compulsory "all work or service which is exacted from any person under the menace of any penalty and for which the person has not offered himself voluntarily'. Paragraph 92 goes on to recognise that forced services are not to be distinguished from forced labour, citing *Van der Müssele v Belgium* (judgment of 23 November 1983, Series A, No 70, para 37) as authority for this position.

127 Paragraph 93 of the Explanatory Report to the CoE Trafficking Convention (n 41) states that: 'Slavery is not defined in the Convention but many international instruments and the domestic law of many countries define or deal with slavery and practices similar to slavery (for example, the Geneva Convention on Slavery of 25 September 1926, as amended by the New York Protocol of 7 December 1953; the Supplementary Convention on the Abolition of Slavery, the Slave Trade, and Institutions and Practices similar to Slavery of 7 September 1956; the ILO Worst Forms of Child Labour Convention (Convention No 182))'.

128 Paragraph 95 of the Explanatory Report to the CoE Trafficking Convention (n 41) states that: 'The ECHR bodies have defined "servitude". The European Commission of Human Rights regarded it as having to live and work on another person's property and perform certain services for them, whether paid or unpaid, together with being unable to alter one's condition (Application No 7906/77 DR17, 59; see also the Commission's report in the *Van Droogenbroeck* case of 9 July 1980, Series B vol 44, 30, paras 78 to 80). Servitude is thus to be regarded as a particular form of slavery, differing from it less in character less than in degree. Although it constitutes a state or condition, and is a "particularly serious form of denial of freedom" (*Van Droogenbroeck* case, judgment of 24 June 1982, Series A No 50, 32, para 58), it does not have the ownership features characteristic of slavery'.

to be interpreted according to the meanings given by the human rights and labour instruments referred to. The preamble of that Convention also specifically refers to the point that 'trafficking in human beings may result in slavery for victims …', and that trafficking 'constitutes a violation of human rights and an offence to the dignity and the integrity of the human being', thereby invoking the language of internationally accepted human rights instruments from the outset.

Also poignant for the purpose of the discussion here, however, is Article 31(3) of the Vienna Convention, which states that when interpreting the terms of treaties, not only should the context be taken into account but, according to subsections (a)–(c) respectively, also 'any subsequent agreement between the parties regarding the interpretation of the treaty or the application of its provisions',[129] 'any subsequent practice in the application of the treaty which establishes the agreement of the parties regarding its interpretation'[130] and 'any relevant rules of international law applicable in the relations between the parties'.[131]

As regards the second point relating to 'subsequent practice' in subsection (b), there is clear evidence in certain case law of human rights standards being applied in human trafficking cases.[132] The third above-mentioned point relating to subsection (c), that is, 'any relevant rules of international law applicable in the relations between the parties', is particularly pertinent here, as it would indicate that regard may be had to pre-existing international law, and also to contemporary law.[133] Simply put, Article 31(3)(c) 'identifies the different circumstances in which the interpreter may use matter from the body of law outside the treaty'.[134] However, 'the formulation eventually adopted offers no guidance for its modern application'.[135] The meaning and exact scope of 'relevant rules of international law' is undefined, but the unqualified nature of the terminology might strongly suggest that treaties are to be included.[136] As Gardiner notes:

129 Vienna Convention art 31(3)(a).

130 ibid art 31(3)(b).

131 ibid art 31(3)(c).

132 See *Rantsev v Cyprus and Russia* [2010] (Application no 25965/04) , although, as stated in the judgment at H30(d): 'It was not necessary for the Court to identify whether the treatment about which the applicant complained constituted "slavery", "servitude" or "forced and compulsory labour". It found that trafficking itself, within the meaning of art.3(a) of the Protocol to Prevent, Suppress and Punish Trafficking in Persons, especially Women and Children ("the Palermo Protocol") and art.4(a) of the Council of Europe Convention on Action against Trafficking in Human Beings ("the Anti-Trafficking Convention") fell within the scope of art.4'. Allain has notably been critical of the ECtHR's approach in that case. See Allain '*Rantsev v Cyprus and Russia*' (n 23) 546–57, 546, where the author states that: '[w]ith the determination of the Court that obligations emanating from art 4 of the ECHR come into play because trafficking is based on slavery, the Court reveals itself as not having truly engaged with the legal distinctions that exist between these two concepts'.

133 Aust (n 110) 195; C McLachlan, 'The principle of systematic integration and Article 31(3)(c) of the Vienna Convention' (2005) 54 *International and Comparative Law Quarterly* 279–320.

134 R Gardiner *Treaty Interpretation* (Oxford University Press, Oxford, 2008) 250.

135 ibid 256.

136 ibid 262.

> Even though not hierarchical, or invariably to be applied sequentially, the general rule in Article 31 is conceptually clear: progression from terms to context, though any agreements at the time of conclusion of a treaty, to subsequent agreements, subsequent practice, and thence to relevant rules of international law.[137]

The European Court of Human Rights (ECtHR) has notably been sensitive to this principle of interpretation. This is exemplified in its application of the meaning of 'slavery' as being that provided within the 1926 Slavery Convention in recent trafficking cases such as *Rantsev*,[138] and similarly in *Siliadin*,[139] where the 'Other International Conventions' part of the 'Relevant Law' section of the judgment referred to the 1926 Slavery Convention[140] and the Forced Labour Convention.[141]

Article 32 of the Vienna Convention further provides that where it is necessary to confirm the meaning of terms resulting from the application of Article 31, or where the interpretation according to Article 31 leads to a meaning which is ambiguous, obscure, manifestly absurd or unreasonable, then '[r]ecourse may be had to supplementary means of interpretation, including the preparatory work of the treaty and the circumstances of its conclusion'. This could therefore include *travaux préparatoires* and/or interpretative notes to the *travaux*, where they exist.[142] Materials such as *travaux* are dealt with by Article 32 of the Vienna Convention since they are not 'primary criteria'[143] for interpretation. Nonetheless, Article 32 provides for the use of materials to 'confirm' meanings borne of Article 31 interpretation or, if there is 'ambiguity' or 'manifest absurdity' such as is referred to above, recourse to supplementary materials[144] under Article 32 may be used to 'determine' the meaning of a treaty provision as opposed to simply having a confirmatory role.[145]

The interpretative notes to the Trafficking Protocol give less explicit signposting, although direct reference to the Supplementary Slavery Convention of 1956[146] is made in the context of the potential for illegal adoption to fall within its scope.

The EU 2011 Directive weaves an interpretational path, which leads us to recognised human rights instruments, in stating that:

137 ibid 251.

138 *Rantsev v Cyprus and Russia* [2010] (Application no 25965/04).

139 *Siliadin v France* (Application no 73316/01) [2005] ECHR 545 (26 July 2005).

140 1926 Slavery Convention (n 6).

141 Forced Labour Convention (adopted 28 June 1930, entered into forced 1 May 1932) 39 UNTS 55, ILO CR 155.

142 See, for example, UN Doc A/55/383/Add.1 (n 72).

143 Aust (n 110) 187.

144 Aust states that this section may include 'other treaties on the same subject matter adopted either before or after the one in question which use the same or similar terms'. See Aust (n 110) 200.

145 Aust (n 110) 197.

146 Supplementary Slavery Convention (n 87).

> This Directive respects fundamental rights and observes the principles recognised in particular by the Charter of Fundamental Rights of the European Union and notably human dignity, the prohibition of slavery, forced labour and trafficking in human beings, the prohibition of torture and inhuman or degrading treatment or punishment ...[147]

Thus, the Directive points us to the human rights standards laid down in the Charter of Fundamental Rights (the EU Charter), which has a specific provision relating to slavery, forced labour, servitude and trafficking.[148] In turn, to interpret the terms enshrined in the trafficking definition contained within the EU 2011 Directive, we are pointed to the EU Charter, and through the preamble of the latter to other sources – international obligations, ECHR rights, and ECtHR jurisprudence.[149]

Owing to the increasing importance of the interpretational rules laid down in Part III, section 3 of the Vienna Convention, coupled with the direct and indirect signposting from the anti-trafficking instruments, it appears that it is possible to draw upon pre-existing international human rights instruments in order to interpret the meanings of some of the terms used within the trafficking definition. With respect to each 'purpose' element of trafficking, then, the obligations of states under the relevant human rights treaties and instruments may be used to interpret, elucidate and supplement obligations arising under the trafficking instruments. This activity can then be criminalised and the needs and rights of victims better identified and protected. Further, these treaties help to identify the obligations of states which are not party to the specific anti-trafficking instruments.

The following sections of this chapter will deconstruct and analyse the specific and non-exhaustive forms of exploitation provided within the definition of human trafficking.

### *3.5.3 Sexual exploitation and the exploitation of the prostitution of others*

Many traffick-specific instruments include 'sexual exploitation' and 'the exploitation of prostitution' as 'purpose' elements of trafficking. Certain of these instruments – even fairly recent ones – solely envisage sexual exploitation or prostitution as the 'purpose' element of human trafficking.

The CoE has seen a fair amount of recent activity in the fight against trafficking. Recommendations concerning trafficking[150] and the sexual exploitation of

147 EU 2011 Directive (n 2) preamble para 33.

148 Article 5 of the EU Charter of Fundamental Rights deals with prohibition of slavery and forced labour, and states that: '1. No one shall be held in slavery or servitude. 2. No one shall be required to perform forced or compulsory labour. 3. Trafficking in human beings is prohibited'. Charter of Fundamental Rights of the European Union [2000] OJ C364/01, reprinted [2010] OJ C83/389 http://www.europarl.europa.eu/charter/pdf/text_en.pdf (last accessed 15 January 2014).

149 Charter of Fundamental Rights of the European Union (n 148) preamble.

150 Council of Europe Committee of Ministers, Recommendation R (2000)11 adopted by the

children and young adults[151] have been issued, as well as the commencement of projects to support regional action to combat trafficking. In a Recommendation in 2000, the Committee of Ministers offered the following definition of human trafficking, which notably only envisaged sexual exploitation as a 'purpose' element of trafficking.[152]

The CoE clearly has a human rights based agenda. The Recommendation states that trafficking is offensive to human dignity, and constitutes 'a violation of human rights'.[153] Although not specifically stated by the definition offered, trafficking was at this point seen by the CoE as an issue predominantly affecting women and girls.[154] The recent EU 2011 Directive furthers this trend by referring to 'the gender-specific phenomenon of trafficking and that women and men are often trafficked for different purposes'.[155]

The terms used within the UN Trafficking Protocol, the CoE Convention and the EU 2011 Directive – 'the exploitation of the prostitution of others' and 'sexual exploitation' – are clearly broader than merely referring to 'prostitution', and are left wholly undefined by the instruments. Today, both remain undefined by international law. Both the interpretative notes for the *travaux préparatoires* to the Trafficking Protocol and the Explanatory Report to the CoE Trafficking Convention indicate that these terms are addressed solely in the context of trafficking in persons, and that this is 'without prejudice to how States Parties address prostitution in their respective domestic laws',[156] reflecting the varied and contrasting views on this matter which are held from state to state.

During negotiations, more than 100 country delegations had input into the UN Trafficking Protocol, and between them were unable to reach agreement upon definition of these two terms; consequently, the decision to leave them undefined was the only viable route to progress. The main reasons behind the disagreement were the differing policies and laws to be found within many countries as regards

Committee of Ministers of the Council of Europe to member states on action against trafficking in human beings for the purpose of sexual exploitation; Council of Europe Parliamentary Assembly, Recommendation 1325 (1997) on traffic in women and forced prostitution in Council of Europe member states; Council of Europe Parliamentary Assembly, Recommendation 1523 (2001) on domestic slavery; Council of Europe Parliamentary Assembly, Recommendation 1526 (2001) on a campaign against trafficking in minors to put a stop to the east European route: the example of Moldova; Council of Europe Parliamentary Assembly, Recommendation 1545 (2002) on a campaign against trafficking in women.

151 Council of Europe Committee of Ministers, Recommendation R (91) 11 adopted by the Committee of Ministers of the Council of Europe on Sexual exploitation, pornography and prostitution of, and trafficking in, children and young adults; Council of Europe Committee of Ministers, Recommendation R (2001)16 adopted by the Committee of Ministers of the Council of Europe to member states on the protection of children against sexual exploitation.

152 Council of Europe Committee of Ministers, Recommendation R (2000)11 adopted by the Committee of Ministers of the Council of Europe to member states on action against trafficking in human beings for the purpose of sexual exploitation, Appendix at I.1.

153 ibid preamble.

154 ibid Appendix II.2.

155 EU 2011 Directive (n 2) preamble para 3.

156 UN Doc A/55/383/Add.1 (n 72) 64.

adult sex work. As with so many treaties, compromise was necessary in order to obtain signatures and ratification. The compromise allows the individual governments of each delegation to treat voluntary adult sex work in the way that it sees fit. The notion that voluntary or non-coerced participation in labour of any form is trafficking was rejected by the majority of those involved.[157]

The institutions of the EU have taken part in some substantial action in the fight against trafficking, including the funding of certain initiatives such as the STOP[158] and Daphne[159] programmes. The European Commission has noted that action to combat human trafficking was restricted because of 'the lack of common definitions of crime, incrimination, and sanctions'.[160] In 2001, Communications were sent from the Commission to the European Council and the European Parliament concerning the subject of human trafficking. The Commission issued a proposal for a Framework Decision on combating human trafficking,[161] which contained trafficking definitions. What is particularly interesting about the definitions proffered is that sexual exploitation and labour exploitation are addressed separately. Article 1 addresses labour exploitation in the following way:

> ... where the fundamental rights of that person have been and continue to be suppressed for the purpose of exploiting him or her in the production of goods or provision of services in infringement of labour standards ...

Article 2 addressed sexual exploitation as:

> ... where the purpose is to exploit him or her in prostitution or in pornographic performances or in production of pornographic materials ...

These definitions include at least some qualification as to what constitutes labour exploitation and sexual exploitation, and are therefore less open-ended than other instruments referred to.

157 A D Jordan states that: 'While such work can be abusive and exploitative, it is only trafficking if it amounts to the internationally recognised human rights violations of forced labour, slavery, or servitude'. See Jordan (n 46) 8.

158 STOP was launched as an incentive and exchange programme to support public officials and NGOs in their actions to combat human trafficking and the exploitation of children. This programme was adopted by the Council of the European Union in November 1996. See EUROPA Press Releases 'Prevention and fight against trafficking in human beings – a European strategy since 1996' http://europa.eu/rapid/pressReleasesAction.do?reference=MEMO/02/191&format=HTML&aged=0&language=EN&guiLanguage=en (last accessed 15 January 2014).

159 This programme was conceived with a view to raising public awareness regarding violence and sexual exploitation and abuse against women and children. Daphne has a broader scope than STOP because it is not solely aimed at victims of trafficking. See EUROPA Press Releases (n 158).

160 Commission communication on combating trafficking in human beings, the sexual exploitation of children and child pornography [2001] OJ C357/11.

161 Proposal for a Council Framework Decision on combating trafficking in human beings [2001] OJ C62 E/324.

In a Recommendation, the CoE viewed sexual exploitation as a 'purpose' element of trafficking as a form of slavery.[162] The overlaps between human trafficking and the slave trade are apparent, but, similarly to labour exploitation, it is not universally accepted that sexual exploitation in the context of trafficking is a form of slavery, as it does not in every instance display the ownership characteristics to the extent that the status of slavery does. Therefore, although sex trafficking may in some or even many cases result in slavery, it will not do so in every case.

Overall, the relevant anti-trafficking instruments provide very little illumination as to the parameters of what may actually constitute 'sexual exploitation'. The 2002 EU Framework Decision included specific mention in the text of 'exploitation of the prostitution of others or other forms of sexual exploitation, including in pornography'.[163] The 2011 Directive does not include this qualification, and gives no guidance as to what constitutes 'sexual exploitation'. The Explanatory Report to the CoE Convention refers to various other Council measures to combat sexual exploitation[164] (which largely apply to children), and provides minimal illumination as to what might constitute sexual exploitation, in referring to '… sexual exploitation … in the form of pornography, prostitution, sexual slavery, sexual tourism and trafficking in human beings …',[165] thereby creating something of a circular definition.

Domestic (UK) cases involving trafficking frequently invoke more than one legal provision; consequently, a case concerning trafficking for sexual exploitation in the UK may include, for example, the offence of trafficking (SOA 2003 section 59A) coupled with the offence of controlling prostitution for gain (SOA 2003 section 53).[166]

One might assume that, provided that a requisite standard of 'exploitation'[167] is met, any work[168] of a sexual[169] nature may be capable of constituting sexual

162 Council of Europe Committee of Ministers 'Recommendation R (2000)11 adopted by the Committee of Ministers of the Council of Europe to member states on action against trafficking in human beings for the purpose of sexual exploitation' (adopted by the Committee of Ministers on 19 May 2000, at the 710th Meeting of the Ministers' Deputies).

163 Council Framework Decision 2002/629/JHA of 19 July 2002 on combating trafficking in human beings [2002] OJ L203/1 art 1(d).

164 Such as Council of Europe Committee of Ministers, Recommendation R (91) 11 adopted by the Committee of Ministers of the Council of Europe on sexual exploitation, pornography and prostitution of, and trafficking in, children and young adults' (Adopted by the Committee of Ministers on 9 September 1991 at the 461st Meeting of the Ministers' Deputies), and Council of Europe Committee of Ministers, Recommendation R (2001) 16 adopted by the Committee of Ministers of the Council of Europe to member states on the protection of children against sexual exploitation' (Adopted by the Committee of Ministers on 31 October 2001 at the 771 Meeting of the Ministers' Deputies).

165 Council of Europe Committee of Ministers, Recommendation R (2001) 16 ibid.

166 See, for example, *R v Nualpenyai (Atchara)* [2010] EWCA Crim 692.

167 A definition of exploitation offset against accepted labour standards in the destination state is proposed in ch 5.

168 Whether or not prostitution constitutes a legitimate form of labour will be discussed in ch 4.

169 What exactly constitutes 'sexual' in this context is unclear, but one might look for guidance in,

exploitation – prostitution, lap dancing, pornography etc. The terms were clearly left broad for a reason, as social and cultural variants may determine certain activities as inherently or not remotely sexual in nature. The same may be said of 'exploitation' – that which is considered exploitative clearly varies between countries; this is evident in the many and varied approaches to prostitution taken within the legislative frameworks of these countries.[170]

### *3.5.4 ... Forced labour or services, slavery or practices similar to slavery, servitude...*

It has been established that current international legal definition of human trafficking includes the 'purpose' elements of forced labour, slavery and servitude as examples of 'exploitation'. Accordingly, Piotrowicz observes that: 'While not all slavery involves (trafficking in human being), (trafficking in human beings) will almost always involve slavery or slavery-like practices'.[171] These elements warrant further exploration.

#### *3.5.4.1 Elucidating some elements of the 'purpose': the international legal framework*

Forced labour is addressed and defined in various instruments, of which the International Labour Organization (ILO) has drafted several. This practice is not defined by the three main anti-trafficking instruments considered in this book; the definition remains that provided by the ILO Conventions. The Forced Labour Convention 1930[172] requires state parties to agree to work towards eradicating the existence of forced labour practices. Article 2 defines 'forced or compulsory labour' as 'all work or service which is exacted from any person under the menace of any penalty and for which the said person has not offered himself voluntarily'. Forced labour is not further defined by the Trafficking Protocol, CoE Trafficking Convention or the EU 2011 Directive.[173] As regards 'forced services', the Explanatory Report to the CoE Trafficking Convention indicates that: '[f]rom

for example, SOA 2003 s 78 which states that: 'For the purposes of this Part (except section 71), penetration, touching or any other activity is sexual if a reasonable person would consider that— (a) whatever its circumstances or any person's purpose in relation to it, it is because of its nature sexual, or (b) because of its nature it may be sexual and because of its circumstances or the purpose of any person in relation to it (or both) it is sexual'.

170 In Sweden, for example, prostitution is seen as violence against women and inherently exploitative, therefore criminal sanction is aimed at the purchaser of sexual services. This can be contrasted with the regulated sex sector which can be seen in operation in the Netherlands.

171 R Piotrowicz 'The legal nature of trafficking in human beings' (2009) 4 *Intercultural Human Rights Law Review* 179.

172 Forced Labour Convention (adopted 28 June 1930, entered into forced 1 May 1932) 39 UNTS 55, ILO CR 155.

173 Paragraph 11 of the preamble to the EU 2011 Directive (n 2), for example, points directly to the 1930 ILO Convention No 29 concerning Forced or Compulsory Labour. Also see section 3.5.1 of this chapter on the interrelation of treaty obligations.

the standpoint of the ECHR ... there is no distinction to be made between the two concepts'.[174] Potentially, then, 'services' could be read to include sex work.

Similarly, as regards the Abolition of Forced Labour Convention 1957,[175] Article 1 requires that ILO members who ratify the Convention undertake to 'suppress and not to make use of any form of forced or compulsory labour'. The Convention does not at any point specifically use the language 'trafficking', neither does it specifically include prostitution or sex work under the overarching term of 'forced labour'. Sexual and labour exploitation in the context of trafficking are dealt with separately in many instruments. A definition proposed by the Organization for Security and Co-operation in Europe (OSCE) makes no explicit mention of sex work at all.[176]

Hernandez-Truyol and Larson[177] propose that prostitution should be studied under a labour paradigm, that is, as an exercise of the right to work, even though it (may) contain elements of servitude. Although addressing both issues within the same definition, the trafficking definition continues the trend of separating prostitution from forced labour. This will continue to be the case unless 'sexual labour'[178] is globally recognised as a legitimate form of labour.

At a similar time to the 1949 Trafficking Convention, the Universal Declaration of Human Rights (UDHR)[179] was drafted. The relevant provision is Article 4, which states that: 'No one shall be held in slavery or servitude; slavery and the slave trade shall be prohibited in all their forms'. The provision does not explicitly include forced labour as a form of, or practice related to, slavery. Forced labour was addressed at this time through the two above-mentioned ILO Conventions.

Such practices were also addressed in a multilateral treaty drafted between 1947 and 1966 – the ICCPR.[180] Article 8 prohibits slavery, servitude and forced labour. As with the UDHR, inclusion of the word 'involuntary' directly to precede 'servitude' was rejected, for reasons mirroring those given during UDHR drafting debates; that one should not be able to contract oneself into bondage.[181] Forced/compulsory labour is explicitly prohibited by Article 8(3) of the ICCPR,

174 Explanatory Report to the CoE Trafficking Convention (n 41) 92.

175 Abolition of Forced Labour Convention (adopted 25 June 1957, entered into force 17 January 1959) 320 UNTS 291.

176 A definition offered by the Organization for Security and Co-operation in Europe 'Supplementary Human Dimension Meeting on Human Trafficking: Final Report' (Vienna, 18–19 March 2002) defines human trafficking as: 'All acts involved in the recruitment, abduction, transport (within or across borders), sale, transfer, harbouring, or receipt of persons, by the threat or use of force, deception, coercion (including abuse of authority), or debt bondage, for the purpose of placing or holding such person, whether for pay or not, in involuntary servitude, forced or bonded labour, or in slavery-like conditions, in a community other than the one in which the person lived at the time of the original deception, coercion or debt bondage'.

177 Hernandez-Truyol and Larson (n 91) 391.

178 ibid.

179 Universal Declaration of Human Rights (adopted 10 December, 1948 UNGA Res 217 A(III)) (UDHR).

180 International Covenant on Civil and Political Rights (adopted 16 December 1966, entered into force 23 March 1976) 999 UNTS 171 (ICCPR).

181 Although this is questioned by some. See Hernandez-Truyol and Larson (n 91) 418–19.

which gives examples of practices deemed not to constitute this, such as work or services required of a person under detention in consequence of a lawful order of a court.[182] Forced/compulsory labour is not defined within the instrument, although during drafting reference was made to Article 2 of the ILO Forced Labour Convention (above). The common element of slavery, the slave trade and servitude in the ICCPR, is that they are prohibited regardless of whether the person concerned has offered consent. Suggestions of addressing forced labour as a wholly separate issue were rejected.

The ICCPR essentially replicates the corresponding UDHR provision, but it takes it further with the separate inclusion of servitude[183] and the explicit inclusion of forced or compulsory labour,[184] thus paving the way for broader scope of inclusion of slavery-related practices. Prostitution and sexual exploitation are not explicitly included under the umbrella of forced labour according to these provisions, yet this may be overcome by developmental interpretation. The development of provisions and definitions relating to slavery and – in particular – its related practices, have appeared to tend toward a more inclusive nature, so further development and expansion of scope is not an impossible or even improbable aspiration.

Slavery and servitude were dealt with separately in the ICCPR, as it has been observed that slavery, in the legal sense, is a technical term which requires strict limited construction, as it 'implied the destruction of the juridical personality … whereas servitude was a more general idea covering all possible forms of man's domination of man'.[185] Once again, this makes a notable effort to separate slavery, the central characteristic of which is ownership, from related practices which are also considered to undermine human dignity. Thus, servitude covers other forms of 'bondage' or human domination that do not constitute slavery.[186]

One interesting point to be drawn from the ICCPR drafting debates is that 'slave trade' is also to be construed in a limited manner. A proposal to substitute the phrase for 'trade in human beings', which may have encompassed the trafficking of women for sexual exploitation, was rejected, as it was thought that the clause should only deal with the slave trade as such.[187]

Respective provisions of the ECHR[188] and the American Convention on Human Rights 1969[189] prohibit slavery, servitude and forced or compulsory labour. Interpretation of the ECHR makes it clear that there are positive obligations on states with respect to dealing with such practices. These positive obligations have

182 ICCPR (n 180) art 8(3)(c)(1).

183 ibid. Article 8(1) addresses slavery, art 8(2) addresses servitude.

184 ibid art 8(3).

185 M J Bossuyt *Guide to the 'travaux préparatoires' of the International Covenant on Civil and Political Rights* (Nijhoff, Dordrecht and Lancaster, 1987) 167.

186 ibid.

187 Y Dinstein 'Liberty: freedom from slavery and forced labour' in L Henkin (ed) *The International Bill of Rights: The Covenant on Civil and Political Rights* (Columbia University Press, New York, 1981) 127.

188 ECHR art 4.

189 American Convention art 6, which also prohibits trafficking in women.

some reach in terms of, for example, Articles 2[190] and 3[191] of the ECHR, and can reasonably include criminalisation of such practices, which would be reflected in the national laws of parties to the Convention.

The 2011 Directive contains a broader definition of the forms of 'exploitation', which may form the 'purpose' element of human trafficking, in that it specifically includes 'begging', and 'the exploitation of criminal activities'. The preamble to the directive justifies inclusion of this element.[192]

### *3.5.4.2 The relationship between slavery and trafficking*

In the context of the trafficking definition, the definition of slavery remains that provided by the 1926 Slavery Convention: 'The status or condition of a person over whom any or all of the powers attaching to the right of ownership are exercised'.[193]

What appears to be common to slavery and its related practices is the element of control, of ownership, which is a central characteristic of slavery. It is the status of commodification – the subject is essentially reduced to a possession which can be bought and sold or ultimately disposed of – which is the defining factor. Related or comparable practices can be distinguished from slavery on this basis. For example, in *Siliadin v France*[194] the subject was effectively used as a domestic servant. It was held by the ECtHR that, since the evidence did not suggest that a genuine right of ownership having the effect of reducing her to an object, had been held over her, Ms Siliadin had not been held in slavery. It was held that she had, however, been subject to forced labour and held in servitude within the meaning of Article 4 of the ECHR.[195]

Subsequent instruments that address the slave trade, such as the ICCPR, solely contained prohibition, thereby accepting the 1926 Convention Slavery definition as adequate. The only real elaboration upon the definition came from the 1956 Supplementary Slavery Convention,[196] which called for the abolition of certain

190 ECHR art 2 addresses the right to life.

191 ECHR art 3 addresses the right to be free from torture and inhuman or degrading treatment.

192 EU 2011 Directive (n 2) preamble para 11 states that: 'in order to tackle recent developments in the phenomenon of trafficking in human beings, this Directive adopts a broader concept of what should be considered trafficking in human beings than under Framework Decision 2002/629/JHA and therefore includes additional forms of exploitation. Within the context of this Directive, forced begging should be understood as a form of forced labour or services as defined in the 1930 ILO Convention No 29 concerning Forced or Compulsory Labour. Therefore, the exploitation of begging, including the use of a trafficked dependent person for begging, falls within the scope of the definition of trafficking in human beings only when all the elements of forced labour or services occur'.

193 1926 Slavery Convention (n 6) art 1(1).

194 *Siliadin v France* (n 139).

195 This can be contrasted with the *Kunarac* judgment, where forced labour was deemed to fall within the remit of 'enslavement'. See *Prosecutor v Dragoljub Kunarac, Radomir Kovac, and Zoran Vukovic* (Appeal Judgment) Case Nos IT-96-23 & IT-96-23/1-A (12 June 2002) 542.

196 Supplementary Slavery Convention (n 87).

practices, 'whether or not they are covered by the definition of slavery contained in article 1 of the Slavery Convention'.[197] The practices referred to include debt bondage[198] and serfdom,[199] as well as situations whereby a woman could be promised for marriage, transferred to another for value or inherited by another on her husband's death.[200]

The words 'trafficking' or 'traffick' in the context of early legal definitions such as that provided within the 1910 Trafficking Convention arguably carried different connotations than they do today. During the Temporary Slavery Commission's deliberations, the actual word 'traffic' only crops up briefly, and is explained as 'the transformation of free men in to slaves'.[201] This loosely covers the entire process of action, means and purpose, to the exclusion of those already enslaved. 'Trafficking', however, was not explicitly defined by the Temporary Slavery Commission, nor was it explicitly included in the 1926 Slavery Convention.

Although the Temporary Slavery Commission appeared to push for a broader definition of slavery than that adopted,[202] as did certain of the governments of respondent countries during the drafting of the 1926 Slavery Convention,[203] the consensus among members was that to address the disguised forms of slavery would take the Commission beyond the ambit of its competence.[204] Consequently, trafficking for the purpose of exploitative sex work or labour was explicitly excluded from the ambit of the 1926 Slavery Convention, and so the resulting chosen definition became the narrow, specific definition of slavery as we know and understand it to be today, exclusive of related 'lesser' forms of exploitation. It is, however, clear that the two related yet distinct practices of slave trading and trafficking have not consistently been viewed distinctly. As well as this confusion being evident in some academic commentary,[205] comments on Article 4 of the UDHR made it clear that 'slavery' was intended to encompass the trafficking

197 ibid art 1.

198 Defined in art 1(a) of the Supplementary Slavery Convention (n 87) as: 'the status or condition arising from a pledge by a debtor of his personal services or of those of a person under his control as security for a debt, if the value of those services as reasonably assessed is not applied towards the liquidation of the debt or the length and nature of those services are not respectively limited and defined'.

199 Defined in art 1(b) of the Supplementary Slavery Convention (n 87) as 'the condition or status of a tenant who is by law, custom or agreement bound to live and labour on land belonging to another person and to render some determinate service to such other person, whether for reward or not, and is not free to change his status'.

200 ibid art 1.

201 League of Nations 6.B.4 Temporary Slavery Commission: Minutes of the First (and Second) Session(s), Geneva (1924–25) 7.

202 ibid.

203 Germany, for example, proposed that conditions resembling slavery, such as trafficking, be included: see League of Nations, Draft Convention on Slavery, Replies of Governments, Reply from the Government of Germany, League of Nations Doc A.10(a).1926.VI (22 July 1926), reprinted in *Publications of the League of Nations*, VI.B. Slavery, 1926. VI.B. 3, 4 (1926).

204 See M Van Rees, League of Nations 6.B.4 Temporary Slavery Commission: Minutes of the First (and Second) Session(s), Geneva (1924–25) 10.

205 See Scarpa (n 22) and Gold (n 22).

of women and children,[206] evidently without explicit mention. The slave trade and the resulting 'purpose' element of slavery amount to a form of exploitation. Trafficking according to current legal definition goes beyond this, in that it covers a broader spectrum of 'purpose' elements, which are all forms of 'exploitation', of which slavery is one.

Allain[207] considers the relative meanings of 'slavery' and 'enslavement' against an international criminal law backdrop, and makes a variety of salient points, noting in particular that the definitions provided in the 1998 Rome Statute[208] of the International Criminal Court and the 2002 Elements of Crimes[209] are somewhat contradictory on the points of slavery and sexual exploitation, and sex trafficking. Article 7 of the former includes 'enslavement' as a crime against humanity,[210] as well as sexual slavery and enforced prostitution.[211] The Article expands upon the meaning of enslavement as: '(T)he exercise of any or all of the powers attaching to the right of ownership over a person and includes the exercise of such power in the course of trafficking in persons, in particular women and children',[212] thereby recognising that enslavement can occur during the process of trafficking in human beings. Aside from that extra consideration, the definition mirrors closely that provided within the 1926 Slavery Convention. The Elements of Crimes provides a somewhat broader definition, and refers to the elements of 'enslavement' as:

> … (the exercise of) any or all of the powers attaching to the right of ownership over one or more persons, such as by purchasing, selling, lending or bartering such a person or persons, or by imposing on them a similar deprivation of liberty.[213]

Further to this, Allain[214] notes that the above-mentioned provision of the Elements of Crimes has a footnote annexed to it, which provides that:

> It is understood that such a deprivation of liberty may, in some circumstances, include exacting forced labour or otherwise reducing a person to servile status as defined in the Supplementary Convention on the Abolition of

206 Report of the Working Group on the Declaration of the second session of the Commission on Human Rights E/CN.4/57, 1947; and summary records of the Third Committee of the third session of the General Assembly, UN Docs A/C.3/SR. 109 and 110 (1948).

207 See Allain, 'The parameters of "enslavement" in international criminal law' (n 26) and Allain 'The definition of slavery in international law' (n 26) 239.

208 Rome Statue of the International Criminal Court, UN Doc A/CONF.183/9.

209 Elements of Crimes under the Rome Statute of the International Criminal Court.

210 Article 7 of the Rome Statute provides a list of acts which will constitute crimes against humanity 'when committed as part of a widespread or systematic attack directed against any civilian population, with knowledge of the attack'.

211 Article 7 of the Rome Statute ss (c) and (g) respectively.

212 Rome Statute of the International Criminal Court art 7(2)(c).

213 Elements of Crimes art 7(1)(c).

214 See Allain 'The parameters of "enslavement" in international criminal law' (n 26) 239.

> Slavery, The Slave Trade, and Institution and Practices Similar to Slavery of 1956. It is also understood that the conduct described in this element includes trafficking in persons, in particular women and children.[215]

This expansion of 'enslavement' reads as though intended to include both slavery and institutions and practices which are similar, such as servitude, but which do not in themselves necessarily constitute actual slavery. Thus, a broader notion of 'enslavement' is apparently postulated, which goes beyond mere 'slavery', as recognised by the 1926 Slavery Convention. Accordingly, the above-mentioned provisions imply that a person who is trafficked can be deemed to be 'enslaved'; a person who is trafficked could be deemed to be a 'slave', even if a person who is trafficked and enslaved is not necessarily a slave in the 1926 Slavery Convention sense. Similarly, the *Kunarac* judgment concluded that:

> … indications of enslavement include exploitation: the exaction of forced or compulsory labour or service, often without remuneration and often, though not necessarily, involving physical hardship; sex; prostitution; and human trafficking.[216]

Literally, to enslave is to 'make (someone) a slave'.[217] Further, to enslave is to 'cause (someone) to lose their freedom of choice or action'.[218] The apparent lack of clarity as to the meanings of 'slavery' and 'enslavement', against a backdrop of trafficking and slavery, does serve to cloud the meaning of 'slavery' as traditionally understood (according to current international legal definition). Although slavery can (according to current international legal definition) occur as a 'purpose' element of trafficking, it is clearly not the sole 'purpose' element of trafficking.

Allain observes that:

> From the preparation of the 1926 definition onwards, attempts have been made to obfuscate the term 'slavery' and to distance its legal definition from a definition that might instead be consonant with any type of exploitation.[219]

Between the variants of 'exploitation' provided within the trafficking definition, such as servitude[220] and slavery,[221] there may be differences of degree[222] but there are also differences of nature. Consequently, trying to assimilate these different forms of exploitation into the definitive terms of 'slavery' is not necessarily possible, if the full reach of illegal trafficking is to be caught. As defined, slavery can

215 Footnote to Elements of Crimes art 7(1)(c).
216 *Prosecutor v Dragoljub Kunarac, Radomir Kovac, and Zoran Vukovic* (Appeal Judgment) (n 195) 542.
217 *Oxford English Dictionary* (2nd edn, Oxford University Press, 2003).
218 ibid.
219 Allain 'The definition of slavery in international law' (n 26) 242.
220 *Siliadin v France* (n 139).
221 *Hadijatou Mani Koraou v Republic of Niger* [2008] ECW/CCJ/JUD/06/08.
222 *Prosecutor v Dragoljub Kunarac, Radomir Kovac, and Zoran Vukovic* (Appeal Judgment) (n 195).

only occur where 'any or all of the powers attaching to the right of ownership are exercised'[223] and forms of human exploitation that fall short of this standard cannot be deemed actual slavery.[224] They may, however, still feasibly be within the scope of the definition of trafficking.

The UN Secretary General in his 1953 report noted the following, which was contained within a governmental communication:

> (A) person is a slave if any other person can, by law or enforceable custom, claim such property in him as would be claimed if he were an inanimate object; and thus the natural freedom of will possessed by a person to offer or render his labour or to control the fruits thereof or the consideration therefrom is taken from him. The term also seems to imply a permanent status or condition of a person whose natural freedom is so taken away, for from the proprietary interest of the other person in the person to whom that status attaches is implied a right of disposal by sale, gift or exchange.[225]

Thus, in the case of *Siliadin v France*[226] this standard was – in the opinion of the ECtHR – not met, as the treatment of the individual had not had the effect of reducing her to an object. This begs the question as to what 'ownership' actually is. Arguably, its characteristics include possession, the right to use, and the right to make income from the object.[227] To own is to be able to buy, sell and perhaps go so far as to destroy, although as Allain observes, the killing of slaves was criminalised under Roman law.[228]

Clearly, ownership relates to established proprietary rights, that is, as rights over property, although in the context of slavery falling short of legal right of possession – the abolition of *de jure* slavery by the 1926 Slavery Convention negates legal right of possession of a human being in states that are party to the Convention. The meaning of '*the powers attaching to* the right of ownership' (emphasis added)[229] in the Convention definition can be taken to mean what would otherwise be powers of actual ownership, if such ownership were legal.[230] Thus, if one treats a human being in a fashion that would be acceptable if that human being was a legally owned object, one is exercising 'the powers attaching to the right of ownership'.

The characteristics of the powers referred to include the above-mentioned characteristics of ownership: the ability to buy, sell or transfer the individual;

223 1926 Slavery Convention (n 6) art 1(1).
224 For further discussion of this issue, see Allain 'The definition of slavery in international law' (n 26) 239.
225 United Nations Economic and Social Council 'Slavery, the slave trade, and other forms of servitude' (Report of the Secretary-General), UN Doc E/2357 (27 January 1953).
226 *Siliadin v France* (n 139).
227 See A M Honoré 'Ownership' in A G Guest (ed) *Oxford Essays in Jurisprudence* (Oxford University Press, Oxford, 1961) 112–24.
228 Allain 'The definition of slavery in international law' (n 26) 258.
229 1926 Slavery Convention (n 6) art 1(1).
230 Allain, 'The definition of slavery in international law' (n 26) 261.

property rights to the fruits of any labour of the individual; and permanence in that the status or condition cannot be terminated by the individual who is subject to it.[231] As recognised by Weissbrodt, the degree of restriction and control exerted is central to determining what practices constitute slavery.[232]

As stated previously, 'exploitation' is a key element of human trafficking. It would seem clear that 'exploitation' per se does not hit the specific standard of slavery, yet it seems clear that trafficking can, in certain circumstances, amount to de facto slavery in the sense of the definition 1926 Slavery Convention, where 'any or all of the powers attaching to the right of ownership are exercised', that is to say, where the powers of ownership are exercised with respect to a trafficked person *as if* that person were legally owned.[233]

Consideration of *R v Tang*[234] may aid this discussion. This recent case, heard by the High Court of Australia, has provided an insight into the application of the above-mentioned definition and characteristics of slavery to a situation of human trafficking. Allain observes that this decision has 'brought much depth of understanding to the parameters of what constitutes "slavery" both in the Australian context, but also in international law'.[235] This case concerned application of the relevant sections of the Australian Criminal Code Act that address slavery.[236] The Act uses a definition of slavery[237] which is very similar to that provided within the 1926 Slavery Convention. Interestingly, Division 270 of the Criminal Code Act has provisions relating not only to slavery, but also to 'trafficking in persons',[238] and to 'sexual servitude'. Section 270.4(1) provides the following definition:

> (1) For the purposes of this Division, *sexual servitude*[239] is the condition of a person who provides sexual services and who, because of the use of force or threats:
> (a) is not free to cease providing sexual services; or
> (b) is not free to leave the place or area where the person provides sexual services.

The Act also has related provisions which address the use of threats[240] and deception[241] in the course of sexual servitude.

231 United Nations Economic and Social Council (n 225).
232 UNHCHR, D Weissbrodt and Anti-Slavery International 'Abolishing slavery and its contemporary forms' (2002 United Nations New York and Geneva) HR/PUB/02/4 para 21.
233 This much is voiced by Hayne J in *R v Tang* [2008] HCA 39 (28 August 2008) 142.
234 ibid.
235 Allain 'The definition of slavery in international law' (n 26) 246.
236 Australian Criminal Code Act ss 270.1–270.3.
237 ibid s 270.1 states that: 'For the purposes of this Division, slavery is the condition of a person over whom any or all of the powers attaching to the right of ownership are exercised, including where such a condition results from a debt or contract made by the person'.
238 ibid s 271.2.
239 Emphasis in the original text.
240 Australian Criminal Code Act s 270.4(2).
241 ibid s 270.7.

The facts of *Tang* concerned five women of Thai nationality who had voluntarily come to Australia to work in the sex industry. On arrival, they discovered that they had been 'bought' and consequently were required to work off the debt, which consisted of more than double their 'purchase' price. Their passports were withheld, and their movement was restricted until their debt was paid off, at which point the restrictions were lifted, travel documents were returned, and they were given freedom of choice with respect to their hours of work.[242] The High Court, rather than defaulting to application of trafficking or sexual servitude provisions, applied section 270 and considered the characteristics of slavery, that is, where 'any or all of the powers attaching to the right of ownership'[243] were exercised.

A distinction was made between exploitative labour conditions and conditions of slavery,[244] and although it was recognised that borderline cases would be problematic,[245] the outcome of the present case indicates that the degree of control exercised over the victims went beyond any level of exploitation which is to be tentatively deemed acceptable, and in fact, went so far as to constitute slavery. Gleeson CJ indicated that the difference lay in the nature and extent of the powers attaching to the right of ownership that were exercised over the victim,[246] and referred to treatment of the individual in terms that echo those explored above with reference to the UN Secretary General in his 1953 report;[247] treating the individual as an object who might be sold – in other words, commodification.

Gleeson CJ also stated that in the present case it was unhelpful to draw boundaries between slavery and related practices such as servitude, as the boundaries are not necessarily clear-cut,[248] and that traffickers 'are unlikely to be so obliging as to arrange their practices to conform to some convenient taxonomy'.[249] This, however, seems inconsistent with the principle of 'representative labelling', so termed by Ashworth,[250] but more commonly referred to as 'fair labelling'.[251] Slavery, servitude, debt bondage and other related practices have, for the most part, consistently been addressed separately[252] and therefore cannot easily be assimilated without further justification. For example, Allain is critical of the ECtHR judgment in *Rantsev* for not adequately engaging with the distinction between different types of human exploitation such as slavery and servitude,[253] as the Court in that

242 *Tang* (n 233) para 17.

243 Section 270.1 of the Australian Criminal Code Act, drawing upon the definition of slavery provided within art 1(1) of the 1926 Slavery Convention.

244 *Tang* (n 233) para 32.

245 ibid para 44.

246 ibid.

247 United Nations Economic and Social Council (n 225).

248 *Tang* (n 233) para 29.

249 ibid.

250 See A Ashworth 'The elasticity of *mens rea*' in C F H Tapper (ed) *Crime, Proof and Punishment: Essays in Memory of Sir Rupert Cross* (Butterworths, London, 1981) 45, 53.

251 G Williams 'Convictions and fair labelling' (1983) 42 *Cambridge Law Journal* 85.

252 Although the *Rantsev* judgment muddied the waters somewhat here. See Allain '*Rantsev v Cyprus and Russia*' (n 23) 546–57.

253 ibid 546.

case determined that trafficking is based upon slavery and therefore invokes the obligations that emanate from Article 4 of the ECHR.[254] There is an inherent need for precision on these matters in a criminal context, particularly in terms of, for example, assessing the rights and needs of victims.

What can be taken from the *Tang* judgment, however, is that the reasoning is sound for the most part, and the law relating to slavery and the elements of the definition therein was consistently applied. This judgment therefore exemplifies that the trafficking process can, in certain circumstances where the high threshold is met, that is, where 'any or all of the powers attaching to the right of ownership' are exercised, result in the condition of slavery, as does the slave trade. However, owing to the myriad types of 'exploitation' envisaged as 'purpose' elements of trafficking, the slave trade and the process of human trafficking may be compared, but cannot and should not be wholly equated. Human trafficking is for 'exploitation' and supersedes definitions of the slave trade and the condition of slavery.[255]

### *3.5.5 The 'purpose': some conclusions*

The terminology used within the criminal anti-trafficking regime is clearly borrowed from human rights law and requires interpretation. Owing to the increasing importance of the principles of interpretation enshrined in the Vienna Convention, elucidation of these elements using internationally recognised human rights standards allows us to gain a sounder understanding of the scope of the types of exploitation outlined in the 'purpose' element of the trafficking definition.

Evidently, the trafficking definition casts its net widely and envisages a spectrum of exploitative activities, so that a variety of 'purposes' fall within the ambit of the international legal definition of human trafficking. The status or condition of slavery, where 'any or all of the powers attaching to the right of ownership are exercised', sits clearly at one end of this spectrum, and represents the most severe form of exploitation which may come about as a 'purpose' element of human trafficking. Along this spectrum sit the multitude of other forms of exploitation that form part of the trafficking process. This confirms that serious exploitation is the central characteristic of the 'purpose'; the non-exhaustive definition of

254 ibid.

255 As a final point on the scope of the UN Protocol, the definition also extends to illegal adoption, where it 'amounts to a practise similar to slavery as defined in Article 1, paragraph (d), of the Supplementary Convention on the Abolition of Slavery, the Slave Trade, and Institution and Practices similar to Slavery'. See United Nations General Assembly 'Report of the Ad Hoc Committee on the Elaboration of a Convention against Transnational Organized Crime on the work of its first to eleventh sessions, Addendum, Interpretative notes for the official records (*travaux préparatoires*) of the negotiation of the United Nations Convention against Transnational Organized Crime and the Protocols thereto' (2000) UN Doc A/55/383/Add.1, 66. In terms of illegal adoption, the 'action' is satisfied, and the issue of consent is irrelevant as the subject of the illegal adoption will be a child, so the 'purpose' element becomes the central focus. Thus, the illegal adoption of a child in order to use the child as a domestic servant, for example, can be caught by the trafficking definition.

'exploitation' provided by the current definition ensures that myriad activities are caught, so that states can make an effective attempt at tackling this global phenomenon and the serious forms of human exploitation that it involves.

## 3.6 Conclusion

The current internationally recognised definition of human trafficking has taken major steps in defining exactly what 'trafficking in persons' is in a legal sense. The definition is comparable to the legal definition addressing the slave trade, which can similarly be broken down into the three elements of 'action', 'means' and 'purpose'. Both the slave trade and human trafficking are exploitative forms of trade in human beings. The fact that the purpose element of trafficking – as provided within the current internationally accepted definition of 'trafficking in humans' – now includes the status of slavery as a relevant form of exploitation, demonstrates that the trafficking definition intends to address severe forms of non-consensual exploitative migration in a broader sense than previously achieved by individual trafficking and slavery-specific instruments. While prostitution is not globally accepted as a form of labour, the definition incorporated within the relevant instruments[256] must remain on the fence by not defining sexual exploitation – the result of a need to secure signatures and ratifications etc to these landmark instruments.

The 'action' element of human trafficking is phrased in necessarily broad terms, to encompass all situations where traffickers come into contact with putative victims. It has been established for the most part that international borders do not necessarily have to be crossed;[257] nonetheless, that cases of 'intra-state' or 'internal' trafficking may well be dealt with according to national law. Furthermore, it has been established that entry into the destination state does not have to be illicit. This extends the scope, applicability and therefore efficiency of the anti-trafficking regime.

The inclusion of the 'means' element into recent trafficking definitions has proven to be a controversial step, as it has the effect that otherwise 'trafficked' persons who have not been subject to force or coercion (or at least where there is no objective proof of such) arguably fall outside the scope of the trafficking definition. This raises further issues that warrant exploration, and so the role of consent (or lack thereof) in the context of human trafficking will be considered further in Chapter 5. The particulars of the 'means' element are not always clearly separable, yet nonetheless go toward establishing the definition of human trafficking as a non-consensual process, or at least a process where any consent given may be rendered ineffective by use of any of the 'means'. This in turn relies upon objective proof of 'coercion' etc being available in order for the 'victim' to

256 See the Trafficking Protocol (n 5); the CoE Trafficking Convention (n 1) and the EU 2011 Directive (n 2).

257 With the caveat under the Trafficking Protocol (n 5) that the activity be 'transnational' in nature.

be formally identified as trafficked – such is the centrality of the consent/coercion spectrum created by the trafficking definition.[258]

Early traffick-specific instruments defined trafficking as a process which entailed a 'purpose' element solely comprised of exploitation of a sexual nature. It is now clear that non-consensual 'exploitation' per se is the defining element of this activity. The detailed trafficking definition works toward clarifying exactly which exploitative situations do and do not constitute human trafficking, and attempts to provide a clearer view of what the 'purpose' element of human trafficking is.

The evolution of the scope of this element of trafficking legislation can only enhance its effectiveness in combating the most severe forms of non-consensual exploitative migration, as it takes what has already been done in human rights and labour law instruments to address slavery and its related forms, sexual exploitation and exploitation of labour, and creates instruments to address all of these aspects by criminalising them as acts committed by private individuals. The 'purpose' element of the anti-trafficking regime is supplemented by the pre-existing instruments that address slavery, forced labour etc, and recourse to these instruments as aids to interpretation of the 'purpose' elements of human trafficking can be justified by reference to Articles 31 and 32 of the Vienna Convention.

The analysis conducted throughout this chapter indicates that all activity which can be deemed human trafficking falls along a spectrum of exploitation, which at an extreme point can cross into the realms of *de facto* slavery. With 'exploitation' being the central 'purpose' element of human trafficking, the definition provided within the relevant instruments takes a 'broad brush' approach, thereby encompassing a multitude of exploitative activities, provided that the other elements of the trafficking definition are present. We now know what human trafficking is in a legal sense. It is a tripartite process comprised of an 'action', 'means' and 'purpose', inclusive of a range of serious exploitative activities. The UN Trafficking Protocol has drawn upon previous instruments and years of debate, and the resulting definition – although not unproblematic – is comprehensive and perhaps even appropriate, in that it sets the standard high enough to encompass the worst forms of exploitation, yet low enough to encompass those which may push the boundaries of the traditionally recognised conditions of slavery and its related practices.

This chapter has established what human trafficking is, including the importance of the fairly new and inherently controversial 'means' element. This provides a sound basis to go on to analyse the specific and problematic relationship between consent and sexual exploitation, which will be dealt with in Chapter 4.

258 The word 'dichotomy' is rejected here for reasons discussed in ch 5, and instead a 'spectrum' of consent and coercion is envisaged.

# 4 Consent in the law, and consent to sexual exploitation

## 4.1 Introduction

As stated by George Fletcher, 'No idea testifies more powerfully to individuals as a source of value than the principle of consent'.[1] Valid consent serves to act as a 'procedural justification' for the doing of 'something', to someone or someone's property.[2] On the face of it, then, the doing of 'something' is defensible provided the conditions for a valid consent (as to the doing of 'something') are present.[3] However, as will be argued throughout this body of work, not only is correct determination of a valid consent inherently problematic in an exploitative facilitated migration and trafficking context, but also that there are limits to the justificatory scope of consent.

Establishing lack of consent is difficult.[4] In basic terms, consent can be defined as 'subsisting, free and genuine agreement to the act in question'.[5] Specifying and determining the scope of the conditions for a valid consent is necessary for discussion of consent in a specific context to take place. It may not seem palatable to all to accept that exploitation can take place with consent, but it is on this issue that the determination of a person as 'trafficked' or otherwise turns.[6]

When we examine consent in the context of sexual activity, prostitution and sexual exploitation, it becomes all the more difficult correctly to determine lack of consent, However it also becomes increasingly important that the correct determination is made because of what is at stake. The harm caused by trafficking,

1 G P Fletcher *Basic Concepts of Legal Thought* (Oxford University Press, Oxford, 1996) 109.

2 D Beyleveld and R Brownsword *Consent in the Law* (Hart Publishing, Oxford, 2007) 125.

3 ibid.

4 As indicated, for example, by the UK experience as regards low conviction rates for rape. The number of reported rapes that result in a conviction currently stands at approximately 6%. See 'The Stern Review' Government Equalities Office 2010 http://www.equalities.gov.uk/pdf/Stern_Review_of_Rape_Reporting_1FINAL.pdf (last accessed 1 August 2010).

5 Law Commission *Consent in Sex Offences: A Report to the Home Office Sex Offences Review* (1998) para 2.12.

6 See S V Jones 'Human trafficking victim identification: should consent matter?' (2012) 45 *Indiana Law Review* 483, who explores a spectrum of victimhood in the context of 'deserving' and 'undeserving' victims.

sexual exploitation (and even consensual prostitution in some circumstances) is undisputable – trafficking for sexual exploitation exemplifies the 'sexualization of power'.[7]

The difficulty lies in the hotly debated matter of consent to prostitution. Farley is not comfortable with the position that prostitution is here to stay: 'These stereotypes about men not only normalize and trivialize prostitution but are also good business strategy …'.[8] It is very true to say that: 'Sexual consent is a complex issue and there are various fields that have seized upon it to decide when it happens, what form it takes, and who is in a position to know'.[9] How we approach the consent (or lack thereof) question in a prostitution and sexual exploitation context clearly has implications for the trafficking debate, as it directly affects who is and is not determined to be a 'victim' or 'worthy' of some form of assistance or protection.

Section 4.2 of this chapter will establish and analyse the basic principles of an integral part of the enquiry made within this work: that of consent. This discussion will draw upon various areas of the law where such a notion is employed, in order to provide an illustration of the problematic nature of determining a valid consent, so that the specific matter of the role of consent in human trafficking can be analysed in depth in Chapter 5.

Section 4.3 will consider the widely debated matter of consent to prostitution, sexual labour and sexual exploitation. This section will explore competing feminist perspectives, which in turn view prostitution as inherently exploitative or violence against women, or alternatively as an expression of the right to work. The issue of whether 'sex work' is a legitimate form of labour and what the implications of this are will be analysed.

Section 4.4 will conclude the analysis in recognising that owing to compelling evidence that lack of consent in the context of prostitution and sexual exploitation is difficult to determine, however may be more frequent than we would like to accept, it would be wise to err on the side of caution in determining lack of consent where there is the potential for 'victimhood', that is to say, we should, wherever possible, assume lack of consent where it is at issue.

## 4.2 The requirements of a 'valid' consent

The Sexual Offences Act 2003 (SOA 2003) defines consent as where 'a person consents if he agrees by choice, and has the freedom and capacity to make that choice'.[10] Additionally, according to the Law Commission, we might explicitly

7 Mackinnon states that: 'The sexualization of power … is particularly visible in prostitution …'. See C A MacKinnon 'Gender: the future' (2010) 17(4) *Constellations* 504, 504.

8 M Farley '"Bad for the body, bad for the heart": prostitution harms women even if legalized or decriminalized' (2004) 10 *Violence Against Women* 1087, 1088.

9 Judith Butler 'Sexual consent: some thoughts on psychoanalysis and law' (2011–2013) 21(2) *Columbia Journal of Gender and Law* 3, 3.

10 Sexual Offences Act 2003 (SOA 2003) s 74.

also ask that the consent should 'subsist',[11] although this putative element has received critique from Temkin and Ashworth.[12]

Accordingly, then, the conditions central to a valid consent to be analysed here can be categorised as follows: the consent must be freely given; it must be informed; the consenting agent must have the capacity and understanding as regards that to which she is consenting; and the consent must subsist at the time of the act consented to. These issues will now be addressed.

### *4.2.1 Consent must be 'freely' given*

An ostensible consent is not necessarily an authentic consent unless it is freely given and is therefore the product of unforced choice.[13] Drawing the line between forced and unforced choice is not always necessarily simple.[14] A defining characteristic of 'forced' choice is the application of external force which bears negatively on the generic interests of the consenting party.[15] As typically understood, this external force would be exerted by the party to whom the consent is to be given. Whether external force can come from other sources will be discussed at a later point in this work.[16]

In a report on Consent in Sex Offences, the Law Commission stated that: 'The essence of consent … is *agreement* to what is done'.[17] The report goes on to state that agreement must be 'free and genuine' in order for it to qualify as consent,[18] and that 'consent should be defined as a subsisting, free and genuine agreement to the act in question'.[19] 'Coercion', 'pressure' and 'influence'[20] may all demonstrate a different level of interference with free consent. However, all have the potential to vitiate it.

As mentioned above, according to the SOA 2003, a person has consented 'if he agrees by choice, and has the freedom and capacity to make that choice'.[21] In a report concerning consent in the context of rape, the Scottish Law Commission proposed that consent should be defined as 'free agreement'. This definition

11 The Law Commission suggested that consent be defined as 'subsisting, free and genuine agreement to the act in question'. See Law Commission *Consent in Sex Offences* (n 5) para 2.12.

12 J Temkin and A Ashworth 'The Sexual Offences Act 2003: (1) Rape, sexual assaults and the problems of consent' (2004) *Criminal Law Review* 328, 337–38.

13 Beyleveld and Brownsword *Consent in the Law* (n 2) 126.

14 Research conducted into sexual relationships and rape in prison indicates in particular how problematic correct determinations of consent/lack thereof can be within a coercive environment. See, for example, Human Rights Watch 'No escape: male rape in U.S. prisons' http://www.hrw.org/legacy/reports/2001/prison/index.htm (last accessed 22 March 2014).

15 Beyleveld and Brownsword *Consent in the Law* (n 2) 126.

16 See ch 7 in particular for discussion of 'economic coercion of circumstances'.

17 Law Commission *Consent in Sex Offences* (n 5) para 2.9.

18 ibid para 2.10.

19 ibid para 2.12.

20 Beyleveld and Brownsword *Consent in the Law* (n 2) 131.

21 SOA 2003 s 74; Crown Prosecution Service 'Sexual Offences Act 2003' http://www.cps.gov.uk/legal/s_to_u/sexual_offences_act/ (last accessed 1 January 2010, link no longer live).

accepts that agreement can be given in situations where it is not 'real', 'full' or 'valid';[22] and it follows that such an agreement would not qualify as valid consent. Consent must be 'free from the influence or opinion of others'.[23] Indeed: 'every consent involves a submission, but it by no means follows that a mere submission involves consent'.[24]

Beyleveld and Brownsword recognise that:

> ... determination of whether 'consent' has been given 'freely' is doubly complex: first, we need a stable and defensible conception of 'free' action; and secondly, employing this conception, we need to be able to interpret actions with some confidence as 'free' or otherwise.[25]

In the most basic sense, where a choice is made against one's will, the 'choice', so-called, does not constitute freely given consent. This may be too simplistic a formula because where either a choice is made as a product of coercion, or where a choice must be made between undesirable alternatives, each constitutes an influenced choice but the consequence, vitiating consent, is not necessarily the same in each case. Further, in neither situation could it necessarily or conclusively be said that the will of the consenting agent was overborne; more that the choice was influenced – by external factors – albeit to different degrees.

The former situation – that of outright coercion, such as threat of physical force – is more clearly capable of invalidating or vitiating consent, whereas the latter less clearly does so. As Philips observes: '... it is difficult to imagine what a society would be like in which a person would invalidate a consent simply by showing that she was placed in a position having to choose between unattractive alternatives'.[26] Every day, choices are made that result in an undesirable outcome but they are made in the absence of a more agreeable alternative. It is difficult to view such choices as 'free', but it is impractical to view such choices as being made wholly without consent. It follows from this that even consent which is legally considered to be valid comes in varying degrees and shades of grey. It is not difficult to argue that direct coercion vitiates consent sufficient to render it invalid. The effect of more indirect forms of coercion on consent is more difficult to categorise – that which is 'persuasive' may not uniformly be considered coercive – in fact it may in some situations simply be deemed to be a material consideration to be taken into account (by the consenting individual) when making a decision.

Clearly, overt forms of coercion such as force or violence may invalidate consent where there is no legal justification for the force, as any agreement cannot be considered to be 'freely' given. Further, psychological forms of coercion may

22 See Scottish Law Commission *Report on Rape and Other Sexual Offences: Report on a reference under section 3(1)(e) of the Law Commissions Act 1965* (Scottish Law Commission No 209, 2007) para 2.38.
23 Beyleveld and Brownsword *Consent in the Law* (n 2) 12.
24 *R v Olugboja* [1981] All ER 443, 448, quoting Coleridge J in *Day* [1841] 9 C&P 722.
25 Beyleveld and Brownsword *Consent in the Law* (n 2) 12.
26 M Philips 'Are Coerced agreements involuntary?' (1984) 3 *Law and Philosophy* 133–45, 140.

invalidate consent – even where there is no overt force.[27] The specific 'means' (such as coercion) through which consent may be invalidated in the context of human trafficking for sexual exploitation were considered in the previous chapter.

### *4.2.2 Consent must be 'informed'*

As stated in the District of Columbia Court of Appeal case *Canterbury v Spence*, '[t]rue consent to what happens to one's self is the informed exercise of a choice, and that entails an opportunity to evaluate knowledgeably the options available and the risks attendant upon each'.[28] This statement was made in the context of medical treatment; however, the basic premise has further reach than purely a medical context. Is it possible to achieve a fixed point on a spectrum of what qualifies as 'informed'? This may be conceptually and evidentially difficult. There is no settled legal meaning of the term 'informed consent',[29] and accordingly the standard may vary according to context. It is, therefore, necessary to consider what qualifies as informed, which will involve consideration of various different areas of the law where informed consent may be treated differently.

In order for consent to operate as a procedural justification for doing 'something',[30] the consenting individual must know what she is consenting to. Early domestic case law in the UK seemed to indicate that consent could operate as a defence, even where the consenting party was unaware of, for example, the fact that she would be exposed to an incidental risk of injury.[31] Subsequent case law[32] took a different approach: in order for a person to give a valid consent, that person must know the 'nature and quality' of that to which consent is being granted. This indicates that consent to a particular something does not equate to consent to incidental 'extras', the risk of which the consenting agent was unaware and therefore uninformed – nonetheless, the consent to the original 'action' remains valid – the principle here is simply that the consent does not extend beyond the exact particulars of the 'action'.[33]

Deception as to the act consented to unquestionably invalidates consent.[34]

27 See, for example, *Olugboja* (n 24), where the rape victim submitted to sexual intercourse through fear, without the defendant using force or making any threats or violence.

28 *Canterbury v Spence*, 464 F.2d 772 (DC Cir 1972).

29 M Jones 'Informed consent and other fairy stories' (1999) 8(2) *Medical Law Review* 103.

30 Beyleveld and Brownsword *Consent in the Law* (n 2) 5.

31 Notably, in *R v Clarence* [1888] 22 QBD 23, the court determined that the wife's consent to sex also extended to any incidental risk of injury which arose from having consensual sex, namely catching gonorrhoea.

32 Such as *R v Dica* [2002] EWCA Crim 1103, [2004] QB 1257. This case involved consent to sexual intercourse, but not to the transmission of HIV, the presence of which in the defendant the victims were unaware.

33 See, for example, *R v B* [2006] EWCA Crim 2945, where the court held that the complainant's consent to sexual intercourse was not invalidated by her ignorance of the defendant's status as HIV positive, so there could be no rape on that basis.

34 See, for example, *R v Williams* [1923] 1 KB 340, where a choirmaster was found guilty of rape where he had sexual intercourse with a girl to whom he was giving singing lessons, under the

Where information is withheld that would be considered material and important to the decision-making process (of the consenting agent), any consent given to the specified act cannot be considered to be informed. This in turn would mean that there was no valid consent – it was vitiated; damaged; no longer subsisting. The seriousness of the outcome is therefore linked to the importance placed upon valid consent. Implied consent may be sufficient for minor risks, but not for risks of a serious magnitude.

It is clearly complex to determine what qualifies as informed when the information relates directly to the agreement. It is useful here to look to other areas of the law which employ a notion of informed consent. The notion of 'free and informed' consent is specifically mentioned and elaborated upon in the Council of Europe's Convention on Human Rights and Biomedicine,[35] and requires that the individual concerned be given 'appropriate information as to the *purpose and nature* (of the intervention) as well as its consequences and risks' (emphasis added).[36]

The Explanatory Report to that Convention emphasises the autonomy of the patient and makes clear reference to restraining 'the paternalistic approaches which might ignore the wish of the patient'.[37] The report builds on this by emphasising the importance of presenting the information clearly to the patient, using terminology that she can understand, which she can use to weigh up the necessity and usefulness against the potential risks. In a medical context, it has been stated that: '…once the patient is informed in broad terms of the nature of the procedure which is intended, and gives her consent, that consent is real'.[38]

Jones states that: '[t]he underlying ethical principle of informed consent is that one should respect the patient's autonomy: the capacity to think, decide and act on one's own thoughts and decisions freely and independently'.[39] The ability to make such decisions depends on information about the chosen course of conduct, and the ability to assess this information, 'i.e. the capacity to act autonomously'.[40] The EU Charter on fundamental rights includes in Article 3 the right to integrity of the person, and paragraph 2 specifically states that: 'In the fields of medicine and biology, the following must be respected in particular: the free and informed consent of the person concerned'. Clearly, where physical and mental integrity is concerned, a high standard of free and informed consent may be required. That

pretence that her breathing was not quite right and that he had to perform an operation to enable her to produce her voice properly.

35 Convention for the Protection of Human Rights and Dignity of the Human Being with regard to the Application of Biology and Medicine: Convention on Human Rights and Biomedicine (adopted 4 April 1997, entered into force 1 December 1999, Oviedo, 4. IV.1997, Council of Europe Treaty Series No 164).

36 Convention on Human Rights and Biomedicine art 5.

37 Explanatory Report to the Council of Europe's Convention on Human Rights and Biomedicine para 34 http://conventions.coe.int/Treaty/EN/Reports/Html/164.htm (last accessed 24 March 2014).

38 *Chatterton v Gerson* [1981] QB 432.

39 Jones 'Informed consent and other fairy stories' (n 29) 103.

40 ibid.

there is social utility in medical intervention in the majority of cases is undisputed here. There is long-standing debate between legal and medical professionals as to the correct approach to informed consent in a medical context[41] – understandably so where self-determination and bodily integrity are concerned.

The notion of informed consent features to varying extents in aspects of family law, and contract law – the examples used here are not mutually exclusive. For example, before an adoption order can be made, all persons with parental responsibility or guardianship must 'freely, and with full understanding of what is involved, agree(s) unconditionally'.[42] Clearly, pressure from, for example, an adoption agency invalidates 'freely' given consent. Consent could not be considered to be 'informed' if adoption was agreed to on the basis of a fundamental mistake, such as in *Re M (A Minor) (Adoption)*,[43] where a father agreed to an adoption of his child by his ex-wife and her husband. However, unbeknownst to him, his wife was in fact terminally ill, and died shortly after conclusion of the adoption. The missing information would have been material to the decision-making of the father, and therefore his consent could not be considered to be informed. Furthermore, informed consent in this context concerns close personal relationships and persons in need of care and protection (that is, children) and, therefore, it is desirable to ask for a high standard of informed consent in terms of all facts which may be material to the decision-making of the consenting agent.

Similarly, consent to marry can be rendered voidable by 'duress, mistake, unsoundness of mind or otherwise'.[44] Mistake in particular goes toward the notion of informed consent. However, the categories of mistake capable of invalidating consent to marriage (and therefore rendering a marriage voidable, although not void) are limited. Primarily, there may be mistake as to the identity of the partner to be married;[45] secondly, there may be mistake as to the nature of the ceremony.[46] In neither situation can the consent given be considered to be informed. Fraud or misrepresentation which led to a mistake can also invalidate consent and render a marriage voidable.

Furthermore, where marital separation is concerned, consent orders may be made. If parties have reached agreement prior to the making of a consent order, then the court will hold a contested hearing and then take the agreement into account.[47] Although there is a strong presumption in each case that the court will implement the agreement,[48] it is recognised that: 'there could be some

41 See, for example, Jones 'Informed consent and other fairy stories' (n 29) 103; Beyleveld and Brownsword *Consent in the Law* (n 2).

42 J Herring *Family Law* (Longman, Pearson Education Limited 2001) 542.

43 *Re M (A Minor) (Adoption)* [1991] 1 FLR 458.

44 Article 16(2) of the Universal Declaration of Human Rights 1984 (adopted 10 December 1948, UNGA Res 217 A(III) (UDHR) states that: 'Marriage shall be entered into only with the free will and full consent of the intending spouses'.

45 See, for example, *Militante v Ogunwomoju* [1993] 2 FCR 355.

46 Herring *Family Law* (n 42) 51, and see for example *Valier v Valier* (1925) 133 LT 830.

47 See *Edgar v Edgar* [1980] 2 FLR 19 (CA).

48 Although the court should still consider all the circumstances of the case: *Smith v Smith* [2000] 3 FCR 374.

circumstances when a party should not be bound by their agreement: namely where there was duress, undue influence, unforeseen circumstances, or injustice'.[49] In particular, the category of 'unforeseen circumstances' goes toward the validity of consent in that it cannot be considered to be 'informed' in that instance. As with the above-mentioned example, these areas of the law concern personal relationships and therefore inherently sensitive issues. Consequently, a high standard of informed consent may be called for. Because the situations above involve intense relationships and significant interventions of a personal kind, the reality of consent seems particularly important. It may not be quite so crucial in economic matters, which are regulated by the law of contract.

A choice to enter into a contract must be an informed choice, in that: '[t]he background informational obligations must be discharged, and so on'.[50] The rules for informed consent in contract law 'function … to ground procedural justification in relation to the agreement reached'.[51] Consent in a contractual sense may be invalidated (in that the contract may be invalidated) by, for example, mental incapacity, duress[52] or undue influence. Bix notes that:

> There is too much at stake – to those seeking to enter agreements as well as to third parties – to set the bar too high too often on contractual consent. Among other problems, making too many commercial transactions subject to serious challenge on consent/voluntariness grounds would undermine the predictability of enforcement that is needed for vibrant economic activity.[53]

Transactions that are purely commercial contracts for 'goods' are more at 'arm's length' when compared with the above-mentioned different aspects and areas of law where some form of informed consent doctrine is invoked, such as marriage or adoption, and is less likely to concern personal relationships or bodily integrity in the way that medical intervention, certain family law matters, and exploitative sex work can do. Where the relationship between the transported woman and the transporting agent (who may be a trafficker or smuggler) is of an economic nature, we might want not to impose too strict a standard of consent, were it not for the sometimes awful consequences that may befall those caught up in the trafficking environment.

On the one hand, 'consent, in terms of voluntary choice, is – or, at least,

49 Herring *Family Law* (n 42) 207.

50 Beyleveld and Brownsword *Consent in the Law* (n 2) 178.

51 ibid 179.

52 Duress occurs where 'where the doctrinal rule allows a party to void a contract if it can show an appropriate combination of wrongful threat on the part of the other contracting party, and a lack of reasonable alternatives to entering the contract on its own part'. See B Bix *The Ethics of Consent: Theory and Practice*, A Wertheimer, Franklin G Miller (eds) (Oxford University Press, Oxford, 2010) Minnesota Legal Studies Research Paper No 08-36 2 at 7. See also H Beale (ed) *Chitty on Contracts 30th edition: Volume 1: General Principles* (Sweet & Maxwell Ltd 2008) 7.

53 Bix (n 52) 5.

appears to be or purports to be – at the essence of contract law'.[54] However, in a contractual sense, a judge may find that even in the absence of (full) consent, a transaction should be enforced, and vice versa:[55] 'the level or kind of consent that might be sufficient to ground enforcement in one type of situation may not be sufficient in another'.[56]

Undue influence may be particularly pertinent to the discussion of informed consent here. As stated succinctly by Beale: '[t]he equitable doctrine of undue influence is a comprehensive phrase covering cases in which a transaction between two parties who are in a relationship of trust and confidence may be set aside if the transaction is the result of an abuse of the relationship'.[57] The doctrine is necessarily broad – Lord Chelmsford LC stated in *Tate* that: '[t]he courts have always been careful not to fetter this useful jurisdiction by defining the exact limits of its exercise'.[58] In 1887, Lindley LJ asked: 'Is it that it is right and expedient to save persons from the consequences of their own folly? or (sic) is it that it is right and expedient to save them from being victimised by other people?'[59] Clearly, there is a question mark regarding just how informed a person has to be within the context of undue influence.

Where there is an allegation of undue influence, it is necessary to show that the influenced party acted with 'free' and 'informed' consent. In *Etridge* (a combined appeal of eight cases), which is a central case here, a wife sought to challenge a transaction into which she had entered on the basis of her husband's undue influence, although 'their relationship did not fall within a special category of case where an irrebuttable presumption of trust and confidence arose'.[60] Lord Nicholls – with the support of the other lordships – referred in that case to 'the taking of unfair advantage',[61] 'misuse' of influence[62] and 'abuse of trust and confidence'.[63] Undue influence may occur not only where the defendant pressured the claimant or subjected her to excessive persuasion, 'but also it seems if the defendant abused the claimant's trust by making a decision for her rather than allowing her to make her own decision'.[64]

The reasoning of the court in *Etridge* can be summarised thus:

> Where a wife proposed to charge her interest in the matrimonial home in favour of a bank as security for her husband's indebtedness or the indebtedness of his company, her solicitor would have to explain the nature and

54 ibid 1.
55 ibid 2.
56 ibid 5.
57 Beale (ed) *Chitty on Contracts* (n 52) 56.
58 *Tate v Williamson* (1866) LR 2 Ch App 55 para 61. See also *Winder* (1940) 3 MLR 97; *Royal Bank of Scotland v Etridge (No 2)* [2001] UKHL 44, [2002] 2 AC 773 para 6.
59 *Allcard v Skinner* (1887) 36 Ch D 145, 182.
60 *Royal Bank of Scotland v Etridge (No 2)* (n 58) 3.
61 ibid para 8.
62 ibid para 9.
63 ibid para 10.
64 H Beale (ed) *Chitty on Contracts* (n 52) 56.

> consequences of the transaction and the seriousness of the risk involved, but he would not have to be satisfied that the wife was free of undue influence.[65]

And, apparently:

> The most that a bank could be expected to do, was to take reasonable steps to satisfy itself that the practical consequences of the proposed transaction had been clearly explained; the decision whether to proceed with the transaction or not had to rest with the wife and it was not a solicitor's role to intervene and attempt to prevent the transaction even if it was thought not to be in her best interests.[66]

Therefore, if the wife is not fully informed as to the particulars, and accordingly she cannot be said to have consented in an 'informed' manner, she may still be held to the contract. It was stated in that case that:

> In holding the balance fairly between the vulnerability of the wife who relies implicitly on her husband and the problems for financial institutions asked to accept a secured or unsecured surety obligation from her for her husband's debts, it has not been assumed that in the ordinary case the wife would necessarily be separately advised at all, or that even in probable undue influence cases the lender should make the taking of separate advice a condition, irrespective of its quality: see the O'Brien case [1994] 1 AC 180. That balance preserves the economic value of residential property as security for lending purposes for small businesses and protects wives in appropriate cases.[67]

This 'balance' referred to is morally if not legally questionable, and the lack of a requirement for separate and full advice for the wife is open to criticism; her consent cannot be considered to be fully informed if she does not have all the facts, particularly where there may be a substantial risk of financial loss. However, such economic loss owing to lack of informed consent is still – although morally questionable – at more of an 'arm's length' nature than in some other areas of the law where an informed consent doctrine is applied. Clearly, different types of agreements create different types of relationships, in which cases the standard or notion of informed consent may be treated differently.

Knowledge – as to the act consented to – is the key element here as regards informed consent. The cases considered in this section show an important aspect of the consent inquiry – it goes to the nature of the decision-making, not to its quality. The question is not: 'Was that a good or bad decision?' but 'Was that decision reached freely and on an informed basis?' We should try to avoid too easily saying that someone did not consent because things (perhaps foreseeably) turned

65 *Royal Bank of Scotland v Etridge (No 2)* (n 58) Case analysis, Westlaw UK.

66 ibid.

67 *Etridge (No 2)* (n 58) 790.

out badly, but it may at times be necessary and/or preferable to take matters of context into account. If a consenting agent has sufficient information to understand what she is consenting to and to weigh up the merits or otherwise of the act, she has the tools to make a decision which can be considered to be consensual and informed. However, '[t]he significance of consent to an individual, and to the society that must decide whether to give effect to it, depends on the circumstances in which it is elicited'.[68] The importance of this statement will become clearer throughout the discussion of informed consent in the context of human trafficking, which will be discussed in Chapter 5.

### *4.2.3 Capacity and understanding*

The consenting agent must have the capacity to give consent, and to understand that to which she is consenting. Essentially, a person – in any context – 'will not have had the capacity to agree by choice where their understanding and knowledge were so limited that they were not in a position to decide whether or not to agree'.[69] Beyleveld and Brownsword provide some insight here:

> If the conditions for an authentic consent are that it is given freely and on an informed basis (however these conditions are interpreted), then the logic is that the specification of a 'subject of consent' – that is, one having the relevant capacity (or competence) to consent – will reflect these conditions. This means, first, that a person with a capacity to consent will be capable of forming their own judgements and making their own decisions free from the influence or opinion of others; and, secondly, that such a person will be able to understand and apply the information that is material to their decision.[70]

This clearly relates to mental capacity to understand and process information, and to use the information when making an informed decision. Where mental capacity to do so is lacking, consent cannot be considered to be valid. Adults may be assumed to have the capacity to consent, although this can be rebutted.[71]

As regards minors (those under 18 years of age, according to domestic law),[72] the basic position is that the capacity of those aged under 16 to consent to, say, sexual intercourse, is not legally recognised.[73] There is, however, a somewhat nuanced position in medical law terms, as the principle of '*Gillick* competence'[74]

68 P H Schuck 'Rethinking informed consent' (1994) *Yale Faculty Scholarship Series*, Paper 2765, 906.

69 P Rook QC and R Ward (eds) *Rook and Ward on Sexual Offences: Law and Practice* (3rd edn, Sweet & Maxwell, 2003) para 1.94.

70 Beyleveld and Brownsword *Consent in the Law* (n 2) 12.

71 This point was made by Butler-Sloss LJ in the context of medical treatment in *Re MB (Medical Treatment)* [1997] 2 FLR 426.

72 Family Law Reform Act 1969 s 1.

73 SOA 2003 s 10.

74 The elasticity of consent in terms of legal acceptance of capacity to consent is demonstrated by

indicates. It is undisputed here that there is a sound basis for legal restrictions as regards the recognition of capacity of minors to consent – such measures are protective.

### *4.2.4 The timing of consent*

The timing of consent can be a relevant factor when determining a valid consent. In a 1998 report the Law Commission stated as regards this matter that:

> … an agreement to an act should not be regarded as a consent to that act unless it is *subsisting* at the relevant time. If what is relied on is past agreement, this will mean *both* (a) that, when previously given, the agreement must have extended to the doing of the act at that later time, *and* (b) that it must not have been withdrawn in the meantime.[75]

This clearly indicates that consent to the doing of 'something' must exist at the time of the act. As a basic principle, then, consent can be withdrawn at any time. UK domestic case law has confirmed this in the specific context of consent to sexual intercourse.[76] Similarly, in a medical law context, consent can be withdrawn even after the signing of a consent form. This position is more desirable than any alternative, as to hold an agent to a past consent would in some situations clearly be unacceptable (save, for example, where a binding contract had been entered). Temkin and Ashworth are critical of the potential for inclusion of the condition that the consent must 'subsist', on the basis that 'would have invited the defence to argue that a consent given previously had not been withdrawn'.[77] Notably, this element is not explicitly included in the definition provided within section 74 of the SOA 2003.

The conditions for a valid consent that have been considered above show a difference in treatment of consent depending on the nature of the relationship. Accordingly, it seems that requiring a high standard of valid consent is more justifiable where close personal relationships and bodily integrity are concerned, than where the relationship is of an economic nature. Consent to exploitative labour or sexual exploitation, for example, presents a situation where we might justifiably set the bar high as regards informed, valid consent. If a liberal perspective were to be embraced, then we might say that an individual has the right to make autonomous choices, and face the consequences of those choices if things go badly.[78] The

the 1985 *Gillick* case in the UK where a Lords majority ruled upon the potential capacity of under 16s to make their own decisions about medical treatment. See *Gillick v West Norfolk and Wisbech Area Health Authority* [1985] 3 All ER 402.

75 Law Commission *Consent in Sex Offences* (n 5) para 2.11.

76 See *Kaitamaki v R* [1984] 3 WLR 137 (PC), where it was confirmed that a person may withdraw consent to intercourse at any time, including whilst intercourse is taking place.

77 Temkin and Ashworth 'The Sexual Offences Act 2003' (n 12) 328, 338.

78 P Cole *Philosophies of Exclusion: Liberal Political Theory and Immigration* (Edinburgh University Press, 2000) 150.

following section will consider the competing feminist arguments regarding the validity of consent to exploitation and sexual exploitation.

## 4.3 Consent to prostitution, sexual labour and exploitation

This body of work does not set out to conflate prostitution with sexual exploitation or trafficking for that purpose. Discourse regarding the trafficking of adults can and does lead to disagreement as to the existence of this distinction. The discussion hinges largely on whether it is possible to accept as valid a consent to prostitution, or sexually exploitative work – that is, should a consent, in such conditions, be recognised. It follows from this that – as will be discussed later – some see prostitution or 'sex work' as inherently exploitative. However, this is resisted here as a comprehensive proposition. Others see prostitution as violence against women in all situations of sold sex.[79] Politically and socially, it is easier to accept a consent to other forms of exploitative work that might otherwise be undertaken in acceptable conditions than it is to prostitution, which has always carried with it implications of exploitation and immorality (and often illegality). Balos contends that one form markets strength, the other markets intimacy.[80] Sixteen-hour days spent working in a field or factory, and 16-hour days spent servicing man after man in a brothel, each for exploitatively low wages, may be perceived and reacted to in very different ways.

This is largely why the trafficking and smuggling-related debate is frequently of a gendered nature – men are smuggled, women are trafficked. The common perception is that men consent to facilitated migration, or smuggling, in order to look for work on arrival in the host state. Trafficking, on the other hand, is perceived as largely affecting females and as being for the purposes of commercial sex work. It is, for some, difficult to accept that any woman would consent to being transported for these purposes.

Although there may exist situations where it is true to say that 'What is oppression feels like freedom',[81] arguments of 'false consciousness' are resisted in this work, and elsewhere.[82] It is not impossible to consider that some may not realise

79 See, for example, C A MacKinnon 'Prostitution and civil rights' (1993) 1 *Michigan Journal of Gender and the Law* 13; MacKinnon 'Gender' (n 7) 504; D M Hughes 'The "Natasha" trade: the transnational shadow market of trafficking in women' (Spring 2000) 53(2) *Special Issue of Journal of International Affairs* 'In the shadows: promoting prosperity or undermining stability?' 625–51; Farley 'Bad for the body, bad for the heart' (n 8) 1087; M Farley 'Theory versus reality: commentary on four articles about trafficking for prostitution' (2009) 32 *Women's Studies International Forum* 311–15; K Barry *The Prostitution of Sexuality: The Global Exploitation of Women* (New York University Press, New York, 1995); S Jeffreys 'Globalising sexual exploitation: sex tourism and the traffic in women' (1999) 18 *Leisure Studies* 179–96.

80 B Balos 'The wrong way to equality: privileging consent in the trafficking of women for sexual exploitation' (2004) 27 *Harvard Women's Law Journal* 137, 151–52.

81 MacKinnon, 'Gender' (n 7) 506.

82 See, for example, J Levy 'Swedish abolitionism as violence against women' Paper presented at the Sex Worker Open University Sex Worker's Rights Festival, Glasgow (6 April 2013) 3; S Schulhofer *Unwanted Sex: The Culture of Intimidation and the Failure of Law* (Harvard University Press, 1998).

how badly they are being exploited, and also that the 'freedom' (which is in turn at times mistakenly conflated with consent) that we impose upon struggling migrants coming from backgrounds of, say, severe poverty is constructed and attributed to those migrants by consent discourse, rather than by each and every individual exploited migrant. The standard of 'freedom (and therefore consent) is imposed, and then from a liberalist perspective these migrants or smuggled or trafficked persons are told that, having made their choices, they must take the consequences of their actions.

In reality, of course, we are not all equally 'free' to make our choices. MacKinnon says that often, '… prostitution [is] defended through standard liberal abstractions like freedom of expression and freedom of choice, as if one can be free while being unequal'.[83] The migrant who leaves home to escape poverty and finds herself 'consensually' exploited is not 'free' in the most qualitative sense. The quality of consent varies significantly in situations of sold sex, and the migratory aspect which brings issues such as language barriers, lack of knowledge of geography of a country, fear of authorities etc, serves to render a consent even more questionable than where those conditions do not exist.

Nonetheless, we should not be too quick to accept or assume consent in the context of the prostitution and trafficking spectrum. However, neither should we be too quick to ignore an ostensible consent. As recognised by Butler:

> … it could prove quite disconcerting to think one has consented and to find that one's consent has been manufactured instead. One thought one was acting freely, but it turns out a discourse has been acting in your place, or constraining your self-understanding in ways that were not clear at the time. It is a much stronger version of that claim to argue that consent is always instrumentalized in the name of coercion, and that consent is therefore actually subjugation, and freedom, if it exists, is something wholly different from the discourse of consent.[84]

Consent in the context of prostitution, sexual exploitation and trafficking does not neatly dispose of itself, and presents problems as regards how these things should be legally addressed. Farley notes that:

> It is confusing to many, including governments, that women in prostitution appear to consent to prostitution. It is only when one looks carefully at the context of the consent, as well as past traumatic abuses, that this apparent consent to and promotion of prostitution by some women in the sex industry can be understood.[85]

83 This is not to suggest that there are not a multitude of issues relating to inequality which are faced by domestic prostitutes – simply to acknowledge that in some cases there are or may be factors affecting migrant prostitutes which exacerbate the severity of their situation.

84 Butler 'Sexual consent' (n 9) 3, 8.

85 Farley 'Bad for the body, bad for the heart' (n 8) 1107–108.

She cites various sources to show that some prostitutes freely admit that they did not consent.[86] Accepting that there are some (perhaps many) prostitutes who do not consent presents little difficulty, as the need for anti-trafficking and pimping laws tells us. Indeed, prostitution is defined within the SOA 2003 in a manner which makes it clear that someone can prostitute his or herself, or be prostituted by another.[87] The other side of the matter – that some prostitutes assert that they do in fact consent – presents more difficulty and is more contentious. Farley warns of 'the clear statements of women in prostitution who tell us that they want to escape it …'.[88] However, we cannot justifiably ignore the assertions of organisations such as the International Prostitutes Collective, which defend their claims that consent to prostitution is indeed possible and can be valid.[89]

Farley refers to the 'dissociated personality'[90] of the prostitute who has endured and 'managed' the suffering caused by her involvement in prostitution, the point being that some prostitutes will talk themselves into accepting and 'being ok' with what they do. The empirical evidence presented in Farley's research may indeed indicate that there exist case study examples where this is true for some prostitutes or ex-prostitutes, but this does not justify a 'one size fits all' situation and turn it into a generally applicable principle/argument of 'disassociation' for all who sell sex. We know that some (perhaps many) prostitutes have been raped, multiple times in some cases.[91] We also know that some women and girls who are raped are already vulnerable owing to background or circumstances, although this is not exclusively the case.[92] However, this must not lead us to consider that consent is lacking for each prostitute in every sold sex situation.

Herzog holds that effective consent requires a reasonable alternative to the withholding of consent.[93] As mentioned earlier, it may and does seem unpalatable to some to consider that meaningful consent to prostitution can be given. It is of the utmost importance when discussing consent in the current context to avoid conflating prostitution with trafficking. Much or all sex trafficking may end in forced prostitution, but it does not follow from this that all prostitution is forced.

86 ibid.

87 SOA 2003 s 51(2).

88 Farley 'Theory versus reality' (n 79) 312.

89 International Prostitutes Collective http://prostitutescollective.net/ (last accessed 22 September 2014).

90 Farley 'Bad for the body, bad for the heart' (n 8) 1087.

91 ibid 1087 at 1095; also G Hunter, T May and the Drug Strategy Directorate 'Solutions and strategies, drug problems and street sex markets: guidance for partnerships and providers' (Home Office, Drug Strategy Directorate, London, 2004) 20.

92 See the Stern Review (n 4), where it is stated at 17 that: 'A pervading theme throughout the evidence was the vulnerability of many of those reporting rape. Their vulnerability means they have less capacity to consent'. These vulnerabilities are, in the review, seen to be caused by many factors, from those with mental health problems, to those with a background of abuse or a background that can be described as 'difficult'. See Baroness Vivien Stern 'A report by Baroness Vivien Stern CBE of an independent review into how rape complaints are handled by public authorities in England and Wales' (Government Equalities Office, 2010).

93 Don Herzog *Happy slaves: a critique of consent theory* (University of Chicago Press 1989) 225.

There are and will be some real, valid consents, but they may be rare, and so we may justifiably take the narrowest possible conception of what is a 'valid' consent here as a protective measure. Although an 'autonomy' stance is supported in this work to an extent, we can still question the validity of consent in some if not many situations involving sold sex.

### 4.3.1 *Autonomy v paternalism*

As to prostitution or 'sex work', competing perspectives are evident, the arguments of which are invoked in detail by various commentators,[94] and which fuel the debate as to whether anyone should be considered capable of consenting to sex work or whether consent to sex work should be recognised (legally). One position is the 'autonomy/empowerment' view, and the other is the 'paternalist/protectionist' view.[95] These views are generally put forward by women, and should be seen in the context of the wider debate about the relationship between women and the law.[96]

The former is based in liberal theory, and maintains that individuals have the capacity and right to consent to prostitution-related activity.[97] Lee states that:

> By and large, religiously inspired and feminist abolitionists consider that prostitution is the worst form of patriarchal oppression and the most intense form of victimisation of women, that it is impossible for a woman to consent to sell sexual services, and that all (migrant) women in prostitution are victims of sexual violence and slavery ...[98]

This view is widely held among some strains of feminist academia.[99] A host of others prefer to focus on the distinction between forced prostitution or trafficking, and prostitution as a form of labour.[100]

94 See, for example, K Abramson 'Beyond consent, toward safeguarding human rights: implementing the United Nations Trafficking Protocol' (2003) 44(2) *Harvard International Law Journal* 473–502, 473 and J Chaung 'Redirecting the debate over trafficking in women: definitions, paradigms and contexts' (1998) 11 *Harvard Human Rights Journal* 65.

95 See Abramson (n 94).

96 See, for example, C A MacKinnon *Feminism Unmodified: Discourses on Life and Law* (Harvard University Press, 1987); C A MacKinnon *Toward a Feminist Theory of the State* (Harvard University Press, 1991); C A MacKinnon *Sex Equality: Family Law* (Foundation Press University Press, 2001); MacKinnon 'Prostitution and civil rights' (n 79) 13; K Mahoney 'Theoretical perspectives on women's rights and strategies for their implementation' (1996) 21(3) *Brooklyn Journal of International Law* 799–856.

97 See, for example, A Murray 'Debt bondage and trafficking: don't believe the hype' in J Doezma and K Kempadoo (eds), *Global Sex Workers: Rights, Resistance and Redefinition* (Routledge, New York, 1998); K Kempadoo 'Victims and agents of crime: the new crusade against trafficking' in J Sudbury (ed) *Global Lockdown* (Routledge, New York, 2005) 35–55; R Kapur 'The tragedy of victimization rhetoric: resurrecting the "native" subject in international/postcolonial feminist legal politics (2007) 15(1) *Harvard Law Review* 1–37.

98 M Lee *Trafficking and Global Crime Control* (Sage, 2011) 27.

99 Barry *The Prostitution of Sexuality* (n 79); S Jeffreys 'Globalising sexual exploitation: sex tourism and the traffic in women' (1999) 18 *Leisure Studies* 179–96.

100 Murray 'Debt bondage and trafficking' (n 97); Kempadoo 'Victims and agents of crime' (n 97) 35–55; Kapur 'The tragedy of victimization rhetoric' (n 97) 1–37.

The 'autonomy' perspective allows for free will and expression of sexual self-determination,[101] and is an example of people, women in particular, seeing a market with the potential for economic gain, and making the most of that opportunity. Essentially, this view says that the choice to partake in commercial sex work is a rational economic choice made by a woman who is simply cashing in on her sexuality by taking advantage of a pre-existing market. After all, prostitution is referred to as the oldest profession, and this market will never be short of consumers. The world has some proportion of willing prostitutes, and the extreme view of a minority would go so far as to hold that '[o]utside of sex trafficking, it seems to me that it's the women exploiting the men'.[102] Although the reality of such a view may be restricted to a small number of sex workers, anecdotal examples of willing prostitutes – such as Belle de Jour[103] – do, infact, exist.

The paternalist/protectionist view, on the other hand, focuses largely on the anti-prostitution debate, and argues that, since the sex trade is based on male dominance and the commodification of women, prostitution is inherently exploitative and any consent by women is irrelevant to its condemnation,[104] including in trafficking law. If prostitution were such a rewarding job and the product of free choice, why, it is asked, is it most often the women with the fewest meaningful or desirable choices who are most often the ones found doing it,[105] and why do traffickers have to 'deceive, coerce and enslave women to get them into and keep them in the sex industry'.[106]

Opposing groups of feminist lobbying targeted the preparation of the UN Trafficking Protocol, each advocating either an autonomy or paternalist stance. This input came predominantly from the Human Rights Caucus (the Caucus),[107] and the Coalition Against Trafficking in Women (CATW). The former were of the view that prostitution is a legitimate form of labour, in which women are capable of consenting to participate. CATW was strongly opposed to this view, advocating that prostitution is inherently exploitative and a violation of women's rights in all circumstances. CATW's position was effectively that consent should

101 J Chaung 'Redirecting the debate over trafficking in women' (n 94) 86.

102 Godfrey Bloom (UKIP MEP) *BBC News* 'UK should outlaw paying for sex' (20 December 2007).

103 A pseudonym used by a high profile call girl who has published several books about her experiences, including Belle de Jour *The Intimate Adventures of a London Call Girl* (Weidenfeld & Nicolson, London, 2005).

104 See, for example, MacKinnon 'Prostitution and civil rights' (n 79) 13; MacKinnon 'Gender' (n 7) 504; Hughes 'The "Natasha" trade' (n 79); Farley 'Bad for the body, bad for the heart' (n 8) 1087; Farley 'Theory versus reality' (n 79); Barry *The Prostitution of Sexuality* (n 79); Jeffreys 'Globalising sexual exploitation" (n 79) 179–96.

105 MacKinnon 'Prostitution and civil rights' (n 79) 13, 28.

106 Hughes 'The "Natasha" trade' (n 79) 632.

107 Human Rights Caucus 1999: Members of the Human Rights Caucus: International Human Rights Law Group, Foundation Against Trafficking in Women, Global Alliance Against Traffic in Women, Asian Women's Human Rights Council, La Strada, Ban-Ying, Fundacion Esperanza, Foundation for Women, KOK-NGO Network Against Trafficking in Women, Women's Consortium of Nigeria, Women, Law & Development in Africa (Nigeria).

be deemed irrelevant, and that trafficking should be comprised solely of 'action' and 'purpose' elements and cover all forms of 'recruitment, transportation …' etc for prostitution. This echoes the all-encompassing sentiments of the 1926 Slavery Convention, which envisaged the subject being brought into the slave trade 'by any means',[108] and goes hand in hand with the idea that one cannot contract oneself into bondage. The Caucus, in keeping with its view of prostitution as a form of labour, felt that prostitution should be placed in the same category as all forms of labour, and that it was therefore necessary to include an explicit 'means' element. The aim of the Trafficking Protocol was to be an anti-human trafficking document, not an anti-prostitution document aimed solely at women.

The autonomy view espouses a liberalist position, and piggy-backs on arguments promoting equality, in turn implying and accepting that those involved are exercising choice. It is necessary to make a distinction between 'free' choice and 'necessary' choice. The former may be enjoyed by those individuals who are less constrained by social and economic factors. Those with more constraints upon their ability to choose freely are more likely to make their decisions out of necessity; for example, those suffering severe economic impoverishment, or turning to prostitution in order to fund drug addiction. Criticism of this view raises the frequently asked question: can there be such a thing as a 'willing prostitute'? The fact is that there exist bodies of sex workers who argue that partaking in sex work is their free and uncoerced choice,[109] and the views of such persons should not be disregarded. However, in recognizing that '… libertarians, who while basing their claims on fixed nature arguments, made a case for the supervening value of sexual freedom for individuals',[110] we should not conflate 'work' with 'exploitation'.[111] Realistically, abuse, violation and physical and mental violence can be highly pervasive in situations of sold sex,[112] the exact proportions of which we cannot know as the data and participants are not clearly and easily visible.

It is argued by some that legalised prostitution blurs the line between what is coerced and what is voluntary, so that traffickers can claim that the woman had full prior knowledge of the nature and conditions of her 'work'.[113] In the most extreme sense, the autonomy view focuses on consenting to prostitution and, therefore, to potentially exploitative activity as a career move from economic motives. Further, the autonomy view accepts it as given that the consumers –

108 League of Nations Convention to Suppress the Slave Trade and Slavery art 1(2) (signed at Geneva on 25 September 1926, entered into force 9 March 1927, in accordance with art 12) 60 LNTS 253, Registered No 1414.

109 Such as the English Collective of Prostitutes. See http://www.prostitutescollective.net/ (last accessed 1 January 2014).

110 Butler 'Sexual consent' (n 9) 3, 3.

111 See Jones 'Human trafficking victim identification' (n 6), who discusses willingness and exploitation, 'happy' slaves, and explores a spectrum of victimhood in the context of 'deserving' and 'undeserving' victims.

112 MacKinnon 'Gender' (n 7) 505.

113 Hughes 'The "Natasha" trade' (n 79) 633.

chiefly male – will always have the need for prostitutes. Acceptance of this stems from and perpetuates the gender imbalance that underpins the sex trade. This idea of capitalising on sexuality may represent part of a skewed ethos that women can gain control of this market. The liberal model of autonomy presumes the giving of consent in a 'free and unfettered' way.[114] Munro states that critics consider that the rhetoric of liberalism has played a role 'in both disguising the complex realities of consent and obscuring the extent to which human agency is curtailed to comply with this artificial framework'.[115] What is required is 'a more realistic account of the constructed operation of choice in specific human situations'.[116]

On the other hand, the paternalist/protectionist view also invites criticism, as it victimises women and deems them to be weaker, sexually passive, and in need of paternalistic protection. Indeed, it can be argued that 'paternalistic ethics impinge on individual self-determination (limiting the significance of consent)'.[117] Commentators such as MacKinnon[118] 'draw … attention to the constraints and cultural pressures that operate on women's ability to make sexual choices'.[119] MacKinnon has produced some heavily paternalistic commentary.[120] She insists that the notion of consent is inadequate, because it ignores the reality that all men and women are not on an equal footing when engaging in sexual encounters or negotiations.[121] Furthermore, she states that: 'women [who] exist as oppressed victims of male power, tokens of heterosexual interest, acquiescence, or even initiative, may be as much a mechanism for survival as an expression of legitimate choice'.[122]

Conversely, Munro observes that:

> … while Mackinnon's claims are perhaps to be commended … her failure to discriminate between the different kinds of pressure and her refusal to engage with the role that (some) women play in perpetuating – or, indeed, resisting – these pressures is theoretically limiting and strategically damaging.[123]

The paternalist stance removes the element of choice advocated by the autonomy view – that women are simply taking advantage of an opportunity for economic gain. However, a quasi-paternalist stance in the context of trafficking and/or consensual migration for the purpose of exploitation, particularly where the latter

114 V E Munro 'Constructing consent: legislating freedom and legitimating constraint in the expression of sexual autonomy' (2008) 41 *Akron L. Rev* 923, 925.
115 ibid 929.
116 ibid.
117 Beyleveld and Brownsword *Consent in the Law* (n 2) 27.
118 See, for example, MacKinnon *Sex Equality: Family Law* (n 96); MacKinnon *Feminism Unmodified* (n 96); MacKinnon *Toward A Feminist Theory of the State* (n 96); MacKinnon 'Prostitution and civil rights' (n 79).
119 Munro 'Constructing consent' (n 114) 939.
120 See, for example, n 92 above.
121 MacKinnon *Feminism Unmodified* (n 96) 100.
122 Munro 'Constructing consent' (n 114) 938.
123 ibid 939.

takes place in a coercive environment, may be preferable in that it can pave the way for a better standard of protection for those who may be coerced. Full autonomy is the luxury of the free and uncoerced agent who exercises choice in an ideal setting.

Consent to exploitation – particularly as a result of severe economic need – may be less a reflection of the exercise of genuine autonomy, and more of a necessary submission. Liberalist perspectives are based upon an abstract conception of free agency, which does not fit comfortably in all situations. Conceding to sex work as a mechanism for survival does not necessarily equate to an acceptable standard of autonomous agency, at least morally. However, the desire here is not to belittle the choices of the autonomous migrant sex worker. Consent to sex work – even exploitative sex work[124] – is recognised as valid in an uncoerced setting, and should not be attributed to 'false consciousness' – as Schulhofer recognises: '[w]e cannot simply dismiss as "false consciousness" the perceptions of women themselves'.[125]

Hernandez-Truyol and Larson state that: '[l]abor measures the legitimacy of work not by the presence of contract or worker consent, but rather by substantive ethical and moral standards of what conditions of work accord with the dignity, health, and liberty of the worker'.[126] Can we say that the voluntary sex worker, owing solely to her choice of work, lacks dignity? The right to work includes the right to work in hard conditions. Nonetheless, it may be that a case can be made for the consideration 'in context' of the validity of certain choices and consents.

A central problem with these competing perspectives is that they do not see the sex trade as a whole; they appear to have been conceived solely with adult women in mind. A fully paternalistic approach is taken with regard to children, who are deemed incapable of making such a choice. Early trafficking instruments dealt only with women being trafficked for the sex trade, and early slavery-specific instruments appear to have envisaged mainly a male subject.[127] Now that trafficking definitions have extended to include other forms of exploitation, the subjects are both male and female. It is questionable as to whether either the paternalist view or the autonomy view would extend to male sex workers. Indeed, advocates of each view have thus far limited their application to women.

These views are polarised at opposite ends of a spectrum, which envisages informed consent in an ideal setting, or purely coerced sex work in an exploitative setting. Prostitution does not always occur in coercive conditions; neither is it always the product of choice.[128] Either way, criminalising prostitution is not

124 A definition of 'exploitation' in this context is offered at a later point in this chapter.

125 Schulhofer *Unwanted Sex* (n 82) 56.

126 B E Hernandez-Truyol and J E Larson 'Sexual labour and human rights' (2006) 37 *Columbia Human Rights Law Review* 391–445, 395.

127 See, for example, League of Nations 6.B.4 Temporary Slavery Commission: Minutes of the First (and Second) Session(s), Geneva, 1924–25.

128 See L L Lim 'Whither the sex sector? Some policy considerations' in L L Lim *The Sex Sector: The Economic and Social Bases of Prostitution in Southeast Asia* (International Labour Office 1998) 212. The ILO concludes that although prostitution may frequently be coercive, it can also be freely chosen.

so much about protecting women or removing their ability to make choices; in reality, it has the effect of criminalising women in the sex sector, a proportion of whom will have become prostitutes owing to a lack of other meaningful choices. Lim recognises that some prostitutes:

> ... freely choose sex work as an expression of sexual liberation, or as an economically rational decision based on income potentials, costs involved and available alternatives. Others are pressured by poverty and dire economic circumstances. Still others are subject to overt coercion from third parties, in the form of deception and/or physical violence or threats.[129]

Although one may accept that, in many cases, prostitution may either be a product of force, coercion, severe economic need or of the absence of other preferable choices, it should also be accepted that it is still a potentially viable economic choice. This is the case as long as there are sex workers who are proponents of this view.[130] In a 2006 report, the Special Rapporteur stated that: 'One of the many benefits of the (Trafficking) Protocol definition is that it provides a foundation upon which anti-trafficking discussion, research, and policy development may transcend the general debate about the rights and wrongs of prostitution to a significant extent'.[131]

Limoncelli notes that in feminist scholarship in the area of trafficking for prostitution: '... ideas themselves then become the main issue to be addressed (e.g., the idea of sex work as repressive or empowering) rather than the actual material practices of paid sexual labor occurring across and within countries'.[132] Clearly, exploitation is wrong – this is something about which all may agree. Prostitution per se presents a more difficult exercise in terms of searching for a uniform approach.

### *4.3.2 Prostitution or 'sex work' as a legitimate form of 'labour'*

Farley recognises that: 'Much of the health sciences literature has viewed prostitution as a job choice'.[133] However, she goes on to say that normalising prostitution as 'work' decreases the visibility of its harm. Reconciliation of the two polarised views that in turn champion autonomy or paternalism, is nigh on impossible. Hernandez-Truyol and Larson[134] propose that prostitution should be studied

129 ibid.

130 See, for example, the International Prostitutes Collective, which maintains that they engage in prostitution consensually http://prostitutescollective.net/.

131 Report on the Special Rapporteur on trafficking in persons, especially women and children, Sigma Huda, Addendum, Mission to Bosnia and Herzegovina 'Integration of the rights of women and the gender perspective' (30 November 2005) UN Doc E/CN.4/2006/62/Add.2.

132 S A Limoncelli 'The trouble with trafficking: conceptualizing women's sexual labor and economic human rights' (2009) 32 *Women's Studies International Forum* 261–69, 265.

133 Farley 'Bad for the body, bad for the heart' (n 8) 1087, 1088.

134 Hernandez-Truyol and Larson 'Sexual labour and human rights' (n 126) 391.

under a labour paradigm, that is, as an exercise of the right to work, even though it might contain elements of servitude. Abramson reaches a similar conclusion, stating that: 'emphasis on the right to consent to a generic livelihood divorced from a sexual context may carry the day in winning support for the autonomy camp'.[135] Similarly, the UN Special Rapporteur on violence against women, in a 2000 report[136] offered a definition of trafficking which omitted inclusion of a separate reference to prostitution – the terminology 'forced labour or slavery like practices' was intended to be inclusive of this.

Viewing prostitution through a labour lens allows us to overcome the stalemate reached by the 'autonomy v paternalism' debate, and to address trafficking for the purpose of exploitation as a whole. Issues of autonomy, morality, sinners and saints have long stood in the way of progress on this particular point. The same factors, such as economic hardship, can lead people to 'choose' any form of exploitative labour, sexual or otherwise. Treating sex work in this way (that is, as a form of labour) may have the additional advantage of ridding consideration of it and the women who engage in it from a moralistic perspective, which can only obscure the genuineness of the consent to participate of some of them and the very real exploitation of others.

Outshoorn asks: '[i]s all "trafficking" forced or is it prostitution-related migration?',[137] thereby highlighting the consent/coercion spectrum of migration-related sexual labour. Early anti-trafficking conventions made the prohibited conduct trafficking for prostitution, and a link between the two has endured and has led to the two practices being all too often seen as indistinguishable. There can be a blurred line as to when prostitution-related migration becomes trafficking. Conflating those who are controlled and seriously exploited with those who have arguably exercised their right to work creates a barrier to making progress in terms of the fight against sexual exploitation. In keeping with this line of argument, Phoenix states the following:

> Take, for instance, the recent identification of the links between global migration and prostitution. Recognition of the mass movement of people (usually women) from around the globe into the sex industry in more affluent Western societies has conditioned the *almost complete collapse of any discursive boundary between human trafficking and prostitution.* In responding to the international call to do something about human trafficking and the misery, exploitation and human tragedies which trafficking often involves, and in an endeavour to stop

135 See Abramson 'Beyond consent' (n 94) 491.

136 Report of the Special Rapporteur on violence against women, its causes and consequences, Ms Radhika Coomaraswamy, on trafficking in women, women's migration and violence against women, submitted in accordance with Commission on Human Rights Resolution 1997/44 'Integration of the human rights of women and the gender perspective: violence against women' (28 February 2000) UN Doc E/CN.4/2000/68.

137 J Outshoorn 'The political debates on prostitution and trafficking of women' (2005) 12(1) *Social Politics: International Studies in Gender, State and Society* 141–55, 142.

illegal migration, governments around the world have focused their attention on prostitution (emphasis added).[138]

Although it cannot be disputed that the two are sometimes linked, 'prostitution' should not be used as a euphemism for 'human trafficking'. Prostitution per se and trafficking for the purpose of prostitution are fundamentally different things – prostitution can be a 'purpose' element of human trafficking; it can also be a result of prostitution-related migration[139] or a wholly separate issue in its own right, that is, concerning domestic prostitutes – coerced or consenting.

This leads us more specifically on to consideration of whether 'sex work' is to be viewed as a legitimate form of labour. It is undisputed that '[t]he legal status of prostitution is an unsettled issue in nations throughout the world, particularly those of the west'.[140] For example, prostitution in Sweden is viewed as a form of violence against women in all situations, and this is reflected in the legislative framework, which criminalises the purchaser of sexual services in all situations.[141] Levy asserts that: 'Prostitution in Sweden has been (re)defined according to a "radical feminist" discourse as a form of gendered violence against women, something that cannot be freely chosen by those who sell sex'[142] and that, according to this 'radical feminist' understanding, 'female sex workers are seen as passive, disempowered victims of violence, their clients as male exploiters'.[143] Levy is not alone in his critique of the Swedish approach,[144] about which there is conflicting commentary and evidence as to its success – some of the evidence strongly suggests that this approach has increased the danger to sex workers.[145]

Accordingly, there is a lack of uniformity as to how 'sex work' is viewed from country to country. Sex work is not 'legitimate' in the UK in the sense that it is not legalised and regulated, in contrast to the system adopted in the Netherlands, which has a fully regulated and legitimised sex sector and has clearly identified sex work as 'labour', like any other form of work. In the UK context then – and those of other countries where a system operates other than one of a regulated sex trade

138 Jo Phoenix 'Frameworks of understanding' in Jo Phoenix (ed) *Regulating Sex for Sale: Prostitution Policy Reform in the UK* (The Policy Press 2009) 7.

139 Outshoorn 'The political debates on prostitution and trafficking of women' (n 137) 142.

140 Hernandez-Truyol and Larson 'Sexual labour and human rights' (n 126) 396.

141 Law (1998:408) Prohibition of the Purchase of Sexual Services; *Lag ou förbund mot köp av sexuella tjänster* (1998): *Dem som mot ersattning skaffar sig en tillfällig sexuell förbindelse, doms – om inte gärningen är belagd med straff enligt Brottsbalken – för köp av sexuella tjänster till böter eller fängelse i högst sex månader. För försök döms till ansvar enligt 23 kap. Brottsbalken.*

142 Levy 'Swedish abolitionism as violence against women' (n 82) 1.

143 ibid 3.

144 See A Jordan 'The Swedish law to criminalize clients: a failed experiment in social engineering' (2012) *Issue Paper 4* Program on Human Trafficking and Forced Labor, Centre for Human Rights and Humanitarian Law.

145 See J Elliott 'Criminalising the purchase of sexual services: the Use of strict liability as a form of risk management?' in J Child, K Doolin, A Beech and J Rain *Whose criminal justice: regulatory state or empowered communities?* (Waterside Press 2011); Levy 'Swedish abolitionism as violence against women' (n 82) 1.

– there remains the philosophical and political question of whether prostitution is 'legitimate' labour.

What, then, is 'labour', and can sex work be viewed through this paradigm? In the most basic sense, labour – specifically waged labour – is the exchange of services for remuneration. An ordinary understanding of the meaning of the word 'prostitution' might be 'the exchange of sex or sexual services for money or other material benefits'.[146] According to section 51(2) of the SOA 2003, a 'prostitute' is:

> … a person (A) who, on at least one occasion and whether or not compelled to do so, offers or provides sexual services to another person in return for payment or a promise of payment to A or a third person; and 'prostitution' is to be interpreted accordingly.[147]

This definition indicates that it is possible to prostitute oneself and also to be prostituted by another, illustrating the potentially coercive and exploitative nature of prostitution in some circumstances. However, prostitution is not always the result of either free will or of coercion or force. These are two opposite points on a spectrum, along which all prostitution-related activities may be placed, including prostitution as a 'purpose' element of human trafficking. 'Sexual labour' may also extend beyond prostitution – for example, '[s]ome sex trafficking victims are forced into the following situations: forced prostitution, pornography, stripping/exotic dancing, mail order brides, and massage parlors'.[148] These forms of 'labour' may also – and indeed in some situations are – undertaken or engaged in, on a voluntary and unforced basis.

In contrast to forced or coerced prostitution, prostitution itself is, as stated by Bakirci, 'when a woman sells her body as a commodity and pockets the income. Prostitutes are not slaves and are not controlled by the traffickers'.[149] Clearly this represents the ideal scenario of fully consenting and uncoerced prostitution. The presence of exploitation in some situations of sold sex – actual or intended – does not render prostitution wholly incapable of being viewed as a legitimate form of labour. The smuggled or trafficked potato picker, for example, may work consensually and in acceptable labour conditions; consensually in exploitative conditions; or involuntarily as a result of coercion etc – as, indeed, may the sex worker. It is, however, potentially necessary (and not entirely unprincipled) to consider that the sex worker may be a more vulnerable person than the potato picker. Sex workers are predominantly female, and anti-trafficking instruments are increasingly making reference to gender as a consideration to be taken in account when considering any or all aspects of the fight against trafficking.[150] This

146 Outshoorn 'The political debates on prostitution and trafficking of women' (n 137) 141.

147 SOA 2003 s 51(2).

148 K Bakirci 'Human trafficking and forced labour: a criticism of the International Labour Organisation' (2009) *Journal of Financial Crime* 160–65, 164.

149 ibid.

150 Notably the Trafficking Protocol refers in its title to 'especially women and children' and the EU

added vulnerability of the sex worker is not solely based upon gender, however; the nature of the 'work' may raise other issues.

Eckberg states that 'prostitution has been normalized by neoliberals as a form of sexual entertainment, with equal players exchanging services for money. 'Working' as a 'sex worker' is seen as a legitimate career path for women'.[151] Although such a realisation may not sit well with all who comment on sex work, the reality is that ultimately, for some individuals, prostitution is a viable choice in terms of 'economic survivalism':[152] a job, a profession, a way of making money – preferable to some other forms of 'legitimate' employment.[153] We should, however, not be too quick to equate 'survival necessity' with 'consent'.[154]

Outshoorn recognises that:

> It should be noted that not all those adhering to the sex work position set prostitution within the same feminist framework. Some are radical liberals who celebrate sexual variety and free choice … whereas others, while analyzing prostitution as (sexual) service work, maintain a feminist critique by contextualizing prostitution within unequal relations of sexual economic exchange …[155]

Hernandez-Truyol and Larson refer to the 'current human rights debate that dichotomises prostitution as either a modern form of slavery or as the exercise of the right to work'.[156] This encapsulates perfectly the problem with prostitution-related discourse – prostitution can involve agency and victimhood[157] – it is not a 'binary'.[158] Indeed, 'the dichotomy between the wholly autonomous subject and the wholly compromised victim'[159] is damaging. Hernandez-Truyol and Larson

2011 Directive refers in the preamble to the 'gender-specific phenomenon of trafficking' para 3. This is not to disregard the potential vulnerability of male sex workers or sex traffick victims – it is accepted here that these men may be similarly vulnerable when compared to their female counterparts. However, the references to gender in the 2011 Directive indicate that female victims may be seen as particularly vulnerable.

151 G Ekberg 'The Swedish law that prohibits the purchase of sexual services: best practices for prevention of prostitution and trafficking in human beings' (October 2004) 10(10) *Violence against Women* 1187–218, 1187–88.

152 Phoenix 'Frameworks of understanding' (n 138) 3.

153 This is certainly not to suggest that the majority of prostitutes feel this way, but that a proportion does. Anecdotal examples of willing prostitutes, such as Belle de Jour and Xaviera Hollander, do, infact, exist and should not be disregarded.

154 MacKinnon 'Gender' (n 7) 505.

155 Outshoorn 'The political debates on prostitution and trafficking of women' (n 137) 146.

156 Hernandez-Truyol and Larson 'Sexual labour and human rights' (n 126) 391.

157 C Hoyle, M Bosworth and M Dempsey 'Labelling the victims of sex trafficking: exploring the borderland between rhetoric and reality' (2011) 20(3) *Social and Legal Studies* 313–92.

158 M Roces 'Prostitution, women's movements and the victim narrative in the Philippines' (2009) 32 *Women's Studies International Forum* 270–80, 271.

159 K Abrams 'Sex wars redux: agency and coercion in feminist legal theory' (1995) 95 *Columbia Law Review* 304–76, 375.

engage in a labour analysis of prostitution, in order to deconstruct the practice and its component parts.[160] It is nonsensical to see prostitution as either bondage or work. The authors refer to prostitution as 'sexual labour' and recognise that like all forms of labour, it can be exploited.[161] This is key to the arguments advanced in this book, as it demonstrates recognition of the delineation between prostitution, exploitative prostitution (which may be uncoerced), and coerced or forced prostitution (which will always be exploitative).

Over the past decade, the ILO's Committee of Experts on the Application of Conventions and Recommendations has made various comments regarding human trafficking (of persons of all ages and genders) for the purposes of labour exploitation, such as that performed in factories, construction, or the sex and entertainment industry.[162] 'Forced *labour* as a result of organised criminal trafficking can be found in the *sex industry* all over the world' (emphasis added).[163] It follows from this that work or services provided within in the sex industry, or 'sexual labour' services, are therefore capable of being viewed as a form of forced labour.

Bakirci states that:

> According to the ILO (2005) supervisory bodies: A woman forced into prostitution is in a forced labour situation because of the involuntary nature of the work and the menace under which she is working, irrespective of the legality or illegality of that particular activity.[164]

It follows from this that sexual labour can be forced, but it can also be undertaken voluntarily. The ECJ ruled in a fairly recent case that 'sex work' such as prostitution is a protected economic activity.[165] The finding of the Court was that: '[t]he activity of prostitution pursued in a self-employed capacity can be regarded as a service provided for remuneration'.[166] The Court went on to state that the economic activity must be 'outside any relationship of subordination … under (the sex worker's) own responsibility; and in return for remuneration paid to that person directly and in full'.[167] It was concluded that in each case it is for the national court to determine whether those conditions were satisfied, in the light of the evidence before it.[168] Granted, this case concerned the Netherlands sex sector which is state legitimised and regulated. However, it is significant in terms of the potential for the 'sex work as labour' debate.

160 ibid.
161 Hernandez-Truyol and Larson 'Sexual labour and human rights' (n 126) n 551, 393.
162 B Andrees *Forced labour and human trafficking: handbook for labour inspectors* (International Labour Office, 2008) 17.
163 ibid 16.
164 Bakirci 'Human trafficking and forced labour' (n 148) 163.
165 Case C-268/99 *Aldona Malgorzata Jany v Staatssecretaris van Justitie* [2001] ECR I-8615 (regarding the refusal of the Netherlands Secretary of State for Justice to grant residence permits for Polish and Czech nationals to engage in self-employed sex work).
166 ibid para 4.
167 ibid para 5.
168 ibid.

Hernandez-Truyol and Larson propose that:

> ... even where prostitution is chosen by an adult woman as a form of work, it may be an intolerably exploitative form of labour analogous to sweatshop, child, or bonded labour, and subject to the same legal and political pressures for extinction or transformation.[169]

Elimination – of prostitution per se – is unlikely; no country in any part of the world has found an approach to dealing with it that has provided the 'magic bullet'. Extinction of exploitative prostitution, that is, where the conditions or rate of pay are exploitative, even in the face of consent, is without doubt highly desirable. There exists research which indicates that prostitution is freely chosen by very few.[170] If this is to include those who engage in prostitution because they need money to get by, then the number will be desperately low. But whether or not economic need can vitiate consent is difficult and goes against orthodox criminal law – this is considered elsewhere in this volume.[171] Nonetheless, if it is indeed true that in practice 'Women in prostitution are treated as if their rapes do not matter',[172] then we do have a convincing body of evidence to suggest that, although genuine consent can exist in a sale of sex situation, it may be lacking or questionable in a proportion of cases which is high enough for the broadest conception of 'victimhood' (where such a label might be needed) to be justifiably used.

### *4.3.3 Consequences of sex work as labour – access to labour rights and standards*

If prostitution is fully legitimised in the UK in the formal sense, sex workers may have access to the economic and social rights that affect all legitimate workers, as well as the civil and political rights from which they already benefit as human beings (where countries are party to the relevant instruments).

There is, however, the potential for 'the presence of the wage labour contract, which manifests the worker's consent, [to] obscure any reality of exploitation or bondage'.[173] The presence of some form of contract may obscure the coercive or bonded reality. At present, since the sex sector is not regulated in UK, there is nothing to ensure that treatment of sex workers is maintained within a fair labour framework. Conversely, a labour framework may still be insufficient to protect prostitutes from harm. Farley states with conviction that it is '... a cruel lie to suggest that decriminalization or legalization will protect anyone in prostitution'.[174] Consent does not necessarily equate to legitimacy:

169 See Hernandez-Truyol and Larson 'Sexual labour and human rights' (n 126) 393.
170 Farley 'Theory versus reality' (n 79) 311.
171 See ch 7.
172 Farley 'Bad for the body, bad for the heart' (n 8) 1087, 1096.
173 Hernandez-Truyol and Larson 'Sexual labour and human rights' (n 126) 394.
174 Farley 'Bad for the body, bad for the heart' (n 8) 1087, 1094.

> A sex worker's consent does not legitimate conditions of work that are otherwise incompatible with her human dignity. We may accept that a labourer is making the best choice she can and still acknowledge that she lacks the bargaining power to insist upon standards of decent work.[175]

To take this one step further, we may accept that 'sexual labourers' may make the best choice they can. However, they can still insist upon and experience decent conditions of work. This may realistically only be a true reflection of a very small proportion of the sex sector, but vehement responses from groups such as the International Prostitutes Collective[176] indicate that a body of sex workers themselves argue for and recognise free consent and that not all sex work takes place in forced or exploitative settings.

If sex work is not viewed as a legitimate and regulated form of labour within a state, then it will fall without the scope of labour inspection systems.[177] Indeed:

> NGOs and other civil society organisations are essential in economic sectors that are not covered by trade unions and that are difficult to reach for labour inspectors or the police. Examples are domestic service, sex and entertainment or other types of work that are out of scope for labour inspectors.[178]

It is the lack of legal legitimacy of sex work as 'labour' in the UK that renders this activity beyond the reach of any enforceable labour standards, and instead places significant aspects of it within the remit of the criminal law, leaving sex workers particularly vulnerable when compared with other forms of labourers. Some would suggest that sex work as labour should be subject to international and national labour standard regulations,[179] thereby creating a clearer legal and political separation between exploited and unexploited sex workers.[180] Further empirical research into the conditions of domestic prostitution is perhaps needed, in order to establish the standards, varied as they may be. Although evidence exists on both sides of the debate as to what proportion of prostitution is forced, we may be able to conclude from earlier analysis that a significant proportion is non-consensual, or at least at risk of being non-consensual.

Labour rights and human rights are clearly intertwined, particularly so where consensual economic migration, consensual exploitative facilitated migration,

175 ibid 395.

176 See International Prostitutes Collective website http://www.prostitutescollective.net/ (last accessed 5 June 2011).

177 B Andrees *Forced labour and human trafficking* (n 162) 21.

178 ibid 36.

179 See Lim 'Whither the sex sector?' (n 128).

180 Hernandez-Truyol and Larson state that: '[w]e believe that the case can be made now for partial decriminalisation as a mandate of international law in order to protect the fundamental labor and human rights of sex workers to organize and freely associate'. The authors are under no illusion, however, that full legalisation would solve all problems associated with sex work, as there is no 'magic bullet'; see Hernandez-Truyol and Larson 'Sexual labour and human rights' (n 126) 440.

and human trafficking (non-consensual by definition) are concerned. In a labour context, civil and political rights are not wholly separate or independent from economic and social rights, as the worker, the exploited worker and the forced labourer draw their rights from these instruments.[181] Together, these rights comprise 'the fundamental guarantees of essential rights inherent in human existence'.[182] The preamble to the ICCPR[183] and the International Covenant on Economic and Social Rights (ICESCR)[184] both state that 'freedom from fear and want can only be achieved if conditions are created whereby everyone may enjoy his civil and political rights, as well as his economic, social and cultural rights', thereby underpinning this point. The UDHR recognises the right to work and the right to 'just and favourable conditions of work'.[185] The ICESCR enshrines the same basic substantive rights, and refers to 'just and favourable conditions'[186] and 'safe and healthy working conditions'.[187]

Analogies with other forms of wage labour may aid the discussion here. Spector states that:

> What is really needed … is a sustained comparison between prostitution and other forms of wage labor, to try to identify what might be troubling about prostitution, or rather, about the way that it is practiced. Schwarzenback likens the prostitute as physical labourer to a dancer, while Nussbaum compares prostitution to a number of jobs … including domestic servant and masseuse … Accordingly, since we treat other such jobs as legitimate choices, we should similarly treat prostitution. For feminist liberalism, it is the worst form of paternalism to preclude the choices of women whose options are already limited.[188]

The intention here, in this book, is not to embrace this 'worst form of paternalism', but instead to recognise the right of sex workers to choose sex work as a legitimate labour choice, albeit against a backdrop of evidence that suggests that the percentage of sex work which is voluntarily undertaken may well be very low.[189] Furthermore, the intention here is to emphasise that there is a spectrum

181 ibid *passim*.

182 ibid 407.

183 International Covenant on Civil and Political Rights (adopted 16 December 1966, entered into force 23 March 1976) 999 UNTS 171 (ICCPR).

184 International Covenant on Economic and Social Rights (adopted and opened for signature, ratification and accession by General Assembly Resolution 2200A (XXI) of 16 December 1966, entry into force 3 January 1976, in accordance with art 27) (ICESCR).

185 Universal Declaration of Human Rights arts 30 and 23(1) (adopted 10 December 1948, UNGA Res 217 A(III) (UDHR).

186 ICESCR art 7.

187 ibid art 7(b).

188 J Spector *Prostitution and Pornography: Philosophical Debate About the Sex Industry* (Stanford University Press, 2006) 426.

189 Farley 'Bad for the body, bad for the heart' (n 8) 1087; Farley 'Theory versus reality' (n 79) 311–15.

of situations, ranging from voluntary sexual labour, through exploitative (but still potentially voluntary and consensual) sexual labour, to coerced or forced sexual labour.

Spector also recognises that:

> … the radical feminist critique of prostitution is both an argument about the harms caused by prostitution and an argument about the fact (or sometimes, about the possibility) of consent to such harms, while the feminist liberal defense of the legitimacy of prostitution is an argument that the harms are not of a different kind than the harms caused by other jobs and, as such, can be subject to meaningful consent.[190]

The position taken in this book plots somewhat of a mid-way path, and recognises that other forms of wage labour may involve different levels of potential harm; prostitution and sexual labour per se can be high risk, and therefore 'safety measures' would need to be taken if it is legitimised – the 'hard hat'[191] of the sex industry, so to speak. There is a plethora of issues with the regulation of prostitution, however, consideration of which goes beyond the ambit of this work.

Askola[192] suggests that trafficking for the purpose of sexual exploitation raises complex issues connected to freedom, sexuality, choice and gender equality, in contrast to trafficking for the purpose of other forms of more traditionally recognised labour.[193] It seems that although sex work may indeed be viewed as a legitimate form of labour in that it comprises an exchange of services for remuneration, it is a complex issue which cannot easily be assimilated with a generic idea of labour – different types of labour raise different issues, and accordingly may require different responses.

### *4.3.4 What constitutes 'exploitative' labour, and is sex work inherently exploitative?*

Gilbert and Moore state that:

> Mostly female prostitutes sell access to their intimate body, sexual service, time, and intellectual and emotional labour for mostly male profit and consumption. This commodification of female characteristics in accord with

190 ibid 427.

191 To draw an analogy with the construction industry and the potential for 'harm' to occur through work in that industry – there is clearly no need for a hard hat when working in the office, therefore different levels of harm, risk etc may be identified within currently recognised and regulated form of 'legitimate' labour.

192 See H Askola *Legal Responses to Trafficking in Women for Sexual Exploitation in the European Union* (Hart Publishing, Oxford, 2007).

193 See A Gilbert and C Moore 'Human trafficking in the United Kingdom: the journey so far and the road ahead' (2010) *Criminal Lawyer* 2–4, 2.

> sexualised gender roles stigmatises women as objects and reaffirms women's subordinate status.[194]

However, must this necessarily lead us to conclude that the sale of sex is inherently exploitative? There is sex work in the ideal setting – safe, consensual, uncoerced, unexploitative (in terms of accepted labour standards). Then, there is exploitative sex work – say, where the would-be economic migrant agrees to work in the UK sex sector for less than UK minimum wage, or for arduously long hours. Finally, there is fully coerced, forced sex work. These are all different things – sexual labour, exploitative sexual labour and forced or coerced sexual labour – and there is not necessarily the same gradation of awfulness of the conditions of the work, although there sometimes will be.

It appears from the discussion in the previous section that sex work (that is, the first category) can therefore – in a philosophical and/or political if not necessarily a legal sense – be viewed as a legitimate form of labour. There is compromised legitimacy in the face of exploitation, and furthermore there is nothing legitimate about force or coercion. These latter categories are not sexual labour or prostitution – they are exploitation of, or force as to, sexual labour or prostitution.

What exactly constitutes 'exploitative' labour remains largely undefined in international law, although the Convention Concerning the Prohibition and Immediate Action for the Elimination of the Worst Forms of Child Labour [195] provides some specific insight as regards exploitative child labour.[196] Hernandez-Truyol and Larson conveniently summarise from that Convention four factors which characterise exploitative child labour. These are:

> (1) work that meets existing standards of slavery or forced labour, (2) culturally stigmatized or degrading work, (3) the illegality of the work itself, and (4) harmful or dangerous conditions that interfere with human development and capacity.[197]

For the purposes of the argument made in this book, a definition of 'exploitation' in a labour context is proposed that explicitly refers to lack of conformity with accepted labour standards in the country where the work is taking place.[198] There exists no international legal instrument that formally defines what is 'exploitative' in an adult labour context.

That sex work is inherently exploitative does not have to be accepted as a given. The Trafficking Protocol does not state that prostitution itself is exploitative; instead, it refers to 'the exploitation of … prostitution'.[199] It is necessary at this

194 Hernandez-Truyol and Larson 'Sexual labour and human rights' (n 126) 441.

195 Convention Concerning the Prohibition and Immediate Action for the Elimination of the Worst Forms of Child Labour (17 June 1999) ILO No 182.

196 ibid arts 3(a)–(d).

197 Hernandez-Truyol and Larson 'Sexual labour and human rights' (n 126) 434.

198 This definition will be further discussed in ch 5.

199 Article 3 of the Protocol to Prevent, Suppress and Punish Trafficking in Persons, Especially

point once again to emphasise the separation between consent to the 'purpose', for example commercial sex work, outside of a trafficking context, and consent to trafficking for that 'purpose'. In terms of domestic prostitution, there are some convincing arguments for recognising consent in that context,[200] including the recognition of prostitution as a legitimate form of labour, and participation in it as an expression of autonomy, as previously discussed.

Autonomy advocates may rely upon an abstract conception of consent to reinforce a freedom which may really be illusory. It is argued that 'the autonomous individual agent is itself a product of social construction'.[201] The disparate power relations inherent in an exploitative relationship have to be taken into account when considering the validity of any consent. In a trafficking context, it should also be acknowledged that there are conditions present which do not affect the domestic prostitute.[202] These include the fact that the trafficked prostitutes are away from their family and friends and therefore their community support network, as well as perhaps being hundreds or thousands of miles from home. They may be illegally present on the soil of the destination state, and therefore unable to approach law enforcement agencies for protection, fearing ill-treatment or deportation. On top of this, their native language may well be different from that of the destination state.

All of these conditions render the putative victim potentially more vulnerable than the domestic sex worker, and therefore arguably more in need of protection; 'sexual exploitation becomes trafficking when the abuse involves forcefully moving women from one location to another'.[203] Similarly, the victim trafficked for forms of labour other than sex work is more vulnerable than domestic labourers for the same reasons. Even those who have consented to the trafficking process may be more vulnerable than the domestic worker for the reasons outlined above. In terms of the realities of determining a valid consent in an exploitative facilitated migration/human trafficking context, an argument can be made for a context-sensitive understanding of, and corresponding standard of, consent.[204]

Nonetheless, although empirical evidence clearly demonstrates that sex work can be exploitative,[205] it also demonstrates that other forms of work or labour can,

Women and Children, Supplementing the United Nations Convention Against Transnational Organized Crime (adopted November 2000 by United Nations General Assembly Resolution A/RES/55/25, entered into force 25 December 2003) (Trafficking Protocol).

200 See, for example, J Doezma 'Who gets to choose? Coercion, consent and the UN Trafficking Protocol' (March 2002) 10(1) *Gender and Development* 20–27.

201 E Frazer and N Lacey *The Politics of Community: A Feminist Critique of the Liberal-Communitarian Debate* (Harvester Wheatsheaf, Hemel Hempstead, 1983) 57.

202 Home Office and Scottish Executive 'UK Action Plan on tackling human trafficking' (March 2007) http://www.homeoffice.gov.uk/documents/human-traffick-action-plan?view=Binary (last accessed 4 January 2008) 47.

203 F Gold 'Redefining the slave trade: current trends in the international trafficking of women' (2003) 11 *University of Miami International & Comparative Law Review* 99, 101.

204 On this point in a sexual autonomy context, see Munro 'Constructing consent' (n 114) 923.

205 See J Raymond '10 reasons for not legalising prostitution' (2003) 2 *Journal of Trauma Practice* 315; C C H Hauge 'Prostitution of women and international human rights law: transforming

too. This does not lead here to a conclusion that all work, or indeed all sex work, is exploitative. In fact, it is submitted here that provided that satisfactory labour conditions are present (that is, those in conformity with the accepted labour standards in the destination state) sex work or sexual labour can be undertaken in an unexploitative way.

### *4.3.5 Consent to harm and/or exploitation*

It is undisputed here that prostitution can result in harm. As regards all forms of exploitation, including sex work (where it is exploitative), it must be considered whether consent to exploitative, abusive and dangerous situations should be recognised as valid or as having legal effect. After all, '[people] may agree to exploitative working conditions, but ... agreement is not tantamount to consent'.[206] What is considered to be consent may in reality more closely resemble 'giving in'. The harm to be considered in the context of sold sex and sexual exploitation is the risk of lack of consent. Indeed: '... conceptual vagueness arises, particularly in circumstances in which individuals, despite knowing the inhumane conditions under which they will labor, consent to remain in the custody of a criminal enterprise or coercive agent'.[207]

In the context of offences against the person, Ormerod asks: '[i]n what circumstances should the acts of the accused which cause injury to the victim be punished when that victim has expressly consented to, or at least knowingly taken the risk of, the injury occurring?'[208] English law does not take a single position on whether or not the 'victim's' consent to otherwise unlawful conduct will be a bar to the criminal liability of the perpetrator. In some circumstances, the law does recognise that this is the effect of consent. In *Wilson*,[209] a husband branded his wife with a hot iron – with her full consent – as an apparent token of his love for her. He was acquitted. Jehovah's witnesses can refuse to consent to blood transfusions,

exploitation into equality' (1995) 8 *New York International Law Review* 23; Home Office 'Tackling the demand for prostitution: a review' (November 2008); Home Office 'Paying the price: a consultation paper on prostitution' (July 2004) http://www.homeoffice.gov.uk/documents/paying_the_price.pdf?view=Binary (last accessed 1 July 2011); Eaves 'Men who buy sex: who they buy and what they know' (2009) http://www.eaves4women.co.uk/Documents/Recent_Reports/Men%20Who%20Buy%20Sex.pdf (last accessed 1 July 2011); L Brussa 'Survey of prostitution, migration and traffic in women: history and current situation' (European Union, EG/PROST (91)2 43); M Coy, M Horvath and L Kelly (Child and Women Abuse Studies Unit), 'It's just like going to the supermarket: men buying sex in East London' (2007) http://www.cwasu.org/filedown.asp?file=17242_LMU_Demand_Report_Text_screen-1.pdf (last accessed 1 July 2011).

206 See Abramson 'Beyond consent' (n 94) 473, regarding the view taken by Ateneo Human Rights Centre, the Philippine-Belgian Pilot Project Against Trafficking in Women.

207 Jones 'Human trafficking victim identification' (n 6) 496.

208 D Ormerod 'Reports: consent and offences against the person: Law Commission Consultation Paper no 134' (1994) *Modern Law Review* 928, 928.

209 *R v Wilson (Alan Thomas)* [1997] QB 47.

a decision which may result in their death,[210] thereby attributing a high level of autonomy to the consenting agent in a situation which can result in harm or death.

In various reports and consultation papers, the Law Commission has considered the effect of consent on criminal liability in the context of offence against the person.[211] In Consultation Paper No 134,[212] the Commission considered the general rule that 'no offence is committed if harm of a minor and limited kind is inflicted with the consent of the victim',[213] which meant that, beyond special categories:[214] 'a person cannot effectively consent to the intended or actual infliction on him of "actual bodily harm"'.[215] This rule was developed through the common law in UK domestic cases, such as *Coney*,[216] *Donovan*,[217] *Attorney General's Reference (No 6 of 1980)*[218] and, most recently, *Brown*.[219]

What these cases illustrate is a quasi-paternal approach: the state puts a limit on the acceptable level of harm to which consent can operate as a defence. A distinction remains, however, between situations such as that which occurred in *Brown* and those of the consenting trafficked victim. Those in *Brown* concerned individuals who were on a more comparably equal footing with each other. In the case of 'consensual' trafficking, one party has a clear advantage over the other. Such is the nature of exploitation, which is why 'consensual' trafficking may appropriately be labelled 'consensual facilitated exploitative migration'. It is important to recognise that the autonomy of those engaging in sex work may in limited situations be valid and real. That is to say, consent to sex work is accepted here as prima facie capable of being valid. Consent to exploitative sex work is also recognised here as the same. But, owing to the nature of the latter – particularly in the context of migration and trafficking – perhaps a quasi-paternalist stance is acceptable in the face of serious exploitation.

These different effects of consent raise the question of whether or not it is possible to recognise the validity of consent to trafficking/exploitative facilitated migration but still retain the criminality of the 'trafficker', and more pertinently for this body of work, whether any concession may be made for the victim who

210 See for example, *R v Blaue* [1975] 3 All ER 446, and more recently Emma Gough, a Jehovah's witness, died following severe blood loss after giving birth to twins, *Times Online* (5 November 2007) http://www.timesonline.co.uk/tol/news/uk/article2809423.ece (last accessed 7 November 2007).

211 See Law Commission *Legislating the Criminal Code: Offences Against the Person and General Principles* (Law Commission No 218, November 1993) and Law Commission *Consent and Offences Against the Person* (Law Commission Consultation Paper No 134, 1994).

212 Law Commission *Consent and Offences Against the Person* (Law Commission Consultation Paper No 134, 1994).

213 ibid at 4.1.

214 Such as sports and medical procedures.

215 Law Commission *Consent and Offences Against the Person* (n 211) 4.2.

216 [1882] 8 QBD 534.

217 [1934] 2 KB 498.

218 [1981] QB 715.

219 *R v Brown* [1993] 2 WLR 556, [1993] 2 All ER 75; *Laskey, Jaggard and Brown v United Kingdom* (1997) 24 EHRR 39.

has ostensibly consented or is ostensibly uncoerced. The latter will be considered in Chapter 7.

## 4.4 Conclusion

This chapter commenced with an analysis of the conditions that should exist where a consent is to be determined 'valid'. The emphasis on the importance of a standard of consent can and does vary within different areas of the law, and it was argued that where a consent is given in situations that are more 'at arm's length', then it may be deemed of less importance that the standard is high. It follows from this that we might expect a high standard of consent where, say, bodily integrity and/or close personal relationships are at issue.

In a trafficking context, Global Alliance Against Trafficking in Women (GAATW) and the Foundation against Trafficking in Women (STV) call for a shift away from focusing on prostitution as the work, and instead focus on the force and coercion. The conditions of work should be the issue, not the type of work.[220] This chapter has argued that sex work can be viewed as a legitimate form of labour. Trúóng argues that the elements of the body that are purely sexual may be used not only for pleasure but also for survival and sustenance.[221] This may not sit well with traditional social norms, that is, sex as intimacy, to be reserved for a 'proper' relationship, but it is nonetheless a modern reflection of the potential for sex work to be viewed as a legitimate form of labour, albeit not in a legal sense in every state.

Any form of labour is capable of being exploited or exploitative. Hernandez-Truyol and Larson state that: 'the premise of labor rights is that consent or voluntariness alone cannot guarantee freedom from bondage'.[222] They go on to recognise that '[w]hat the wage labourer sells is control over the body, energy, will and time'.[223] They consider 'relations within which an individual consents to conditions of labour that cannot be reconciled with human dignity'.[224] It is the conditions of the sale, the agreement, which make the different between slavery, consensual exploitation and consensual labour resulting from an agreement or sale. Arguably, the law should provide additional protections to those who are potentially more vulnerable – clearly this category includes children, it may also include women, or sex workers in general.

During the drafting of the Trafficking Protocol, organisations such as the GAATW[225] did not want the instrument to be overprotective or too paternalistic. But, even in the face of consent, exploitative activity should be criminalised and

220 M Lee 'Human trade and the criminalization of irregular migration' (2005) 33 *International Journal of the Sociology of Law* 1–15 at 6.

221 See T-D Trúóng *Sex, Money and Morality: The Political Economy of Prostitution and Tourism in South East Asia* (Zed Books, London, 1990) 67–92.

222 Hernandez-Truyol and Larson, 'Sexual labour and human rights (n 126) 418.

223 ibid 420.

224 ibid 394.

225 See Global Alliance Against Trafficking in Women http://www.gaatw.net/ (last accessed 29 March 2009).

addressed. Consent may well be deemed probative as to the existence of human trafficking, but it should not be deemed probative as to the existence of serious exploitation. Consensual or forced, exploitative labour undermines human dignity.

There is a body of evidence that addresses the effects of legal and decriminalised prostitution,[226] and it would be foolhardy to allow the consent of the minority to be taken as a suggestion that prostitution is not harmful, or that it is a 'safe' profession. This in turn, however, would not justify a conclusive determination that all prostitution should be viewed as non-consensual.

There is a need to move away from the ideas and 'discourse' and toward the practicalities – we know from the evidence that a proportion, possibly a high proportion, of prostitution is coerced. On this basis, when looking for lack of consent, we must lean toward lack of consent wherever there is evidence – no matter how small – to suggest lack of consent, and we should not too easily accept that simply because some prostitution is consensual, that most or much of it is. Some will warn that we should be wary of the 'common but erroneous theory that prostitution is simply work ...',[227] whereas others clearly support the view of prostitution as 'work'.[228] It may be justifiable to have a high standard of consent to be met when there is a question of 'victimhood'.

The standard of proof cannot be adjusted for an offender, but since there is clearly evidence that forced prostitution can appear to be consensual prostitution, we must err on the side of caution when determining whether or not a person is a 'victim' in this context, and in difficult or borderline cases, for the purposes of anti-trafficking and anti-exploitation law and policy, we should come down on the side which determines that someone is a victim (where such a determination may be needed and to the victim's benefit), rather than the opposite. On this basis, in a trafficking nexus, it is not unjustifiable to argue in favour of a presumption of trafficking or exploitation, as opposed to the opposite.

226 For consideration of some such material, see Farley 'Theory versus reality' (n 79).
227 ibid 311.
228 Levy 'Swedish abolitionism as violence against women' (n 82).

# 5 The effect of consent in human trafficking

## 5.1 Introduction

The discussion throughout previous chapters has established that lack of consent/ presence of coercion etc is a necessary condition to establish the existence of trafficking according to legal definition, whether as an offence, as a condition for criminal cooperation, or to identify victims of trafficking. The issue of consent is a much-debated consequence of the requirement imposed by the 'means' element of trafficking – human trafficking is now defined explicitly with reference to lack of (full and genuine) consent, and the presence of factors invalidating consent. Correct determinations as to the presence or lack of consent are made all the more important where 'social relationships are framed by a respect for human rights',[1] as is the case in a smuggling/trafficking/exploitation nexus.

While it is evident through lack of inclusion of a 'consent' element in slave trade provisions that one may not contract oneself into bondage in the context of slavery, the potential to contract oneself into a form of bondage in the context of human trafficking means that consent has come to play a pivotal role in trafficking debate. Where the 'means' element of human trafficking is not deemed to be satisfied, the activity falls outside of the scope of the trafficking definition, and this issue is left to be addressed by individual governments.

Apparent lack of coercion or other 'means' renders the activity prima facie consensual for adults. Here, 'trafficking' becomes consensual facilitated migration for sex work or labour in exploitative conditions, and we are left with a body of 'consensually trafficked' persons. Consent in such a situation, if it can even be clearly deemed valid,[2] does not necessarily render the activity harmless or justified; the exploitative conditions still exist.

The aim of anti-trafficking legislation is to combat trafficking through imposing criminal responsibility on the traffickers and obligations on the state to protect the rights (including the human rights) of trafficked persons. The difficulties inherent in establishing consent in the context of human trafficking may constitute a barrier to obtaining successful prosecutions against traffickers, and an obstacle

1 D Beyleveld and R Brownsword *Consent in the Law* (Hart Publishing, Oxford, 2007) 2.

2 This would turn on each individual situation.

to protecting the rights of the 'victims' as the consequence of an individual being accorded, or not being accorded, victim status under the instruments that form the anti-trafficking regime. Correct determinations of valid consent are paramount to securing adequate identification, treatment and protection of victims.

Consequently, consent seems to serve to negate, or at least mitigate, the exact wrongfulness of transporting people and benefiting from their exploitation. If a person consents to border crossing in order to work under the control of another in exploitative conditions, then under the anti-trafficking instruments the act or process is not criminalised; therefore, this consent serves to operate as a defence for the putative trafficker. The (unofficial) Guide to the explanatory notes to the Protocol attempts to expand upon the issue of consent within the context of human trafficking, stating that:

> … despite evidence that that the victim consented to migrate, to carry false documents and to work illegally abroad, defendants cannot argue that the victim 'consented' to work in conditions of forced labour, slavery or servitude. By definition, these three crimes mean there is no consent. For example, a woman can consent to migrate to work in prostitution in a particular city, at a particular brothel, for a certain sum of money. However, if the defendant intended actually to hold the woman in forced or coerced sex work, then there is no consent because everything the defendant trafficker told the woman is a lie. No one can consent to a lie. Even if a person agrees to work in very bad conditions, for very little money, with very little freedom, he would still be a victim of trafficking if the trafficker intended to hold him in debt bondage, involuntary or forced conditions.[3]

This excerpt takes its cue from the trafficking definition, which recognises that consent to exploitation may be given.[4] The question for the purposes of trafficking are whether or not that consent can be deemed relevant or valid. For trafficking to exist, it would appear that exploitative conditions alone are not sufficient. In order for the crime to constitute trafficking, there must be an element of force, or some form of broken agreement, which will suffice to satisfy the 'means' element of human trafficking and therefore vitiate any initial consent.

None of the central legal instruments[5] using the recognised definition of human

3 A D Jordan 'Annotated guide to the complete UN Trafficking Protocol' (May 2002, updated August 2002) Ann D Jordan Director, Initiative Against Trafficking in Persons, International Human Right Law Group, 11.

4 This is evident through the explicit statement in the trafficking definition that: 'The consent of a victim … to the exploitation … shall be irrelevant where any of the means … has been used'.

5 Including the Trafficking Protocol, the CoE Trafficking Convention and the EU 2011 Directive: Protocol to Prevent, Suppress and Punish Trafficking in Persons, Especially Women and Children, Supplementing the United Nations Convention Against Transnational Organized Crime (adopted November 2000 by United Nations General Assembly Resolution A/RES/55/25, entered into force 25 December 2003); Council of Europe Convention on Action against Trafficking in Human Beings and its Explanatory Report (adopted 3 May 2005, entered into force 1 February 2008) Warsaw, 16.V.2005, Council of Europe Treaty Series No 197; Directive 2011/36/EU of the

trafficking adequately provides for situations of 'consensual' human trafficking. Exploiting a person – and profiting from the exploitation – seems to be almost acceptable in terms of the trafficking definition, as long as no one was deceived and the exploitative situation was not enforced or altered from what was agreed. The definition seems to shift the focus from the end result of the offence to the nature of the offence; how the end result, that is, exploitation, was brought about. It has been suggested that the focus should surely be not on the consent of the victim but on the harm done.[6]

Through the inclusion of the consent element, what we are left with is a category of persons who, through the giving of (or the appearance of) consent, have been 'less than trafficked', but 'more than smuggled'. These persons – the 'consensually trafficked' – may have recourse to ordinary human rights law and domestic criminal law for protections and standards of treatment, but are currently entitled to no specific provision under the anti-trafficking regime.

This chapter aims to analyse the role of consent (or lack thereof) in human trafficking. Section 5.2 will revisit and draw upon the conditions for a valid consent that were discussed in Chapter 4, with the discussion here focusing specifically on valid consent in a trafficking context. Section 5.3 will consider how the inclusion of the 'consent' element in human trafficking came about, and section 5.4 will discuss the reality of consent in human trafficking while challenging the dichotomous approach that some take to the consent/coercion debate in a trafficking context.[7] The effects of recognising consent in a trafficking context will then be addressed in section 5.5, which will include consideration of the potential for consent to act as a defence for would-be traffickers, and a barrier to securing adequate support and protection for putative victims. Finally, alternatives to the current situation offered by the anti-trafficking regime will be suggested in section 5.6.

## 5.2 The requirements of a valid consent in the context of human trafficking

The various aspects of a valid consent were analysed at an earlier point in this book. These aspects will now be considered and applied in the specific context of human trafficking. As will be seen from the analysis which follows in this chapter, it may not necessarily be appropriate in the context of trafficking and sexual exploitation to base determinations of valid consent upon a 'consent threshold

European Parliament and of the Council of 5 April 2011 on preventing and combating trafficking in human beings and protecting its victims, and replacing Council Framework Decision 2002/629/JHA [2001] OJ L101/1.

6 B Balos 'The wrong way to equality: privileging consent in the trafficking of women for sexual exploitation' (2004) 27 *Harvard Women's Law Journal* 137, 149.

7 See, for example, J Doezma 'Forced to choose: beyond the voluntary v. forced prostitution dichotomy' in J Doezma and K Kempadoo (eds) *Global Sex Workers: Rights, Resistance and Redefinition* (Routledge, New York, 1998) and J Bhabha 'Trafficking, smuggling and human rights' (March 2005) *Migration Information Source: Special Issue on Migration and Human Rights* http://www.migrationinformation.org/Feature/display.cfm?id=294 (last accessed 21 January 2014).

that centres on such theoretically contested, and malleable, concepts as "freedom" (and) "capacity"'.[8]

### *5.2.1 Consent must be 'freely' given*

As established in Chapter 4, the Law Commission and Scottish Law Commission view 'freely' given consent as '... *agreement* to what is done'[9] and that this agreement must be 'free and genuine agreement to the act in question'.[10] Furthermore, that 'agreement' can be given in situations where it is not 'real', 'full', or 'valid'.[11] In the most basic sense in a trafficking context, 'free' consent is that which is free from any form of coercion or other 'means', or more specifically as stated in the trafficking definition, that which is free from:

> ... threat or use of force or other forms of coercion, of abduction, of fraud, of deception, of the abuse of power or of a position of vulnerability or of the giving or receiving of payments or benefits to achieve the consent of a person having control over another person ...[12]

The meaning of each of these terms was explored in Chapter 3. The 'consensually trafficked' person (that is, one who cannot show that he or she was subject to coercion etc) must, therefore, give clearly uncoerced consent, and must exercise autonomous agency, free from the influences of external pressure such as force etc being applied by the trafficker. This, as will be argued, is not without its complications.

Abramson asserts that the existence of full, free consent in the context of human trafficking is problematic, as it 'ignores the real difference in choices between rich and poor, male and female, and educated and uneducated'.[13] This statement extends beyond consideration of lack of consent in the face of more obvious forms of coercion, such as force, and raises the issue of the relevance of coercion of circumstances, in which case it could be argued that the notion of 'free' consent is morally suspect where the consenting agent was motivated by, for example, severe poverty.[14] We might conclude, in a metaphorical sense, that no matter how hungry a person is he or she may not steal the loaf, although this involves taking a highly simplistic view – this matter (as to coercion of circumstances) is dealt with further in Chapter 7.

8 V E Munro 'Constructing consent: legislating freedom and legitimating constraint in the expression of sexual autonomy' (2008) 41 *Akron Law Review* 923, 926.

9 Law Commission *Consent in Sex Offences: A Report to the Home Office Sex Offences Review* (1998) para 2.9.

10 ibid para 2.12.

11 Scottish Law Commission *Report on Rape and Other Sexual Offences: Report on a reference under section 3(1)(e) of the Law Commissions Act 1965* (Scottish Law Commission No 209, 2007) para 2.38.

12 UN Trafficking Protocol art 3, CoE Trafficking Convention art 4 and EU 2011 Directive art 2.

13 K Abramson 'Beyond consent, toward safeguarding human Rights: implementing the United Nations Trafficking Protocol' (2003) 44(2) *Harvard International Law Journal* 473, 475.

14 See ch 7 for discussion of this matter.

The problem of 'free' consent in a trafficking context is further exacerbated by a tendency for those who may have been trafficked to be viewed simply as 'another smuggled prostitute'. The smuggling/trafficking divide raises its head again,[15] as does the politics of tackling irregular economic migration. Establishing the lack of 'freely' given consent in a trafficking context is clearly no easy task. This is the case not least because of the intricacies of the 'means' element of the trafficking definition, but also in the face of external pressures – such as those of an economic form – which do not come from the trafficker.[16] Nonetheless, it would appear that, in a trafficking context, invalidation of 'freely' given consent is dependent upon some form of positive action from another agent, which would require some objective proof of activity interfering with the freedom of any consent given.

Furthermore, it can be argued that the standard of interference (with consent) may be set too high in certain circumstances, such as in a trafficking or sex trade context that comprises an inherently coercive environment,[17] which may obscure the coercive reality and lead to the appearance of freely given consent. Ostensible forms of coercion such as force can more clearly render ineffective any consent given, but where the force used is not sufficiently evident to the objective observer, this renders genuine 'freely' given consent difficult to determine here.

### *5.2.2 Consent must be 'informed'*

In the context of consent to exploitation, one might ask whether 'where a choice touches on a person's most basic interests … do we (or should we) set a higher threshold for free and informed consent than where lesser interests are at stake …'.[18] Exploitative conditions of any type of work may encroach upon a person's basic interests. Therefore, it may be possible to ask for a higher standard of free and informed consent here, particularly in light of the discussion in Chapter 4 regarding consent to prostitution and sexual exploitation.

In a trafficking context, the definition provides that the existence of any of the stipulated 'means' will render invalid a consent 'to the intended exploitation'.[19] Therefore, the parameters of the 'exploitation' are relevant to the idea of the putative victim being considered to be 'informed'. Here, the notion of informed consent raises the question of exactly what the putatively trafficked person will be consenting to, and how informed she has to be – particularly when bearing in mind that she may have little or no knowledge of the 'typical' conditions to be faced in the sex sector of the destination state. The law – and those executing it – must take care to distinguish between genuine consent and situations where there

15 See ch 2.

16 See ch 7.

17 As regards discussion of 'free' consent in an inherently coercive environment, see Human Rights Watch 'No escape: male rape in U.S. prisons', in particular see the section entitled 'Consent and Coercion in prison' http://www.hrw.org/legacy/reports/2001/prison/index.htm (last accessed 17 January 2014).

18 Beyleveld and Brownsword *Consent in the Law* (n 1) 11

19 UN Trafficking Protocol art 3, CoE Convention art 4, EU 2011 Directive art 2.

is merely the appearance of consent.[20] Human trafficking against a backdrop of illicit economic migration and people smuggling renders it more difficult to distinguish between real and apparent consent.

Addressing this question (as to how well informed the putative victim must be) a person 'will not have had the capacity to agree by choice where their understanding and knowledge were so limited that they were not in a position to decide whether or not to agree'.[21] In the context of human trafficking, given the tripartite nature of trafficking, then for the consent to be considered informed and genuine, the nature, quality and purpose of the act or process must be agreed upon and the facts on which it was based must be maintained.

Some subsequent change in conditions from those that were agreed will potentially satisfy the 'means' element, and render the activity capable of being caught by the trafficking definition. This will be easier to establish where for the 'purpose' element of human trafficking, the objective standards of 'slavery' or 'servitude',[22] for example, are met. By definition, apparent initial consent would surely be rendered ineffective by a change from what was agreed, which led to circumstances where the characteristics of these practices were endured. There will, however, exist cases of a more borderline nature.

Jordan states that:

> A woman can consent to migrate to work in prostitution in a particular city, at a particular brothel, for a certain sum of money. However, if the defendant intended actually to hold the woman in forced or coerced sex work, then there is no consent ...[23]

This goes toward establishing a standard of informed consent in a trafficking context. In this context, then, consent to be transported from point A to point B in order to work in the sex industry as a prostitute is prima facie capable of constituting a valid consent. Nonetheless, this is too simple a formula, which does not take full account of the intricacies of smuggling and trafficking of humans. Accordingly, a consent to be transported to work as a prostitute can be valid but if the conditions of 'work', such as pay, are different from those agreed, then this no longer qualifies as informed consent, and the consent is invalidated – there is deception. The initial giving of consent no longer subsists; it is damaged, changed

20 The Anti-Trafficking Monitoring Group notes that: 'In many cases, victims may *appear* "free". Sometimes, they might get paid some money. However, often these appearances merely mask the coercion: debt bondage, control over people's identity or immigration status, threats and other psychological pressures are very real factors that control behaviour as much as any physical imprisonment. These forms of coercion leave serious psychological consequences'. See Anti-Trafficking Monitoring Group 'Wrong kind of victim: One year on: an analysis of UK measures to protect trafficked persons' (June 2010) 17.

21 P Rook QC and R Ward *Rook and Ward on Sexual Offences: Law and Practice* (3rd edn, Sweet & Maxwell, London, 2003) para 1.94.

22 See ch 3 for a full discussion of these 'purpose' elements of the trafficking definition.

23 Jordan 'Annotated guide to the complete UN Trafficking Protocol' (n 3) 11.

from the initial state in which it was offered – it can no longer be considered to be informed, owing to the change from what was agreed.

In order for consent to be real and informed, sufficient of the conditions of 'work' must have been agreed upon, free from the constraints of any form of coercion. Research conducted into victims of trafficking into Israel estimates that in '… 70% of the cases the women are aware of the fact that they will be selling their bodies in prostitution but they are not aware of the harsh conditions that await them when they arrive in Israel'.[24] If we ask for a higher standard of informed consent here, it is rendered more palatable to respect the autonomous choices of the migrant prostitute/would-be trafficked person.[25]

There may be some responsibility on the consenting individual to gather information prior to giving consent. We might query how much responsibility is to be placed upon the migrant to determine the details of the arrangement to which they are consenting. It cannot be assumed that all putative victims, particularly those living in rural areas,[26] will have an adequate understanding of the risks associated with migration and trafficking. It may also not be suitable to expect the putative victim to have sound knowledge of the conditions of sexual labour or sex work in the destination state.

While retaining a stance that recognises the autonomy of the individual to consent to engaging in prostitution (even where it is exploitative), a sufficiently paternalistic stance – which requires a higher, more stringent standard of informed consent – is not an unreasonable proposition where exploitation, which interferes with the basic interests of human beings, is the intended outcome of the activity in question. Autonomy is a difficult matter in terms of the choice to engage in exploitative sex work; that is, sex work in conditions that meet a standard of 'exploitation',[27] as opposed to sex work *per se*. In the context of exploitation, the exploiter cannot be said to have the best interests of the exploited at heart.

Various areas of the law that employ notions of informed consent were explored in Chapter 4. The notion of 'informed consent' in certain contexts concerns different issues. For example, informed consent in a medical, family or contractual context may raise issues of bodily integrity, personal relationships and harm to an individual. These are clearly of a less 'arm's length' nature than

24 L G Gold and N B Ami 'National NGOs Report to the Annual UN Commission on Human Rights: Evaluation of national authorities' activities and actual facts on the trafficking in persons for the purpose of prostitution in Israel' (on behalf of Awareness Centre, Machon Toda'a, Representative of the IAF in Israel, 2004) 8.

25 Furthermore, many women who are exploited in the sex trade, whether or not trafficked, are dependent upon drugs – the economic need to fund their habits and the possibility that any decisions are less than genuine and informed ought to be taken into account if consent is so crucial a matter.

26 It has been reported that those from rural areas are more likely to underestimate the risk of being trafficked, see GfK Ukraine 'Human Trafficking Survey: Belarus, Bulgaria, Moldova, Romania, and Ukraine', Kyiv, Ukraine (December 2006), prepared by GfK Ukraine for the International Organization for Migration, 5.

27 A definition of 'exploitation' is proposed later in this chapter, as offset against accepted labour standards in the destination state, is proposed.

informed consent in a commercial contractual sense, and therefore more fitting as basis of comparison in a sex trafficking context, particularly when considering the nature of the 'work' to be undertaken and the risks involved. The trafficking/smuggling type of 'transaction' or agreement needs to be treated more tentatively. Furthermore, it needs to be treated so because of the potentially risky nature of such a 'transaction', and also potentially because women (or perhaps sex workers in general) are more vulnerable (note the 'gender perspective', or similar, alluded to in some of the main anti-trafficking instruments discussed in this book),[28] and, ultimately, because of the inherently personal nature of the 'work' or 'services' to be provided.

Notably, 'informed consent is a normative variable, not an empirical constant'.[29] If it is treated as an empirical constant, then the law serves as something of a blunt tool in terms of protecting the vulnerable. To reiterate what was stated in Chapter 4, 'the level or kind of consent that might be sufficient to ground enforcement in one type of situation may not be sufficient in another'.[30] Borderline cases of trafficking may, in the absence of a requirement of a high standard of informed consent, otherwise simply be deemed as cases of human smuggling or economic migration. Because the consequences for the victim are so serious, the putative victim should have been informed as to many aspects of the process before it can be said that she has consented. Only then can she be said to have demonstrated the 'informed exercise of a choice, and [had] an opportunity to evaluate knowledgeably the options available and the risks attendant upon each'.[31]

On the basis of the analysis in this section and, as noted by Jordan, it is not entirely unprincipled to ask that the requisite standard of informed consent may at the absolute minimum be that: '… a woman can consent to migrate to work in prostitution in a particular city, at a particular brothel, for a certain sum of money'.[32] Expected hours of work, for example, may also need to be agreed upon. The purpose and nature of the act(s) consented to must be maintained as agreed, so that the consent elicited can be considered to be informed. The fact that establishing such matters is resource intensive, and demanding evidentially, is not necessarily sufficient to lower the standard required here, particularly if effective protection of victims of trafficking and sexual exploitation is to be achieved.

28 Notably, the UN Trafficking Protocol refers in its title to 'especially women and children', and the EU 2011 Directive refers in the preamble, para 3, to the 'gender-specific phenomenon of trafficking'.

29 P H Schuck 'Rethinking informed consent' (1994) Yale Faculty Scholarship Series, Paper 2765, 906 at 956.

30 B Bix 'The ethics of consent: theory and practice' in A Wertheimer, Franklin G Miller (eds) (Oxford University Press, Oxford, 20110) Minnesota Legal Studies Research Paper No 08-36, 2, 5.

31 *Canterbury v Spence*, 464 F.2d 772 (DC Cir 1972).

32 Jordan 'Annotated guide to the complete UN Trafficking Protocol' (n 3) 11.

### *5.2.3 Capacity and understanding*

This clearly relates to mental capacity – the consenting agent must have the capacity to understand that which she is consenting to. A consistent theme is how trafficking definitions deal with minors – namely that those under 18 are not to be deemed capable of consenting in this context. Although the competence of minors to make their own decisions may at times be recognised in certain areas of the law, there is to be no grey area resembling '*Gillick* competence'[33] here. Where mental capacity to consent is lacking in an adult, a consent cannot be considered to be valid. As stated in Chapter 4, adults may be assumed to have the mental capacity to consent, but this assumption can be rebutted.[34]

### *5.2.4 The timing of consent*

Migration situations will frequently be difficult to categorise. The 'means' element of trafficking fundamentally distinguishes this activity from smuggling, as the latter requires no form of coercion. This element of trafficking demonstrates the involuntary nature of this activity, whereas the fact that there is no need to demonstrate 'means' where smuggling is concerned implies activity of a more voluntary nature.[35]

Whether a person has been trafficked or smuggled, whether a person has consented or been coerced, are questions of both interpretation and timing, and any consent given must subsist at the time of the act consented to.[36] Initial consent may indeed be given in many circumstances. However, what a putative victim has 'consented' to will frequently be far from the realities facing the migrant on arrival. Is her position at the point of departure or the point of arrival a better indicator of the migrant's intentions? From a human rights perspective, for victims of human trafficking, it is surely the point of arrival.[37] It my even come later than that, as the deception etc of the trafficker may still not be apparent on arrival in the destination country. In order to cater adequately for victims, it is submitted here that, provided there is at least some suspicion that a woman is putatively a victim (the problems with which are addressed in Chapter 6), we should start from a presumption of trafficking (and therefore lack of consent, for adults).

It has been established that in a trafficking context there may frequently be an

33 The elasticity of consent in terms of legal acceptance of capacity to consent is demonstrated by the 1985 *Gillick* case in the UK where a Lords majority ruled upon the potential capacity of under 16s to make their own decisions about medical treatment. See *Gillick v West Norfolk and Wisbech Area Health Authority* [1985] 3 All ER 402.

34 This point was made by Butler-Sloss LJ in the context of medical treatment in *Re MB (Medical Treatment)* [1997] 2 FLR 426.

35 T Obokata 'Smuggling of human beings from a human rights perspective: obligations of non-state and state actors under international human rights law' (2005) 17(2) *International Journal of Refugee Law* 394–415, 394.

36 Law Commission *Consent in Sex Offences* (n 9) para 2.11.

37 Bhabha 'Trafficking, smuggling and human rights' (n 7).

initial consent, but if this consent is obtained through, or followed by, subsequent deception, then it can no longer be accepted as a valid consent. If the deceptive intention was always present, the consent was never valid. If consent must be subsisting, then it follows that it can be withdrawn at any point,[38] although this may not always be straightforward in principle and in practice. Any belief by the authorities that trafficked victims are often in fact 'complicit' is damaging.[39] Accordingly, belief by, say, law enforcement authorities in the giving of consent by the 'victim', can rest on the giving of initial consent by the victim, and fail to take into account the scope for subsequent vitiation of consent by deceptive or coercive conditions.

The difficulty inherent in determining this matter is exemplified in an account provided in Chapter 3,[40] which refers to a victim who agreed (and therefore consented) to be recruited (the 'action') in order to work in the Israeli sex industry (the 'purpose'), and yet subsequently received no money from her pimp. There was no deception about the nature of the 'work'.[41] However, it may be argued that the deception as regards the nature of the payment occurred at a later point in the process, or was perhaps the intention of the exploiter all along. Whether this is sufficient to vitiate consent and therefore render a situation of otherwise consensual facilitated migration – possibly into an exploitative situation – one of human trafficking, is a central factor and further highlights the problematic nature of the consent requirement in this part of the sex trade.

A female co-trafficker cited in the UK Action Plan on Tackling Human Trafficking makes the following observation:

> The girls I've met … some of them don't even have a clue what they're doing, why they came … some of them know why they're coming … right, some of

38 The Law Commission in 1998 stated that: '… an agreement to an act should not be regarded as a consent to that act unless it is *subsisting* at the relevant time. If what is relied on is past agreement, this will mean *both* (a) that, when previously given, the agreement must have extended to the doing of the act at that later time, *and* (b) that it must not have been withdrawn in the meantime'. See Law Commission *Consent in Sex Offences* (n 9) para 2.11.

39 Research conducted in Birmingham, UK, indicates that local police believe that many 'victims' of trafficking are complicit in the process, and knew what they were getting into. Statement by Sarah Garrat (Personal Communication on 14 February 2008, following research conducted by the Asylum and Immigration Research Team, Birmingham, into the treatment of victims of human trafficking once discovered in the destination state).

40 The example used was as follows: 'A young woman was studying in Tashkent and living in a hostel. A woman she did not know said that she was recruiting girls for summer jobs in the Israeli sex industry. When the young woman arrived she worked for several months and received no payment. When she raised this, her pimp ("balobay") said she had been earning a percentage all along, but that he had been saving it for her. After eight months, she was picked up by the police for overstaying her visa. Her pimp promised to bring the money she was owed (€9000) to the jail. He never came and she wants to return to claim her money, but has been told by the Israeli authorities that if they pick her up again they will prosecute her'. See International Organization for Migration 'Fertile fields: trafficking in persons in Central Asia' (a report prepared by Liz Kelly, Child and Woman Abuse Studies Unit, London Metropolitan University April 2005) 67–68.

41 See International Organization for Migration 'Fertile fields' (n 40) 68.

> them knew that they were going to work as prostitutes but they didn't know they were going to be controlled by Albanians to start with, or some of them thought they were going to work for themselves as prostitutes.[42]

The Explanatory Report to the CoE Trafficking Convention provides further illumination on this point of the timing of consent:

> The question of consent is not simple and it is not easy to determine where free will ends and constraint begins. In trafficking, some people do not know what is in store for them while others are perfectly aware that, for example, they will be engaging in prostitution. However, while someone may wish employment, and possibly be willing to engage in prostitution, that does not mean that they consent to be subjected to abuse of all kinds.[43]

The above qualifications make for a broad view as to when, and for what, consent must be given. This encompassing view recognises that initial consent to migrate in order to work in prostitution can potentially be rendered ineffective by deception with respect to factors other than solely the strict nature of the 'work' to be undertaken. This indicates that the scope of the consent must be determined, that is, the specific extent of what has been consented to. The excerpts illustrate the point that consent to sex work does not equate to consent to exploitation. The justificatory scope of consent in such situations should be limited.

## 5.3 The move toward inclusion of a 'consent' element in human trafficking definitions

The relevant instrument preceding the Trafficking Protocol, namely the 1949 Trafficking Convention,[44] deemed consent irrelevant through inclusion of the words 'even with the consent of that person'. The Convention simply focused upon the 'action' and the 'purpose' elements of trafficking as they are understood today, although at the time the 'purpose' element was limited to prostitution or the exploitation of the prostitution of others. Since there was no clear 'means' element, it was not necessary to establish lack of consent.

The 1949 Convention had followed the pattern set by the 1933 Trafficking Convention,[45] which states that trafficking of a woman or girl occurs 'even with her consent', by including no list of specific 'means' and thereby providing that traffickers could not rely upon consent as a defence to the crime contained in the

42 Female co-trafficker, cited in Home Office and Scottish Executive 'UK Action Plan on tackling human trafficking' (March 2007) 27.

43 Explanatory Report to the Council of Europe Trafficking Convention (n 5) 97.

44 Convention for the Suppression of the Traffic in Persons and of the Exploitation of Prostitution of Others (approved by General Assembly resolution 317(IV) of 2 December 1949, entered into force 25 July 1951) (1949 Trafficking Convention).

45 International Convention on the Suppression of the Traffic in Women of Full Age (11 October 1933, entered into force 24 August 1934) 150 LTS 431 (1933 Trafficking Convention).

treaties. Prostitution itself was not considered illegal under the 1949 Convention, and thus the emphasis was taken away from the perceived immorality of prostitution and prostitutes and placed upon punishment of those responsible for the trafficking. This approach accepts that, even if there is consent, there is also the simultaneous existence of inherently exploitative activity.

Some more recent definitions of trafficking in persons concentrate solely on commercial sex work.[46] Others envisage trafficking for a wider 'purpose', such as the definition offered by the UN General Assembly in 1994, which described trafficking as:

> ... the illicit and clandestine movement of persons across national and international borders, largely from developing countries and some countries with economies in transition, with the end goal of forcing women and girl children into sexually or economically oppressive and exploitative situations, for the profit of recruiters, traffickers and crime syndicates, as well as other illegal activities related to trafficking, such as forced domestic labour, false marriages, clandestine employment and false adoption.[47]

During drafting debates surrounding the trafficking Protocol, non-governmental organizations (NGOs) offered their own definitions. Many combined an element of 'action', such as movement or transport with an element of 'purpose', such as exploitative labour of some sort. Trafficking has – as we know – now evolved to become a strict combination of all three constituents of 'action', 'means' and 'purpose'.

Hernandez-Truyol and Larson state that: '[t]he presence of consent or voluntariness alone is not enough to fend off the dispossession, exploitation, and alienation of human bondage: "mere exemption from servitude is a miserable idea of freedom"'.[48] To allow consent of the transported woman to exclude from trafficking the movement of women to conditions of exploitation (in the context of exploitative facilitated migration), would create a body of persons who risk serious exploitation or who have been seriously exploited, yet who fall outside of the scope of the international legislation enacted to combat trafficking.

Nonetheless, trafficking according to the current legal definition consisting of all three elements of the process, and 'trafficking' (if it can be so called), consisting only of the 'action' and 'purpose' elements, are not the same. Although both situations result in exploitation and should be legally addressed, it is questionable whether they should be deemed identical and therefore capable of being

46 See, for example, art 1(3) of the South Asian Association for Regional Cooperation Convention on Preventing and Combating Trafficking in Women and Children for Prostitution (done at Kathmandu on 5 January 2002).

47 'Traffic in women and girls' UNGA Resolution 49/166 (24 February 1995) UN Doc A/RES/49/166.

48 Rep. Holman of Indiana, Cong. Globe, 38th Cong. 1st Sess. (2962 1864), speaking in the debate over the enactment of the Thirteenth Amendment, cited in B E Hernandez-Truyol, and J E Larson 'Sexual labour and human rights' (2006) 37 *Columbia Human Rights Law Review* 391–445, 424.

addressed in the same way by the same instrument(s), with the same definition. This is particularly so when framed in terms of the principle of 'fair labelling'.[49] The concern of this normative principle is, as Ashworth states:

> … to see that widely felt distinctions between kinds of offences and degrees of wrongdoing are respected and signalled by the law, and that offences are subdivided and labelled so as to represent fairly the nature and magnitude of the law-breaking.[50]

Accordingly, application of this principle would determine that those who facilitate migration into an exploitative situation where consent has been given, and those who traffick humans, should indeed not be treated in the same way in terms of criminal sanction. These two activities signal different degrees of wrongdoing; therefore, this should be reflected in the legislative response. However, this does not avoid the problems inherent in determining the existence of a valid consent in either context. If anything, it would make the enquiry more important, particularly in terms of the effect of such a determination upon the victim.

## 5.4 The consent/coercion 'dichotomy': the reality of consent in the context of human trafficking

### *5.4.1 The consent/coercion 'dichotomy'*

In a trafficking context, the consent debate is frequently flawed owing to the supposition that there are only two situations: consent or coercion/force. The reality is a spectrum with one of the two states at either end. Munro states that the excessive and inherent ambiguity of consent 'means that it is simply not useful in the delineation of the law itself'.[51] Coercion, force, or other 'means' elements of the trafficking definition are capable of vitiating consent; that is, they can impair the quality of consent. In some circumstances they may go so far as to negate consent; that is, to invalidate it fully. These respective terms – vitiate, negate – also sit on a spectrum as to what degree they damage the quality of consent.

The perceived coercion/consent 'dichotomy' assumes a rather clean line between cases. In his 2000 Report, the UN Special Rapporteur on Violence against Women states that it is 'the non-consensual nature of trafficking that distinguishes it from other forms of migration';[52] thus, trafficking is largely characterised

49 Initially identified as 'representative labelling' by Ashworth, and re-named 'fair labelling' by Glanville Williams. See G Williams 'Convictions and fair labelling' (1983) 42 *Cambridge Law Journal* 85.

50 A Ashworth *Principles of Criminal Law* (5th edn, Oxford University Press, Oxford, 2006) 88–90.

51 Munro 'Constructing consent' (n 8) 940.

52 United Nations Economic and Social Council, Report of the Special Rapporteur on violence against women, its causes and consequences, Ms Radhika Coomaraswamy, on trafficking in women, women's migration and violence against women, submitted in accordance with Commission on Human Rights Resolution 1997/44 'Integration of the human rights of women

by the lack of consent, whereas smuggled persons are considered to have 'willingly engaged in a criminal enterprise'.[53]

Bhabha[54] also points out the flawed distinction made by the trafficking definition through its presupposition of only the two states of either consent or coercion. It is this distinction and the grey area in between that tempers the trafficking debate. The internationally recognised definition of human trafficking already provides us with a sliding scale of severity of activity, all of which constitutes trafficking. Initially, we have the example of the victim abducted fully against her will. Further along the spectrum, we have the situation where consent is given, but some event occurs to render the consent irrelevant or invalidated. This could come about where one of the 'means' elements of the current definition of 'trafficking in persons' is employed; say, the nature of 'work' or conditions agreed to are changed and therefore deception has occurred, rendering the victim trafficked (by definition), even though initial consent was given. These cases illustrate differences of degree, rather than nature.

Finally, at the far end of the spectrum, we have the person who has consented to every part of the process (or the appearance is such because objective proof of any coercion etc is lacking), even though the person is to be performing exploitative work in perhaps dangerous conditions. The presence of ostensible consent illustrates differences of both degree and the nature of the activity. This person has not been trafficked. Neither has the person been smuggled, at least in a moral sense, as the activity goes beyond the ambit of the Smuggling Protocol. What we are left with is a body of persons who come within a larger spectrum of 'facilitated exploitative migration', or 'facilitated migration for the purpose of exploitation', which although exploitative and potentially illegal in nature, cannot currently be said to be human trafficking in a legal sense.

In the context of the definitional gap between trafficking and smuggling, these persons exist in a legal vacuum. They may have experienced the comparable levels of exploitation and abuse of rights as many persons who are deemed to have been trafficked. However, the state is unable to obtain prosecution against the migration facilitator as a 'trafficker', and the exploited migrants are not afforded 'victim' status and, consequently, the protection offered to trafficked persons by the state. One might ask whether there are likely to be any persons at all who can really be said to have truly given their consent, and therefore consideration of this category of persons is unnecessary. However, in response, one would say that the drafters of the Trafficking Protocol clearly envisaged the potential to consent in this context, and considered it to be relevant as to the determination of the existence of trafficking.

As outlined above, older traffick-specific instruments did not deem consent to

and the gender perspective: violence against women' Commission on Human Rights, Fifty-sixth session, Agenda item 12(a) of the provisional agenda (2000) E/CN.4/2000/68 http://www.unhchr.ch/Huridocda/Huridoca.nsf/0/e29d45a105cd8143802568be0051fcfb?Opendocument (last accessed 1 July 2011).

53 Bhabha 'Trafficking, smuggling and human rights' (n 7).

54 ibid.

be relevant or probative of human trafficking. Slavery-related instruments make it clear that a person cannot contract herself into bondage in a slavery context. The Trafficking Protocol presents somewhat of an anomaly – the ability to contract oneself into an exploitative and potentially harmful situation. The nature and degree of the exploitation in question, and relevant factors such as coercion and deception, are clearly relevant to determining on which side of a blurred line (the blurred element of which may be very broad) the activity in question will fall.

### *5.4.2 The 'spectrum' of consent/coercion: the reality of consent in the context of human trafficking*

As the above discussion indicates, the 'dichotomy' of consent/coercion is rejected here. It is submitted instead that these inherently malleable concepts sit at opposite ends of a spectrum. Along this spectrum and between these concepts there are varying shades of grey as to what constitutes valid consent or coercion sufficient to render consent ineffective or invalidated in any given situation.

Drew asserts that, in the case of smuggling, the human being is the consumer, whereas in the case of trafficking, the human being is the commodity.[55] However, the division between trafficking and smuggling is not clear-cut. One can give polarised such as the kidnapped victim juxtaposed against the willing migrant sex worker. These examples may represent how one perceives 'pure'[56] cases of smuggling or trafficking, but in reality cases are rarely this simple.

The concepts of consent and coercion are particularly problematic when considered within a coercive environment, as indicated by research conducted into prison rape.[57] Where there is the potential that individuals enjoy limited autonomy, such as in a potentially exploitative sex work environment, the appearance of valid consent can obscure the reality of coerced consent. The power imbalance that can occur in such relationships further problematises determinations of valid consent. This hierarchical relationship of exploiter and exploited further means that a valid consent can become a coerced consent and yet, to an objective observer, there has been little or no change in the relationship.

Consequently the potential for, and effects of, exploitation and abuse may be exacerbated. In such a coercive environment there may be little need for overtly and obviously coercive acts, and there is the further issue that the exploited individual may not view herself as coerced or trafficked.[58] Human Rights Watch states that, as regards rape in prison environments:

> … in instances where the victim makes little apparent effort to escape the abuse, both prisoners and prison authorities often fall into the trap of viewing

55 S Drew 'Human trafficking: a modern form of slavery?' (2002) 4 *European Human Rights Law Review* 481–92, 484.

56 J Bhabha 'Reforming immigration policy: start by protecting rights, not borders' (2005) *Boston Review*. See http://bostonreview.net/bhabha-immigration-policy.

57 See Human Rights Watch 'No escape' (n 17).

58 See ch 7.

> non-consensual [sic] sexual activity as consensual, ignoring the larger context in which the activity takes place.[59]

Similarly, the apparently willing smuggled prostitute may in fact be labouring under coercion or threats – thereby rendering her formally 'trafficked' – but this may not be apparent. Valid consent requires the power to refuse – it may not be clear where this is lacking. Unwanted could still equate to unforced, but this does not necessarily equate to a valid consent.

In realistic terms, we might ask what degree of coercion or deception (and about what issues) is necessary in order to establish that a woman has been trafficked. Let us proceed on the basis that someone can consent to sex work, even in exploitative conditions where pimps and exploiters take their inflated cut of the earnings. In this situation, if the usually willing sex worker is persuaded to service one more client that she wants to on a particular day, does that mean she has been coerced significantly for her to have been trafficked? The *Moir* case would suggest that, in some circumstances, she will have been so coerced.[60] Even if it were concluded that she had been coerced, whether or not the coercion is sufficient to invalidate consent is a further issue and would turn on the facts. If, for example, on arrival in the agreed destination state the rate of remuneration is lower than that which was agreed but the victim cannot logistically withdraw consent and get herself back home, engaging in sex work may give the appearance of consent to the nature and degree of exploitation.

The consent/'means' aspect of the trafficking definition leaves the question unanswered as to how severe the interference with consent has to be – we have no specific pinpoint on the spectrum.[61] This allows for states to interpret and implement the anti-trafficking regime differently. This will potentially allow for significant difference in terms of the identification and treatment of putative victims in destination states.[62] If the terms are to be interpreted inclusively, the putative victim benefits, and the pool of recognised victims is wider. If the terms are to be interpreted exclusively and stringently, then the reach of the anti-trafficking regime is more limited.

Where an individual agrees to be smuggled for exploitation, there is prima facie a valid consent. Where the conditions of exploitation agreed to are changed, that is, where there was deception as to some conditions of the 'work' such as hours or rate of pay, then this vitiates the initial consent. However, it is questionable as to whether destination states would view this individual as trafficked, since she had consented to the transport and to the exploitation, but in different terms to those that she eventually experienced. Prima facie, this is trafficking, yet the willingness of states to recognise trafficking in such a situation where the initial

59 ibid, particularly the section entitled 'Consent and coercion in prison'.

60 *R v Moir (Sharon Carol)* [2007] EWCA Crim 3317.

61 Although Jones tried to identify such a point. See S V Jones 'Human trafficking victim identification: should consent matter?' (2012) 45 *Indiana Law Review* 483.

62 See ch 6.

giving of consent has played such an important part in the process, is uncertain; if anything, it is doubtful that they would.[63] The consent is damaged, but is the damage sufficient to negate the consent fully, therefore rendering the individual a trafficked victim who has the entitlement to rights and protections provided by the anti-trafficking regime?[64]

The difference here is less one of nature and more of quality or degree. The agreement as regards the latter, deceived, individual was always to undertake sex work, and therefore the nature remains the same. The quality and degree of the exploitation, however, is changed – deception as to the rate of pay, for example, would alter the quality of the acts consented to. This should be sufficient to vitiate consent.[65] The theory and application may vary depending upon the context, as states' legitimate interests in border protection may colour the perception of consent with respect to some putative trafficking victims.

Clearly, then, the quality of the act consented to is relevant, as domestic cases such as *Tabassum*[66] have indicated. Similarly, the nature and degree of the harm caused is relevant to consent – as domestic cases such as *Brown*[67] have shown us. *Brown* is a clear illustration of the importance of public policy in the making of decisions regarding the potential for consent to operate as a defence.[68] The transnational criminal regime applicable to human trafficking does not allow exploitation where consent to it has been obtained by significant deception, coercion etc. It does, however, allow exploitation where there is no apparent or significant deception or coercion and, therefore, there is deemed to be a valid consent.

The nature and degree of harm caused in situations of consensual and non-consensual trafficking varies sufficiently for the situations to receive different treatment. It is unfortunate, however, that the treatment of consensually exploited persons is left to be addressed wholly by domestic law. In, for example, a medical law context, the consent of a patient renders lawful the touching etc that takes place in medical procedures. Consent in a trafficking context does not negate the wrong, morally or legally – exploitation cannot be justified. In a legal sense, the migration facilitator is still in breach of legislation relating to the facilitation of the illicit border-crossing of humans,[69] and potentially also accepted domestic

63 On this point, see specifically the Anti-Trafficking Monitoring Group 'Wrong kind of victim?' (n 20) 12, where the point is made that those who agreed to come to the UK to engage in work yet were subjected to abuse and/or deception have all too often been identified as 'not trafficked', even though the trafficking definition would intend for such persons to be formally identified as 'trafficked'.

64 The bespoke rights and protections available to formally trafficked victims are discussed in ch 6.

65 See, for example, *R v Tabassum (Naveed)* [2000] 2 Cr App R 238.

66 ibid .

67 *R v Brown* [1993] 2 WLR 556, [1993] 2 All ER 75; *Laskey, Jaggard and Brown v United Kingdom* (1997) 24 EHRR 39.

68 Although it is recognised here that the decision in *Brown* is very open to criticism. See, for example, C F Stychin 'Unmanly diversions: the construction of the homosexual body (politic) in English law' (1994) 32(3) *Osgoode Hall Law Journal* 503–36.

69 Including smuggling offences. The Immigration Act 1971 s 25 (substituted by the Nationality, Immigration and Asylum Act 2002 s 143) creates an offence of assisting unlawful immigration

labour standards,[70] although the position as regards the latter depends upon how prostitution is dealt with by the legislative framework of the destination state.

As a matter of public policy, the transnational criminal regime applicable to trafficking and smuggling could go further and provide for criminalisation of would-be traffickers who fall into the grey area between trafficking and smuggling, as the extent of the harm caused should be the concern of the criminal law. What this means for the 'victim' who has been 'less than trafficked' but 'more than smuggled' (at least in a moral sense) is another matter, and will be discussed later. As a protective measure or a matter of public policy, then, the law may be framed so as not to deem relevant the giving of consent in certain situations (which fall below the formal 'trafficking' threshold and 'means'), at least to the extent that the justificatory scope of consent is limited and the broadest possible conception of 'victim' can be drawn upon.

## 5.5 The effects of recognising consent

In order for the trafficker to be convicted, the prosecution must show that women have been transported for exploitation as a result of coercion or otherwise have not consented to being brought to the destination state. Similarly, in order for a putative trafficked victim to be conclusively deemed to be a trafficked victim, those charged with identifying her as such need to be able to determine whether or not she was forced or coerced etc. This test poses several difficulties.

The first is the evidential burden produced by the need to show lack of consent and the presence of coercion. It cannot be assumed that the criteria, indicators and training provided to the authorities charged with identifying victims of trafficking will always be adequate in this respect. The second problem is the potential for the existence of consent to act as a defence for the would-be trafficker. The third is the most pertinent for the discussion in this book and concerns the denial of victim status as regards the trafficked person who is deemed to have consented. This feeds into the fourth problem: that of the potential criminality of the victim as a result of her role in breaching domestic law(s).

### *5.5.1 The evidential problem*

Primarily, there is the evidential problem. One might ask whether, 'where consent is equivocal or uncertain, (should) we take a precautionary approach or do we

(known as facilitation) and also covers acts previously dealt with under the old offence of 'harbouring'. Immigration Act 1971 s 25A (also substituted by the Nationality, Immigration and Asylum Act 2002 s 143) creates an offence of knowingly facilitating the arrival or entry of another into the UK for gain, coupled with knowledge or reasonable cause to believe that the individual is an asylum seeker. Immigration Act 1971 s 25B(1) (also substituted by the Nationality, Immigration and Asylum Act 2002 s 143) addresses assisting entry into the UK in breach of deportation of exclusion order. Immigration Act 1971 s 25B(3) provides for assisting entry/remaining of an excluded person.

70 As regards, say, the provision of a minimum wage, or other conditions of the 'work' undertaken.

treat the consent as given?'[71] Coercion of some form must be shown in order to vitiate consent, but what of those cases where this simply is not clear? The problems associated with determining the presence of, or lack of, consent in rape cases provides an example of the difficulties presented here.[72] Bhabha makes the following observation as regards consent or coercion in situations of human trafficking:

> The distinction between coercion and consent remains useful in some circumstances. There are clear-cut cases that fall at one or the other end of the spectrum, and they should be treated accordingly. Where the distinction is not clear, however, significant investment of administrative resources will be necessary to ensure that basic human-rights protections are not violated by thoughtless categorizations designed to serve exclusionary agendas and improve deportation statistics.

Wherever the lines are drawn, they must involve the discretion of experienced and skilled professionals. Determining who is coerced and who has consented – whether at the border or in the workplace – requires detailed case histories and considerable background knowledge about states of origin, states of transit and employment arrangements within particular industries. Once this process has been undertaken – and grass-roots border-patrol agents, immigration officials, NGOs, community associations, newspaper reporters, trade unions and other labour rights groups should be involved as consultants – then sensible determinations can be made.[73]

As the above statement illustrates, proving coercion is likely in many cases to be an arduous and difficult task. As a result, the coercion/consent debate provides

71 Beyleveld and Brownsword *Consent in the Law* (n 1) 22.

72 At present, 6% of reported rapes result in prosecution in the UK. See Home Office 'The Stern Review' Government Equalities Office (2010) http://www.equalities.gov.uk/pdf/Stern_Review_of_Rape_Reporting_1FINAL.pdf (last accessed 1 May 2011). See also *R v A* [2001] UKHL 25, where tensions between s 41 of the Youth Justice and Criminal Evidence Act 1999 (YJCEA 1999) (which prohibits the giving of evidence and cross examination about any sexual behaviour of the complainant except with leave of the court, in certain circumstances outlined throughout the subsections of the provision) and art 6 of the ECHR were apparent. The relevant provision was s 41(3)(c), which states that: 'This subsection applies if the evidence or question relates to a relevant issue in the case and either … it is an issue of consent and the sexual behaviour of the complainant to which the evidence or question relates is alleged to have been, in any respect, so similar (i) to any sexual behaviour of the complainant which (according to evidence adduced or to be adduced by or on behalf of the accused) took place as part of the event which is the subject matter of the charge against the accused, or (ii) to any other sexual behaviour of the complainant which (according to such evidence) took place at or about the same time as that event, that the similarity cannot reasonably be explained as a coincidence'. It was held in that case that the YJCEA 1999 s 41(3)(c) should, where necessary, be construed according to the interpretative obligation under the Human Rights Act 1998 s 3, and furthermore by considering the need to aim to protect complainants from humiliating questions, or indignity. It was found that evidence of a complainant's previous sexual history was admissible where that evidence, and any questioning which concerned it, was so relevant to the issue of consent that to not include it would raise art 6 concerns.

73 J Bhabha 'Reforming immigration policy' (n 56).

an opportunity for legal representatives that could provide a real barrier to the successful prosecution of those facilitating migration and subsequently exploiting the putative 'victim'.

### *5.5.2 Consent as a defence for the trafficker*

As regards the second problem identified above, whether or not consent should act as a defence in a trafficking context, the matter is debatable. It is necessary to make the point that 'consent' here is not, as it usually is in the criminal context to do with the *mens rea* of the defendant or giving him a defence but with establishing an element of the *actus reus*, such as coercion or deception. In the most basic sense, one would generally accept that the presence of consent indicates a lack of any crime. The reality is not quite this simple.

Harmful activities were consented to in the domestic case of *Wilson*,[74] and also in the case of *Brown*,[75] which concerned consensual sado-masochistic activities between adults. In the former, consent was accepted as a defence to the harm caused. In the latter, the domestic courts found that consent was not a defence to the crime. The European Court of Human Rights (ECtHR) allowed that the identification of criminal harm that could not be lawfully consented to was largely for each state to decide.[76]

It can be contended that:

> When individuals consent to undergo medical operations, to engage in sexual intercourse, to open their homes to police searches, or to testify against themselves in court, they convert what would otherwise be an invasion of their person or their rights into a harmless or justified activity.[77]

This view is overly simplistic. Some activities require strong justification in order for them to be rendered harmless, and as to what these activities are there is some disagreement in academic discussion.[78] It is questionable whether exploitation can ever be justified. Consent can be transformative; it can, in an extreme sense, as suggested by Hurd, work its 'moral magic' and – according to the example that Hurd gives – transform rape into love-making, and trespass into a dinner party.[79] Not every situation is capable of being disposed of with such a simplistic formula.

If consent is simply seen as justification for the doing of 'something', then this does not go far enough. This justification does not take into account whether the doing of this 'something' is right or wrong, at least in a moral if not in a legal

74 *R v Wilson (Alan Thomas)* [1997] QB 47.

75 *R v Brown* (n 67); *Laskey, Jaggard, and Brown v United Kingdom* (n 67).

76 *Laskey, Jaggard, and Brown v United Kingdom* (n 67).

77 G P Fletcher *Basic Concepts of Legal Thought* (Oxford University Press, Oxford, 1996) 109.

78 See, for example, M M Dempsey and J Herring 'Why sexual penetration requires justification' (2007) 27(3) *Oxford Journal of Legal Studies* 467–91.

79 H Hurd 'Was the frog prince sexually molested? A review of Peter Westen's "The logic of consent"'(2005) 103 *Michigan Law Review* 1329, 1329.

sense. Exploitation of human beings unquestionably has a moral dimension. Does consent in a trafficking context render the exploitative activity harmless or justified? Few would answer 'yes'; 'consent functions as a "procedural" rather than as a "substantive" (or, "on the merits") form of justification'.[80] Should consent in a trafficking context provide a legal 'flak-jacket'[81] to protect the would-be trafficker? If the answer were 'yes', then this surely would not be a wholly satisfactory situation. Paternalism in this context does have its place. It is for this reason that, even in the face of an ostensible consent, we can ask for consideration of concessions for the 'consensually trafficked'.[82]

There is argument to be drawn upon from a public interest perspective; the 'wider social harm' must be considered – consent should be no defence if it is 'injurious to the public, as well as the person injured'.[83] Consent should not preclude an otherwise trafficked person from asserting that he or she has been wronged – a line must be drawn, beyond which consent is no defence. Where the trafficker stands trial, the burden of proof is on the prosecution to show coercion in order to prove lack of consent. Uncertainty as to the limits of what constitutes 'coercion' in this context, coupled with the fact that initial consent is often given, renders the issue more difficult to prove.

### *5.5.3 Denial of victim status*

As regards denial of victim status under the trafficking instruments, the three main instruments considered in this book all make provision for some form or another of consideration of support (or requirement of support and protection) for victims, whereas the Smuggling Protocol extends no such status to the smuggled person. Chapter 2 outlined the basic provisions contained within the main instruments considered in this book, and Chapter 6 will go on to consider these victim-specific provisions in depth, while Chapter 7 will address the concerns of those who fall into the void between trafficking and smuggling.

The would-be trafficked person who is deemed to have consented falls in the grey area between the trafficking and smuggling definitions and is left in limbo. This allows the potential for destination states, in the situation where coercion cannot be shown, to deny the ostensibly 'consenting' trafficked person protection and support, the outcome of which may include criminalising the person for offences that have been committed by the person through trafficking-related compulsion.[84] In terms of maintaining border integrity, controlling immigration and meeting quotas, this may well be in the state's interests.

Under the continuing existence of a definition that recognises consent, it is

80 Beyleveld and Brownsword *Consent in the Law* (n 1) 61.

81 Lord Donaldson in *Re W (A Minor) (Medical Treatment)* [1992] 4 All ER 627, 635.

82 See ch 7.

83 Stephen J in *R v Coney* (1882) 8 QBD 534, 549.

84 This is evidenced through case law, as discussed in ch 6. See *R v O* [2008] EWCA Crim 2835, Re *LM* [2010] EWCA Crim 2327, [2011] 1 Cr App R 12, [2011] Crim LR 425 and *R v N and LE* [2012] EWCA Crim 189.

possible to argue that the consenting trafficked person both does, and does not, deserve to be accorded victim status. Arguments 'for' include the fact that consent does not necessarily cancel out the existence of serious abuse through exploitation. The consenting trafficked person is still potentially a victim of unacceptable circumstances flowing from the exploitative conditions of her 'labour'. Arguments 'against' include the perspective that the consenting trafficked person has not been coerced in the manner of the non-consenting trafficked person. In fact, the person has willingly and knowingly agreed to breach borders and domestic immigration laws. This brings us to the third issue: that of the potential criminality of the trafficked person.

### *5.5.4 Criminality of trafficked victims and of the 'consensually trafficked'*

The focus of anti-trafficking legislation must be borne in mind. It should offer a combination of the criminalisation of the activities of the trafficker, coupled with protective human rights-based measures as regards the trafficked person. None of the Smuggling or Trafficking Protocols, the CoE Trafficking Convention or the EU 2011 Directive envisages criminality for the migrant in terms of his or her illicit entry into the destination state, even though smuggling is viewed as being of a largely consensual nature on the part of the migrant. The question of criminality is left for states to determine where smuggled migrants are concerned. Neither does the international anti-trafficking regime envisage criminalisation of victims where they have been compelled to commit offences as a result of having been trafficked – this particular matter is addressed in depth in Chapter 6.

With respect to the 'consenting' trafficked person, it can be argued that, on the face of it, it is difficult to justify criminalisation for, say, immigration offences, as this undermines the purpose of anti-trafficking legislation, one of the aims of which is to combat exploitation. However, tensions will arise in this respect concerning breaches of immigration law, and border integrity. Conversely, if there is existence of true consent, then the 'consensually' trafficked person will often have committed an immigration offence. It is difficult here to maintain an argument for non-criminalisation, and it might be suggested that as a matter of course, prosecutorial discretion – whether prosecution is in the public interest – should be used, particularly where women have been exploited and remain vulnerable. This will be addressed further in Chapter 7.

Essentially, the issue seems to be not whether consent in a trafficking context should be deemed meaningless, more whether or not it should be deemed irrelevant, even in the face of coercion or force etc. Alternatives to the current situation created by the trafficking and smuggling definitions, which encompass the above-mentioned problems, will now be considered.

## 5.6 Where next? Alternatives to the current situation

The consent debate could potentially leave genuinely trafficked persons in a state of limbo, on the wrong side of the law, and denied any victim status. They may be subject to legal sanctions and/or peremptory removal, with the destination state struggling to obtain prosecution against the trafficker. This aspect of human trafficking legislation is a contentious issue, but ultimately the inclusion of this issue in legal definition takes major steps in clarifying what trafficking actually is in a legal sense.

Inclusion of the consent element in the trafficking definition creates a hierarchy of severity of exploitative migration. This means that those who have ostensibly consented to migrate and be subjected to exploitative conditions are indeed exploited in a way that undermines human dignity but they have not, in a current legal sense, been trafficked. The trafficking and smuggling definitions, therefore, have created a loophole. The definition of smuggling includes solely an 'action' element.[85] The definition of trafficking includes 'action, 'means' and 'purpose'. Where there is consent, we are left with 'action' and 'purpose'.

The above-mentioned situation is not simply smuggling, as it goes beyond the ambit of the Smuggling Protocol. It also may not be trafficking, as it falls short of the requirement for ostensible coercion or some other 'means'. It is, therefore, unclear what exactly this type of exploitative migration is and where it falls on the spectrum. That which may tentatively (yet perhaps realistically) be deemed a 'lesser' form of exploitative migration than trafficking, that is, where consent has been given, can and should be addressed by international legislation. Consent lends legitimacy to traffick-related activity. Even in the face of consent, such activity still merits suppression and punishment, beyond simply addressing the breach of immigration laws that it may involve.

Hernandez-Truyol and Larson consider 'relations within which an individual consents to conditions of labour that cannot be reconciled with human dignity'.[86] In a smuggling context, the focus is on the smuggler, his illegal activity and the damage that it does. Consent in the context of the trafficking definition shifts the focus from the damage done, and keeps the focus on the victim and the existence or otherwise of ostensible consent or lack thereof.

Consent exists largely to protect the stereotypical 'perfect' trafficked victim,[87] the woman who is abducted and forced into prostitution wholly against her will, and who clearly does not comprise the entire victim pool. The following proposals suggest alternatives to the current situation created by the definition provided within the UN Trafficking Protocol and reproduced within the other main instruments considered in this book.[88] These alternatives will potentially mean that those who – on application of the criteria used to identify victims of human

85 See art 3 of the Protocol against the Smuggling of Migrants by Land, Sea and Air, Supplementing the United Nations Convention against Transnational Organised Crime (adopted November 2000 by United Nations General Assembly Resolution A/RES/55/25, entered into force 28 January 2004) (Smuggling Protocol).

86 Hernandez-Truyol and Larson 'Sexual labour and human rights' (n 48) 394.

87 See R Uy 'Blinded by red lights: why sex trafficking discourse should shift away from sex and the "perfect victim" paradigm' (2011) *Berkeley Journal of Gender, Law and Justice* 204–19.

88 That is, the CoE Trafficking Convention and the EU 2011 Directive.

trafficking[89] – do not display ostensible 'indicators' or signs of coercion and so are deemed to have consented are not left in a legal vacuum.

Progress can realistically follow one of two routes. Either consent must be deemed irrelevant in a trafficking context, even in the absence of coercion or other 'means', or specific measures must be taken or legislation enacted to address situations of 'consensual facilitated migration for the purposes of labour exploitation', as a category separate to both smuggling and trafficking.

### 5.6.1 Rendering consent irrelevant in the context of human trafficking

Abramson states that the Trafficking Protocol 'offers the opportunity to urge state party compliance in a way that protects trafficked people without making a formal pronouncement on their ability or inability to consent'.[90] However, deeming consent to be irrelevant in a trafficking context is not about denial of the capacity to make choices about one's own life. Rather, it is about effectively combating a phenomenon that constitutes criminal activity coupled with serious exploitation. Feinberg considers reconciliation of the prohibition against contracting oneself into slavery with maintaining respect for freedom of contract. He suggests that when faced with fallible tests of voluntariness, then a presumption of involuntariness is more preferable than the alternative.[91]

If this route were to be taken, and consent were deemed to be irrelevant in the context of trafficking, it would be necessary to draft an instrument providing a definition of 'trafficking in humans' that recognised trafficking as an activity involving an element of transport, and an element of exploitation of labour, including sexual labour, 'regardless of consent' or 'by any means'. An instrument that supersedes both the trafficking and smuggling definitions is a possible option, but smuggling is not characterised by exploitation in the same way that trafficking is and so this may not be the most comprehensive way to proceed. However, a definition that covers a wider group of people retains what should be the essential focus of anti-trafficking legislation; the criminalisation of perpetrators and the protection of exploited persons. Even if valid consent only exists in a very limited number of situations, the current existence of this element excludes some – perhaps many, and at times incorrectly – from the protection offered by the legal instruments forming the anti-trafficking regime, and makes it harder for others who did not consent to get the protection that they need and deserve under these instruments.

A definition tailored to fit this proposal might read along the following lines:

> 'Trafficking in persons' shall mean the recruitment, transportation, transfer, harbouring or receipt of persons, by any means, for the purpose of

89 See ch 6.

90 Abramson 'Beyond consent' (n 13) 497.

91 J Feinberg 'Legal paternalism' in *Rights, Justice, and the Bounds of Liberty* (Princeton University Press, Princeton, 1980).

> exploitation. Exploitation shall include, at a minimum, the exploitation of the prostitution of others or other forms of sexual exploitation, forced labour or services, slavery or practices similar to slavery, servitude or the removal of organs …

Such an approach would no doubt be unpopular with state parties who were considering signing a treaty with provisions to that effect, and consequently this may not be the best way to proceed.

### *5.6.2 The creation/recognition of a new category: concessions for the 'consensually trafficked'*

Consent operates as a 'transformative channel between the harmful and the harmless, and also thereby between the permissible, the condemnable, and the criminal'.[92] Consequently, addressing formal trafficking and 'consensual' trafficking for the purpose of sexual exploitation both in the same way, with the same instruments, may not provide a satisfactory answer. Although the two do not sit at opposite ends of a spectrum of what is harmful and what is harmless, they do indicate different degrees of harm and therefore, in a 'fair labelling' sense, they need to be addressed separately, however unsatisfactory this may be in some cases.

As opposed to rendering consent irrelevant in the context of human trafficking, the other potential route to be taken involves recognition of a third category as wholly separate from trafficking and smuggling: that of 'consensual facilitated migration for the purpose of exploitation', or 'smuggling for the purpose of exploitation', or similar. This approach is less paternalistic than the one outlined above, as it accepts that there may be valid consent, even to exploitative work in the sex trade; however, it does not allow it to negate the wrongness of exploitation fully. If it must be maintained that, legally speaking, human trafficking cannot involve any consensual transportation for the purpose of exploitation, then this new category allows for criminalisation of serious exploitative activity that undermines human dignity, even in the face of consent. Furthermore, this new category allows the potential for concessions to be made for victims in borderline cases of trafficking, or where, for example, ostensible evidence of coercion etc cannot be shown. Smugglers, in the most basic sense, commit a wrong against the country whose borders have been breached. Those who 'traffick' even consenting persons commit a wrong that far exceeds the breach of borders and involves harm to human beings and undermines the dignity of the human.

To determine a precise point on a spectrum of consent and submission, or free consent and coerced consent, is a 'philosophical conundrum'.[93] In the context of the creation of a new category of consenting trafficked persons in the broad spectrum of facilitated migration, it is perhaps possible to achieve some concession as to allow support and assistance (for 'victims') without fully going into the realms of

92 Munro 'Constructing consent' (n 8) 924.

93 R Stone *Offences Against the Person* (Cavendish Publishing, London, 1999) 147.

paternalism (that is, not opting for ignoring the autonomous choice of a consenting agent to consent to migrate to work in the sex trade). It is undoubtedly possible to achieve criminalisation (of would-be traffickers).

In terms of policy, more people may benefit if it is not accepted that consent may be given by a trafficked person to transport into exploitative conditions.[94] However, some may find it difficult to concede fully that consent should be rendered irrelevant. If we take the following completely polarised examples: at one end of the spectrum, we have the person who is abducted and forced into some form of exploitative labour. At the opposite end of the spectrum is the person who is earning low wages at home – although enough to survive – who consents to be 'trafficked' to, say, Cornwall to pick turnips for 16 hours a day for low/exploitative pay but at a higher rate of pay than the person was receiving while working at home. The second person has given full consent, but is still being exploited by working long hours for very low pay. Since these polarised scenarios differ in both degree and nature, it is difficult to concede that they can be deemed identical and, therefore, properly addressed in the same way, by the same instrument. Coerced trafficking can include elements of violence and control that go beyond the scope of 'trafficking' against a backdrop of consent. Someone who trafficks an inanimate object, such as firearms,[95] should not be seen in the same light as one who trafficks human beings who are capable of choice.

A potential definition tailored to fit this proposal might read as follows:

> 'Facilitated migration for the purpose of labour exploitation' shall mean the recruitment, transportation, transfer, harboring, or receipt of persons, with the consent of that person, for the purpose of exploitation.

In order for this proposal to be implemented, the meaning of 'exploitation' or 'labour exploitation' – both to include commercial sex work – would have to be considered in some depth. This issue would either have to be determined as 'a question of degree depending on circumstances'[96] or, alternatively a minimum level would have to be established. It is suggested here that a suitable definition of 'exploitation' could be offset against a standard compliant with domestic labour legislation. This definition would also cover the exploitation of prostitution, on the basis that sex work is 'sexual labour' and should be viewed as a form of labour. Abramson offered a definition of trafficking in persons which, although intended to address trafficking regardless of consent, proposed the following as regards 'exploitation of labour':

94 Abramson 'Beyond consent' (n 13) 493.

95 See, for example, Protocol against the Illicit Manufacturing of and Trafficking in Firearms, Their Parts and Components and Ammunition, supplementing the United Nations Convention against Transnational Organized Crime (adopted June 2001 by United Nations General Assembly Resolution A/RES/55/255), which defines illicit trafficking as: 'the import, export, acquisition, sale delivery, movement or transfer of firearms …', thus demonstrating only an 'action' element.

96 Stephen J in *R v Coney* (n 83).

> … for the purpose of the exploitation of their labor, as defined through illegal work or legally recognized work that is carried out in a pattern of serious non-conformity with existing labor laws.[97]

Similarly, labour exploitation as a 'purpose' element of human trafficking was considered in a European Union Commission Proposal for a Framework Decision on combating human trafficking.[98] Article 1 defined it as:

> … the purpose of exploiting him or her in the production of goods or provision of services in infringement of labour standards governing working conditions, salaries and health and safety.

Exploitation, then, depends not on the nature of the work, but on the degree; that is, voluntary prostitution juxtaposed against exploitative prostitution, with the latter falling below the accepted labour standards of the state in question. Both of the above-mentioned examples provide a sound basis from which to proceed in developing a definition of 'exploitation' in the context of sex work as an accepted form of labour.

The recognition of 'consensual' trafficking and what it means for the 'victims' (if they can be so called) is addressed in depth in Chapter 7.

### *5.6.3 The effect of the implementation of these proposals*

Either of the above proposals recognises the potential for validity of consent in a trafficking context, but they differ in how the presence of consent is to be legally addressed. The implementation of either of these proposals allows for some resolution of the four problem areas identified above. If the first proposal is followed (that is, that consent be deemed irrelevant), then the evidential problem is eradicated as it is not necessary to prove lack of consent. However, in terms of the second proposal the evidential problem still exists, as it is still necessary to determine lack of consent in order to determine which category the individual case falls into: either that of 'trafficking' (non-consensual) or 'consensual facilitated migration for the purpose of exploitative labour', that is, where one has been 'consensually trafficked'.

Either proposal cancels out the potential for consent to serve as a full defence for the perpetrator, as there is criminality of his activity in both instances – and not simply that resulting from breaches of immigration law. Some may struggle to accept criminalisation in the face of consent, on the basis that if a person voluntarily accepts exploitative labour conditions, there is no wrong to be remedied.

97 Abramson 'Beyond consent' (n 13) 499.

98 European Union (2001) Communication from the Commission to the European Council and the European Parliament: Combating Trafficking in Human Beings and Combating Sexual Exploitation of Children and Child Pornography, Proposals for a Council Framework Decision on Combating Trafficking in Human Beings and on Combating Sexual Exploitation of Children and Child Pornography COM(2001) 854.

However, it can be contended that as a defence it should only go so far – without being overly paternalistic, there can realistically be limits on what is considered 'harmless' in the face of consent. In *Donovan*,[99] it was argued that:

> If an act is unlawful in the sense of being in itself a criminal act, it is plain that it cannot be rendered lawful because the person to whose detriment it is done consents to it. No person can license another to commit a crime. So far as the criminal law is concerned, therefore, where the act charged is in itself unlawful, it can never be necessary to prove absence of consent ...[100]

If we transpose the above into a trafficking/exploitative migration context, the movement of persons and the exploitation of these persons, regardless of consent, potentially infringes domestic immigration and labour laws. Facilitating illicit border-crossing and exploiting the labour of another are unacceptable, irrespective of the giving of consent. Arguably, 'Where human dignity is independently compromised, irrespective of whether the act in question is freely performed, consent is not material'.[101]

Owing to the difficulties of determining a valid consent or the presence of coercion, and the obvious gap between those who are trafficked and those who are smuggled, international law should provide for criminalisation of the would-be trafficker despite the presence of ostensible consent, and perhaps treat the lack of evidence of coercion as a 'mitigating factor' or similar. The effect of this would be that the would-be trafficker is not simply treated as a smuggler – he must pay for his part in the exploitation of the 'victim'. Consent does not negate the wrong that undermines human dignity and the basic values of society and, therefore, it should not absolve the trafficker of any responsibility for his actions.

As regards the denial of victim status, the former proposal eradicates this issue, as 'victims' will be victims regardless of consent, although their treatment may vary according to which instruments are ratified by each state and what those instruments provide for. It would be difficult to maintain an argument for exactly the same access to the same rights for those who ostensibly consented, unless the instrument was drafted so that no line was drawn between 'types' of victim. If consent is deemed irrelevant, the 'victim' is more likely to be portrayed as a victim, and therefore the state will be more likely to accord 'victim' status.[102]

The latter proposal is more problematic in terms of the denial of victim status (and therefore the bespoke rights created for victims of trafficking) as not all would agree that the exploited migrant who falls into this category deserves comparable victim status. Those who have given an ostensible consent (which may possibly be

99 [1934] 2 KB 498.
100 ibid 507.
101 Beyleveld and Brownsword *Consent in the Law* (n 1), 17.
102 J Chaung 'Redirecting the debate over trafficking in women: definitions, paradigms and contexts' (1998) 11 *Harvard Human Rights Journal* 65, 85.

merely 'assumed' owing to lack of adverse indicators) might be left less deserving of full victim status and the protection that this provides.

On the one hand, it can be argued that consent does not destroy the duty on the state to protect the otherwise-trafficked person. On the other hand, as Bhabha notes: 'Having *chosen* to migrate illegally, smuggled illegals are considered less deserving of protection'.[103] Thus, the voluntary nature of consensual trafficking forms a potential barrier to victim status. However, consensually trafficked people have been more than smuggled – they have also been exploited, thus placing them in a grey area, somewhere between victim and complicit actor. The exploitation taking place against a backdrop of consent arguably benefits both parties – the 'consensually trafficked' person earns more than she did back at home, and the migration facilitator/trafficker profits from the exploitation of that person, although both parties cannot be said to be on an equal footing.

Denial of victim status will, however, adversely affect those who did not consent but were unable to show lack of consent. Balos states that: 'The evolution of language in human rights documents has increasingly made the choice or consent of the trafficked woman the linchpin to determine if a human rights violation has occurred'.[104] It may be desirable to allow consent to determine the presence of human trafficking, but not necessarily that which may arguably be deemed a lesser 'wrong' – exploitative consensual migration. The fact remains that the consenting 'victim' has been the object of serious ill-treatment at the hands of her exploiter(s). There may be, at the least, a case to be made for a sympathetic 'victim of exploitation' based approach to be considered on a case-by-case basis. Depending on various factors, such as the nature and degree of exploitation experienced, different 'victims' will have different needs. Issues such as the potential for reprisals from the would-be-traffickers or similar would justify consideration of protection in the same way as it would where legally recognised non-consenting trafficked victims are concerned. The treatment and protection of victims of human trafficking, and those who might be deemed 'consensually trafficked', will be discussed in Chapters 6 and 7.

As regards the potential criminality of the trafficked person, once again the former proposal fully eradicates this issue. Consideration of this issue under the latter proposal necessitates return to the justification laid down previously; that the focus of anti-trafficking legislation and anti-smuggling legislation is to criminalise the agent, not the trafficked or smuggled individual.[105] This is particularly true as regards the Organised Crime Convention and the Smuggling and Trafficking Protocols thereto, as these instruments are intended to combat organised crime and the activities flowing from it. Therefore, the organised crime groups are the intended targets for criminalisation. Further, the existence of exploitative labour undermines human dignity and constitutes intolerable treatment of individuals, and so these are the central issues that need to be tackled – not the potential

103 Bhabha 'Reforming immigration policy' (n 56).

104 Balos 'The wrong way to equality' (n 6) 173.

105 This matter is considered further in ch 7.

criminality of the migrant. Of course, that is not the end of the story. States have a legitimate concern in maintaining border integrity and therefore require the potential to criminalise and prosecute those who willingly flout immigration laws. This issue will be specifically examined in terms of trafficked and 'consensually' trafficked persons in Chapters 6 and 7.

## 5.7 Conclusion

The aim of the consent caveat in the trafficking definition in the Protocol is apparently '... to pre-empt a possible defence that there has been no trafficking because the alleged victim was a willing participant'.[106] To remove this issue entirely, trafficking could have been classified as an offence regardless of consent, but then this would not reflect the level of culpability of the trafficker in all cases. The consent caveat also causes the opposite problem to arise – the corollary is that consideration of lack of consent allows for victims to be classified as otherwise owing to evidential problems.

We know that consent provides a 'procedural justification' for an act or omission.[107] Whereas consent may lend legitimacy to trafficking-related activity, the use of coercion, force or other relevant factors will damage that consent and render it ineffective. The introduction of a lack of consent element as determinative as to the existence of human trafficking places the emphasis firmly on the coerced or uncoerced nature of the activity. In a given 'trafficking' situation, where none of the coercive 'means' is proved to have been used, and therefore lack of consent cannot be shown, the individual is deemed to have consented. The transformative nature of consent therefore means that that which would otherwise be termed 'trafficking' now becomes a form of consensual facilitated migration for sex work or labour in exploitative conditions. The resulting legal status of the 'consenting' individual is that she is viewed as merely another illicit migrant or smuggled sex worker.

The consent/coercion 'dichotomy' created by the trafficking definition has been a subject of debate in recent years. The most basic approach would simply say: '[t]hat which in the absence of consent would be wrong is rendered permissible by the giving of consent'.[108] This approach has been shown to be too simplistic in the context of trafficking and facilitated migration for the purpose of sexual exploitation. The trafficking definition shifts the focus so that consent or the absence thereof is the central issue, as opposed to the subsequent exploitation of the trafficked person. It assumes 'pure' cases of coerced and uncoerced trafficking whereas, in reality, cases are rarely this clear-cut.

The current situation with the legal anti-trafficking regime recognises the traffickers who are the criminals, the trafficked persons who are the victims and

106 R Piotrowicz and J Redpath-Cross 'Human trafficking and smuggling' in B Opeskin, R Perruchoud, J Redpath-Cross (eds) *Foundations of International Migration Law* (Cambridge University Press, 2012) 234–59, 239.

107 See Beyleveld and Brownsword *Consent in the Law* (n 1) 125.

108 See D Archard 'Book reviews' (2007) 24(2) *Journal of Applied Philosophy* 209.

the trafficked persons who consent, and therefore by definition have not been trafficked and therefore are not 'victims' in this context. The latter comprises a category of persons who have uncertain status.[109] As a result, anti-trafficking legislation has the potential to act as a barrier to obtaining prosecutions and protecting victims of exploitation and human rights abuse. An ability to give valid consent in this context should be recognised, but we should not be too quick to do so in any case, and the real point at issue is whether consent should ever be deemed irrelevant. From a 'fair labeling perspective', consent must be deemed relevant. However, consent must be valid – care is needed, as full and informed consent may be rare and the appearance of consent may obscure the coercive reality.

The exercise of self-determination and free (or 'free') choice does not preclude the existence of exploitation that has been consented to. Simply because a woman agrees, in the absence of a preferable choice, to work as a prostitute for an exploitatively low wage does not mean that she does not suffer 'harm', or at least that she does not have needs – for example – for assistance and support once discovered. This is particularly the case as it is evident that correct identification of victims of human trafficking is not always straightforward.

If it is to be accepted that exploitation is the focus and that consent is irrelevant, then there is the potential to draft an instrument that supersedes the definition provided within the Trafficking Protocol and other relevant instruments,[110] and which addresses trafficking regardless of consent. This approach, however, is rejected here – one who trafficks a human being who is deemed capable of choice cannot be treated in the same fashion as one who trafficks an inanimate object. On this basis, a distinction must be made between the agent who kidnaps his victim, and the agent who aids the 'victim' in her migration into exploitative circumstances. This illustrates the fact that, where human beings are concerned, responsibility must be apportioned accordingly: if it is accepted in a given situation that full, informed consent has been provided, then the 'agent' who would otherwise be labelled a trafficker is perhaps little more than a facilitator in the exploitative migration process. However, he must be held to account for his part in the facilitated migration and subsequent exploitation of the person in question.

If it is to be accepted that a person can give full, informed consent in a trafficking context, then 'consensual facilitated migration for the purpose of exploitation', or 'smuggling of humans for the purpose of exploitation', is a new category existing as a result of the loophole created by the grey area between the Trafficking and Smuggling Protocols (and therefore the other main instruments discussed in this book that form the anti-trafficking regime). As the discussion in this chapter has highlighted, the lines between these categories are often blurred anyway, without there being a need for a black spot category created by the consent debate. However, this black spot category clearly exists – either because consent is clearly given, consent is ostensible, or the presence of any coercion etc is not clearly, objectively present according, for example, to the 'indicators' used by those

109 Abramson 'Beyond consent' (n 13) 500.

110 Including the CoE Trafficking Convention and the EU 2011 Directive.

charged with identifying trafficked persons.[111] This is inherently problematic, and exactly what this means for the consenting 'victim' will be discussed in Chapter 7.

However we are to proceed on this issue, the focus on the harm done[112] must be retained, and the aim of anti-trafficking legislation must be borne constantly in mind: 'There is … abundant authority for saying that no consent can render that innocent which is in fact dangerous'.[113] The public interest surely lies more in combating exploitative trafficking and migration-related activity than in becoming tangled up in the issue of consent.

The following chapter will consider – in more depth than previously done in this book – the international legal regime applicable to victims of trafficking. This will include discussion and analysis of the bespoke regime applicable to formally trafficked victims, the international legal protection regime that is applicable to all human beings in states who are party to these regimes and, finally, recommendations for dealing with trafficked persons.

111 See ch 6.
112 See Balos 'The wrong way to equality' (n 6) 149.
113 Mathew J in *R v Coney* (n 83) 547.

# 6 The 'victim-centred' approach to tackling trafficking: determining who the victims are and how they should be treated

## 6.1 Introduction

In the UK there are an undetermined but considerable number of irregular migrants. It must be borne in mind from the outset that states have a very broad right to set the policy and adopt the law to control the entry to and to regulate the residence in and removal from their territory of non-nationals.[1] Some of these people will, however, be entitled to some protection against removal, despite their irregular entry. These entitlements may be general – all persons in the UK are, for example, entitled not to be removed to a destination where there is a real risk of serious ill-treatment. The entitlements may apply only to members of a specific class, such as refugees, who enjoy a more nuanced protection against removal. To this list of groups to which these considerations apply, we can now add victims of human trafficking.

The instruments considered throughout this book, which form the anti-trafficking regime, include Articles outlining the purpose of the instrument, which includes protecting and assisting victims – and respecting their human rights. The growing recognition of this criminal activity and the human rights abuses that it involves have resulted in legislation and action on an international, European and domestic level. Policy objectives, however, have until recently been predominantly geared towards the criminalisation and prosecution of traffickers. Efforts to provide victim support and to show adequate consideration for the many trafficked victims, who may be unable or unwilling to cooperate with state authorities in criminal proceedings and give evidence against their traffickers, have been insufficient. A human rights-based, victim-centred approach should take account of the effect that trafficking and any subsequent sexual exploitation has on the victims, and provide for their support and rehabilitation.

The drafting and enactment of any legislation to deal with trafficking must cover the prohibition, prosecution and punishment of traffickers, as well as the protection of victims. Legislation that deals with only some of these aspects must be complemented by legislation to address the other(s). Piotrowicz correctly observes that these two aspects of trafficking – namely the prosecution of traffickers and

1 *Moustaquim v Belgium* (Application no 12313/86) [1991] ECHR 3, (1991) 13 EHRR 802.

the protection of victims – are not separable, and therefore should not be dealt with separately.[2] All too often, trafficking victims are treated not as victims but as criminals,[3] either because of their involvement in prostitution or their status as illegal immigrants.

In some cases, trafficked victims may be deported because of their immigration status, with insufficient regard for the gravity of their situation. This may be particularly so where the 'indicators'[4] used by those charged with identifying victims are lacking, or fail to bring to the surface the presence of 'coercion' etc, giving the trafficked victim the appearance of being yet another 'smuggled' (and willing) prostitute. It is not impossible to conceive of borderline cases, or cases where genuine victims will be misidentified.[5]

This chapter aims to analyse the international, European and UK stance taken with respect to providing for victims of trafficking for the purpose of sexual exploitation to date. Although this chapter necessarily enquires into the range of benefits that the victim might be entitled to, it also raises and considers the centrally important matter of how we decide effectively who is a victim and how we deal with those who are victims. Ultimately, conclusions will be drawn to the effect that the danger is that the implementation of the state obligations as regards victim support measures in the UK still does not go far enough in achieving adequate victim protection. It will be shown that there are gains to be made from adopting measures that are yet more sympathetic to the victim than those in place at present.

Primarily, section 6.2 will consider the previous poor performance of the UK Government as regards implementation or consideration of victim support measures. It will address why there is a need for a victim-centred approach, and is followed by consideration of the effects (upon state parties and trafficked victims) of ratification of the Council of Europe Convention on Action against Trafficking in Human Beings,[6] in section 6.3. Section 6.4 will address recent EU activity – specifically the 2011 Directive,[7] and the victim assistance measures provided for within. Section 6.5 will deal with the all-important issue of victim identification and will outline the procedure currently in place, as well as its shortcomings. Section 6.6 will address the issue of non-criminalisation of trafficked persons who

2 R Piotrowicz 'European initiatives in the protection of victims of trafficking who give evidence against their traffickers' (2002) 14 *International Journal of Refugee Law* 263–78, 263.

3 See *R v O* [2008] EWCA Crim 2835; *R v LM* [2010] EWCA Crim 2327, [2011] 1 Cr App R 12, [2011] Crim LR 425; *R v N and LE* [2012] EWCA Crim 189.

4 Including the criteria or 'signals' to look out for when determining whether someone may be a trafficked victim.

5 J Elliott '(Mis)Identification of victims of human trafficking: the case of *R v O*' (2009) 21(4) *International Journal of Refugee Law* 727–41.

6 Council of Europe Convention on Action against Trafficking in Human Beings and its Explanatory Report (adopted 3 May 2005, entered into force 1 February 2008) Warsaw, 16.V.2005, Council of Europe Treaty Series – No 197 (CoE Trafficking Convention).

7 Directive 2011/36/EU of the European Parliament and of the Council of 5 April 2011 on preventing and combating trafficking in human beings and protecting its victims, and replacing Council Framework Decision 2002/629/JHA [2001] OJ L101/1 (EU 2011 Directive).

have committed offences as a result of having been trafficked; section 6.7 will consider international protection for the trafficked person available beyond the bespoke regime implemented as a result of the main anti-trafficking instruments, and section 6.8 will offer recommendations for improving how trafficked persons are dealt with.

## 6.2 Victim protection: the UK's previous poor performance

It has been suggested that the UK is one of the main destination countries for victims of human trafficking,[8] thereby necessitating a regime that provides for victim assistance and protection. However, consistent poor performance in respect of these victims' rights in the UK has meant that even an adequate minimum standard has not previously been achieved. Limited initiatives have been in existence, such as the Poppy Project,[9] yet even this project has had limited reach in terms of actually assisting and supporting victims of trafficking.[10] This consistent poor performance in respect of victims' rights in UK will now be considered, with reference to the relevant legislation and policy.

8 See Europol 'Trafficking of women and children for sexual exploitation in the EU: the involvement of Western Balkans organised crime', public version, Crimes Against the Person Unit, 5, where this claim is made, and see also Nick Davies 'Inquiry fails to find single trafficker who forced anybody into prostitution' *The Guardian* (20 October 2009) http://www.guardian.co.uk/uk/2009/oct/20/government-trafficking-enquiry-fails (last accessed 20 October 2009), which suggests that the results of Operation Pentameter 2 potentially show that trafficking into the UK has been somewhat overestimated.

9 The Poppy Project is funded by the Office for Criminal Justice Reform and offers accommodation and support to female victims of trafficking. This project has played a valuable role in identifying and supporting victims of human trafficking. See http://www.eaves4women.co.uk/POPPY_Project/POPPY_Project.php (last accessed 15 January 2014).

10 The criteria for receiving help and support from this organisation have previously been quite restrictive and therefore lacked applicability in respect of many trafficking victims (see, for example, Home Office and Scottish Executive 'UK Action Plan on tackling human trafficking' (March 2007) 51). Criteria included having worked as a prostitute within the last 30 days, and having shown the will to co-operate with the authorities. A four-week period of support is provided while the victim makes this decision. Beyond the Poppy Project, various independently funded organisations have set up victim support schemes (see UK Action Plan on tackling human trafficking, 52). Victims have had the option, regardless of whether they choose to cooperate with the authorities, to apply for asylum or humanitarian protection (see UK Border Agency 'Humanitarian protection' http://www.ukba.homeoffice.gov.uk/sitecontent/documents/policyandlaw/asylumpolicyinstructions/apis/humanitarianprotection.pdf?view=Binary (last accessed 21 February 2010). Also within recent years, parliamentary debate within the UK has at times focused upon victim incentive schemes and evidence for residence bargaining in a human trafficking context (see, for example, Lord Filkin, Written Answers, *Hansard* HL vol 645 col WA143 (10 March 2003)), although not all were in favour of this approach. Indeed, it was felt by some that support for victims should in no way be dependent upon their cooperation in the criminal process (see, for example, the Earl of Sandwich, *Hansard* HL vol 652 col 555 (10 July 2003)).

### 6.2.1 EU activity: Council Directive 2004/81/EC

Activity within the EU resulted in a Council Directive in 2004 on the residence permit issued to third country nationals who are victims of trafficking in human beings or who have been the subject of an action to facilitate illegal immigration, who cooperate with the competent authorities.[11] Article 6(1) requires the establishment by Member States of a reflection period, during which the victim may temporarily remain in the destination country (for a period of time to be determined by national law)[12] in order to consider whether or not that to cooperate with the relevant authorities. This directive has been subject to criticism from various corners for the lack of incentive for victims to cooperate,[13] and also because, as the title implies, it offers protection to victims only in exchange for cooperation with state authorities.[14] Trafficking is a matter of both criminal law and human rights law, and this directive appears to exist predominantly to satisfy the former.

This type of 'evidence for residence' bargaining is a 'victim inducement scheme',[15] which at best envisages a quasi-sympathetic approach to victims in return for their cooperation with state authorities in the criminal proceedings, and provides no scope at all for victim support measures outside those necessary effectively to induce the victim into such cooperation. Further to this, the offer of victim support is qualified in that even a willingness to cooperate is inadequate for the granting of a residence permit if the victim is not considered to be sufficiently 'useful' to the criminal proceedings.[16] Furthermore, the duration of the residence permit, if granted, is 'linked to the length of the relevant national proceedings'.[17] During this period, the victim's residence in the destination state

11 Council Directive 2004/81/EC of 29 April 2004 on the residence permit issued to third country nationals who are victims of trafficking in human beings or who have been the subject of an action to facilitate illegal immigration, who cooperate with the competent authorities [2004] OJ L261/19 (2004 Council Directive).

12 ibid. Article 6(1) states that: '[t]he duration and starting point of the period referred to in the first subparagraph shall be determined according to national law…', thereby allowing for much variation in the actual recovery and reflection periods adopted by different Member States.

13 R Piotrowicz 'The legal nature of trafficking in human beings' (2009) 4 *Intercultural Human Rights Law Review* 179, 263.

14 See, for example, Human Rights Watch Briefing Paper 'Commentary on the European Commission Proposal for a Council Directive 'on the short-term residence permits issued to victims of action to facilitate illegal immigration or trafficking in human beings who cooperate with the competent authorities' (1 July 2002).

15 Piotrowicz 'European initiatives' (n 2) 263.

16 Article 10 of the Commission Proposal for a Council Directive on the residence permit issued to third country nationals who are victims of trafficking in human beings or who have been the subject of an action to facilitate illegal immigration, who cooperate with the competent authorities.

17 Article 1 of the 2004 Council Directive (n 11).

is merely 'tolerated, until such time as the competent authority can rule on their future status'.[18] Such an attitude of temporary 'tolerance' appears to view the presence of victims as a mere expedient, and once they have been deemed useful or otherwise, their presence may be terminated forthwith.

The 2004 Council Directive was an attempt to tackle growth in illegal immigration and the increasing development of human trafficking and smuggling networks, and the Commission Proposal for the Council Directive openly admitted that it is not concerned with victim protection.[19] This approach is less victim-centred and more functional in terms of securing border integrity. Many international human rights instruments envisage enforcement measures against illegal migrants, but a human rights-based, victim-centred approach should take better account of victim vulnerability, rather than simply regarding him or her as a nuisance who is on the wrong side of the law.

The directive offers a form of bargain that is inappropriate with respect to the gravity of harm potentially suffered by victims of trafficking activity. Not only is it unsatisfactory on this basis, but also on the basis that the incentives offered to those who choose to give evidence are limited and inadequate; this is ultimately a one-sided bargain.

Although many EU Member States are subject to this directive, the UK unfortunately chose to 'opt out', and therefore is not subject to its content and is consequently not required to observe the 'reflection period' provided for by the directive. A tough stance on immigration has at times meant that victims of serious abuse, such as trafficked persons, have been swept aside in favour of the interests of UK border integrity.[20]

The unspecified period of reflection offered by the 2004 Council Directive, and similarly the 30-day period provided through the UK Poppy Project can be compared with the slightly more accommodating 45 days that were provided for in Belgium under the 1994 Circular,[21] and contrasted with the three-month reflection period provided for under the B9 regulation[22] in the Netherlands. Both

18 Article 8 of the Proposal for a Council Framework Decision on combating the sexual exploitation of children and child pornography, COM(2000) 854 Final 2.

19 Commission Proposal for a Council Directive on the residence permit issued to third country nationals who are victims of trafficking in human beings or who have been the subject of an action to facilitate illegal immigration, who cooperate with the competent authorities, Explanatory Memorandum 2.3, COM(2002) 71 Final states that: 'This proposal for a Directive is concerned with a residence permit and defines the conditions for its issue. In this sense, and to the extent that certain provisions on the conditions of residence constitute protective measures (starting with the residence permit itself, which offers *de facto* "protection" against deportation), *the proposal may appear to serve to protect victims. This is not, however, the case: the proposed Directive introduces a residence permit and is not concerned with protection of either witnesses or victims.* This is neither its aim nor its legal basis' (emphasis added).

20 See, for example, *R (Limbuela, Tesema, Adam) v Secretary of State for the Home Department* [2005] UKHL 66, [2006] 1 AC 396.

21 Circular regarding the issuance of residence documents and work permits to migrant victims of trafficking in human beings (7 July 1994, Belgium).

22 Circular for immigrants: regulation B9 (2000) (formerly B17 (1988), the Netherlands).

Belgium and the Netherlands recently ratified the CoE Trafficking Convention.[23] The reflection period is essential not only to the wellbeing of the victim but also in enabling the victim to make a properly thought-out decision regarding whether or not to cooperate with state authorities in the criminal proceedings. However, the requirements of adequate victim protection go well beyond the provision of a minimum period of recovery and decision-making.

### *6.2.2 The UN Trafficking Protocol*

Guidelines on International Protection state that the Trafficking Protocol[24] 'represents a crucial step forward in efforts to combat trafficking and ensure full respect for the rights of the individuals affected by trafficking'.[25] The Trafficking Protocol comes from a crime control and law enforcement perspective and its strength lies in the multi-lateral nature of the agreement, that is, it signifies the willingness of many countries to mobilise jointly in the fight against trafficking. However, its weakness lies in the fact that it was never clearly intended fully to address the needs of victims or governmental responsibility for addressing these needs: 'There may be significant consequences for victims of trafficking if states see the practice primarily as a matter of criminal law because they may fail fully to appreciate the ramifications for victims, whether in source, transit or destination states'.[26] The Trafficking Protocol evidently envisages some form of victim assistance, as it states in Article 2 that one of the aims is '[t]o protect and assist the victims of such trafficking, with full respect for their human rights', although the Trafficking Protocol did little to yield a particularly favourable approach as regards victims of trafficking.

The relevant provisions on the treatment of victims are Articles 6, 7 and 8, located in Part II of the Protocol. Article 6(3) states that: 'Each State Party shall *consider* implementing measures to provide for the … recovery of victims of trafficking in persons…'[27] The tentative language used does not provide a solid

23 List of signatures and ratifications available at http://conventions.coe.int/treaty/Commun/ChercheSig.asp?NT=197&CM=0&DF=&CL=ENG (last accessed 1 January 2014).

24 Protocol to Prevent, Suppress and Punish Trafficking in Persons, Especially Women and Children, Supplementing the United Nations Convention Against Transnational Organized Crime (adopted November 2000 by United Nations General Assembly Resolution A/RES/55/25, entered into force 25 December 2003) (Trafficking Protocol).

25 'Guidelines on international protection: the application of Article 1A(2) of the 1951 Convention and/or 1967 Protocol relating to the Status of Refugees to victims of trafficking and persons at risk of being trafficked' (2007) 19 *International Journal of Refugee Law* 372, para 2.

26 R Piotrowicz and J Redpath-Cross 'Human trafficking and smuggling' in B Opeskin, R Perruchoud, J Redpath-Cross (eds) *Foundations of International Migration Law* (Cambridge University Press, Cambridge, 2012) 234–59, 235.

27 The full text provides that: 'Each State Party shall consider implementing measures to provide for the physical, psychological and social recovery of victims of trafficking in persons, including, in appropriate cases, in cooperation with non-governmental organizations, other relevant organizations and other elements of civil society and, in particular, the provision of…' (housing, counselling – see full text of the article for exhaustive list).

obligation for states actually to take any action, and this minimum standard envisaged by the Protocol may be interpreted as little more than an afterthought by some state parties: only a limited few willingly implemented noteworthy victim-friendly schemes of their own volition, with Italy, particularly in Rimini,[28] providing a particularly favourable victim-centric system,[29] which has received praise from the Joint Committee on Human Rights (JCHR).[30]

The issuance of temporary or permanent residence may once again be 'considered' by states, by virtue of Article 7(1), with Article 7(2) requesting that this be done with 'appropriate consideration (given) to humanitarian and compassionate factors'. Article 8 addresses repatriation of victims.[31]

The UK implemented no bespoke victim assistance measures to speak of.[32] In order to achieve signatures and ratifications, concessions must at times be made.[33] Yet overall, in terms of support, assistance and protection for victims of trafficking, the Trafficking Protocol has a lack of bite and therefore may be termed somewhat of a toothless instrument in this particular respect. The tentative language of the

28 M Ventrella 'Protecting victims of trafficking in human beings in the UK: the Italian "Rimini method" that could influence the British approach' (2007) 3(2) *Journal of Migration and Refugee Issues* 64–86.

29 Article 18 of Legislative Decree 286/1998 provides for issuance of a special residence permit 'enabling the foreign citizen to escape from a situation of abuse and conditioning perpetrated by a criminal organisation and to participate in a social assistance and integration programme'. See STOP Programme 'Article 18: Protection of victims of trafficking and fight against crime (Italy and the European scenarios) research report', 41. Furthermore, sections 7.2 and 7.3 provide that a permit can be issued whether or not the victim chooses to cooperate with law enforcement authorities. Baroness Elles sees the Italian regime as 'a means of extracting the individual from an intolerable situation without imposing legislative cooperation', Baroness Elles, *Hansard* HL vol 651 col 549 (10 July 2003).

30 The JCHR stated that: '... we were highly impressed by the way in which the proactive victim-centred approach adopted in the country has allowed such high numbers of trafficking victims to be supported and ultimately integrated into Italian society'. Joint Committee on Human Rights Twenty-Sixth Report (Session 2005–2006) [78/205] http://www.publications.parliament.uk/pa/jt200506/jtselect/jtrights/245/24507.htm#n109 (last accessed 1 July 2011).

31 In summary, art 8 of the UN Trafficking Protocol (n 24) and its relevant subsections provides for origin states to 'facilitate and accept ... the return of that person without undue or unreasonable delay'; that repatriation 'shall preferably be voluntary'; that origin states 'verify whether a (trafficked victim) is its national or had the right of permanent residence'; that where proper documentation is lacking, the origin state of whom the victim was a national or resident will issue (on request) the necessary documents for travel etc; that: '[t]his article shall be without prejudice to any right afforded to victims of trafficking in persons by any domestic law of the receiving State Party'; and also 'without prejudice to any applicable bilateral or multilateral agreement or arrangement that governs, in whole or in part, the return of victims of trafficking in persons'. This must all be done consistently with 'due regard for the safety of that person'.

32 Beyond the Poppy Project, which was set up post signature but pre-ratification of the Trafficking Protocol (n 24).

33 Take, for example, the Convention on the Elimination of All Forms of Discrimination against Women (adopted in 1979 by the United Nations General Assembly, entered into force 3 September 1981), which is one of the most highly ratified yet also most highly reserved Conventions in existence today.

Protocol requires and therefore achieves little in the way of victim protection and support.

### *6.2.3 The need for a victim-centred approach*

The JCHR observes that with respect to anti-trafficking legislation, '[t]he focus should be shifted from immigration control to the prevention of exploitation of migrants and workers, and care of victims'.[34] The legislative framework within the UK has lacked this focus, and immigration legislation and policy has presented an obstacle to the protection of victims' rights – the UK has demonstrated tough policies, with trafficked victims at times being subject to rapid (and at times wholly unprincipled) deportation.[35] Notably, the reference by the JCHR to the exploitation of migrants and workers makes no mention of consent. Since the UK was not subject to the above-mentioned Council Directive or (until recently) subject to any obligations arising from the CoE Trafficking Convention, or the EU 2011 Directive, and the requirements of the UN Trafficking Protocol in respect of victim protection were minimal, no comprehensive victim protection framework existed and victims drew their rights from the Refugee Convention and the ECHR. This highlights the needs for an approach that caters for victims of trafficking, for whom the impact of trafficking is exacerbated by factors such as: isolation; language barriers; cultural differences; unfamiliar surroundings; and irregularity of immigration status.[36]

The UK Border Agency (UKBA) has issued general guidance on handling victims of human trafficking to staff in asylum screen units and regional asylum teams,[37] in which it highlights various issues such as the potential distressed or traumatised state of the victim, and resulting trauma-induced mental or physical illness. For these reasons, amongst others, trafficked victims constitute a particularly vulnerable body of persons. Balance must be struck between fighting crime and providing aid to victims.[38]

Ventrella calls for the provision of permanent residence permits to victims of trafficking as opposed to consideration of the needs of each victim on a case-by-case basis.[39] It cannot be said that destination states have an absolute duty to provide for rehabilitation or residence as regards victims of trafficking, although

34 Joint Committee on Human Rights Twenty-Sixth Report (n 30) para 118.

35 See, for example, Alan Travis 'Sex trafficking victim wins substantial damages from Home Office' *The Guardian* (April 2011) http://www.guardian.co.uk/uk/2011/apr/11/sex-trafficking-home-office-damages?INTCMP=SRCH (last accessed 1 May 2011).

36 See Home Office and Scottish Executive (n 10) 47.

37 UK Border Agency 'Victims of trafficking' http://www.ukba.homeoffice.gov.uk/sitecontent/documents/policyandlaw/asylumprocessguidance/specialcases/guidance/victimsoftrafficking.pdf?view=Binary (last accessed 15 April 2010).

38 Commissioner for Justice and Home Affairs, Europa Press Releases, Combating illegal immigration and trafficking in human beings: Commission's proposal for a residence permit for victims who cooperate with the authorities reminds the Member States that the phenomenon cannot be tackled at national level alone (Brussels, 12 February 2002).

39 Ventrella (n 28) 64.

they have some duties towards these people that cannot be satisfied if they are peremptorily removed under ordinary immigration law. What is needed is a human rights-based, victim-centred approach, which has procedures adequate enough to determine who is a victim and to identify what the person's rights are, so that they might be effectively assessed. Such a regime requires positive action by destination state authorities to seek out potential victims and to assist them in gaining access to the facilities that the state provides.

Recently, international recognition of the rights of victims of crime and human rights abuses is increasingly evident,[40] and a domestic response is evident through various government measures such as the introduction of a Statutory Code of Practice for Victims of Crime[41] and signature and ratification of the CoE Trafficking Convention. At first blush, the CoE Trafficking Convention contains much stronger provisions and obligations with respect to victim protection than the UN Trafficking Protocol, which appear to be much more onerous to states, and of considerable benefit to the victim. The success or otherwise of implementation in the UK of this Convention with respect to improved victim support will be evaluated later in this chapter.

## 6.3 Ratification of the CoE Trafficking Convention

The UK signed the Council of Europe Convention on Action against Trafficking in Human Beings[42] on 23 March 2007, thereby meeting the first point of action proposed in the UK Action Plan on Tackling Human Trafficking.[43] Ratification took place on 18 December 2008, and the Convention entered into force on 1 April 2009. Implementation is monitored by a group of experts on action against trafficking in human beings (GRETA),[44] and the Committee of the Parties;[45] effective implementation is essential in order for the requirements of the Trafficking Convention to have any force in national courts.[46]

UK Government spokespersons responded positively as regards this milestone event.[47] Ratification of the Convention constitutes part of a UK agenda geared

40 See M Cherif Bassiouni 'International recognition of victim's rights' (2006) 6 *Human Rights Law Review* 203–79.

41 Home Office 'Statutory code of practice for victims of crime' http://www.homeoffice.gov.uk/documents/victims-code-of-practice (last accessed 12 May 2011).

42 CoE Trafficking Convention (n 6).

43 Home Office and Scottish Executive (n 10) 76.

44 CoE Trafficking Convention (n 6) art 36.

45 ibid art 37.

46 A Harvey 'Human trafficking: the road to ratification of the Council of Europe Convention against Trafficking in Human Beings in the UK' (2008) *Journal of Immigration Asylum and Nationality Law* 218–35, 219.

47 Jacqui Smith, then Home Secretary, stated with respect to this important event: 'We have reached a major milestone today in the fight against trafficking by implementing measures that help us build on our existing efforts to turn the tables on traffickers and provide victims with protection, support and a voice in the criminal justice system. It is vital that European member states work together to stop this awful crime and I am determined that the UK will continue to play its part

toward victim protection and punishment of the exploiters,[48] and the decision to sign and ratify came after measuring the risks against the wider benefits to be gained. The main concern was in respect of border integrity and immigration control as trafficking policy and ratification of the Convention inevitably impacts upon government targets.[49]

The UK Government showed initial reluctance to sign and ratify the Trafficking Convention, notably because although the aims of the Convention were broadly supported, there were concerns that 'some of the provisions, such as the automatic granting of reflection periods and residence permits for trafficking victims, might act as 'pull' factors to the UK'.[50] The JCHR, however, rejected this argument in its Twenty-Sixth Report, stating that such concerns may be largely or entirely 'unfounded'.[51]

### *6.3.1 The CoE Trafficking Convention: a victim-centred approach*

It is recognised in the UK Action Plan on Tackling Human Trafficking that support for victims 'should go beyond providing safe and secure accommodation to include help in their recovery, and prevent re-trafficking or re-victimisation'.[52] The CoE Trafficking Convention requires the implementation of minimum standards in respect of victim protection and support, involvement of victims in the criminal justice system, increased prosecution of traffickers, and increased prevention of trafficking activity.[53] Furthermore, the Convention provides for the possibility of non-prosecution of victims of human trafficking who, in the course of their trafficking, have been compelled to commit offences.[54] This indicates a

by supporting victims and bringing the perpetrators to justice'. See UK Border Agency 'New measures to boost United Kingdom fight against human trafficking' (1 April 2009) http://www.ukba.homeoffice.gov.uk/sitecontent/newsarticles/boosttoukfightaginsthumantraffic (last accessed 3 July 2009, link no longer live).

48 Home Office and Scottish Executive (n 10) 76.

49 Such as the aim to 'ensure fair, controlled migration that protects the public and contributes to economic growth'. See Home Office 'Impact Assessment of ratification of the Council of Europe Convention on Action against Trafficking in Human Beings' (6 October 2008) 3 http://www.ialibrary.berr.gov.uk/ImpactAssessment/?IAID=da0f3cecd6214381bef9e9514cb46afd (last accessed 23 January 2009, link no longer live).

50 Home Office/Scottish Executive 'Tackling human trafficking: consultation on proposals for a UK Action Plan' (2006) 6.

51 The JCHR stated that: 'The bulk of the evidence submitted by NGOs in this inquiry suggests ... that such concerns are largely, if not entirely, unfounded. Nor did we find any evidence of a pull factor resulting in fraudulent claims to have been trafficked arising from Italy's Article 18 procedure. Safeguards exist within the Convention itself, so that reflection periods do not have to be provided if fraudulent claims are made. We therefore do not accept that there is any realistic likelihood that the Convention's provisions relating to reflection periods and residence permits would act as a pull factor for migration into the UK'. See Joint Committee on Human Rights, Twenty-Sixth Report (n 30) para 200.

52 Home Office and Scottish Executive (n 10) 47.

53 Home Office (n 49) 1.

54 CoE Trafficking Convention (n 6) art 26.

move toward a holistic approach to combating human trafficking, as protecting and providing for victims as well as creating a hostile environment for traffickers complements the aim for reducing the harm caused by illegal immigration.

There is a difference, however, between an obligation to provide a systematic response and the obligation to protect individual rights. Systems, however efficient, may not prevent some exploitation. Where an individual complains that the system has not protected her, ideally, there would be an accessible and effective remedy to test whether she were right or not. The Human Rights Act 1998 and the ECHR might do this, so long as potential deportees were given access to informed lawyers and there was a process by which adverse decisions could be challenged.

Article 39 of the CoE Trafficking Convention specifically refers to the relationship between itself and the Protocol, stating that the Convention '... is intended to enhance the protection afforded by (the Protocol) and develop the standards contained therein'. As regards assistance to and protection of victims of trafficking, implementation of the Convention required policy changes in various areas, which will now be considered.

### *6.3.1.1 Recovery and reflection period*

Where there are 'reasonable grounds' to believe that an individual is a victim of trafficking, the CoE Trafficking Convention calls for the provision of a recovery and reflection period of at least 30 days.[55] Initial response in the UK was to provide a recovery and reflection period of 45 days, which could be extended in certain circumstances.[56] Amnesty International, amongst others, calls for a more substantial period of 90 days,[57] particularly owing to the alarming figures that relate to the various types of trauma suffered by trafficked persons.[58]

It is envisaged that the decision as to whether 'reasonable grounds' exist in respect of each individual will be made in an average of five days following initial contact between a potential victim and a 'first responder'.[59] The latter is envisaged as being the police, the UKBA and certain NGOs.[60] The 'first responder' then refers the victim on to a 'competent authority'.[61] A positive 'reasonable grounds' decision will result in the imposition of the 45-day rest and recovery period, at the end of which a 'conclusive grounds' decision as to whether or not the person is

55 ibid art 13.

56 Home Office (n 49) 5. It is not specified what these 'certain circumstances' may be.

57 Amnesty International 'UK: Startling new report on trafficked women's health published, urgent call for protection of trafficked women' (June 2006) http://www.amnesty.org.uk/news_details.asp?NewsID=17013 (last accessed 12 August 2007).

58 ibid.

59 Home Office (n 49) 5.

60 An exhaustive list of first responders is provided on the National Crime Agency website: http://www.nationalcrimeagency.gov.uk/about-us/what-we-do/specialist-capabilities/uk-human-trafficking-centre/national-referral-mechanism (last accessed 9 June 2014).

61 In the UK these are UK Border Agency (UKBA, now UK Visas and Immigration) and the UK Human Trafficking Centre (UKHTC).

indeed a victim of trafficking, will be reached. Therefore, a process is established for correct identification of an individual as a potential victim of trafficking (to be discussed later), an essential prerequisite to being granted a recovery and reflection period. While this decision is being made, temporary accommodation will be provided to those possible victims who are destitute. Correct and timely identification clearly has implications for the possible victim.

#### *6.3.1.2 Temporary residence permits and other victim assistance and support measures*

On the face of it, the policy changes in the UK following implementation of the requirements of the Convention demonstrate a notable improvement when compared to the pre-Convention position, particularly in respect of the accommodating terms relating to the provision of residence periods. When the above-mentioned reflection period has passed and it has been concluded that an individual is a victim of human trafficking, a residence permit should be granted where a victim is cooperating in criminal proceedings or an investigation, and/or, notably, where provision of a residence permit is deemed necessary owing to the victim's 'personal situation'.[62]

The meanings of these terms are expanded upon in the Explanatory Report to the Convention, where it is stated that: '[t]he personal situation requirement takes in a range of situations, depending on whether it is the victim's safety, state of health, family situation or some other factor which has to be taken into account'.[63] The Home Office/Border and Immigration Agency judge stated that, in respect of the second category relating to the 'personal situation' of the victim, 'a combination of our existing obligations on asylum and human rights and our Discretionary Leave policy already cover situations where an individual's personal circumstances ... make it necessary for them to remain in the UK'.[64] Consequently, there is a lack of clear implementing legislation. It is further stated that: 'we intend to extend discretionary leave to explicitly cover the first category as well'.[65]

Where an individual qualifies for a residence permit, it will be granted for a minimum of one year.[66] This exceeds the provisions of the UN Trafficking Protocol. Although victim involvement in investigation and criminal proceedings is an integral part of the fight against human trafficking,[67] securing prosecution against the trafficker must not be the only focus of anti-trafficking legislation and policy. Participation in criminal proceedings or investigation may also be dependent upon the mental or physical wellbeing of the victim, which provides yet

62 CoE Trafficking Convention (n 6) art 14.

63 Explanatory Report to the CoE Trafficking Convention, para 184, http://conventions.coe.int/Treaty/EN/Reports/Html/197.htm (last accessed 1 January 2014).

64 Home Office (n 49) 6.

65 ibid.

66 ibid.

67 By late 2008, only one recorded prosecution had been secured in the UK without the involvement of the victim. See Home Office (n 49) 8.

another reason for improving efforts regarding treatment and support of victims. Prosecution rates for trafficking offences in the UK are frequently cited as being low;[68] victim engagement plays a role in this.

For some, however, the provisions of the CoE Trafficking Convention do not go far enough. The Convention for the Elimination of all Forms of Discrimination against Women (CEDAW) Committee Report 'invites the State party to give consideration to granting victims of trafficking indefinite leave to remain'.[69] Ventrella calls for the imposition of permanent residence permits for trafficking victims.[70] The practical implications of this mean that it is really not a viable option; the CoE Trafficking Convention attempts to offer a more practical and realistic approach, that is, residence permits where needed, and repatriation where a more lengthy or permanent measure is not needed. The UN Trafficking Protocol refers to the repatriation of victims '… without undue or unreasonable delay',[71] but that return should preferably be voluntary.[72] CoE Trafficking Convention also states that repatriation shall preferably be voluntary, and be done 'with due regard for the rights, safety and dignity of that person and for the status of any legal proceedings related to the fact that the person is a victim'.[73] Not all trafficking victims necessarily wish to remain in the destination country,[74] although a good few might.[75] The CoE Trafficking Convention position is that involuntary removal or repatriation is a last resort, and will only take place where it is safe to do so.[76]

Under the CoE Trafficking Convention, states are required to protect the identity and private life of victims.[77] Furthermore, states are required to 'such legislative or other measures as may be necessary to assist victims in their physical, psychological and social recovery'[78] that include giving assistance in terms of providing accommodation and medical treatment and access to counselling and interpreters etc. Obligations are also imposed as regards providing access to legal assistance and free legal aid, as well as to compensation from the perpetrators.[79]

68 See First Annual Report of the Inter-Departmental Group on Human Trafficking, CM8421 (2012).

69 OHCHR 'Concluding Observations of the Committee on the Elimination of Discrimination against Women: United Kingdom of Great Britain and Northern Ireland' (Committee on the Elimination of Discrimination Against Women, Forty-first session 30 June–18 July 2008) 36 http://www2.ohchr.org/english/bodies/cedaw/docs/CEDAW.C.GBR.CO.6.pdf (last accessed 1 July 2009).

70 Ventrella (n 28) 69–70.

71 CoE Trafficking Convention (n 6) art 8(1).

72 ibid art 8(2).

73 ibid art 16(2).

74 Home Office and Scottish Executive (n 10) 59.

75 L Hales and L Gelsthorpe 'The criminalisation of migrant women: research findings and policy and practice implications' (2013) 206 *Prison Service Journal* 25, 25.

76 Home Office and Scottish Executive (n 10) 59.

77 CoE Trafficking Convention (n 6) art 11.

78 ibid art 12.

79 ibid art 15.

## 6.4 Recent EU activity: the Directive of the European Parliament and of the Council on preventing and combating trafficking in human beings and protecting victims

Recent EU action on trafficking has culminated in the directive of the European Parliament and of the Council on preventing and combating trafficking in human beings, and protecting victims.[80] The UK Government initially proposed not to opt in to this directive.[81] As well as the claim that the UK was already compliant, it was stated that opting in would have the effect of making provisions mandatory that are currently discretionary.[82] The government was therefore keen to avoid being bound by provisions that would apparently be 'against our interests'.[83] This continues the pattern of the government showing a certain reluctance to concede to provisions that are sufficiently accommodating the needs of victims of human trafficking.

The response from CARE[84] was highly critical of this position on various bases,[85] including that the UK: 'was not compliant in a number of key areas and that without the directive (or some other identical provision) British provisions for the victims of trafficking would become weaker than those of other Member States'.[86]

In March 2011, the government announced that it had reviewed its position and that it had the broad intention to apply to opt in to the directive now that there was a finalised text, stating that: 'The new text still does not contain any measures that would significantly change the way the UK fights trafficking'.[87]

80 EU 2011 Directive (n 7).

81 The Prime Minister on 15 September 2010 justified the choice not to opt in on the basis that that the directive would add nothing of value to British anti-trafficking law, stating that: '[w]e have put everything that is in the Directive in place'. See *Hansard* HC, col 873 (15 September 2010).

82 It was stated that: '[o]pting in now would also require us to make mandatory the provisions which are currently discretionary in UK law. These steps would reduce the scope for professional discretion and flexibility and might divert already limited resources'. See Home Office 'Home Office defends position on human trafficking' (31 August 2010) http://www.homeoffice.gov.uk/media-centre/news/trafficking-directive (last accessed 1 December 2011).

83 ibid.

84 A registered UK charity. See, for example, CARE 'EU Directive on human trafficking: why the Government should opt in' http://www.care.org.uk/wp-content/uploads/2011/02/EU-Directive-on-Human-Trafficking-Why-the-UK-should-opt-in-7-Feb-2011.pdf (last accessed 25 March 2011).

85 Such as the point that through not opting in, the extended scope of the trafficking definition provided within the directive would not apply in the UK. Furthermore, as regards the establishment under art 19 of a 'National Rapporteur or equivalent mechanism', CARE were critical of the 'equivalent mechanism' in the UK, which is the Inter-Departmental Ministerial Group on Trafficking, on the basis that: 'This group … is, by definition, part of the Government and so cannot constitute the conventional meaning of a rapporteur which is supposed to be independent'. Criticism was also levelled at the lack of UK power to prosecute where the activity takes place beyond UK borders, and at the potential for victim protection and assistance measures to be weaker than in other Member States as a result of opting out. See CARE (n 84).

86 ibid.

87 Home Office (Minister of State for Immigration, Damian Green) 'EU Directive on Human

### 6.4.1 'Vulnerability' and aggravating factors

The preamble to the directive states that: 'When the offence is committed in certain circumstances, for example against a particularly vulnerable victim, the penalty should be more severe'.[88] The directive goes on to state that certain factors relating to vulnerability in this context include, for example, gender,[89] thereby building or expanding upon previous instruments,[90] and the preamble refers directly to situations where the offence is 'particularly grave' being 'reflected in a more severe penalty'.[91] The CoE Trafficking Convention has a similar provision,[92] yet does not use the terminology of 'vulnerability'.

Thus it appears that a form of 'aggravated' trafficking is envisaged, therefore drawing delineations between the severity of experiences of different trafficking victims. As will be argued later, such an approach, taken by the 2011 Directive, which focuses upon vulnerability and spectrum of severity of treatment and exploitation of victims, may leave open the possibility that situations of exploitation that fall much further down the spectrum – perhaps falling short of even the formal trafficking threshold – may still need to be scrutinised, and at least some of the 'victims' thereof need some form of assistance beyond that of the perceived average 'smuggled migrant prostitute'.[93]

### 6.4.2 The 'gender' perspective

The directive has some interesting additions to the current anti-trafficking framework. Article 1 refers directly to 'taking into account the gender perspective'. The preamble expands upon this in stating that:

> This Directive recognises the gender-specific phenomenon of trafficking and that women and men are often trafficked for different purposes. For this reason, assistance and support measures should also be gender specific where

Trafficking: Written Ministerial Statement' (22 March 2011) http://www.homeoffice.gov.uk/publications/about-us/parliamentary-business/written-ministerial-statement/eu-direct-human-trafficking-wms/ (last accessed 12 April 2011).

88 EU 2011 Directive (n 7) preamble para 12.

89 ibid.

90 The UN Trafficking Protocol (n 24) notably refers to 'Women and Children' in its title.

91 The preamble states that: '[w]hen the offence is particularly grave, for example when the life of the victim has been endangered or the offence has involved serious violence such as torture, forced drug/medication usage, rape or other serious forms of psychological, physical or sexual violence, or has otherwise caused particularly serious harm to the victim, this should also be reflected in a more severe penalty'. EU 2011 Directive (n 7) preamble para 12.

92 CoE Trafficking Convention (n 6) art 18 states that: 'Each Party shall ensure that the following circumstances are regarded as aggravating circumstances in the determination of the penalty for offences established in accordance with Article 18 of this Convention: (a) the offence deliberately or by gross negligence endangered the life of the victim; (b) the offence was committed against a child; (c) the offence was committed by a public official in the performance of her/his duties; (d) the offence was committed within the framework of a criminal organisation'.

93 This is discussed in ch 7.

> appropriate. The 'push' and 'pull' factors may be different depending on the sectors concerned, such as trafficking in human beings into the sex industry or for labour exploitation in, for example, construction work, the agricultural sector or domestic servitude.[94]

Specific reference in this directive to gender and the potential for gender-specific assistance and support measures, coupled with the fact that 'women and children' are explicitly mentioned in the very title of the Trafficking Protocol further raises the issue of the potential for recognition of the particular vulnerability of certain parties.[95] Not only does such an approach bring the particular vulnerabilities of women to the forefront of sex trafficking debate, but it may also have ramifications for those women who may be deemed 'consensually trafficked', who, owing to their vulnerability, may have specific needs.[96]

### 6.4.3 Victim assistance, support and protection

As regards victim assistance and protection, mechanisms for early identification[97] of and assistance to victims are required by Article 11, which envisages safe accommodation and medical treatment, and access to counselling, information and interpretation services where needed. Provisions relating to non-prosecution of victims 'for their involvement in criminal activities which they have been compelled to commit as a direct consequence of being subjected to (trafficking)'[98] are also included, and are a welcome development, as cases such as *R v O*[99] have shown us.

#### 6.4.3.1 Recovery and reflection period

There is no new, bespoke recovery and reflection period for trafficked persons contained within the 2011 Directive – the period remains that set down in the 2004 Council Directive on the residence permit issued to third country nationals who are victims of trafficking in human beings or who have been the subject of an action to facilitate illegal immigration, who cooperate with the competent authorities,[100] the exact length of which was to be left to individual governments to determine.

94 EU 2011 Directive (n 10) preamble para 3.
95 This book does not aim specifically to address child trafficking, and therefore an in-depth consideration of this issue would go beyond the ambit of the work.
96 See ch 7.
97 The mechanism for identifying victims is discussed later in this chapter.
98 EU 2011 Directive (n 10) art 8.
99 *R v O* [2008] EWCA Crim 2835. The case is discussed later, and the specific issue of prosecutorial discretion as regards criminal offences committed by trafficked victims, as a result of having been trafficked, is discussed with reference to this case too.
100 2004 Council Directive (n 11).

#### *6.4.3.2 Temporary residence permits*

As to residence permits, the 2011 Directive does not impose similarly onerous obligations on states as in the CoE Trafficking Convention, and asks for little beyond the recovery and reflection period.[101] Article 11(2) states that:

> Member States shall take the necessary measures to ensure that a person is provided with assistance and support as soon as the competent authorities have a reasonable-grounds indication for believing that the person might have been subjected to (trafficking offences).[102]

The directive also states that: '[w]here necessary, assistance and support should continue for an appropriate period after the criminal proceedings have ended'.[103] It is surprising that the measures relating to temporary residence permits appear to be less accommodating than those provided for within the CoE Trafficking Convention, given the statement that victim assistance and support is one of the primary objectives of the directive, coupled with the specific mention of the 'gender perspective'.

The current residence permit obligations go no further than those provided within the 2004 Council Directive discussed earlier. Nonetheless, Article 11(3) of the 2011 Directive states that:

> Member States shall take the necessary measures to ensure that assistance and support for a victim are not made conditional on the victim's willingness to cooperate in the criminal investigation, prosecution or trial, without prejudice to Directive 2004/81/EC or similar national rules.

This paves the way for measures that are somewhat more accommodating, and which will in any case have been adopted by those who ratified the CoE Trafficking Convention and are therefore bound by its more sympathetic victim assistance and support provisions.

As previously mentioned, effective protection is dependent upon correct and timely identification of victims. This issue will now be considered.

101 In para 18 of the preamble to the EU 2011 Directive (n 7), it is stated that: 'In cases where the victim does not reside lawfully in the Member State concerned, assistance and support should be provided unconditionally at least during the reflection period. If, after completion of the identification process or expiry of the reflection period, the victim is not considered eligible for a residence permit or does not otherwise have lawful residence in that Member State, or if the victim has left the territory of that Member State, the Member State concerned is not obliged to continue providing assistance and support to that person on the basis of this Directive'.

102 EU 2011 Directive (n 7) art 11(2).

103 Paragraph 18 of the preamble to the EU 2011 Directive (n 7) goes on to provide examples: 'for example if medical treatment is ongoing due to the severe physical or psychological consequences of the crime, or if the victim's safety is at risk due to the victim's statements in those criminal proceedings'.

## 6.5 Victim identification

All people who enter the UK illegally are entitled to a fair trial before conviction for any immigration offence. Those entitled to this protection will be identified by the decision to prosecute them. Trafficked victims might have special characteristics that require special treatment in the fair trial context, and prosecutors and defence lawyers should be aware of these possibilities. It is, therefore, imperative that those putatively entitled to these protections be accurately and rapidly identified and provided with competent legal advice where necessary. It cannot be assumed that those officials charged with policing the immigration regime have the interests of these kinds of people at the head of their priorities. Matters of border security and economic protection are also significant concerns.

In these circumstances, the provision of effective processes to bring to the attention of people their rights and to decide on contested claims of eligibility are of crucial importance. Correct identification of trafficking victims is paramount to securing their effective protection, and effective protection of their rights. Ill-effects flowing from misidentification include lack of protection and opportunity to recover, as well as detention, expulsion,[104] or criminalisation as a result of being in breach of immigration law, as demonstrated by cases such as *R v O*, decided pre-ratification of the CoE Trafficking Convention,[105] considered below.

### *6.5.1 (Mis)Identification of victims of human trafficking: the case of* R v O

That national law might not have been as effective as subsequently required by the UK's international obligations, has been demonstrated by the recent decision in *R v O*,[106] which was decided prior to ratification of the CoE Trafficking Convention by the UK.

The appellant was apprehended on her way out of the UK and was found to be carrying false identity documents. Between speaking to passport control officers and subsequently to her legal representatives, it soon became clear that there were questions to be ascertained as to her age.[107] She stated that she had come to

104 See A Pacurar 'Smuggling, detention and expulsion of irregular migrants: a study on international legal norms, standards and practices' (2003) *5 European Journal of Migration and Law* 259–83.

105 *R v O* [2008] EWCA Crim 2835.

106 *R v O* [2008] EWCA Crim 2835. See also Elliott '(Mis)Identification of victims of human trafficking' (n 5) for full consideration of this case.

107 At interview the day following her apprehension at French passport control in the UK, she admitted that the identity card she had in her possession was not her own, and she proceeded to give her actual name and asserted that her nationality was Nigerian. She had initially stated that she was 31, but later had given her year of birth as 1985. Notably, she was described by two officers as 'very young' and, in one instance, 'possibly juvenile'. Several days prior to her trial date of 17 March 2008 at the crown court, she informed her legal representatives that she was 17. From various meetings between the appellant and her legal representatives which took place prior to the trial, the latter obtained information to the effect that her actual date of birth was 10

England with her boyfriend in order to escape her father, who would have killed her if she had not proceeded with an arranged marriage in Nigeria. She also stated that, once in England, she was 'given to be a prostitute' and consequently ran away.

Several days prior to her trial date, the appellant's legal representatives received information from the Poppy Project to the effect that O was potentially a victim of human trafficking for the purpose of prostitution, although they failed to act upon this information. O was initially convicted at the crown court on 17 March 2008, resulting in imposition[108] of a sentence of eight months' imprisonment, less 16 days spent on remand. Leave to appeal was granted by Cox J on 26 June 2008.

The grounds of appeal related to O's age;[109] the potential for her to rely on the defence of duress;[110] and the lack of appreciation by the appellant's lawyers of her position as a victim of trafficking.[111] Consideration of this issue by her legal representatives was largely non-existent,[112] as was any awareness by legal representatives on both sides of two CPS Protocols that provided guidelines on 'Prosecution of Defendants Charged With Offences Who Might Be Trafficked Victims' and 'Prosecution of Young Defendants Charged With Offences Who Might Be Trafficked Victims'.[113] The appeal was allowed.[114]

December 1991, which would have made her only 16 rather than 17 as she had claimed. The crown court was not informed of this.

108 By Adele Williams J.

109 CoE Trafficking Convention (n 6) art 10(3) provides that the victim will be presumed to be a child if his/her age is uncertain and there are reasons to believe that he or she is a child. Further to this, since the age of the defendant was in doubt, then if she were indeed 16 she should have been tried in the youth court rather than in the crown court. It is also clear that her legal representatives had ample opportunities and reasons to question the age of the defendant. The UK also has obligations under the Convention on the Rights of the Child 1989 (adopted and opened for signature, ratification and accession by General Assembly Resolution 44/25 of 20 November 1989, entered into force 2 September 1990, in accordance with Article 49), state parties are committed to protecting children from sexual exploitation, etc: see art 34.

110 As regards any criminal charge for her potential complicity in breaching immigration laws.

111 This was due to the fact that – despite receiving communication that O was a putative victim of trafficking –her legal representatives took no steps to act upon this information.

112 The seventh and final ground of appeal was actually an application to admit fresh evidence in the following categories: a report by the Poppy Project prepared after the trial date of 17 March; the file of the trial solicitors; correspondence between the appellant's present solicitors and her trial lawyer. The second category was admitted under s 23 of the Criminal Appeal Act 1968. As regards the first category, the Poppy Project report is dated 23 June 2008. It provides that after the trial date of 17 March, the appellant was assessed by a senior outreach worker and was deemed to be a victim of trafficking. A detailed history included showed that she was held in debt bondage, raped and forced to work as a prostitute until she escaped a month later. This report was admitted as fresh evidence to the appeal.

113 Crown Prosecution Service 'Prosecution of defendants charged with offences who might be trafficked victims' and 'Prosecution of young defendants charged with offences who might be trafficked victims' http://www.cps.gov.uk/legal/h_to_k/human_trafficking_and_smuggling/ (last accessed 25 February 2009).

114 The complete lack of consideration given to the possibilities of the appellant being a victim of trafficking or being a child/young person, coupled with the lack of awareness on the part of the prosecutors of the above-mentioned protocols meant that the appeal had to be allowed.

Since the UK had not at that time ratified the CoE Trafficking Convention, it was not bound by its provisions and could not have been held legally accountable for any failure to act according to the standards of the CoE Convention,[115] which includes a 'non-punishment' provision with regard to victims,[116] yet the facts of the case show that the then existing provision of protection for such people as the applicant in *R v O* was deficient. It was recognised in *R v O* that the UK had taken measures expressly in support of the purpose of the CoE Convention,[117] although these were clearly insufficient to protect O at first instance. Instead, Laws LJ found a way to get the most desirable outcome through drawing upon the sources that were available to be used at that point in time: the two CPS Protocols, the common law,[118] and Article 6 of the ECHR.[119] He recognised that both the common law and Article 6 of the ECHR required standards of procedural protection that were much higher than those that had been accorded to the defendant in the present case. O had not had a fair trial. Her conviction was ultimately declared unsafe.[120]

Although the UK could not be held to account for deficiencies as regards the CoE Trafficking Convention which it had yet to ratify, *R v O* still provides a shocking insight into the lack of training, acknowledgement and formal procedure for victim identification pre-ratification. Clearly, a formalised procedure that is tailored to the identification or and catering for the needs of trafficking victims, such as the CoE Convention requires, was a much needed feature. However, more recent domestic case law[121] indicates that, following ratification of the CoE Convention, there is still much work to be done as regards both identifying victims correctly and engaging in active consideration of whether or not to prosecute them for offences committed owing to trafficking-related compulsion.

115 Beyond art 18 of the Vienna Convention, which states that signatory states must 'refrain from acts which would defeat the object and purpose of [the] treaty'. Such an obligation – pre-ratification – cannot possibly exist, because, as Aust observes: 'the act of ratification would then have little or no purpose, the obligation to perform the treaty being then not dependent on ratification and entry into force'. See A Aust *Modern Treaty Law and Practice* (2nd edn, Cambridge University Press, Cambridge, 2007) 117.

116 CoE Trafficking Convention (n 6) art 26 provides for a requirement of active consideration of whether or not it is in the public interest to proceed with prosecutions against victims who have been compelled to commit an offence.

117 Notably through the criminalisation of trafficking by Sexual Offences Act 2003 (SOA 2003) ss 57 and 58, and by introducing the two above-mentioned CPS Protocols, yet as the facts indicate, these were of little help to O at first instance. It may be noted at this point that some of these measures taken 'expressly in support' of the Trafficking Convention were taken four years prior to signing of the Convention by the UK.

118 ibid para 26.

119 ibid.

120 *R v O* [2011] EWCA Crim 2226.

121 *R v O* [2008] EWCA Crim 2835; *R v LM* [2010] EWCA Crim 2327, [2011] 1 Cr App R 12, [2011] Crim LR 425; *R v N and LE* [2012] EWCA Crim 189; *OOO v Commissioner of Police of the Metropolis* [2011] EWHC 1246 (QB).

### *6.5.2 The identification of victims: the 'National Referral Mechanism'*

Article 10 of the CoE Trafficking Convention has some particular stipulations that go toward providing a victim identification mechanism, to be executed by competent authorities and trained staff to identify putative victims with whom they come into contact.[122] Article 10 of the CoE Trafficking Convention provides that:

> Each Party shall provide its competent authorities with persons who are trained and qualified in preventing and combating trafficking in human beings, in identifying and helping victims.

The EU 2011 Directive has a similar stipulation in Article 11(4),[123] yet the Trafficking Protocol has no such corresponding provision. Such systems can only be effective if properly implemented and adhered to.[124]

Implementing measures as regards Article 10 of the CoE Trafficking Convention required the creation of a process that is often referred to internationally as a 'National Referral Mechanism'[125] (NRM), whereby:

122 CoE Trafficking Convention (n 6) art 10 in full states that: '(1) Each Party shall provide its competent authorities with persons who are trained and qualified in preventing and combating trafficking in human beings, in identifying and helping victims, including children, and shall ensure that the different authorities collaborate with each other as well as with relevant support organisations, so that victims can be identified in a procedure duly taking into account the special situation of women and child victims and, in appropriate cases, issued with residence permits under the conditions provided for in Article 14 of the present Convention; (2) Each Party shall adopt such legislative or other measures as may be necessary to identify victims as appropriate in collaboration with other Parties and relevant support organisations. Each Party shall ensure that, if the competent authorities have reasonable grounds to believe that a person has been victim of trafficking in human beings, that person shall not be removed from its territory until the identification process as victim of an offence provided for in Article 18 of this Convention has been completed by the competent authorities and shall likewise ensure that that person receives the assistance provided for in Article 12, paragraphs 1 and 2; (3) When the age of the victim is uncertain and there are reasons to believe that the victim is a child, he or she shall be presumed to be a child and shall be accorded special protection measures pending verification of his/her age; (4) As soon as an unaccompanied child is identified as a victim, each Party shall: (a) provide for representation of the child by a legal guardian, organisation or authority which shall act in the best interests of that child; (b) take the necessary steps to establish his/her identity and nationality; (c) make every effort to locate his/her family when this is in the best interests of the child'.

123 CoE Trafficking Convention (n 6) art 11(4) states that: 'Member States shall take the necessary measures to establish appropriate mechanisms aimed at the early identification of, assistance to and support for victims, in cooperation with relevant support organisations'. Paragraph 4 of the preamble to the directive also refers to 'the development of general common indicators of the Union for the identification of victims of trafficking, through the exchange of best practices between all the relevant actors, particularly public and private social services'.

124 CoE Trafficking Convention (n 6) art 10 also provides for protection against peremptory removal until the identification process is complete, and makes some specific provision for the treatment of children.

125 Defined as 'a procedure in which trained/qualified staff within 'competent authorities' can

> Front-line professionals will use indicators to consider whether an individual could be a victim of trafficking before referring their details to a designated competent authority to make a decision on whether there are reasonable grounds to believe that the individual has been trafficked.[126]

Examples of 'competent authorities' are given in the Explanatory Report to the Convention as 'public authorities which may have contact with trafficking victims, such as the police, the labour inspectorate, customs, the immigration authorities and embassies or consulates'.[127]

The NRM has been in place in the UK since 1 April 2009, and the relevant designated competent authorities are the UKBA – (now Visas and Immigration) and the UK Human Trafficking Centre (UKHTC).[128] Once a possible victim is identified, specialist staff will be assigned to assess the individual case.[129] Training and guidance are imperative as regards victim identification – *R v O* (above) demonstrates that the ramifications of misidentification can be severe for the victim. CPS guidelines state that: 'Guidance has been issued to police and immigration officers on identification of victims and what might constitute a credible trafficked victim'.[130] The NRM, however, lacks a formal route of appeal, which may give rise to Article 6 challenges and judicial review claims concerning those who are not found to be a credible trafficked victim.

The UKBA has also produced information as regards 'indicators' that those who come into contact with potential traffick victims should look out for.[131] These include: signs of physical or psychological harm or debt bondage; signs of fear or anxiety; and whether the testimony of the potential victim includes elements of coercion, deception or threat. The list provided is far from exhaustive. Further guidance is provided by the UKHTC and by Anti-Slavery International,[132] who

identify victims of all forms of trafficking and ensure their access to appropriate levels of support' – see 'Explanatory Memorandum on the Council of Europe Convention on Action against Trafficking in Human Beings', Report CM 7465 at http://www.fco.gov.uk/en/about-the-fco/publications/treaty-command-papers-ems/explanatory-memoranda/explanatory-memoranda-2008/humantrafficking (last accessed 7 April 2009, link no longer live). Information on the NRM is now available through http://www.crimereduction.homeoffice.gov.uk/humantrafficking005overview.pdf (last accessed 7 April 2009).

126 Home Office (n 49) 5.

127 Explanatory Report (n 63) para 129.

128 See UK Human Trafficking Centre website http://www.nationalcrimeagency.gov.uk/contact-us/contact-the-ukhtc (last accessed 15 January 2014).

129 See Home Office 'Overview of the implementation of the National Referral Mechanism' http://www.crimereduction.homeoffice.gov.uk/humantrafficking005overview.pdf (last accessed 1 July 2011, link no longer live).

130 Crown Prosecution Service (n 113).

131 See Home Office/UK Border Agency 'Enforcement Instructions and Guidance, Chapter 9 – Identifying victims of trafficking'. http://www.ukba.homeoffice.gov.uk/sitecontent/documents/policyandlaw/enforcement/oemsectiona/chapter9?view=Binary (last accessed 1 April 2014).

132 This includes extensive lists of identification criteria under various headings relating to, *inter alia*, personal belongings, violence and working conditions. See Anti-Slavery.

include extensive lists of identification criteria under headings such as 'Personal documents and belongings', 'Violence or threat of violence' and 'Working conditions'. Although these criteria and lists of 'indicators' are useful, they are geared toward identification of the 'perfect victim';[133] the victim who displays the correct, obvious indicators and presents conveniently as 'trafficked'. Ideal victim stereotypes are damaging[134] and are one of the many barriers to successful victim identification.

As outlined previously, where there are 'reasonable grounds' to believe that an individual is a victim of trafficking, a recovery and reflection period of at least 30 days is called for by the CoE Trafficking Convention.[135] The above-mentioned criteria go toward the establishment of 'reasonable grounds' as regards any putative victim. Secondly, there is a notable improvement as regards the rather accommodating terms relating to the provision of residence periods.

However, the granting of a residence permit is wholly dependent upon correct determination of the first stage; that is, there being 'reasonable grounds' to believe that an individual is a victim of trafficking. Because the identification of an individual as a possible victim of trafficking is a prerequisite even to being granted a recovery and reflection period, an essential period of time and space for the potentially severely traumatised victim, it is necessary that those who are likely to come into contact with victims of trafficking are alert to the indications that are signs of this possibility. The circumstances in the above-mentioned *R v O* were such that – even after ratification and after full implementation of the Convention – O may not have been in a position to enjoy the benefits conferred by the Convention because there was no recognition of her trafficked-victim status at a sufficiently early stage.

It would be welcome at this stage to be able to adduce evidence to show that the situation of victim identification has improved post-ratification of the CoE Convention, but subsequent case law indicates clearly that the victim identification problem is not going away. This particular issue is discussed further at a later point in this chapter. We now turn to consideration of the deficiencies of the victim identification regime, and the barriers to victim identification that are increasingly becoming apparent. There exist numerous barriers to identification, each with its own requirements as to how it may be tackled.

133 See R Uy 'Blinded by red lights: why trafficking discourse should shift away from sex and the "perfect victim" paradigm' (2011) *Berkeley Journal of Gender, Law and Justice* 204–19.

134 C Hoyle, M Bosworth and M Dempsey 'Labelling the victims of sex trafficking: exploring the borderland between rhetoric and reality' (2011) 20(3) *Social and Legal Studies* 313–92, 314.

135 CoE Trafficking Convention (n 6) art 13.

### *6.5.3 Identification of victims of trafficking: barriers to identification and the need for effective procedures*

Recent domestic case law[136] has compounded the continuing need for a better response, including improved victim identification procedures in the UK. The nuanced regime for victim identification and assistance is there, but awareness of trafficking and the myriad issues surrounding it, as well as general understanding of victim behaviour and victimology,[137] is lacking. It is stated in the UK Action Plan on Tackling Human Trafficking that support for victims 'should go beyond providing safe and secure accommodation to include help in their recovery, and prevent re-trafficking or re-victimisation'.[138] The CoE Trafficking Convention requires the implementation of minimum standards in respect of victim protection and support, involvement of victims in the criminal justice system, increased prosecution of traffickers, and increased prevention of trafficking activity.[139] Although the UK was apparently largely compliant with the Convention at the point of signature,[140] implementation required some legislative changes,[141] and policy changes in various areas, notably the development of the formal NRM process for referring and identifying victims of trafficking.[142] There is, however, a lack of clear implementing legislation following ratification of the Convention. This could be taken as an indication of the UK's continuing reluctance to concede too much for even those formally identified as trafficked, let alone those borderline cases where there is lack of ostensible coercion, etc, according to UKBA 'indicators'.

Evidently, trafficking is the kind of crime that places some responsibility on third parties with respect to victim identification. These parties range from police, border authorities and organisations such as the Poppy Project to sexual health services, prostitute users and beyond. Clearly, various barriers exist with respect to victim identification. Some of these arise from the predicament of the victim;[143]

136 *R v O* [2008] EWCA Crim 2835; *R v LM* [2010] EWCA Crim 2327, [2011] 1 Cr App R 12, [2011] Crim LR 425; *R v N and LE* [2012] EWCA Crim 189; *OOO v Commissioner of Police of the Metropolis* [2011] EWHC 1246 (QB).

137 See Hales and Gelsthorpe (n 75); Hoyle and others (n 134).

138 Home Office and Scottish Executive (n 10) 47.

139 Home Office (n 49) 1.

140 ibid 3.

141 Implementation required legislative amendments to the Criminal Justice and Immigration Act 2008 to ensure that automatic deportation of victims of trafficking under the UK Borders Act 2007 cannot take place where this would breach obligations under the Trafficking Convention; and to the Asylum and Immigration (Treatment of Claimants, etc.) Act 2004 to correct a cross-reference to human tissue legislation has been made through the Human Tissue (Scotland) Act 2006 (Consequential Amendment) Order 2008 (SSI 2008/259). Also, Secondary legislation by way of the National Health Service (Charges to Overseas Visitors) Regulations 2008 which amend reg 4(1) of the National Health Service (Charges to Overseas Visitors) Regulations 1989 (SI 1989/306) and ensure the UK meets obligations in relation to medical treatment under the Convention.

142 Home Office (n 49) 1.

143 The Anti-Trafficking Monitoring Group states that: 'Myths about trafficking still exist and often

others arise from the responsibilities of the relevant persons charged with identification of victims. There are myriad reasons why trafficked persons may not be identified as such by those that they encounter in the criminal justice process, some of which are considered below.

### *6.5.3.1 Victims do not self-identify*

Drew observes that: '[w]aiting for a client to self-identify will not suffice. Many clients will be unwilling or unable to raise the issue first, because of fear, ignorance or linguistic barriers'.[144] The circumstances in which human trafficking occurs mean that, despite an increasingly victim-centred approach, there is a low level of self-reporting on the part of victims.[145] Self-identification places a lot of responsibility on these vulnerable victims of abuse, and there are many barriers standing in the way of self-identification.

The clandestine nature of human trafficking means that outreach to victims is not easily achieved. The UK Action Plan on Tackling Human Trafficking goes so far as to recognise that some trafficked persons may not perceive themselves as such, which is a clear barrier to identification.[146] The Action Plan states that:

> ... [s]ome victims do not self-identify because they may not recognise that the situation in which they are in actually constitutes a recognised crime against their person, or they may have been in an exploitative situation for such a long period of time that they have built up a psychological dependency on their exploiters.

Accordingly, the victim may not be familiar with the terminology of 'trafficking', but more importantly, she may not be aware that she is even a 'victim' – she may be aware that she is being exploited and/or badly treated, but simply perceive herself as a prostitute, potentially with irregular immigration status. The reference to 'psychological dependency' of the victim, upon the trafficker, is also poignant

impede identification. For example, to understand the real nature of forced labour, we need to understand the link between coercive exploitation and the abusive treatment that workers might be subjected to as a result of "rational" choice (Speech by the Roger Plant, the head of the Special Action Programme on Forced labour of the ILO, at a conference "Work – Migration – Rights; Strategies against Trafficking in Women", Vienna, October 2008.) Traffickers have become more sophisticated and the coercion they apply more complex and "invisible". Instead of kidnapping, physical violence, and keeping victims under lock, traffickers tend to use methods that create a complex web of control, through debt bondage, psychological violence and threats, use of modern information technologies and intimidation to put their victims into a situation of total dependence, where victims are scared or too intimidated to escape or reveal what happened to them'. See Anti-Trafficking Monitoring Group 'Wrong kind of victim? One year on: an analysis of UK measures to protect trafficked persons' (June 2010) 17.

144 S Drew 'calls to raise the game against human trafficking' (4 December 2008) 46 *Law Society Gazette* Articles.

145 Home Office/Scottish Government 'Update to the UK Action Plan on Human Trafficking' (October 2009) 25.

146 Home Office and Scottish Executive (n 10).

as it highlights one of the complexities arising with regard to understanding of victim behaviour in a trafficking nexus. The victim may have a close and dependent relationship with her controller which presents a barrier in the form of a psychological web that must be untangled in order to identify the individual as a victim of trafficking.

Furthermore, it is becoming apparent that the expectations placed upon putative victims at an early stage in the identification process are far too high. Research conducted by Hales and Gelsthorpe identified failure by arresting police to provide appropriate responses to disclosures of victimisation and to 'understand the impact of ongoing threats on the arrestee's ability to fully and freely disclose all that had happened at their initial interview'.[147] Victims may feel '... socially isolated, vulnerable, traumatised, subject to flashbacks, ashamed to tell others what had happened and finding difficulty in knowing whom to trust'.[148] On top of this, victims may be less likely to identify themselves to male personnel. Increased representation of women involved in, for example, border management could be a factor in successfully identifying more female sex trafficking victims.[149]

The UK Action Plan also states that:

> Some victims may be unwilling to identify themselves to the authorities due to a fear of reprisal from their traffickers, whilst others may fear that they will be penalised for their immigration status. There are also a number of victims who have a distrust of the authorities due to past negative experiences or possible levels of corruption in their home countries.[150]

Threats from traffickers are very real. These threats, for many, do not disappear once the victim is discovered or arrested.[151] Hales and Gelsthorpe's research found that in two cases encountered, children of the victim had been under threat from traffickers and reprisals had been attempted and carried out on family members.[152] Victims may agree to and begin to take part in the criminal process, and disengage at a later point owing to fear of reprisals. Article 28 of the CoE Trafficking Convention calls for states to 'adopt such legislative or other measures as may be necessary to provide effective and appropriate protection from potential retaliation or intimidation in particular during and after investigation and prosecution of perpetrators' as regards victims, witnesses and other relevant persons. The Metropolitan Human Trafficking Team has run an initiative along with the Poppy Project in order to communicate sensitively with women who choose to disengage in order to gain a better understanding of their reasons for doing so,

147 Hales and Gelsthorpe (n 75) 27.
148 ibid 26.
149 OSCE 'Border management and gender', Geneva Centre for the Democratic Control of Armed Forces (2008) http://www.osce.org/publications/odihr/2008/02/29669_1035_en.pdf (last accessed 21 January 2009, link no longer live).
150 Home Office and Scottish Executive (n 10) 48.
151 Hales and Gelsthorpe (n 75) 26.
152 ibid 28.

purportedly with a view better to meet the needs of victims who take part in criminal proceedings and to provide better support in order to encourage continued engagement. Threats from traffickers also come in more hidden psychological forms, such as the use of, for example, Juju rituals to secure victim compliance.[153]

We know from cases such as *R v O* that trafficked victims are penalised for immigration offences. Furthermore, as the Action Plan recognises, victims may be disinclined to trust those who they come into contact with, be it the police, immigration officials or NGOs. Feder notes that mistrust of the authorities is often present in migrants who have experienced sexual violence, for example.[154] For adult victims, consent is required so that they can be referred into the NRM. Hales and Gelsthorpe's research found that 43 women in the target group were identified as trafficked victims by the researchers. Only 11 of these were referred into the NRM, and two of them were not processed until they had already served their sentences for their offences.[155] The traumatic experiences of trafficked victims do not render them easily amenable to providing full, reliable testimony[156] as to their experiences at an early stage following their discovery, if at all.

### *6.5.3.2 Lack of understanding of victim behaviour and the perception of consent*

The UK Action Plan on Tackling Human Trafficking recognises that the relevant persons coming into contact with victims of trafficking may not correctly identify them, and this is borne out in the case law.[157] This may lead to the perception of compliance of the victim, that present a barrier here – be the perception (by another) of the victim's consent be drawn from evidence, or from assumptions and poor attitudes toward 'irregular migrants'. Lack of understanding of the behaviour of victims of abuse and exploitation can lead to incorrect assumptions about the consent of that person, within and without of a trafficking nexus. In some

153 See *R v O* [2011] EWCA Crim 2226; Sarah Bell 'Trafficked girls controlled by Juju magic rituals' (2011) *BBC News online* http://www.bbc.co.uk/news/uk-14044205 (last accessed 14 January 2014); see also 'Breaking the spell of Juju: Detective Constable Andy Desmond, from London's Metropolitan Police's Human Exploitation and Organised Crime Command, explains how his team's investigation into the use of 'juju' (voodoo) in trafficking from Nigeria, helped lead to the successful conviction of Ikponmwosa Omuruyi, also known as Anthony Harrison, for the trafficking of two teenage girls into prostitution' http://www.antislavery.org/includes/documents/cm_docs/2012/1/13_autumn_2011_feature.pdf (last accessed 9 June 2014).

154 B Feder 'A credible judge of character? A psycho-legal analysis of credibility assessments for asylum applicants with a history of sexual violence' (2010) 24(4) *Journal of Immigration Asylum and Nationality Law* 295–323.

155 Hales and Gelsthorpe (n 75) 26.

156 Inconsistent testimonies provided by putative victims can influence the perception of that person as 'not trafficked', when in fact it can be an indicator of trafficking. Research conducted by Hales and Gelsthorpe noted the inability of asylum officials, for example, to be sensitive to the impact of trauma (sexual or otherwise) on the victim's ability to provide consistent and comprehensive testimony as to their experiences. See Hales and Gelsthorpe (n 75) 28.

157 See, for example, *R v O* [2008] EWCA Crim 2835; *R v LM* [2010] EWCA Crim 2327, [2011] 1 Cr App R 12, [2011] Crim LR 425; *R v N and LE* [2012] EWCA Crim 189; *OOO v Commissioner of Police of the Metropolis* [2011] EWHC 1246 (QB).

situations where control is exerted over another, the 'willingness' of a victim may be examined in some detail for the purpose of determining the full complement of offences to be brought against the perpetrator.[158] The appearance of compliance and/or autonomy plays a significant role in which side of the line on which each putative victim will fall – that of 'trafficked' or that of 'not trafficked'.

The appearance of consent or compliance comes about in a variety of ways, such as when victims are seen to have had an opportunity to escape or call externally for help, but have not done so. The truth of the matter may be that, for some victims, the struggle ceases to be about escape and instead turns into one of survival. For example, in the case of *R v N and LE*,[159] one of the defendants (who was a putative victim of trafficking and was on trial for his part in cannabis cultivation) was found to have a mobile phone and some money on him. This was initially taken to indicate a level of autonomy that would not be present in a 'true' victim of trafficking. However, research by Elliott and McCartan indicates that it is not unusual for victims of trafficking in the UK to have a mobile phone, many of which are given to the victims by their traffickers.[160] The very item that is seen as an indicator of freedom is in fact the very tool that the trafficker uses to maintain control over their victims – to contact them, check up on them and keep them in contact with clients.[161]

Hoyle's research found that victims would be asked questions by UKBA staff such as '… was there a window in the room? Was it locked? Were you on the top floor?'[162] The unfortunate reality is that, although some victims will be permitted, for example, to leave the premises alone, they will not try to run or escape. An analogy brought out by the research is that of victims of domestic abuse.[163] There is a lack of understanding of how these victims do or 'should' behave, and why they do not run or call for help when presented with the opportunity to do so. This does not mean that they consent; it means they are controlled through violence, threats, psychological coercion or some other means to a point that renders it impossible for them to leave. If the behaviour of these victims is incorrectly interpreted, and if the formal 'indicators' that officials are told to look out for are applied too stringently, it is not impossible to conceive of a significant amount of genuine victims slipping through the net and being misidentified.

158 Colleen Stan, for example, was sexually abused and held in servitude for several years, during which time her kidnapper (Hooker) gradually gave her more and more latitude in her movements to the point where she was allowed to visit her family, and then returned to her kidnapper in an ostensibly willing manner. It was also alleged at trial that she consented to sexual activity with him. Expert evidence from a specialist in coercion was offered to help the jury understand how Stan could have acted as something resembling a 'compliant' victim in light of what she had been through. See J B Green *Colleen Stan: The Simple Gifts of Life* (*iUniverse.com*, 2009) 25.

159 *R v N and LE* [2012] EWCA Crim 189.

160 J Elliott and K McCartan 'The reality of trafficked peoples access to technology' (2013) 77(3) *Journal of Criminal Law* 255–73.

161 ibid.

162 Hoyle and others (n 134).

163 Elliott and McCartan (n 160); Hoyle and others (n 134) 323.

### *6.5.3.3 Lack of training amongst officials*

That awareness and training among officials as regards identification of trafficked victims may still be somewhat deficient is exemplified by the recent case of *OOO et al v Commissioner of Metropolitan Police*,[164] in which there were a number of occasions where police officers were asked to investigate the situation of the women involved, although they failed to do so. Had they done so, it would potentially have been discovered that the victims had been subjected to slavery-like practices. In summary, it was held that police duties to investigate alleged breaches of an individual's Article 3 and Article 4 ECHR rights was not limited solely to where an alleged victim had made a complaint. The duty was triggered as soon as a credible allegation was received, however that information was brought to their attention. That case provided a particularly shocking insight into the potential for information relating to trafficking to be ignored – one officer, when informed by a concerned party about a suspected trafficked victim, responded by saying: 'If I were you I wouldn't get involved'.[165] The officer also told the informant that:

> ... there were a lot of people ... who try to use the police to get out of situations that they have got themselves into. The officer appeared to think that [the fifth claimant] was partly to blame for coming into the UK illegally even though she was a child and said that the police see a lot of people in [the fifth claimant's] position.[166]

This ill-conceived perception of victim compliance is highly damaging to the identification process and demonstrates a need for education and training among certain officials. One putative victim encountered by Hales and Gelsthorpe in their research questioned: 'Why after all I have been through are you the first person to listen to my whole story?'[167] In some cases victims are simply neither seen nor believed. For the effective protection of victims, it is clearly imperative that the relevant authorities charged with identifying the victims have heightened awareness of and sensitivity to the exploitative, coercive and clandestine nature of trafficking. Intense scrutiny as regards any potential instance of trafficking is essential. Border officials will similarly have training needs.[168]

Although already theoretically compliant with the victim protection and assistance provisions of the anti-trafficking regime, the Anti-Trafficking Monitoring Group[169] has noted various problems occurring under the current system,[170]

164 *OOO et al v Commissioner of Metropolitan Police* [2011] EWHC 1246 (QB).

165 [2011] EWHC 1246 (QB) para 38.

166 ibid.

167 Hales and Gelsthorpe (n 75) 28.

168 Guidance exists for 'frontline staff'; see, for example, Home Office 'Victims of human trafficking: guidance for frontline staff' (21 January 2013).

169 The Anti-Trafficking Monitoring Group 'Call for evidence' http://www.antislavery.org/english/what_we_do/programme_and_advocacy_work/anti_trafficking_monitoring_group.aspx (last accessed 1 June 2011).

170 See Anti-Trafficking Monitoring Group 'Wrong kind of victim?' (n 143) http://www.antislavery.

particularly with the identification system used in the UK – the NRM. The report states that:

> The system appears to be relying excessively on the discretion of officials who receive minimal training to staff a mechanism supported by flawed legal guidance relating to who should be identified as victims of trafficking, and without a formal appeals process. This fails to consistently identify and assist people who have been trafficked. Furthermore, the system appears to be putting more emphasis on the immigration status of the presumed trafficked persons, rather than the alleged crime committed against them.[171]

If this is indeed the case, then the current system is deficient – lack of consistent identification and a lack of formal route of appeal leaves the NRM and the assistance and protection measures beyond reach for those not correctly identified as trafficked persons, and this in turn leaves the entire process with a lack of bite.

As considered in Chapter 3, the specifics of the 'means' element of trafficking are not always clearly separable, although they nonetheless go toward establishing the definition of human trafficking as a non-consensual process, or at least a process where any consent given may be rendered irrelevant by use of any of the 'means'. This in turn relies upon objective proof of 'coercion' etc being shown by the state in order to prosecute a trafficker. The victim stands in her own metaphorical trial in terms of establishing the same, as she is assessed by 'indicators' that are given to those charged with identifying her. These 'indicators' are used to decide whether she was coerced, for example, and is therefore a victim or, if there are a lack of 'indicators' of such treatment, she may simply be rendered merely another 'smuggled prostitute'. In the words of Raymond, '[n]o woman should be punished for her own sexual exploitation',[172] although this is what incorrect or misidentification of trafficked victims has the effect of doing.

### *6.5.3.4 Emphasis on immigration*

Early statistics indicate that there is a significant disparity between rates of 'conclusive grounds' decisions being granted that correlate with the (ir)regularity of immigration status of the victim. The Anti-Trafficking Monitoring Group Report of 2010 found that:

> The UK citizens referred were speedily identified as having been trafficked with a rate of 76 per cent of cases positively identified as trafficking, in contrast with the rate of cases positively identified as trafficked as a whole of 19 per cent. The rate of nationals from other EU states identified as trafficked

org/includes/documents/cm_docs/2010/a/1_atmg_report_for_web.pdf (last accessed 1 July 2011).

171 ibid 9.

172 J Raymond '10 reasons for not legalising prostitution' (2003) 2 *Journal of Trauma Practice* 315.

was 29.2 per cent, while that of nationals from countries outside the EU was only 11.9 per cent.[173]

Although this cannot be interpreted conclusively as evidence of discrimination against third country nationals, the difference is startling.[174] The report goes on to state that: 'these figures merit further investigation by the Home Office, to check that individuals from outside the EU are not being subject to discrimination in the decision-making process'.[175] However, more recent figures from GRETA, compiled two years after the NRM had been implemented, suggest that, although the identification rate for EU nationals has improved significantly, the situation for third country nationals has not improved as significantly. The UK Country-specific GRETA report stated that 86 per cent of UK nationals, 71 per cent of other EU/EEA nationals, and 21 per cent of non-EU/EEA nationals received conclusive grounds decisions.[176] On the evidence, it would appear that the UK may not be doing enough to meet its obligations under the CoE Trafficking Convention as regards these putative victims.

The use of two separate authorities to deal with putative victims' origination from inside or outside of the EEA is questionable from the outset. The Centre for Social Justice in the UK states that: 'We recommend that better engagement with the National Referral Mechanism is fostered through investing competent authority decision-making powers into one body'.[177] The use of the UKBA to identify third country nationals, while all other putative victims are dealt with by the UKHTC, sends out a message that there is a division or hierarchy of victims dependent upon their country of origin. This is borne out by the statistics above; it seems that a finding of trafficking (where it becomes necessary – for adults – to determine the coercion/consent question), is less likely to come about where the putative victim is a third country national. Hales and Gelsthorpe found that: 'On the whole, evidence gathered on immigration case management for those in the target group indicated that they were viewed as illegal migrants, rather than victims of trafficking or abuse by others'.[178] It seems that immigration status may be being treated as a significant determining factor as regards victimhood.

## 6.6 Non-criminalisation of victims of human trafficking

The prosecution of trafficked victims who have committed offences as a direct consequence of having been trafficked is taking place in the domestic courts, as

173 The Anti-Trafficking Monitoring Group (n 143) 9.

174 ibid.

175 ibid.

176 GRETA, Council of Europe 'Report concerning the implementation of the Council of Europe Convention on Action against Trafficking in Human Beings by the United Kingdom' (2012) 6 para 217.

177 Centre for Social Justice 'It happens here: equipping the United Kingdom to fight modern slavery' (March 2013) 12.

178 Hales and Gelsthorpe (n 75) 28.

case law tells us.[179] The use of criminal law against some migrants – particularly involuntary migrants – can be inappropriate to say the least.[180] All too often, trafficked victims are treated not as victims but as criminals, as demonstrated by *R v O*, above. The JCHR has voiced concerns, notably that:

> Section 2 of the Asylum and Immigration (Treatment of Claimants, etc.) Act 2004 makes it an offence to enter into the UK without valid passports and visas. This, it was claimed, is detrimental to trafficked victims as many of them use false documentation to enter.[181]

Offences other those related to immigration could feasibly also be committed by trafficked persons as a result of trafficking-related compulsion.[182]

The CoE Trafficking Convention addresses the issue of non-criminalisation of victims of trafficking, by explicitly stating that: 'Each Party shall, in accordance with the basic principles of its legal system, *provide for the possibility* of not imposing penalties on victims for their involvement in unlawful activities, to the extent that they have been compelled to do so' (emphasis added).[183] Notably, the language employed here is weak,[184] and is not framed in terms of an obligation. Instead, it creates a duty actively to consider whether or not prosecution should be pursued. In *R v LM*, it was recognised that:

> (Article 26) does not say that no trafficked victim should be prosecuted, whatever offence has been committed. It does not say that no trafficked victim should be prosecuted when the offence is in some way connected with or arises out of trafficking. It does not provide a defence which may be advanced before a jury. What it says is no more, but no less, than that careful consideration must be given to whether public policy calls for a prosecution and punishment when the defendant is a trafficked victim and the crime has been committed when he or she was in some manner compelled (in the broad sense) to commit it. Article 26 does not require a blanket immunity from prosecution for trafficked victims.[185]

179 *R v O* [2008] EWCA Crim 2835; *R v LM* [2010] EWCA Crim 2327; *R v N and LE* [2012] EWCA Crim 189.

180 Of particular note here is the theme of 'Crimmigration' – the 'convergence of criminal and immigration law in marking out the boundaries of who is an accepted member of society'. See J P Stumpf 'The crimmigration crisis: immigrants, crime and sovereign power' (2006) *ExpressO* 1.

181 Joint Committee on Human Rights Twenty-Sixth Report (n 30) para 116.

182 Including, but not confined to, causing or inciting/controlling prostitution for gain (provided for within SOA 2003 ss 52 and 53); keeping a brothel (Sexual Offences Act 1956 s 33 or s 33a); theft in organised pickpocketing gangs (Theft Act 1968 s 1); or cultivation of cannabis plants (Misuse of Drugs Act 1971 s 6).

183 CoE Trafficking Convention (n 6) art 26.

184 A Gallagher 'Recent legal developments in the field of human trafficking: a critical review of the 2005 European Convention and related instruments' (2006) 8 *European Journal of Migration and Law* 163–89, 178.

185 *R v LM* [2010] EWCA Crim 2327 para 13.

Nonetheless, this remains a very important provision. The EU 2011 Directive has a similar provision.[186] The impact of this provision, however, turns on whether and how it is drawn upon, and this issue is in turn affected by how the provision is implemented domestically.

As noted by Laws LJ in *R v O*,[187] there are the CPS Protocols[188] that cover the commission of immigration offences, such as possession of a false passport or forged identity document, by trafficking victims who have been coerced by someone else. According to these Protocols, if the suspect is a 'credible trafficked victim', that is, 'the investigation officers have reason to believe that the person has been trafficked',[189] then the prosecutor must consider whether pursuing a prosecution for the immigration offence best serves public interest.[190] As regards the latter Protocol, which deals with 'Prosecution of Young Defendants Charged With Offences Who Might Be Trafficked Victims',[191] evidence of duress will lead to the case being discontinued and, where the evidence is less clear, 'further details should be sought from the police and youth offender teams, so that the public interest in continuing a prosecution can be considered carefully'.[192] The Court of Appeal noted in *R v O* that these protocols – although incorporated into the Code for Crown Prosecutors – did not at the time appear in standard criminal law practice books.

Once again, rather tentative language is employed in the CPS Protocols, and the possibility of continuing with the prosecution remains. As the UK Action Plan on Tackling Human Trafficking observes: 'It is difficult to envisage circumstances where it would be in the public interest to prosecute genuine victims of human trafficking for immigration offences'.[193]

186 Article 8 of the EU 2011 Directive (n 7) states that: 'Member States shall, in accordance with the basic principles of their legal systems, take the necessary measures to ensure that competent national authorities are entitled not to prosecute or impose penalties on victims of trafficking in human beings for their involvement in criminal activities which they have been compelled to commit as a direct consequence of being subjected to any of the acts referred to in Article 2'.

187 *R v O* [2008] EWCA Crim 2835 para 14.

188 Crown Prosecution Service (n 113).

189 ibid.

190 In doing so, the following factors should be taken into consideration: the role that the suspect has in the immigration offence; was the immigration offence a direct consequence of their trafficked situation; were violence, threats or coercion used on the trafficked victim to procure the commission of the offence; was the victim vulnerable or put in considerable fear. See Crown Prosecution Service (n 113).

191 ibid.

192 The Protocol goes on to state that: 'Prosecutors should also be alert to the fact that an appropriate adult in interview could be the trafficker or a person allied to the trafficker. Any youth who might be a trafficked victim should be afforded the protection of our childcare legislation if there are concerns that they have been working under duress or if their well-being has been threatened. In these circumstances, the youth may well then become a victim or witness for a prosecution against those who have exploited them. The younger a child is, the more careful investigators and prosecutors have to be in deciding whether it is right to ask them to become involved in a criminal trial'.

193 Home Office and Scottish Executive (n 10) 57.

The pre-Convention ratification case, *R v O*, is a clear example of the consequences of misidentification. More recent case law, decided post-ratification of the Convention, provides illumination as to whether or not the Article 26 duty of active consideration is indeed being discharged. *R v LM*,[194] a combined appeal with five appellants, concerned individuals who had previously been trafficked, and three of whom were convicted for then playing a part in the 'controlling of prostitution for gain'[195] of other prostitutes or trafficked persons.

References were made to Articles 26[196] and 10[197] of the CoE Trafficking Convention, as there were to the CPS Protocols[198] and to *R v O*. The appellants contended a breach of Article 10 of the CoE Trafficking Convention, on the basis that they had never been advised about the relevant referral agency which could have aided their identification as formally trafficked persons, and that this failure had rendered the prosecution unlawful. The appeal in *R v LM* was allowed, but not on this basis. It was instead allowed because the Article 26 duty (to consider non-prosecution) was ignored at the crucial point where the crown had, at a late stage, accepted a basis of plea that the appellants had been trafficked and violently coerced into prostitution themselves, and that their part in anything comprising or resembling 'controlling prostitution' had been done under pressure, that is, as a result of being trafficked, although falling short of duress. The initial reaction in cases such as *R v LM* suggest a lack of understanding – of the inherently coercive nature of human trafficking, the hold that the trafficker has over the victim and the consequent victim behaviour – on the part of the officials charged with identifying them, and with prosecuting traffickers, who are the true creators of the harms in a trafficking situation.

It seems that the lessons to be learned from *R v O* are still being learned now that a formal system is in place, and it is clear that the same mistakes as to referral to relevant agencies etc by counsel is still an issue, consequently raising the need for constant and improved awareness raising and training of all of those involved in the victim identification process. Perhaps, the offence in *R v O* arguably being of a lesser nature (that is, immigration offences as opposed to controlling prostitution) means that had *R v O* occurred post-ratification of the CoE Convention then the case may have been decided differently at first instance, although one can only speculate on this matter.

These cases provide evidence that the system has flaws and required 'kid gloves' treatment – *R v LM* in particular illustrates the effects of perceptions of consent in an inherently coercive environment, coupled with lack of knowledge and understanding of the legal representatives involved in the case. More recently we have

194 *R v LM* [2010] EWCA Crim 2327, [2011] 1 Cr App R 12, [2011] Crim LR 425.

195 Contrary to SOA 2003 s 3.

196 Article 26 of the CoE Trafficking Convention provides for the possibility of non-prosecution of trafficked victims for offences committed as a result of having been trafficked.

197 Article 10 of the CoE Trafficking Convention provides for the identification of victims of trafficking.

198 Crown Prosecution Service (n 113).

the case of *R v N and LE*,[199] which concerned two defendants, both Vietnamese minors who had been arrested in cannabis farms and sentenced to 20 months' imprisonment. Both saw their convictions confirmed, after the custodial sentences had been completed. Identification of the victims did not occur until after the custodial sentences had been carried out in any case. Guidance that existed at the time relating to trafficked persons and cannabis production was ignored or not known about or consulted.[200]

The evidence of trafficking was more questionable in this case than in either *R v O* or *R v LM* yet still, the fact that a conclusive grounds decision was finally reached points to an inadequate identification system, inadequate awareness of trafficking amongst those who are part of that system, and continuing lack of awareness of the non-punishment principle. Hales and Gelsthorpe's research determined that: 'Even where referrals were made to the NRM that resulted in a positive decision and non-prosecution, the victims spent on average four months in custody'.[201] These cases are illustrative of the deficiencies of the identification system, which in turn exacerbate the ongoing lack of awareness and consideration of the non-punishment principle.[202] Furthermore, that non-prosecution is wholly dependent upon correct victim identification, to which there exists numerous barriers. In this manner, the misidentified are victimised twice. These cases can at the most – to a limited extent – tell us how future similar cases should be conducted and at the very least, we can continue to learn from them.

The following section will discuss the international protection regime available to the victim, beyond the bespoke provisions of the anti-trafficking regime.

## 6.7 International protection for the trafficked person

International protection may apply to anyone who is in need of it. Specifically in the context of human trafficking, the CoE Trafficking Convention clearly envisages situations where it may be necessary for trafficking victims to remain in the destination state beyond simply taking part in the criminal proceedings against their traffickers. The potential vagueness of the 'personal situation' referred to in the CoE Trafficking Convention as regards temporary residence permits, for example, may mean that the current standards (of the anti-trafficking regime) are deficient, particularly in the UK context where it was perceived that there was

199 *R v N and LE* [2012] EWCA Crim 189.

200 Association of Chief Police Officers of England, c/o The Child Exploitation and Online Protection (CEOP) Centre 'Position from ACPO leads on child protection and cannabis cultivation on children and young people recovered in cannabis farms', and Association of Chief Police Officers of England 'UK national problem profile: commercial cultivation of cannabis 2012'.

201 Hales and Gelsthorpe (n 75) 27.

202 ibid, who state that: 'In cases where the defence did not raise the issue of trafficking in defence but in mitigation, there were only two examples where the CPS adjourned proceedings for an NRM assessment, resulting on a decision as to whether it was in the public interest to continue with the prosecution. This did not happen in court proceedings for any of those charged in relation to cannabis production'. See Hales and Gelsthorpe (n 75) 28.

barely a need for implementing legislation. This is not to suggest that the UK Government is legally at fault (although perhaps falling 'below par', so to speak) as regards implementation of the CoE Trafficking Convention, but that the provisions of the Convention itself could have been drafted more conclusively and stringently, so that assistance and protection required owing to a 'personal situation' may have more clarity of scope[203] and therefore be more inclusively applied.

Such issues, that is, the potential deficiency of the current system, become relevant when considering complementary protective measures, such as those available through international protection regimes. This is particularly so when considering the potential for retrafficking and revictimisation on return to the country of origin, as well as the threat of reprisals from the traffickers or persecution from the local community as a result of having been a prostitute. The destination state must take various factors into account and make the decision as to whether the best action to take is to expel the victim, or allow her to remain. The same regime would apply to any human being in a country where the relevant instruments have been ratified. Such matters undoubtedly invoke human rights concerns, as will be discussed below.

### *6.7.1 Trafficked victims as refugees?*

The purpose of asylum law and policy, and related matters such as discretionary leave, is twofold. Primarily, there is the focus of giving aid to those who are in need of it. On the other hand, the reduction and control of numbers entering and staying in the UK is also at the heart of this. Any system that is intended to benefit a body of persons will inevitably be subject to abuse; therefore procedures must be in place that aid the determination as to who is, and who is not, genuinely in need.

The first point of call for many persons with a potential need to remain in the destination state would be to claim asylum, relying upon the Convention Relating to the Status of Refugees (Refugee Convention).[204] As noted by the JCHR in its Tenth Report, there are 'human rights issues raised by the treatment of asylum seekers, from the time when they first claim asylum in the UK, through to either the granting of asylum, or, for asylum seekers whose claims are refused, their departure from the UK'.[205] Clearly, efficient application of the Refugee Convention criteria is paramount to securing protection of certain vulnerable persons.

203 The terms used in the Explanatory Report to the Trafficking Convention as regards the victim's 'personal situation' refer directly to the 'victim's safety, state of health, family situation or some other factor' which can be interpreted broadly, although they do appear to be drafted in a way which relates to human rights standards under, say Articles 3 and 8 of the ECHR, which were indeed already part of the UK's human rights obligations under the ECHR.

204 Convention Relating to the Status of Refugees (adopted 28 July 1951, entered into force 22 April 1954) 189 UNTS 137 (Refugee Convention).

205 Joint Committee on Human Rights Tenth Report (Session 2006–2007), 'The treatment of asylum seekers' 5 http://www.publications.parliament.uk/pa/jt200607/jtselect/jtrights/81/81i.pdf (last accessed 30 January 2011).

#### 6.7.1.1 The Refugee Convention: qualifying criteria

In order to come within the scope of the Refugee Convention, an individual must demonstrate a 'well-founded fear of being persecuted for reasons of race, religion, nationality, membership of a particular social group or political opinion'.[206] Some such persons may well have sought out the services of traffickers or smugglers in order to leave the origin state where they are being subjected to persecution, in which case they may have grounds to make an asylum claim in the same way that non-trafficked asylum seekers would. It is, however, worth exploring if, how and when the Refugee Convention may apply to trafficked victims, that is, the circumstances in which such persons may claim asylum because they have been trafficked.

Both the UN Trafficking Protocol[207] and the CoE Trafficking Convention[208] implicitly recognise the potential for the entitlement of a proportion of trafficked victims to international refugee protection. The conditions contained within the Refugee Convention are somewhat limited, and there is likely to be a body of trafficked persons who may have a need to not be returned to the origin state but fall outside of the scope of the Refugee Convention.

A trafficked victim or putative victim may make claims for international protection in several circumstances. For example, she may have escaped her traffickers and be seeking protection in the destination state; she may have been trafficked within national territory, and have fled abroad; or the individual may fear becoming trafficked and therefore flees abroad.[209] The victim may also fear persecution on return to the origin state as a result of having worked in the sex trade, albeit unwillingly. If a victim is to make a claim for international protection under the Refugee Convention, then she must fulfil the two-step criteria in order to qualify for refugee protection.

Primarily, the victim must demonstrate a well founded fear of persecution. Secondly, there must be a causal link[210] between this persecution and one of the Convention grounds of 'race, religion, nationality, membership of a particular social group or political opinion',[211] hence the words 'for reasons of' membership of a particular social group, for example. It is not difficult to envisage trafficked persons who do not fall into those categories but nonetheless require some form of help instead of deportation. At present, those who do not qualify for refugee status can be considered for humanitarian protection[212] or discretionary leave[213] if

206 Refugee Convention (n 204) art 1(a)2.

207 ibid art 14(1).

208 ibid art 40(4).

209 'Guidelines on international protection' (n 25) para 13.

210 ibid part f.

211 Refugee Convention (n 204) art 1(A)(2).

212 UK Border Agency 'Humanitarian protection' http://www.ukba.homeoffice.gov.uk/sitecontent/documents/policyandlaw/asylumpolicyinstructions/apis/humanitarianprotection.pdf?view=Binary (last accessed 21 February 2010, link no longer live).

213 UK Border Agency 'Discretionary leave' http://www.bia.homeoffice.gov.uk/sitecontent/documents/policyandlaw/asylumpolicyinstructions/apis/discretionaryleave.pdf?view=Binary (last accessed 16 January 2014).

they need to remain in the UK. Nonetheless, there exist some established trafficking cases where refugee status has been attributed to the victim as a result of, for example, the inability of the origin state to protect the victim from retrafficking,[214] or where trafficked women have been considered to constitute a 'social group' for the purposes of the Refugee Convention.[215] This is therefore not a novel concept.

#### *6.7.1.2 The scope of 'persecution': trafficking, retrafficking, reprisals and social ostracism*

Guidelines on International Protection state that 'persecution' in the context of the Refugee Convention can involve 'serious human rights violations, including a threat to life or freedom, as well as other kinds of serious harm or intolerable predicament, as assessed in the light of the opinions, feelings and psychological make-up of the asylum applicant'.[216] With respect to trafficked victims or possible future trafficked persons, harm feared as a result of trafficking or its anticipation may amount to persecution in the context of the Refugee Convention.[217]

Along the same vein, various characteristics inherent in the trafficking process, such as sexual enslavement, forced prostitution and rape, may amount to persecution. The ongoing effects of past trafficking, such as psychological trauma, may in extreme cases qualify as persecution and render it sufficient to recognise an individual as a refugee, provided that a causal link with a Convention ground may be established.[218]

The threat of reprisals, retrafficking or ostracism from the community in the origin state may also amount to persecution. A recent and somewhat groundbreaking decision taken in the UK High Court recently awarded substantial damages to a Moldovan victim of repeated trafficking, who now has refugee status in the UK, 'for failing to take steps to protect her and for sending her back to Moldova despite substantial grounds to believe she was at risk from her traffickers'.[219] Aside from the risk of other harm, the risk of retrafficking is very real. A study conducted by the Poppy Project in Britain indicated that 19 per cent of victims who had been assisted by the project had been retrafficked,[220] while a multi-country survey in South-east Europe suggested that between 3 and 34 per cent of victims who were assisted had been retrafficked.[221] Bearing all of the above in mind, it seems clear that persecution can as such occur before, during and post-trafficking.

Of course, evidence will be required to establish persecution or the possibility

214 See, for example, Travis (n 35).

215 See, for example, *SB (PSG – Protection Regulations – reg 6) Moldova CG* [2008] UKAIT 00002, where it was stated that: '"Former victims of trafficking" and "former victims of trafficking for sexual exploitation" are capable of being members of a particular social group within regulation 6(1)(d) because of their shared common background or past experience of having been trafficked'.

216 'Guidelines on international protection' (n 25) para 14.

217 ibid para 15.

218 ibid para 16.

219 See Travis (n 35).

220 Poppy Project (2004) 'We women are trafficked: quantifying the gendered experience of trafficking in the UK', London, Poppy Project.

221 M Lee *Trafficking and global crime control* (Sage 2012).

thereof in terms of asylum applications. In *PO (Nigeria)* it was stated that the 'AIT erred in law by requiring her to prove by personal evidence that her trafficker had operated as part of a gang in Nigeria as a necessary element in establishing that she would be at risk on return'.[222] Requiring such a level of evidence in asylum claims to be personally provided by the putative trafficked victim seems to be putting the threshold too high, to say the least. However, the requirement of providing evidence of fear of risk on return is a necessary part of the asylum process; this case is simply illustrative of the bar being set too high,[223] particularly with the onus placed directly on the putative victim.

The basis for the requisite 'well-founded fear' of persecution relates to the circumstances at the time in the country of origin. The United Nations High Commissioner for Refugees (UNHCR) Guidelines on International Protection[224] state that:

> … where a state fails to take such reasonable steps as are within its competence to prevent trafficking and provide effective protection and assistance to victims, the fear of persecution of the individual is likely to be well founded. The mere existence of a law prohibiting trafficking in persons will not of itself be sufficient to exclude the possibility of persecution.[225]

Trafficking victims overwhelmingly originate from countries either suffering political upheaval, economic impoverishment or at least with economies in transition;[226] therefore it is not unreasonable to consider that those originating from such states may be at an increased risk of being trafficked than otherwise. Such states are ideal source countries for trafficked persons as a result of poverty, displacement and vulnerability to organised crime gangs. Many sex trafficking victims are female. Therefore, this particular body of persons – females from impoverished states with poor employment opportunities – may have significant cause to apprehend, fall subject to, or suffer the after effects of, sex trafficking sufficient for a well founded fear of persecution. Applicability of the Refugee Convention of course depends on satisfying the second stage; that of the causal link between persecution and one of the Refugee Convention grounds.

#### *6.7.1.3 Applicability of Refugee Convention grounds to victims of trafficking: establishing a causal link*

The relevant Convention grounds are 'race, religion, nationality, membership of a particular social group or political opinion'.[227] Such grounds may be difficult to

222 *PO (Nigeria) v Secretary of State for the Home Department* [2011] EWCA Civ 132 para 10.

223 The evidence required was referred to as imposing an 'unrealistic burden' on the appellant, *PO (Nigeria)* para 33.

224 'Guidelines on international protection' (n 25).

225 ibid para 23.

226 See ch 1 for discussion of the underlying 'push' factors affecting the decision to migrate.

227 Refugee Convention (n 204) art 1A(2).

establish with respect to asylum claims made by trafficked persons, particularly if trafficking is predominantly motivated by economic motives on the part of the trafficker.

Although it is necessary for one of the above grounds to be satisfied, 'it is sufficient that the Convention ground be a relevant factor contributing to the persecution; it is not necessary that it be the sole, or even dominant, cause'.[228] Various, even numerous, Refugee Convention grounds may apply to victims of sex trafficking. Race and nationality are particularly relevant from the perspective of demand for sexual services from different and 'exotic' women. All of the grounds potentially become relevant in the context of internal or cross border conflict in and between countries leading to sex trafficking as a form of 'weapon', so to speak, such as took place in the former Yugoslavia, in which context sex trafficking (in a war context) was specifically referred to as a crime against humanity.[229] The Refugee Convention was designed to be inclusive, rather than exclusive. Of particular interest is the matter of whether women per se are capable of constituting a 'social group' for the purposes of the Refugee Convention, in the context of human trafficking.

#### *6.7.1.4 The scope of 'social group'*

Early discussion during the drafting of Article 1A(2) of the Refugee Convention envisaged a narrower scope[230] than that which was ultimately adopted. 'Social group' as a Convention ground was included on the basis that an exhaustive list proved impossible to achieve.

In order for this element to be satisfied and for the causal link to be established, the actual persecution must not be a defining factor of the social group,[231] that is, the group must not be defined by reference to persecutory conduct. They are not members of a social group because they are persecuted; they must be persecuted because they are members of a social group. However, it was noted in *Applicant A v Minister for Immigration and Ethnic Affairs* that: 'while persecutory conduct cannot define the social group, the actions of the persecutors may serve to identify or even cause the creation of a particular social group in society'.[232]

It is not unreasonable to consider that gender could be an influential factor with respect to the type of persecution suffered.[233] If this analysis succeeds, then those who fear trafficking, and those who fear being retrafficked, simply because

228 'Guidelines on international protection' (n 25) para 29.

229 See, for example, Obokata (n 48). T Obokata, 'Smuggling of Human Beings from a Human Rights Perspective: Obligations of Non-State and State Actors Under International Human Rights Law' (2005) *International Journal of Refugee Law*, 17(2) 394–415, 394.

230 Convention relating to the Status of Refugees '1951 Conference of Plenipotentiaries on the Status of Refugees and Stateless Persons (*Travaux préparatoires*)' http://www.unhcr.org/pages/49da0e466.html (last accessed 23 May 2011).

231 *A v Minister for Immigration and Ethnic Affairs* [1997] 2 BHRC 143, High Court of Australia.

232 ibid (McHugh J).

233 *Guidelines on Gender Issues for Decision-Makers in 1996* (DIMA 1996).

they are women, may have the option to claim asylum on those grounds. Certain social subsets of women in particular may qualify as a social group such as single women, illiterate women, divorced women,[234] or women who have worked in the sex trade, or as 'sex slaves'[235] – the latter subset in particular is of note, as this potentially encompasses those who fear social ostracism if returned to their community in the origin state. According to the *dicta* from *Applicant A*, above, 'trafficked women' as such may also constitute a 'social group', by virtue of having been trafficked,[236] and indeed have been so classed in decided cases. In *SB (PSG – Protection Regulations – reg 6) Moldova CG*, it was stated that:

> Former 'victims of trafficking' and 'former victims of trafficking for sexual exploitation' are capable of being members of a particular social group … because of their shared common background or past experience of having been trafficked.[237]

It follows from this that those at risk of retrafficking may constitute 'persecution' for Refugee Convention purposes, therefore establishing both the persecution and the causal link to the Convention ground of 'social group'.

In order to satisfy this Convention ground in terms of 'women' as a social group, women would have to show that they feared persecution, that is, trafficking simply by virtue of their gender. The above-mentioned 'former victims of trafficking' become a 'social group' as a result of having been trafficked and being at risk of being retrafficked. This demonstrates 'after the event' (that is, post-trafficking) recognition of a 'social group'. However, can we establish 'women' as a freestanding 'social group' before the event (that is, prior to trafficking, because they are at risk of being trafficked)?

In order to constitute a social group, it is necessary that the members of the particular group 'either share a common characteristic other than their risk of being persecuted or are perceived as a group by society'.[238] Women share unchangeable characteristics, that is, that of being female, and frequently experience different treatment to men; it may therefore be feasible to argue that they constitute a particular social group in this context.[239]

234 'Guidelines on international protection' (n 25) para 38.

235 See *R on the Application of P v Secretary of State for the Home Department* [2008] EWHC 2447 (Admin).

236 See R Piotrowicz 'Victims of people trafficking and entitlement to international protection' (2005) 24 *Australian Yearbook of International Law* 167–70, 159.

237 *SB (PSG – Protection Regulations – reg 6) Moldova CG* [2008] UKAIT 00002, 'Determination and reasons' para 2. See http://www.nrcentre.org.uk/index.php?option=com_content&view=article&id=130:victims-of-trafficking-can-get-refugee-status&catid=13:Policies%20&%20Rulings&Itemid=9 (last accessed 4 May 2011).

238 'Guidelines on international protection' (n 25) para 37.

239 UNHCR Guidelines on International Protection '"Membership of a particular social group" within the context of Article 1A(2) of the 1951 Convention and/or its 1967 Protocol relating to the status of refugees' para 14 http://www.unhcr.org/3d58de2da.html (last accessed 15 February 2011).

'Women' as a 'social group' may on the face of it be deemed too broad. However, if women of a particular race (thereby satisfying the Convention ground) may be trafficked (and therefore persecuted) because of demand for the sexual services of exotic women, by the same token women as a social group, who share the immutable characteristic of being female, may equally be persecuted, that is, trafficked for sexual exploitation, simply by virtue of being women. Although demand for trafficked women for the purpose of sexual exploitation is 'often further grounded in social disparities of race, nationality, caste and colour',[240] the demand is, overall, for women.

The potential for women to be recognised as a 'social group' is becoming increasingly evident through examples such as *Canada v Ward*,[241] where it was recognised that a 'social group' could be constituted in various ways, including primarily '[g]roups defined by an innate or unchangeable characteristic'.[242] The case goes on to state that: 'The first category would embrace individuals fearing persecution on such bases as *gender*, linguistic background and sexual orientation' (emphasis added).

Nonetheless, if women as a social group were to be deemed too broad, an argument can still potentially be made in terms of economically impoverished women or unemployed women – particularly in certain geographical regions where the feminisation of poverty is evident – as social subsets, reflecting the fact that many trafficked women come from economically impoverished areas where female unemployment rates are high. Further weight is added to this argument by the judgment in *Islam v Secretary of State for the Home Department* and *R v Immigration Appeal Tribunal, ex parte Shah*,[243] where a majority in the House of Lords found that 'women in Pakistan' and/or 'Pakistani women' constituted a social group for Refugee Convention purposes; clearly, this is defined largely by reference to gender.

Difficulties in making such a claim can be envisaged, as it requires a departure from the norm, although the above-mentioned examples indicate that there is the potential for claims to be made here.

Beyond the Refugee Convention, we have ordinary human rights law, which is the focus of the following section.

### 6.7.2 Article 3 of the ECHR – expulsion/ deportation and the ECHR

If a trafficked person is sent back to a place where there is a serious risk that he or she will be retrafficked, then that person should not be returned to that

240 See Report on the Special Rapporteur on trafficking in persons, especially women and children, Sigma Huda, Addendum, Mission to Bosnia and Herzegovina 'Integration of the rights of women and the gender perspective' (30 November 2005) UN Doc E/CN.4/2006/62/Add.2 paras 48 and 66.

241 *Canada (Attorney General) v Ward* [1993] 2 SCR 689.

242 Other ways included groups whose members voluntarily associate for reasons so fundamental to their human dignity that they should not be forced to forsake the association; and groups associated by a former voluntary status, unalterable owing to its historical permanence.

243 [1999] 2 AC 629.

place.[244] There is undoubtedly a link between non-refoulement and Article 3 of the ECHR, as indicated by cases such as *Jabari*.[245] In *Kacaj*,[246] the Immigration Appeal Tribunal noted that:

> We recognise the possibility that Article 3 could be violated by actions which did not have a sufficiently systematic character to amount to persecution, although we doubt that this refinement would be likely to be determinative in any but a very small minority of cases.[247]

Victims of human trafficking have the potential to expand this 'very small minority of cases' – the treatment that they may face on return to their country of origin may fall short of the requisite standard of persecution of a systematic character, although they may still face serious ill-treatment.

As mentioned previously, the UKBA judge stated that, in respect of the issuance of a residence permit owing to the 'personal situation' of the victim, 'a combination of our existing obligations on asylum and human rights and our Discretionary Leave policy already cover situations where an individual's personal circumstances … make it necessary for them to remain in the UK'.[248] Obligations under the ECHR are obviously a relevant factor, where matters such as support or expulsion of victims trafficked for the purpose of sexual exploitation are concerned – most notably Articles 3 and 8.[249] Article 4 undoubtedly has significance for trafficking victims, as demonstrated in *Siliadin v France*.[250]

Article 3 of the ECHR becomes particularly relevant when considering the

244 In *M v UK* (Application no 16081/08) it was found that the victim of trafficking would be at significant risk of real harm if returned to the country of origin, and was therefore granted three years leave to remain in the UK. The UK had initially refused to grant her leave to remain in the UK despite the real risk of ill-treatment if she returned to Uganda.

245 See *Jabari v Turkey* (Application no 40035/98) 9 BHRC 1, [2001] INLR 136, where the individual concerned used a false passport to gain entry to Turkey following accusations of adultery in Iran, from where she originated. Initially, she was detained for deportation and refused asylum. Jabari was subsequently granted refugee status under the 1951 Refugee Convention, and she went on to lodge an application against her deportation in a Turkish court. This application was refused. She applied to the ECtHR, on the basis that there had been violations by Turkey of arts 3 and 13 of the ECHR, since if deported to Iran she faced the possibility of death by stoning or flogging, and furthermore that by the Turkish authorities had denied her an effective remedy. Her application was allowed, and violations of both Articles were found.

246 *Kacaj (Article 3 – Standard of Proof – Non-State Actors) Albania v Secretary of State for the Home Department* [2001] UKAIT 00018, United Kingdom: Asylum and Immigration Tribunal/ Immigration Appellate Authority (19 July 2001).

247 ibid para 19.

248 Home Office (n 49) 6.

249 Expulsion could result in breaches of art 3 where there was risk of ill-treatment on return to the origin state, and of art 8 where, for example, 'there was a serious risk of the persons concerned suffering an adverse effect on their health or their physical or moral integrity'. J McBride 'Irregular migrants and the European Convention on Human Rights' (AS/Mig/Inf (2005) 21) para 127.

250 *Siliadin v France* (2006) 43 EHRR 423, and *Rantsev v Cyprus and Russia* [2010] (Application no 25965/04).

potential for retrafficking and revictimisation on return to the country of origin, as well as the threat of reprisals from the traffickers, or perhaps the more general threat of organised crime, which has known links with human trafficking activity. These things may suffice to establish a need not to be returned to that country. The Article states that: 'No one shall be subjected to torture or to inhuman or degrading treatment or punishment'. This right forms part of the fundamental basis of any democratic society, and this value is enshrined in the ICCPR,[251] the American Convention on Human Rights[252] and the United Nations Convention Against Torture and other Cruel, Inhuman or Degrading Treatment of Punishment,[253] the last of which explicitly states that: 'No State Party shall expel, return ("refouler") or extradite a person to another State where there are substantial grounds for believing that he would be in danger of being subjected to torture'.[254]

Invoking Article 3 in the context of victims of trafficking involves consideration of the existence of potential[255] as well as actual violations. The country of proposed return would have to be unable to provide sufficient protection itself to the victim.[256]

Liability under the ECHR concerns the deporting state, as it is the direct consequence of the action of deportation that will lead to exposure of the individual concerned to treatment contrary to Article 3, albeit in the receiving state. The JCHR observes that repatriation into a situation of poverty does not bode well for victims of trafficking, who may fall subject to the same conditions or organised criminals who facilitated their trafficking in the first place.[257] Such measures are therefore counter-productive. Those who have been trafficked may even by their own actions fall back into the hands of traffickers, through seeking out a 'migration broker' to help them migrate, in the belief that either they could not be unlucky enough for it to happen a second time or that they have learned enough from their experience to avoid making the same mistakes again.

When considering this issue transplanted into a trafficking context, it is useful

251 ICCPR art 7.

252 American Convention on Human Rights art 5(2).

253 United Nations Convention against Torture and other Cruel, Inhuman or Degrading Treatment of Punishment (adopted by the General Assembly of the United Nations on 10 December 1984 (Resolution 39/46) entered into force on 26 June 1987).

254 United Nations Convention against Torture and other Cruel, Inhuman or Degrading Treatment of Punishment art 3(1).

255 See *Soering v UK* (1989) 11 EHRR 439; R Lillich 'The Soering case' (1991) 85 *American Journal of International Law* 128; Harris, O'Boyle and Warbrick in D J Harris, M O'Boyle, E P Bates and C M Buckley (eds) *Law of the European Convention on Human Rights* (Oxford, 2009) 79–90 for discussion of the implications of this case.

256 See, for example, *R on the Application of P v Secretary of State for the Home Department* [2008] EWHC 2447 (Admin), where it was alleged on behalf of the applicant that, if she were returned to Cyprus, she would suffer ill-treatment on the basis that she was a trafficked victim and had therefore worked as a 'sex slave', para 9.

257 Joint Committee on Human Rights Twenty-Sixth Report (n 30) para 49.

to look to the standard set down in the *Soering*[258] case, in which it was stated that Article 3 comes into play 'where substantial grounds have been shown for believing that the person concerned, if extradited, faces a real risk of being subjected to torture or to inhuman or degrading treatment or punishment in the requesting country'.[259] Although originally applied to extradition, it has been established in subsequent case law that the *Soering* principle extends to expulsion.[260] A 'mere possibility' of ill-treatment is insufficient to satisfy this standard.[261] Analogies can be brought where trafficking is concerned. After all, 'the Convention is a living instrument which ... must be interpreted in the light of present day conditions'.[262] Therefore, a modern day application of Article 3 may indeed be stretched to accommodate victims of trafficking, who are at risk of ill-treatment on return to the origin state, where necessary.

However, the high standard of proof required by the ECtHR means that Article 3 may have limited applicability in practice.[263] In its *Cruz-Varas*[264] judgment, the Court noted several principles with regard to the assessment of the risk of ill-treatment. Primarily, in determining whether the *Soering* principle is satisfied, the Court will assess the issue in light of all of the material placed before it. Secondly, the existence of the risk of ill treatment must primarily be assessed with reference to the facts which were known, or ought to have been known, by the contracting state at the time of the expulsion. Finally, the assessment of the risk of treatment in breach of Article 3 must be a rigorous one, given 'the absolute character of this provision and the fact that it enshrines one of the fundamental values of the democratic societies making up the Council of Europe'.[265]

The Commission in *Soering* noted that: '[i]t is only in exceptional circumstances that the removal of a person will give rise to an issue under Article 3 and the burden lies on the applicant to substantiate his fear that he will be exposed to treatment or punishment falling under that Article'.[266] The Court stated in that case that:

> As is established in the Court's case-law, ill-treatment, including punishment, must attain a minimum level of severity if it is to fall within the scope of Article 3 (art. 3). The assessment of this minimum is, in the nature of things, relative; it depends on all the circumstances of the case, such as the nature

258 See *Soering v UK* (1989) 11 EHRR 439.

259 ibid para 91.

260 See, for example, *Cruz-Varas v Sweden* (1992) 14 EHRR 1.

261 See, for example, *Vilvarajah and Others v United Kingdom* (1991) 14 EHRR 248 para111. On the point of 'mere possibility' being insufficient, this includes situations where there is some risk to some people but no evidence to single out the applicant from a group, only a small (and unidentified) proportion of whom are at risk – here, they may be considered to be no or insufficient 'real risk'.

262 *Tyrer v United Kingdom* (1979–80) 2 EHRR 1 para 31.

263 See S Egan 'Protecting the victims of trafficking: problems and prospects' (2008) *European Human Rights Law Review* 106–119.

264 *Cruz-Varas v Sweden* (1992) 14 EHRR 1 paras 75–76 and 83.

265 *Vilvarajah and Others v United Kingdom* (1991) 14 EHRR 248 para 108.

266 Opinion of the Commission in *Soering v UK* (1989) 11 EHRR 439 para 94.

> and context of the treatment or punishment, the manner and method of its execution, its duration, its physical or mental effects and, in some instances, the sex, age and state of health of the victim.[267]

*Dicta* from subsequent case law has added to this.[268] The language used in the above-mentioned paragraph, coupled with part of the actual basis of *Soering*'s claim, that is, the 'increasing tension and psychological trauma'[269] that would be suffered as a result of the 'death row phenomenon',[270] opens the door to consider the relevance of the mental state of the trafficked victim, although the standard to be met is clearly – and justifiably – high.

As mentioned previously, the Trafficking Convention envisages the granting of residence permits as a result of the victims 'personal situation', which may include their 'state of health … or some other factor which has to be taken into account'.[271] Further, according to the two CPS Protocols addressing prosecutorial discretion where offences were committed by trafficked persons as a result of having been trafficked,[272] where there is evidence such as medical reports, relating to a person who is suspected of committing immigration offences, which indicate post-traumatic stress as a result of their being trafficked, the prosecutor should consider whether prosecution is in the public interest or whether it should be discontinued.[273] Evidently, the mental state of the trafficked victim is a very real concern. This, coupled with the potential for reprisals or retrafficking,[274] arguably constitutes 'substantial grounds' and 'real risk' for the purposes of the *Soering* principle. It would appear that the mental state of the victim on return would be insufficient alone to qualify for the standard set down in *Soering*.[275] The danger of retrafficking and reprisals is assessed by the host state, and is a matter of degree and judgment.

267 See *Ireland v United Kingdom* (1978) 2 EHRR 25 para 162; and *Tyrer v United Kingdom* (1979–80) 2 EHRR 1 paras 29 and 80. At para 167, the Court goes on to state that: 'Treatment has been held by the Court to be both "inhuman" because it was premeditated, was applied for hours at a stretch and "caused, if not actual bodily injury, at least intense physical and mental suffering", and also "degrading" because it was "such as to arouse in [its] victims feelings of fear, anguish and inferiority capable of humiliating and debasing them and possibly breaking their physical or moral resistance'.

268 See *Tyrer v United Kingdom* (n 267) paras 29 and 30, where it was stated that: '[i]n order for a punishment or treatment associated with it to be "inhuman" or "degrading", the suffering or humiliation involved must in any event go beyond that inevitable element of suffering or humiliation connected with a given form of legitimate punishment'.

269 *Soering v UK* (1989) 11 EHRR 439 para 105.

270 See Harris, O'Boyle and Warbrick (n 255) 79–90 for discussion of *Soering* and subsequent case law.

271 Explanatory Report to the CoE Trafficking Convention (n 63) para 184.

272 Crown Prosecution Service (n 113).

273 ibid.

274 A string of cases clarifies here that the risk of ill-treatment may come from individuals or private groups as well as public authorities. See, for example, *HLR v France* (1997) 26 EHRR 29; *Ahmed v Austria* (1996) 24 EHRR 278.

275 See, for example, *Cruz-Varas v Sweden* (1992) 14 EHRR 1.

The cases cited have required the applicant to bring evidence of the potential for treatment contrary to Article 3 to occur in the receiving state, and so would any person who was seeking to rely on this Article. Previous Article 3 jurisprudence indicates that a wealth of evidence is necessary.[276] An IOM study indicates that many trafficking organisations operate in the same countries of origin,[277] which makes the potential for reprisals and retrafficking a very real threat.

There is also the potential for Article 2 of the ECHR to be invoked,[278] as ill-treatment on return might be that victims risked being killed by the traffickers, organised criminals operating in the area, or even by their own community. Evidence of threats to trafficking victims or their family, or with respect to revictimisation on return, would need to be brought forward, coupled with evidence that the receiving state was not able adequately to protect the victim from such threats or revictimisation. Evidence of high rates of organised crime, high trafficking rates from the victim's origin state, and/or proof that the origin state is a known source country, could be cited.

The UN High Commissioner for Human Rights has expressed the view that:

> ... safe and, as far as possible, voluntary return must be at the core of any credible protection strategy for trafficked persons. A failure to [provide] for safe (and to the extent possible) voluntary return would amount to little more than an endorsement of the forced deportation and repatriation of trafficked persons. When trafficking occurs in the context of organised crime, such an endorsement presents an unacceptable safety risk to victims.[279]

The links between trafficking and organised crime are well known, therefore this is a very real concern. It must be borne in mind as well that as well as the substantive tests for refugee status and human rights protection being different, there are also important procedural differences. No procedure is specified in the Refugee Convention, and so it is up to states as to what to provide.[280] The ECHR at least provides the right to an Article 13 remedy, and the Article 6 right to a fair trial may be relied upon where relevant. Furthermore, unlike all the other instruments considered, the ECHR provides an international mechanism of accountability, the ECtHR, to which individuals have access.

There is real difficulty in obtaining reliable statistics about this clandestine

276 See, for example, *Chahal v United Kingdom* (1997) 23 EHRR 413; *Vilvarajah and Others v United Kingdom* (1991) 14 EHRR 248.

277 International Organization for Migration 'Changing patterns and trends of trafficking in persons in the Balkan region' (2004) 105.

278 Links between arts 2, 3 and 14 of the ECHR in terms of gender-based violence were made in the recent judgment in *Opuz v Turkey* (2009) (Application no 33401/02).

279 United Nations General Assembly 'Informal note by the United Nations High Commissioner for Human Rights' UN Doc A/AC.254/16 para 20.

280 Information on the UK asylum appeals process can be found at: Information Centre about Asylum and Refugees (ICAR) 'Asylum appeals process: thematic briefing prepared for the Independent Asylum Commission' (September 2007) http://www.icar.org.uk/download/Appeals.pdf (last accessed 8 December 2009).

activity, as regards, for example, incidences of retrafficking from certain regions, or evidence of reprisals from traffickers against other victims and/or their families. Victims may also be known to traffickers or trafficking networks who operate in that area, which could increase their chances of being retrafficked or subject to threats and reprisals. Increased protection for victims will be necessary if they do qualify for a right to remain in the destination state in order to cooperate in criminal proceedings, as a result of the threat of reprisals from traffickers.[281]

With respect to the delicate balance between maintaining border integrity, immigration control and adequate protection of victims, the public interest should lie primarily in providing for victims of trafficking and exploitation. When weighing up a balance of interests, one might consider the potential harm to the UK resulting from abuse of the system by those falsely claiming to be victims of trafficking, although how problematic this will actually be remains to be seen,[282] particularly given that the residence permit is not automatically granted; there are many steps to the process.

If a trafficked victim has not been granted the one-year residence permit and is not in a position to apply for asylum, the next point of call is to consider whether they qualify for humanitarian protection. The qualifying criteria under the Immigration Rules[283] state that humanitarian protection may be granted to an individual in the UK who is not a refugee if 'there are substantial grounds for believing that the person would face a real risk of suffering serious harm in the country of return (this refers to a country or territory listed in paragraph 8(1)(c) of Schedule 2 to the Immigration Act 1971); and the person cannot obtain effective protection from the authorities of that country (or will not because of the risk of suffering serious harm).[284] 'Serious harm' in this context includes, most poignantly for victims of human trafficking, 'torture or inhuman or degrading treatment or punishment in the country of return',[285] thereby mirroring the language of Article 3 of the ECHR. Humanitarian protection once granted does not imply permanence – it will be revoked or not renewed once the Secretary of State is satisfied that the conditions that led to the granting of humanitarian protection in the first place have ceased to exist or improved to an acceptable degree so that protection is no longer needed.[286]

281 An empirical study conducted in Rimini, Italy, whereby the head of the investigative office of Polizia di Stato in Rimini was interviewed, and drew conclusions that verify this. See Ventrella (n 28) 82.

282 See Travis (n 35). Damian Green reacted to this case by stating that the rights of victims have been strengthened, and that: 'This very disturbing case shows why our approach to human trafficking has changed significantly since 2003'. See Home Office, 'Damian Green reacts to "disturbing" trafficking case' (12 April 2011) http://www.homeoffice.gov.uk/media-centre/news/trafficking-case?version=1 (last accessed 29 February 2014). Also see *SB (PSG – Protection Regulations – reg 6) Moldova CG* [2008] UKAIT 00002.

283 Home Office/UK Border Agency 'Immigration rules' http://www.ukba.homeoffice.gov.uk/policyandlaw/immigrationlaw/immigrationrules/ (last accessed 10 March 2014).

284 UK Border Agency 'Humanitarian protection' (n 212).

285 ibid.

286 Home Office/UK Border Agency 'Immigration rules' (n 283).

A final category under which a trafficked victim may be able to qualify for the right to remain is discretionary leave. This category comes into play where humanitarian protection is not available to an individual, simply because he or she is not in need of 'protection' per se. Discretionary leave may be granted in limited situations, such as where severe humanitarian conditions in the country of origin or an individual's serious medical condition[287] would render return contrary to Article 3. The threshold is, predictably, very high indeed, and severe mental stress as a result of having been trafficked and forced to work in the sex industry would be unlikely to suffice. Similarly, poor humanitarian conditions on return would have to be exceptionally severe for discretionary leave to be granted; therefore, this category is only of use to a very small group of persons.

### *6.7.3 Consequences of not granting asylum, humanitarian protection, or discretionary leave*

Delays in processing asylum claims are not uncommon, and such delays can result in the asylum seeker becoming destitute in the interim period. One would hope that this situation would not occur with respect to trafficked victims, given the strict deadlines in the identification procedure, that is, five days from initial contact to decide whether 'reasonable grounds' to believe that an individual is a victim of trafficking exist, followed by the 45-day recovery and reflection period during which decisions about the future of the victim and any right to remain on his or her part will be made.

As well as Article 3 concerns, those who are awaiting a decision as regards a right to remain for any period of time may also have concerns that are capable of invoking Article 8, which includes the right to respect for physical or moral integrity.[288] Egan observes that:

> Given that the rights in the Convention apply to all persons within the jurisdiction of the contracting states, it could well be argued that a failure by any contracting state to provide adequate shelter to a trafficked person, to fail to meet his or her psychological or physical needs or to supply emergency medical assistance would be a failure to respect that person's physical or moral integrity.[289]

It would appear that, under the conditions of the CoE Trafficking Convention, support and medical assistance will at first be available to trafficked victims, although delays in procedures could raise issues here.

Those trafficked victims who are not granted any right to remain beyond the 45-day recovery period owing to the fact that they are neither useful to the criminal process or do not meet the criteria with respect to their 'personal situation' do

287 See *D v United Kingdom* (1997) 24 EHRR 423.
288 See *X & Y v Netherlands* (1986) 8 EHRR 235.
289 See Egan (n 263) 117.

not appear to be entitled to any support from the state. Trafficked persons often may not comply with the asylum system, and may 'disappear' soon after making asylum applications.[290] Refusal of asylum, humanitarian protection or discretionary leave does not necessarily result in expulsion, although the individual may be expected to leave the UK. This opens up the potential for a proportion of trafficked victims to 'fall through the cracks' and become homeless or destitute – a problem which is not unknown as regards asylum seekers[291] and, according to the JCHR, the government's treatment of individuals may in some cases amount to inhuman and degrading treatment within the scope of Article 3 of the ECHR.[292] It is those trafficked victims who are not 'useful' to any criminal proceedings, and who do not qualify for any right to remain yet who do not choose to leave, who will suffer. Failed asylum seekers – some of whom will be genuine, but could not bring forward sufficient proof of their situation – slip through the net and become destitute. This is well known. Some of them will be trafficked victims, who have only sought help from NGOs and charities long after their asylum claim has failed, and are afraid to give basic information about themselves that would help them to obtain such support.[293]

The Asylum Support Programme Inter-Agency Partnership (ASP)[294] conducted a Destitution Tally in the UK in January 2008[295] and a Second Destitution Tally in May 2009,[296] and recognised a substantial[297] number of asylum seekers – either refused or at some point in the asylum process. It is estimated that more than 40 per cent of people using refugee support agencies are destitute.[298] It is inevitable that there is the potential for the same to happen to trafficked persons or 'consensually trafficked' persons who are unable to bring the requisite proof of a need to remain and therefore do not qualify for any right to remain. A previous ASP representative states that, primarily: 'ASP experience … is not with those who have admitted that they have been trafficked and then not been granted leave, but with

290 Statement by Kate Smart, Director of Policy, Communications and Advocacy, Welsh Refugee Council (personal communication, 3 March 2009).

291 See *R (Limbuela, Tesema, Adam) v Secretary of State for the Home Department* [2005] UKHL 66, [2006] 1 AC 396; also see *Asylum seekers 'living off hand-outs' BBC NEWS UK* (14 May 2009) http://news.bbc.co.uk/1/hi/uk/8049300.stm (last accessed 14 May 2009).

292 Joint Committee on Human Rights Tenth Report (n 205) 5.

293 K Smart, (n 290).

294 The Asylum Support Programme Inter-Agency Partnership (IAP) consists of five agencies: Refugee Council, Refugee Action, Migrant Helpline, Scottish Refugee Council and Welsh Refugee Council.

295 K Smart and S Fullegar in Refugee Agencies Policy Response 'The destitution tally: an indication of the extent of destitution among asylum seekers and refugees' (January 2008) 2 http://www.refugeecouncil.org.uk/Resources/Refugee%20Council/downloads/policy_responses/IAP_Destitution_Tally_Jan08.pdf (last accessed 1 July 2011).

296 See Kate Smart, Asylum Support Partnership Policy Report: The Second Destitution Tally 'An indication of the extent of destitution among asylum seeker, refused asylum seekers and refugees' Policy and Development Adviser (May 2009).

297 The first destitution tally recognised 1524 destitute cases recorded in four weeks. See K Smart and S Fullegar (n 295) 5.

298 ibid 2.

those that we suspect have been trafficked but who don't admit to it'.[299] The ASP recognises an individual as destitute who is 'currently with no access to benefits/ BIA support/income and are either street homeless or staying with friends only temporarily'.[300] A less stringent definition is provided within section 95(3) of the Immigration and Asylum Act 1999.[301]

Although 'A general duty to house the homeless or provide for the destitute cannot be spelled out of Article 3',[302] inaction in the face of conditions that are deemed unacceptable can suffice with respect to the Article 3 standard.[303] In order for any claim to be made, destitution must be the result of state action as opposed to the individual's own volition. Failed asylum seekers may also be denied access to NHS treatment.[304] Phil Woolas, Border and Immigration Minister, gave the following response to the ASP report on destitute asylum seekers:

> If someone has no right to be here they must return home. I do not believe the taxpayer should be funding those with no grounds to stay in the United Kingdom. Our policies ensure that no person who has sought protection need be destitute whilst they have a valid reason to be here – everyone is entitled to apply for support at every stage of the process. Our asylum process is fair and humane, with oversight by the independent courts, decisions made quicker than ever, and those in genuine need of protection offered refuge.[305]

And so, with respect to those trafficked persons who cannot satisfy the relevant criteria or bring forward the relevant proof that they are at risk on return of ill-treatment, we reach a stalemate, as is the case with failed asylum seekers divorced from a trafficking context. Failed asylum seekers may be eligible for section 4 or 'hard case' support, but only as long as one of the following conditions apply:[306]

1. S/he is taking all reasonable steps to leave the UK or place her/himself in a position in which s/he is able to leave the UK, or

299 K Smart, (n 290).
300 Smart and Fullegar (n 295) 1.
301 Immigration and Asylum Act 1999 s 95(3) states that: '… a person is destitute if – (a) he does not have adequate accommodation or any means of obtaining it (whether or not his essential living needs are met); or (b) he has adequate accommodation or the means of obtaining it, but cannot meet his other essential living needs …'.
302 *R (Limbuela, Tesema, Adam) v Secretary of State for the Home Department* [2005] UKHL 66 para 7; also see *O'Rourke v United Kingdom* (Application no 39022/97) (unreported, 26 June 2001).
303 See *Napier v Scottish Ministers* (2004) Scot CS 100.
304 See *R (on the application of A) v Secretary of State for Health* [2009] EWCA Civ 225.
305 UK Border Agency 'Asylum Support Partnership report on destitute asylum seekers – UK Border Agency response' (14 May 2009) http://www.ukba.homeoffice.gov.uk/sitecontent/newsarticles/asp-report-ukba-response (last accessed 1 June 2009, link no longer live).
306 See Immigration and Asylum (Provision of Accommodation to Failed Asylum Seekers) Regulations 2005 SI No 930.

2. S/he is unable to leave the UK because of a physical impediment to travel or for some other medical reason, or
3. S/he has applied for judicial review of the decision on his/her asylum claim and s/he has been granted permission to proceed, or
4. There is no viable route of return.

Once again, the conditions are – perhaps necessarily with respect to immigration control – very stringent. Evidence suggests that section 4 is not providing an adequate safety net for failed asylum seekers.[307] Some destitute, failed asylum seekers remain because they genuinely feel that they will be subject to serious ill-treatment or that their lives will be threatened on return to their country of origin, but have not been able to meet the standard of proof required for a successful claim.[308] This situation will undoubtedly occur with respect to a proportion of trafficked victims if they do not consider returning home to be 'safe'.[309] There seems no simple way around this real problem, short of adopting an all-encompassing Italian *Rimini*-style outright granting of a right to remain.[310]

Some destitute trafficked victims who do not qualify for any right to remain yet who have chosen to remain in the destination state may simply end up being retrafficked within or out of the destination state, or simply fall back into sex work independently, or perhaps become 'pimped', because they have nowhere else to turn. Some form of resolution for this unsatisfactory situation must be achieved.

With respect to destitute failed asylum seekers, the Asylum Support Partnership requests specific action or conditions to be taken or imposed by the UKBA.[311]

307 See Smart (n 296) 9.

308 See, for example, Welsh Refugee Council Press Release 'Down but not out: refused asylum seekers in Wales choose years of destitution over return to their unsafe homelands' http://www.welshrefugeecouncil.org/documents/pressreleases/May_09/Press%20Release%20Destitution%20Tally.doc (last accessed 24 January 2010, link no longer live).

309 In their research with criminalised migrant women, Hale and Gelsthorpe found that the greatest fear of most of those interviewed was the prospect of return to their home country. See Hales and Gelsthorpe (n 75) 28.

310 See Ventrella (n 28).

311 These are: (1) to accept the evidence that destitution does not lead refused asylum seekers to return to their country of origin; (2) to adopt the principle that destitution should not be a feature of the UK asylum system; (3) to explore solutions to destitution for those currently not entitled to support. Options made available should include provision of support, the right to work and regularisation of status, depending on circumstances; (4) to regularise the status of destitute refused asylum seekers from the most frequently occurring countries of origin; (5) to provide cash support without delay for all destitute refused asylum seekers with dependent children regardless of whether the children were born after the asylum application was refused (see Refugee Council 'More token gestures' (Refugee Council, 2008); (6) to improve significantly processes to end destitution among those with entitlements to support, by implementing various measures. See Smart (n 296). With respect to the 6th point made above, 'various measures' include: enable asylum claims to be lodged locally in order to avoid destitution among those who wish to claim asylum but cannot travel to the Asylum Screening Unit; simplify procedures for applying for asylum support and section 4 support, in particular, ensure that eligibility for sup-

The suggestions made raise some interesting issues with respect to the potential for trafficked persons to become destitute, particularly the requested actions that states should:

> ... explore solutions to destitution for those currently not entitled to support. Options made available should include provision of support, the right to work and regularisation of status, depending on circumstances; and ... regularise the status of destitute refused asylum seekers from the most frequently occurring countries of origin.[312]

As regards the first point above, destitution among asylum seekers and failed asylum seekers is a very real problem, and this body of destitute persons has the potential to be added to by trafficked persons who do not qualify for any right to remain, but who are afraid to return because of risk of ill-treatment. As regards the second point, there are known source countries for many trafficked victims,[313] and therefore it must be recognised that victims from these countries are going to continue to appear in destination countries.

## 6.8 Recommendations for dealing with trafficked persons

As regards formally trafficked persons, the main downfalls of the UK approach to implementation of the CoE Trafficking Convention concern the flawed NRM, and the right of the victim to remain in the host state owing to their 'personal situation'. The statement by the UK Government that it was already largely compliant with Convention provisions[314] indicates that largely, everything that was needed was already in place, which explains a lack of clear implementing legislation. Therefore, the phrase 'personal situation' in this context has the potential to be (or perhaps already has been) interpreted stringently, even to the point that implementation of the Trafficking Convention in this respect will lead to little or no change or improvement at all with respect to the treatment of trafficked victims in the UK.

Progress in terms of rest and recovery periods and temporary residence permits can logically follow one of three paths. Primarily, at a minimum, the recovery and

port does not require evidence, which is impossible for applicants to provide; set tight timescales for processing asylum support applications and section 4 support applications and introduce management systems to ensure that these are met; ensure that there are effective procedures for providing temporary emergency support and accommodation to counteract delays in processing support applications; ensure that there are effective channels of communication for applicants and voluntary agencies to resolve queries about the handling of asylum support applications; ensure seamless transition between support for asylum seekers and support for refused asylum seekers; ensure seamless transition to mainstream benefits for those granted refugee status or leave to remain.

312 See Smart (n 296).

313 See ch 2.

314 Home Office 'Impact Assessment of ratification of the Council of Europe Convention on Action against Trafficking in Human Beings' (6 October 2008) 5.

reflection period should be longer for all victims of trafficking, once discovered. 30 days as a minimum standard (or even 45, as offered by the UK) is not an unfair starting point in terms of obtaining signatures and ratifications, but realistically it still does not offer a particularly sympathetic approach. Three months would potentially be a more appropriate standard, and the added time could prove invaluable in terms of securing cooperation by the victim in criminal proceedings against traffickers.

Secondly, a middle-of-the-road approach could see ratifying states, such as the UK, providing all victims of human trafficking with temporary residence permits, if so desired by victims. Such a model would allow for increased opportunity for recovery, and encourage participation in criminal proceedings.

Finally, the most accommodating proposal, and therefore most likely to be rejected in favour of immigration control and border integrity, would be to grant permanent residence permits for all. This would involve taking a *Rimini*-style approach further than in the country where it was pioneered.

Of these suggestions, the first and second are more workable and therefore preferable. In terms of any of the recommendations, there are potentially other gains to be made from allowing temporary residence. It is not impossible to conceive of victims coming forward in order to help initiate or assist with criminal proceedings against traffickers once they have been allowed to remain in the host state for a period of time (exceeding the minimum of 30 days stipulated by the Convention) and have had the benefit of a period of recovery without an imminent expiry date being stamped on their foreheads.

Perhaps more pertinently, there is the issue of victim identification, the mechanism in the UK for which – as identified by the Anti-Trafficking Monitoring Group[315] – appears to be deficient. It does not seem unreasonable at this point to require a more encompassing system that does not ostensibly discriminate on the basis of origin state (of the victim),[316] and also uses the widest feasible interpretation of the 'means' element of trafficking, which will be assessed through the current UKBA 'indicators' as to whether an individual has been trafficked or not.

## 6.9 The Modern Slavery Bill

The Modern Slavery Bill[317] may make some changes which affect victims of human trafficking. At the time of writing this book,[318] the Bill is being considered and has

315 See Anti-Trafficking Monitoring Group 'Wrong kind of victim?' (n 143).

316 See Anti-Trafficking Monitoring Group 'Wrong kind of victim?' (n 143), where it was suggested that the lower identification statistics relating to third country nationals was not probative of discrimination. However, a sceptical approach might consider that discrimination here is indeed a possibility and that border integrity is being placed above the concerns of the trafficked victim.

317 Home Office, Draft Modern Slavery Bill, December 2013, available at https://www.gov.uk/government/uploads/system/uploads/attachment_data/file/266165/Draft_Modern_Slavery_Bill.pdf (last accessed 1 June 2014).

318 June 2014.

been subject to reports and responses by the Joint Parliamentary Committee on the Draft Modern Slavery Bill[319] and the Government[320] respectively. Various issues surrounding the Bill and the 'strategic response'[321] to be taken to combating trafficking may have ramifications for the treatment and identification of trafficked persons.

Revised guidance as regards the non-punishment principle is proposed,[322] as is the possibility of the principle being placed on a statutory footing.[323] With respect to the latter, the wording of such a statutory defence will have to be very carefully considered. The Government response to the Parliamentary Committee's report states that for the defence to be available, '… the individual must have been compelled to commit the offence as a direct result of their trafficking/slavery situation, and a reasonable person in the same situation would have no realistic alternative but to commit the offence.' The use of terminology such as 'reasonable' is questionable and potentially inappropriate in the context of human trafficking, as the trafficked victim should not realistically be compared to a 'reasonable' person, albeit one in the same situation.

Recognising that some victims will not want to be referred into the NRM, the Joint Parliamentary Committee states that '… we have included an order-making clause in the Committee Bill that gives power to the Secretary of State, in consultation with the Anti-Slavery Commissioner, to publish and maintain guidance on the provision of assistance and support to victims of modern slavery.'[324] If such guidance were to be published and used then this would represent a step forward in the treatment of victims, who, as has been established earlier in this body of work, may have many and varied reasons for not wanting to be referred.

The Joint Parliamentary Committee states that '… the real issue is not statutory protection from prosecution, but improved identification of victims …'[325] and

319 Joint Committee on the Draft Modern Slavery Bill, Report, Session 2013–14, HL Paper 166, HC 1019, available at http://www.publications.parliament.uk/pa/jt201314/jtselect/jtslavery/166/166.pdf (last accessed 1 June 2014).

320 The Government Response to the Report from the Joint Committee on the Draft Modern Slavery Bill session 2013–14 HL Paper 166/ HC 1019, June 2014, available at https://www.gov.uk/government/uploads/system/uploads/attachment_data/file/318771/CM8889DraftModernSlaveryBill.pdf (last accessed 19 June 2014).

321 Home Office, Draft Modern Slavery Bill, December 2013, 12, available at https://www.gov.uk/government/uploads/system/uploads/attachment_data/file/266165/Draft_Modern_Slavery_Bill.pdf (last accessed 1 June 2014).

322 Home Office, Draft Modern Slavery Bill, December 2013, 11, available at https://www.gov.uk/government/uploads/system/uploads/attachment_data/file/266165/Draft_Modern_Slavery_Bill.pdf (last accessed 1 June 2014).

323 The Government Response to the Report from the Joint Committee on the Draft Modern Slavery Bill session 2013–14 HL Paper 166/ HC 1019, June 2014, 19, available at https://www.gov.uk/government/uploads/system/uploads/attachment_data/file/318771/CM8889DraftModernSlaveryBill.pdf (last accessed 19 June 2014).

324 Joint Committee on the Draft Modern Slavery Bill, Report, Session 2013–14, HL Paper 166, HC 1019, para 71, available at http://www.publications.parliament.uk/pa/jt201314/jtselect/jtslavery/166/166.pdf (last accessed 1 June 2014).

325 Joint Committee on the Draft Modern Slavery Bill, Report, Session 2013–14, HL Paper 166,

suggests that it may be appropriate for the NRM be enshrined in statute.[326] The Government response indicates that a review of the NRM is currently underway and the findings of which will be reported in October 2014.[327] Until then at the very least, we do not know the full extent or effect of any potential changes which are on the horizon.

## 6.10 Conclusion

The flaws identified in the current victim identification system indicate a lack of awareness of trafficking, the nature of trafficking, and the nature of victim behaviour. These flaws highlight the need for, amongst other things, improved training of those who may come across victims of trafficking, such as immigration authorities and legal representatives. The UKBA provides guidance on identifying victims of trafficking for sexual exploitation, which states that: 'During operations, enquiries into whether a person is a victim of trafficking should take precedence over enquiries into the individual's immigration status'.[328] However, it is found that: '... law enforcement is often confused as to how to proceed, perceiving incorrectly the issue as one of immigration'.[329] Adequate victim protection requires that putative victim status be accepted primarily at face value, with sanctions or prosecution being pursued later if victim status is not accorded. Immediate detention is likely to be inappropriate for potential trafficked victims.

Particular reference was made in the *R v O* judgment to paragraph 134 of the Twenty-Sixth Report of the JCHR, which states that that: 'the main criticism levelled against the government's approach by witnesses to our inquiry is that the first arm of the "twin-track" approach, the protection of victims, has not been promoted and implemented effectively'.[330] In order for victims of human trafficking to have access to the rights to which they are entitled under the CoE Trafficking Convention such as a period for recovery or temporary residence rights, then clear implementing legislation may be necessary that clarifies that victims of trafficking have these specific rights in English law that are in accordance with what is required by the CoE Trafficking Convention.

The importance of correct and timely identification of victims is clear, so that the process of recovery might begin as soon as is possible. The focus of British

HC 1019, para 62, available at http://www.publications.parliament.uk/pa/jt201314/jtselect/jtslavery/166/166.pdf (accessed 1 June 2014).

326 Joint Committee on the Draft Modern Slavery Bill, Report, Session 2013–14, HL Paper 166, HC 1019, para 82, available at http://www.publications.parliament.uk/pa/jt201314/jtselect/jtslavery/166/166.pdf (accessed 1 June 2014).

327 The Government Response to the Report from the Joint Committee on the Draft Modern Slavery Bill session 2013–14 HL Paper 166/HC 1019, June 2014, 18–19, available at https://www.gov.uk/government/uploads/system/uploads/attachment_data/file/318771/CM8889DraftModernSlaveryBill.pdf (last accessed 19 June 2014).

328 Home Office/UK Border Agency (n 131) 9.1.

329 Centre for Social Justice (n 177) 12.

330 Joint Committee on Human Rights Twenty-Sixth Report (n 30) para 134.

policy has been on criminalisation and prosecution of traffickers for far too long, with victim protection often falling well short of any acceptable minimum standard. The CoE Trafficking Convention represents a welcome – and long overdue – step in the right direction, and although it has not currently been ratified by a large number of countries, those who have ratified it must now provide the minimum standard of treatment to victims of trafficking who are discovered in their territory, which includes identification of victims of human trafficking at the earliest possible juncture. Neither implementation of the CoE Trafficking Convention nor reliance on the ECHR Act 1998 can do all that is required to provide an effective regime for the protection of victims of human trafficking; nor can the matter be left entirely to the courts.

Procedures allowing for correct and timely identification of victims of human trafficking are key, but beyond that there is a host of issues to be dealt with. Trafficking victims and victims of serious exploitation (even in the face of what is, or may appear to be, consent) are a highly vulnerable body of persons, as are asylum seekers and others in need of assistance, support and protection. They need to be given an appropriate level of treatment and care, as necessary, and repatriation while trafficking activity and organised crime is still rife in the country or specific area of origin serves little purpose other than the immediate immigration control interests of the destination state.

Governments will have to tread very carefully indeed when trying to repatriate women. It is clear from the considerations made during the determinations of asylum cases that conditions in the country of origin can change, and that this is considered by the courts – wars end, political shifts occur, safe areas emerge and a level of 'peace' can sometimes be achieved, thereby facilitating the return of the individual who has claimed asylum. Similarly, considerations will be made in determining the fate of identified trafficked victims – as long as trafficking and organised crime continues in the origin state, there will be risks on return of varying degree to the trafficked victim, including to those who may have 'consented' to the process.

Trafficking is arguably similar to slavery or servitude, and is about profit and less the result of conflict and persecution. At the extreme, some of these trafficked victims face risks of slavery or ill-treatment on return, and the state has to consider this. Victims should not have to be shoehorned into a pre-existing and therefore inappropriate legal framework that was not designed to suit their needs. In stating that everything that is needed is already in place, this is what the UK may have done.

Although improved victim assistance and support could be achieved in the UK, the more encompassing regime in Italy – the *Rimini* method, has not, as Ventrella asserts, 'defeated' human trafficking.[331] It has simply provided safe havens for victims who have been trafficked, although such victims will continue to appear unless a multi-pronged, global attack on this abhorrent activity continues and succeeds. Victim protection is the closest thing to a 'cure', but with effective

331 Ventrella (n 28) 64.

prevention, there is no need for a cure. The demand for sold sex will not go away simply because victims are granted leave to remain, rights to work etc in the destination state. So long as the criminal law aspects of the regime do not eliminate trafficking, it will be necessary for the victim protection aspects to be taken equally seriously as the criminalisation ones – so long as there is trafficking, there will be victims.

In order to adopt a more accommodating approach to treatment and protection of victims of human trafficking, it is necessary to weigh up the public interest concerns of immigration control versus giving immediate protection and sympathetic treatment to victims, and protecting victims from ill-treatment on return to the destination state, regardless of whether they can show sufficient evidence to be granted some form of leave to remain in the UK. Adopting a *Rimini*-style method is extreme, in that it does not depend upon considering the merits of individual cases, although it is evident that a more accommodating approach than that currently envisaged and in place may be needed. Therefore, some sort of balance must be struck.

On the face of it, consent will render trafficked victims outside the protective confines of the CoE Trafficking Convention. However, if determinations as to whether a person is a possible victim of trafficking are indeed made rapidly (within five days, as envisaged) there is the possibility that even those who may have consented or whose status is unsure may at least initially fall within the 'possible trafficked victim' category, although certain sources cited throughout this chapter clearly indicate that the opposite may indeed be the case,[332] and it is a possibility that increases in 'grey area' cases. In any event, they should fall within this category, until there is sufficient proof to indicate that they are truly irregular migrants, rather than 'victims', whether formally trafficked or 'consensually trafficked' victims.

It is clear that there are a multitude of barriers standing in the way of victim identification. Case law examples indicate how serious the ramifications of misidentification or late identification can be of victims of human trafficking can be,[333] and underpin the need for a legal and administrative framework that offers protection to victims or those who might become victims.[334] Hales and Gelsthorpe stated that: 'A key question of [their] research was … why so few of those, whose disclosures at interview with the researchers exemplified the key indicators of being a victim of trafficking, had been identified as such within the criminal justice system'.[335] We know that the victims are here (although we may not know how many) and, in the case of some misidentified victims, we know that they did not consent, although they are still not being formally identified as 'trafficked'. So, in any case, either we are setting the 'trafficked victim' threshold too high or, if

332 See, for example, Anti-Trafficking Monitoring Group (n 143).

333 See *R v O* [2008] EWCA Crim 2835; *R v LM* [2010] EWCA Crim 2327, [2011] 1 Cr App R 12, [2011] Crim LR 425; and Elliott (n 5).

334 *Rantsev v Cyprus and Russia* [2010] (Application no 25965/04).

335 Hales and Gelsthorpe (n 75) 27.

it has to be high, we are not providing for a broader, more inclusive and realistic 'secondary' threshold of victimhood, the need for which, the evidence suggests, is not unjustified. How legally to address those who fall short of the formal trafficking definition – either genuinely or through misidentification – will be discussed in Chapter 7.

# 7 Less than trafficked, more than smuggled: dealing with the 'consensually trafficked'

## 7.1 Introduction

The previous chapter established that there are difficulties inherent in the identification of victims, stemming from, amongst other things, a lack of evidence of coercion etc, or lack of consent. Further to this, there may be borderline cases of trafficking, or cases where the conditions experienced by the exploited individual have been so harsh that, although she may have (or appear to have) ostensibly consented and therefore not be formally trafficked, she is still in need of some support and assistance. We do not know the proportions of consenting women to smuggled women to trafficked women, but we do know that the number of trafficking convictions is small,[1] and yet there is evidence of the presence of large numbers of foreign sex workers in the UK.[2]

It seems unlikely, to say the least, that all of these will be consenting prostitutes. There is, thus, a real problem – which a strict application of the trafficking law would appear to make worse – of what to do about 'victims' of exploitation, who, for one reason or another, are not able to bring themselves within the formal trafficked category. Chapter 5 argued that there may be the possibility for recognition of a new category, that is, those who are 'less than trafficked' but 'more

1 See Department of Justice *First Annual Report of the Inter-Departmental Ministerial Group on Human Trafficking* (Cm 8421, 2012) which states on page 4 that: 'the number of convictions on a principal offence basis in England and Wales for 2011 was 8; however, there were 142 defendants charged with offences related to human trafficking in 2011/12 of which two thirds were prosecuted'. Also see Mr Hanson, Written Answers to Questions, *Hansard* HC, col 935W (30 March 2010) and, for example, UK Human Trafficking Centre 'United Kingdom Pentameter 2, Statistics of Victims recovered and Suspects arrested during the operational phase', which cites 15 convictions for trafficking offences secured as a result of the operation. http://www.soca.gov.uk/about-soca/library/doc_download/122-uk-pentameter-2-statistics.pdf (last accessed 1 July 2011).

2 Barbara Follet MP stated in November 2007 that: '10 years ago 85 per cent of women in brothels were UK citizens; now 85 per cent are from outside the UK'. See Barbara Follet MP, *Hansard* HC vol 467 col 537W (19 November 2007). Also see Project Acumen: ACPO Migration and Associated Matters 'Setting the record: the trafficking of migrant women in the England and Wales off-street prostitution sector' (August 2010) and UK Human Trafficking Centre 'United Kingdom Pentameter 2, Statistics of Victims recovered and Suspects arrested during the operational phase', which draws on statistics from 2009.

than smuggled'. This chapter will explore the idea of victimhood in the face of consensual trafficking, and what this could mean for the 'consensually trafficked'.

There are two clear reasons for mitigation for this category. Primarily, as the previous chapters have established, there are a multitude of ways in which genuine victims will and do get misidentified. Secondly, owing to the emphasis on consent and the nature of the forms of 'exploitation' employed as a 'purpose' element of trafficking, it is not impossible to conceive of genuine borderline or 'hard' cases where one who is viewed (perhaps incorrectly) as 'consensually trafficked' will require some form of treatment or assistance, rather than criminalisation or deportation, for example.

As regular migration routes become restricted, illicit routes will increasingly be chosen and the culture of restriction may also have adverse consequences for trafficked victims and smuggled persons who are victims of exploitation and/or human rights abuses, both of whom may be viewed through a crime control lens owing to complicity in subverting immigration laws (say, through use of false documents). Political attitudes to migration reflect a fear of floods of non-nationals entering a country or area. This fear is in some cases unfounded. For example, in the EU:

> … data of 2010 indicate that third-country nationals in the EU area constitute only approximately 4% of the total EU population. Also, data concerning the period of 2008 to 2011 indicate that irregular migration is, in fact, in decline in many EU member states, the major migrant recipients … Available early 2012 data concerning apprehensions of irregular migrants indicated a similar downward trend.[3]

It is telling that the UK, along with many other European Union Member States, has neither signed nor ratified the International Convention on the Protection of the Rights of All Migrant Workers and Members of their Families.[4] Although states may have a legitimate interest in, to put it crudely, keeping people 'out', a focus is also needed that takes account of the different categories of persons who need access to some nuanced regime once they are 'in'. Victims and others who may be in need do not always fit convenient stereotypes or taxonomies, and so we might consider a more inclusive approach to dealing with vulnerable migrants who fall below the formal threshold of 'trafficking'.

In this chapter, a case will be sketched out for consideration of offering concessions in the form of support and assistance to the 'consensually trafficked', for reasons which will be elucidated throughout the chapter. The intention to sketch out such a case is to consider provision both for the sake of the misidentified

3 Keynote speech by Nils Muižnieks, Council of Europe Commissioner for Human Rights 'Addressing the human rights challenges underlying the criminalisation of irregular migrants and national minorities in Europe' The Commissioner – CommDH/Speech (2013) 2. The Centre for European Policy Studies Seminar, Brussels (22 February 2013).

4 Signatures and ratifications available at http://treaties.un.org/Pages/ViewDetails.aspx?src=TREATY&mtdsg_no=IV-13&chapter=4&lang=en (last accessed 10 June 2014).

trafficked victim, and the borderline and the consensually trafficked, but that it does not set out to conflate these categories. The intention is to explore what can be done to address the fact that they are at times barely and perhaps even rarely distinguishable.

The final section makes recommendations for dealing with the 'consensually trafficked', thereby considering potential improvements to the current system beyond those addressed in Chapter 6, and explicitly calling for a more inclusive regime that makes concessions for the ostensibly consenting trafficked person.

## 7.2 The liberalist perspective

It has been established at an earlier stage in this book that there are problems arising from the trafficking/smuggling dichotomy.[5] Lee says of the Trafficking and Smuggling Protocols that: '[t]his line of thinking maps onto a neat dichotomy between two oppositional categories of migration – voluntary and consensual versus involuntary and non-consensual migration'.[6] The presupposition of these 'either/or' states creates a harsh line in a blurred situation, which allows for no shades of victimhood. A liberal perspective would hold those who have voluntarily been 'smuggled' as 'undeserving' victims who are responsible for their rational, autonomous choice and who must face the consequences.

The control of labour is a direct form of power.[7] Trafficking and exploitation are paradigm examples of interference with liberty, but one might question whether the state or society should interfere where the exploitation occurs with ostensible consent. Arguably, there may be a place for paternalism in dealing with trafficked persons and 'consensually trafficked' exploited migrants. This may seem incongruent and indefensible in the face of liberalism, as liberalists argue that: 'Autonomy embodies the idea of free will'.[8] Accordingly, 'Freedom is the condition in which a person is not under the control of an alien will … The love of freedom is part of the avoidance of enslavement to another, which is the opposite of power'.[9]

So, the ideal existence is, according to this perspective, the one that is the most free from social and state interference. Some form of societal order and control involving the state, perhaps through means of legislative measures, is necessary to prevent threats to members of society such as enslavement. However, when this falls into the realm of paternalism, it flies in the face of liberalism. As regards the interference of society in the actions of an individual, it has been argued that:

> … there is no room for entertaining any such questions when a person's conduct affects the interests of no persons besides himself, or needs not affect

5 See ch 2.
6 M Lee *Trafficking and Global Crime Control* (Sage 2012) 9.
7 R M Unger *Knowledge in Politics* (Free Press, 1976) 65.
8 I Jones 'A beastly provision: why the offence of "intercourse with an animal" must be butchered' (2011) 75(6) *Journal of Criminal Law* 528–44, 530.
9 Unger *Knowledge in Politics* (n 7) 64.

> them unless they like (all the persons concerned being of full age, and the ordinary amount of understanding).[10]

Mill argues that this is not 'selfish indifference' but that, in fact, lack of interference promotes the good of others.[11] As a yardstick, lack of interference is preferable to the alternative in many situations. But where we find that an individual makes choices owing to their vulnerability, or is susceptible to vulnerability (and therefore to potential abuse of this vulnerability) as a result of her choices, then an argument for what some may view as 'interference' can be made.

If freedom is 'the power to choose arbitrarily the ends and means of one's striving',[12] then that choice must be made without pressure or unacceptable influence in order for it to be meaningfully categorised as 'free'. Freedom is a relative concept. Migrants have the 'freedom' in varying degrees to choose to migrate, but the laws that are also intended to protect the 'freedom' and order relative to those with a right to be on state soil can adversely affect the vulnerable migrant and, in fact, remove her freedom, where, for example, a custodial sentence is imposed for inter alia possession of false identification documents. This respect for 'freedom' is not entirely in keeping with situations of 'less than trafficked, more than smuggled', where there may be some exercise of consent and freedom but this is curtailed through exploitation, falling short of, or treading a thin line aside, the coercive exploitation required for a finding of 'trafficked' for any putative victim.

Liberalism champions individual freedom of action. However, exclusive immigration practices can lead to the criminalisation both of trafficked victims (as was explored in the previous chapter) and, more easily, those who have been exploited but who fall short of the trafficking definition, and liberal theory requests that these people face the consequences of their actions, the voluntariness of which is questionable from the outset.

Jones states that:

> … individuals … have a natural right to determine for themselves the direction of their lives without interference; individuals are not only entitled to the rewards produced by their decisions, but they are also responsible for any negative outcomes or consequences of their choices.[13]

The liberalist perspective is suitable for those ideally situated to exercise judgment and actions free from constraint and influence, although it does not take adequate account of nuanced situations such as that of the exploited migrant from whom consent may be questionable, or perhaps should be examined as to its relevance in any given case. Even where consent (to exploitation and trafficking situations)

10 J S Mill *On Liberty and Other Essays* (Oxford, 1869) 84.

11 ibid 84.

12 Unger *Knowledge in Politics* (n 7) 66.

13 S V Jones 'Human trafficking victim identification: should consent matter?' (2012) 45 *Indiana Law Review* 483, 486 and 499.

does not appear dubious, relying upon liberal arguments of autonomy in order to avoid giving assistance or taking account of the plight of vulnerable migrants is morally questionable. As has been established in earlier chapters, it is difficult if we place too much emphasis on autonomy when dealing with situations and circumstances that by their very nature may be coercive. It may be that a paternalist perspective – to some extent – is more appropriate – as: '[m]ore often than not the economic and political pressure to move are so closely linked that a distinction between "economic migrants" and "political refugees", or between "voluntary" and "involuntary" movements of population, is no longer tenable'.[14]

Paternalistic interference needs strong justification, as: 'The spirit of improvement is not always a spirit of liberty, for it may aim at forcing improvements on an unwilling people …'.[15] We should not presuppose, however, that not one single 'consensually' trafficked and/or exploited person will want or need assistance following his or her exploitation. Although certain exploited persons may fall below the formal standard of trafficking owing to their compliance or perceived compliance with the traffickers and/or controllers, this should not render each of them beyond needing assistance as a result of their experiences. If the political climate and societal opinion casts all irregular migrants as 'the other', regardless of any individual concerns, we fall short of giving assistance and protection where it is needed.

## 7.3 The 'deserving' and 'undeserving' victim

Cole states that we can hold an individual responsible for her situation, dire as it may be, where we can attribute that situation to her voluntary actions.[16] On this basis, the state makes a distinction between voluntary and involuntary migration, and therefore those who are deserving of protection and assistance and those who are not. A liberalist perspective therefore supports the position that exploited migrants who do not meet the trafficking threshold should have no access to any nuanced regime or system of rights or assistance.

Hoyle and others, in research focusing on the labelling of trafficked victims, refer to Christie's five attributes of the ideal victim. She is weak or sick; carrying out a respectable undertaking; somewhere she could not be blamed for being; the offender was big and bad; and he was not known to her.[17] The 'perfect' trafficked victim will probably satisfy enough of these to be considered a 'deserving' victim. She may not necessarily be weak or sick, and she may not always satisfy the final

14 A H Richmond 'International migration and global change' in J H Ong, K B Chan and S B Chew (eds) *Crossing Borders: Transmigration in Asia Pacific* (Prentice Hall, New York, 1994) 36.

15 Mill *On Liberty and Other Essays* (n 10) 78.

16 P Cole *Philosophies of Exclusion: Liberal Political Theory and Immigration* (Edinburgh University Press, Edinburgh, 2000) 150.

17 C Hoyle, M Bosworth and M Dempsey 'Labelling the victims of sex trafficking: exploring the borderland between rhetoric and reality' (2011) 20(3) *Social and Legal Studies* 313–92, 315.

condition, as trafficking by someone known to the victim is not unusual.[18] Where consent as to trafficking and exploitative migration is at issue, the second and third conditions of Christie's 'ideal' victim are also problematic. Prostitution, for example, may not constitute a 'respectable' undertaking, and being in dangerous situations is not a stranger to prostitutes either.

This emphasis on victims' responsibility for placing themselves in a dangerous situation is continued in CPS guidance that contains criteria for prosecutors to consider where the criminality of a putatively trafficked person is at issue. Criteria such as the following are included:

> Did the defendant *put himself into a position* in which he was likely to be subject to threats made to persuade him to commit an offence of the seriousness of the charge, eg getting involved in a criminal gang likely to subject him to threats to commit criminal offences?[19]

This places a high degree of responsibility upon the victim and is couched in veiled language of complicity and consent. This goes toward determining culpability and therefore how deserving an individual is of being attributed the status of victimhood.

Mill states that (in reference to minors): 'Those who are still in a state to require being taken care of by others, must be protected against their own actions as well as against external injury'.[20] The application of such an approach to persons other than minors is not unreasonable, as vulnerability is not solely age-dependent. Many migrants, both voluntary and involuntary, are vulnerable to exploitation. Exploitation undermines human dignity, even where it takes place ostensibly with consent.

Lee, amongst others,[21] recognises a 'hierarchy of victimhood'.[22] This is why an alternative conception of both victimhood and consent in a trafficking context, and a broader context of exploitative consensual migration, is justified. Indeed, there may be victims who are 'less deserving' of assistance etc, but we should not proceed too quickly to label them as 'undeserving'.

Jones refers to 'isolating the normative point at which the shift from consenting participant to human trafficking victim occurs'.[23] This does not take into account the fact that the appearance of consent will lead to some falling on the wrong side of that point, and also that there is not one fixed point where consent is sufficiently vitiated by coercion – it varies from case to case. Also that even those who will have given consent sufficient to satisfy the ordinary requirements of the concept

18 See L Brown *Sex Slaves: The Trafficking of Women in Asia* (Virago Press, 2001), where many anecdotal examples of the experiences of trafficked women are provided.

19 Crown Prosecution Service *Human Trafficking and Smuggling* (updated 2010) (emphasis added).

20 Mill *On Liberty and Other Essays* (n 10) 14.

21 See, for example, Lee *Trafficking and Global Crime Control* (n 6); Jones 'Human trafficking victim identification' (n 13) 486.

22 Lee *Trafficking and Global Crime Control* (n 6) 12.

23 Jones 'Human trafficking victim identification' (n 13) 486.

and the law may still have suffered serious exploitation so that harsh treatment and denial of all victimhood may not be the best way in which to proceed.

Jones identifies five categories of potential victim who sit on the exploitative smuggling/trafficking spectrum and who are not equally 'deserving' of victim status. The first, Category A, is that of 'standard human trafficking' and is unproblematic in terms of the 'deserving' victim. This is the individual who is most likely to resemble the stereotypical 'perfect victim'.[24] Category B, that of 'standard migrant smuggling', is similarly unproblematic in that it represents a 'pure' smuggling case – the migrant is transported for the agreed sum, and any involvement between the smuggler and the smuggled ceases at the end of the journey.[25] Category C is also a category of person who is prima facie trafficked; that of 'fraudulently induced smuggled migrant and human trafficking victims'. This category includes those who gave initial consent, the validity of which becomes highly questionable owing to subsequent force, coercion or deception. Category D takes us into the more questionable realm of 'the consenting debtor'. These people willingly engage in work as payment for their cross-border transportation. Jones recognises that this category may resemble Category C, because:

> ... the somatic distinction between one who is enslaved by a coercive agent and one who consents to being a slave is not readily discernible. Consequently, persons who are forcibly enslaved on a marijuana farm to pay off their smuggling debts, after willingly entering ... illegally, are easily perceived as criminals who freely consent to engage in such work rather than as victims of coercive agents.[26]

On this basis, we might ask for the widest possible conception of 'victim', so that the latter may be included. Furthermore, we might consider what can be done for the consenting debtor to mitigate the effect of his or her apparent consent to exploitation. This will be discussed further at a later point in this chapter. Finally, we have Category E: 'the consenting participant'. According to Jones, there may not be a border crossing where this category is concerned, but there will be dire economic need that leads the individual to engage in exploitative labour in order to meet that need. These might be termed the 'economically coerced', which is discussed further below.

Jones states that: 'The consent and voluntary nature of the individuals in Categories D, E and perhaps C, shape their moral culpability and consequently encourage the apportionment of blame despite the harm suffered by the individual'.[27] Their moral culpability may indeed weaken their claim to victim-

24 See R Uy 'Blinded by red lights: why sex trafficking discourse should shift away from sex and the "perfect victim" paradigm' (2011) *Berkeley Journal of Gender, Law and Justice* 204–219.

25 Other problems may arise here as the smuggled person may be vulnerable to trafficking, as demonstrated in *R v N and LE* [2012] EWCA Crim 189, but for legal purposes that would likely be treated as a new situation of 'trafficking', which may be separate to the initial smuggling.

26 Jones 'Human trafficking victim identification' (n 13) 497.

27 ibid 499.

hood. Here and throughout this work, the idea that this moral culpability should always preclude victimhood is questioned. It is recognised that, although classifications of 'categories' such as those postulated by Jones are useful in a theoretical sense, they do little to address the central problem: that of correctly determining the presence or lack of consent in any possible trafficking situation. Neither do they go toward suggesting what to do with the 'consensually trafficked'; these categories simply seek to establish that certain categories should be seen as 'underserving' victims, and this chapter aims to challenge this.

Can we approach from a paternalist perspective the matter of what is to be done with a person who willingly places herself in an exploitative situation? 'Liberals would question ... why the desire to impose good welfare upon an individual should trump his right to autonomy.'[28] Trafficked and exploited persons are vulnerable and can be harmed, rendering them deserving of protection and assistance. If there is not sufficient certainty of consent, then its absence should be assumed.

We may find some support for a more inclusive approach in cosmopolitan literature.[29] This term has been used to describe a significant breadth of important views both in moral philosophy, and socio-political philosophy: '[t]he nebulous core shared by all cosmopolitan views is the idea that all human beings, regardless of their political affiliation, are (or can and should be) citizens in a single community'.[30] The central premise is contribution to the common good. Cosmopolitans argue for 'community' among human beings, with matters such as social and political affiliation being put aside: '[f]or some, what should be shared is simply moral community, which means only that living a good human life requires serving the universal community by helping human beings as such, perhaps by promoting the realization of justice and the guarantee of human rights'.[31]

In his work, Kant[32] argued that genuine world peace is dependent upon the self-organisation of states according to 'republican' principles. This involves *inter alia* respecting the human rights of foreigners as well as citizens of the state. This approach considers that individuals are right-bearing as 'citizens of the earth', as opposed to as citizens of particular states. The idea of moral community, the promotion of justice and the guarantee of human rights lends support to a more inclusive model of how we should deal with consenting (real or actual) exploited migrants.

28 Jones 'A beastly provision' (n 8) 4.

29 The word 'cosmopolitan' derives from the Greek word kosmopolitês ('citizen of the world'). Cynic Diogenes in the fourth century BCE apparently referred to himself thus: 'I am a citizen of the world [kosmopolitês]' (Diogenes Laertius VI 63).

30 *Stanford Encyclopaedia of Philosophy* 'Cosmopolitanism', first published 23 February 2002; substantive revision 1 July 2013 http://plato.stanford.edu/entries/cosmopolitanism/#2 (last accessed 14 February 2014).

31 ibid.

32 See S V Jones 'The ethics of letting civilians die in Afghanistan: the false dichotomy between Hobbesian and Kantian rescue paradigms' (2010) 59 *Depaul Law Review* 899 and I Kant 'Toward perpetual peace' (1795).

Vertovec and Cohen refer to the 're-emergence of cosmopolitanism' and states that this re-emergence 'arises by way of a proposed new politics of the left, embodying middle-path alternatives between ethnocentric nationalism and particularistic multiculturalism'.[33] The argument advanced later in this chapter for more sympathetic treatment of victims of exploitation draws upon such an approach and attempts to propose the beginning/recognition of a framework, in order to address the realities of trafficking and exploitative migration. Taking into account the effect of exploitative migration-related activity on the migrant, postulating 'moral' commitment to aid our fellow human beings here is perhaps not unreasonable, although unlikely to be politically popular.

The previous chapters have established that there is enough of a problem in determining lack of consent as to genuine victims, as in identifying them as such. This chapter focuses on how we might mitigate the treatment of misidentified victims or those who fall short of the formal trafficking threshold. However, 'freedom' and 'consent' should not be conflated. The following section explores the role of 'economic coercion' in trafficking and 'consensual' trafficking, in order to illustrate that idea that 'consent' may be given, but that, owing to, say, severe economic hardship, it might not be considered to be given in a manner that is 'free'. This may not be sufficient to render a consent sufficiently lacking for the purposes of the anti-trafficking regime, although since poverty plays a central factor in many situations of trafficking-related exploitative migration,[34] it is worth exploring the potential effect of severe economic coercion on the recognition of a person as a 'victim' or otherwise.

## 7.4 The role of economic coercion in trafficking and consensual exploitative migration

With regard to views that are heavily paternalistic as regards consent – particularly in a sexual context – Hernandez-Truyol and Larson note that: '[w]ith characteristic boldness, (MacKinnon) suggests that "rape law takes women's usual response to coercion – acquiescence, the despairing response to hopelessness to unequal odds – and calls that consent".[35] Coercion as more typically understood comes from an external agent, although those who suffer more greatly from poverty and lack of opportunity for economic gain will have fewer options than those who do not, and therefore less ability to exercise truly 'free agency', and instead 'acquiesce' or make a 'choice' in the face of hopelessness. It is difficult to

33 S Vertovec and R Cohen 'Introduction: conceiving cosmopolitanism' in S Vertovec and R Cohen (eds) *Conceiving Cosmopolitanism: Theory, Context and Practice* (Oxford University Press, Oxford, 2002) 1.

34 Hoyle and others refer to research by the Poppy Project in 2008, in which it was stated that 58 per cent of victims spoken to described themselves as being 'poor' or 'very poor' prior to being trafficked. See Hoyle, Bosworth and Dempsey 'Labelling the victims of sex trafficking' (n 17) 319.

35 B E Hernandez-Truyol and J E Larson 'Sexual labour and human rights' (2006) 37 *Columbia Human Rights Law Review* 391–445 citing C A MacKinnon *Toward A Feminist Theory of the State* (Harvard, 1991) 168.

view consent in such a situation as truly being 'freely' given. However, this may be insufficient according to present definitions, in order to invalidate consent and render the putative victim as formally trafficked.

Following the analysis in Chapter 3 regarding 'abuse of a position of vulnerability', it seems that there may indeed be scope for invalidation of consent where the exercise of authority of, say, a community leader is abused. Furthermore, where the trafficker(s) take advantage of the economic or social vulnerability of the victim in order to recruit him or her, there may also be the potential for ineffective or invalidated consent, although this may turn on the facts of each case. The use of abuse of a position of vulnerability based upon persuasive tactics (on the part of the trafficker) as regards the lure of good fortune in the sex trade abroad may be less persuasive to states than in the case where the 'victim' is already in a situation of exploitation – which may have been entered consensually at first – and is then subjected to abuse of a position of vulnerability or authority through economic-based threats or coercion, such as in the *Moir* case.[36] The use of such tactics in that case clearly rendered the 'consent' of the sex workers invalidated as it was not 'freely' given.

Can severe 'economic coercion of circumstances' serve to invalidate consent in an exploitative migration context? Furthermore, can a trafficker taking advantage of that person's economic vulnerability equate to an 'abuse of a position of vulnerability', as included as a 'means' element in the trafficking definition? The following sections will explore these questions.

### *7.4.1 The role of severe 'economic coercion of circumstances'*

It has been established that the body of persons who are trafficked or smuggled are unlikely to come from affluent backgrounds, where choice of, and access to, education and employment is abundant and free from the constraints of gender discrimination.[37] Persons from an economically impoverished country or area may have an effective lack of opportunity when it comes to education or employment, particularly if they are female, and therefore have no effective 'choice'. Such an oppressive situation might result in making the decision to be smuggled, trafficked or something between the two, but it cannot easily be said that the woman 'freely chooses' her fate. After all, 'it's better to go and earn money to spend than to stay home and starve'.[38] In 1994, a definition offered by the UN General Assembly acknowledged the potential role of economic hardship in the trafficking process: '[Trafficking is the] illicit and clandestine movement of persons … largely from developing countries with economies in transition …'.[39]

36 *R v Moir (Sharon Carol)* [2007] EWCA Crim 3317.

37 See ch 2.

38 S Skrobanek and others *The Traffic in Women: Human Realities of the International Sex Trade* (Zed Books, London, 1997) 91.

39 Report of the Special Rapporteur on Violence Against Women, its Causes and Consequences (1994) UN ESCOR E/CN.4/1997/47/Add.4 Commission on Human Rights, 53rd Session, Provisional Agenda Item 9(a) at 19 http://www.awf.or.jp/pdf/h0010.pdf (last accessed 11 January 2007).

Accordingly, the potential for recognition of 'economic coercion of circumstances' as a form of 'means' can be examined.

On the face of it, it is legitimate to recognise that: 'we do not treat an ostensible consent as invalidated simply because the agent was faced with a choice between unattractive options'.[40] Nonetheless, the role of extreme economic hardship in migration and trafficking situations should not be underestimated, as it has clearly a bearing on the decision to enter a migration/trafficking situation (and therefore has a bearing on the consent of the decision-maker). Indeed, full consent requires a rational and autonomous agent: '[t]he scope for self-determination afforded to the disempowered is radically reduced ... by informal mechanisms that render certain choices too costly – financially, socially, or personally – to be realistic options'.[41]

The Proposal for the recent EU 2011 Directive recognised that:

> Social vulnerability is arguably the principal root cause of trafficking in human beings. *Vulnerability derives from economic and social factors such as poverty*, gender discrimination, armed conflicts, domestic violence, dysfunctional families, and personal circumstances such as age or health conditions or disabilities. Such vulnerability is used by international organised crime networks to facilitate migration and subsequently severely exploit people by use of force, threat, coercion, or various forms of abuse such as debt bondage. In fact the high level of profits generated is a major underlying driver. The demand for sexual services and cheap labour is a concurrent driver.[42]

Nonetheless, some commentators are critical of the 'victim' stereotype. Murray holds that women are well aware of the terms and nature of their work when they opt to enter trafficking-related situations, and that 'false promises' are rare.[43] Others are of a similar opinion: that trafficking typically involves women who voluntarily migrate to a country that is more economically prosperous than her origin state.[44] Clearly, there is a tension between how these women – trafficked and smuggled prostitutes – are perceived by different bodies or persons.

40 D Beyleveld and R Brownsword *Consent in the Law* (Hart Publishing, Oxford, 2007) 126.

41 V E Munro 'Constructing consent: legislating freedom and legitimating constraint in the expression of sexual autonomy' (2008) 41 *Akron Law Review* 923, 930.

42 Proposal for a Directive of the European Parliament and of the Council on preventing and combating trafficking in human beings, and protecting victims, repealing Framework Decision 2002/629/JHA (CO (2010) 95 Final) 1.2 (emphasis added).

43 See A Murray 'Debt bondage and trafficking: don't believe the hype' in J Doezma and K Kempadoo (eds) *Global Sex Workers: Rights, Resistance and Redefinition* (Routledge, New York, 1998).

44 See, for example, N V Demleitner 'The law at a crossroads: the construction of migrant women trafficked into prostitution' in D Kyle and R Koslowski (eds) *Global Human Smuggling: Comparative Perspectives* (The Johns Hopkins University 2001) 257, 264. Similarly, empirical research conducted in Birmingham where police were interviewed regarding their thoughts on trafficked women found that the prevailing attitude was that they had consented (source: Statement by Sarah Garrat, Personal Communication on 14 February 2008, following research conducted by the Asylum and Immigration Research Team, Birmingham, into the treatment of victims of human trafficking once discovered in the destination state).

Beyleveld and Brownsword note that:

> … as relationships become less guided by paternalistic considerations or by status and, correspondingly, more guided by notions of individual freedom and right, the importance of consent will be increasingly voiced.[45]

Accordingly, if we are to follow a liberalist, 'autonomy' stance and recognise the ability and right to contract oneself into exploitative sex work (which this book does), then it is of utmost importance that true consent is present. Owing to the elasticity of the notion of consent, lack of valid consent – particularly in a coercive environment such as that of prostitution – is difficult to determine. Consequently, and somewhat paradoxically, then, a paternal and protectionist stance that requires a high standard of informed consent in order for the autonomous decision of the sex worker to be recognised as valid, is perhaps needed.

This tension merits enquiry into the motivations for consent. As Bhabha asks: 'How should coercion be characterised? Does someone with a gun to their head consent to hand over money when robbed? Most would say no'.[46] Such a choice is 'tainted by compulsion, undesirableness (in the sense that neither option is desirable) and threat'.[47] Bhabha goes on to consider this analogy in a migration context, and asks whether 'persecution, destitution, and … prolonged family separation constitute "guns" to the head'.[48] As regards different types of pressure and graduations of forced choice, it has been stated that:

> At one end of a spectrum, the pressure applied may be characterised as 'strong' while, at the other end, the pressure applied may be characterised as 'weak'. Operating with such a construct, we might characterise the gunman's threat to life as 'strong', threats to property (unless life-threatening) as less strong, and threats of a purely economic nature as relatively 'weak'.[49]

This reflects the more orthodox criminal law position, which would hold that 'economic coercion of circumstances' – although material to making a decision – does not invalidate consent. Coercion or compulsion as typically perceived would come directly or indirectly from another person.[50] However, it is clearly possible that someone who makes the choice to migrate in order to work in exploitative conditions is doing so simply as the result of a lack of other, meaningful or preferable choices, or perhaps as a consequence of a severe lack of options and dire economic circumstances.

45 Beyleveld and Brownsword *Consent in the Law* (n 40) 3.

46 J Bhabha 'Trafficking, smuggling and human rights' (March 2005) *Migration Information Source: Special Issue on Migration and Human Rights* http://www.migrationinformation.org/Feature/display.cfm?id=294 (last accessed 21 August 2007).

47 Beyleveld and Brownsword *Consent in the Law* (n 40) 128.

48 Bhabha 'Trafficking, smuggling and human rights' (n 46).

49 Beyleveld and Brownsword *Consent in the Law* (n 40) 139.

50 ibid 127.

Domestic and international prostitution debates highlight the difficult economic backgrounds of many who engage in it.[51] This can probably be applied to many trafficking victims of all kinds: male and female, sex worker or labourer of another kind. Consent can be seen through an overly generic lens; it does not come with uniform ease or quality, and individual situations may not always be taken into account. Beyleveld and Brownsword consider the effect of external pressure that is applied by a person (or 'agent') to the consenting party, and state that: '[a]ssuming that the external force or pressure is a causative factor in the choice made, this is the ideal-typical case of forced choice by reason of external pressure'.[52] Can this be transplanted into a context where either (a) the pressure comes from circumstances rather than an 'agent', or (b) where the agent indirectly takes advantage of the circumstances but perhaps does not directly apply external pressure? The former situation will now be addressed; the latter will be discussed in the subsequent section.

The majority of the 'means' listed in the trafficking definition would largely be seen as threats or actions coming directly from the trafficker, but, 'other forms of coercion' or 'abuse … of a position of vulnerability' have the potential to be more broadly interpreted. Full consent requires the actor to be fully autonomous. If the conditions for a valid consent require 'free agreement',[53] then 'an agreement secured by duress will not suffice'.[54] Could, for example, the potentially broad scope of the term 'coercion' include 'economic coercion of circumstances'; that is, the making of the choice to be trafficked, motivated by severe economic hardship, as opposed to coercion coming directly from the trafficker? This matter may have specific implications for the consent debate.

Several commentators support the position that 'economic coercion' should be included in the generic meaning of 'coercion' in the context of international trafficking instruments.[55] The Supreme Court of India in 1982 conceded that 'force'

51 See J Doezma 'Forced to choose: beyond the voluntary v. forced prostitution Dichotomy' in J Doezma and K Kempadoo (eds) *Global Sex Workers: Rights, Resistance and Redefinition* (Routledge, New York, 1998); L L Lim 'Whither the sex sector? Some policy considerations' in L L Lim *The Sex Sector: The Economic and Social Bases of Prostitution in Southeast Asia* (International Labour Office 1998); J Outshoorn 'The political debates on prostitution and trafficking of women' (2005) 12(1) *Social Politics: International Studies in Gender, State and Society* 141–55; N Lacey 'Beset by boundaries: the Home Office review of sex offences' (2001) *Criminal Law Review* 3; J Phoenix *Making Sense of Prostitution* (MacMillan Press, London, 1999); *Justis- og Politidepartementet* (Ministry of Justice and the Police) 'Purchasing sexual services in Sweden and the Netherlands: legal regulation and experiences, an abbreviated English version, a report by a Working Group on the legal regulation of the purchase of sexual services' (issued on 8 October 2004) http://www.regjeringen.no/upload/kilde/jd/rap/2004/0034/ddd/pdfv/232216-purchasing_sexual_services_in_sweden_and_the_nederlands.pdf (last accessed 11 July 2011).

52 Beyleveld and Brownsword *Consent in the Law* (n 40) 137.

53 See Scottish Law Commission *Report on Rape and Other Sexual Offences: Report on a reference under section 3(1)(e) of the Law Commissions Act 1965* (Scottish Law Commission No 209, 2007) paras 2.38, 2.10.

54 Law Commission *Consent in Sex Offences: A Report to the Home Office Sex Offences Review* (1998) para 2.10.

55 K Hyland 'Protecting human victims of trafficking: an American framework' (2001) 16 *Berkeley*

in the context of 'forced labour' could feasibly not only include physical force but also 'compulsion arising from hunger or poverty, want and destitution'.[56] (Although once again, the compulsion may be linked to the external agent, as opposed to coming from circumstances independent of any compulsion from a human being.) If it is to be accepted that trafficked victims come 'largely from developing countries with economies in transition …',[57] then consideration must be given to 'economic coercion' as an issue potentially vitiating consent, but bearing in mind that the circumstances of the particular incident will be decisive.

Spector notes that:

> The radical feminist sees the prostitute who appears to 'consent' to prostitution as so affected by systematic gender oppression that her choices are distorted – and even her sense of self shaped – by it. Whereas the liberal believes in the individual's ability to transcend her oppressive circumstances somewhat by making a rational decision to do the best she can, considering. And to choose to do the best one can, considering, is to be free.[58]

Liberal 'autonomy'[59] advocates do not see poverty as coercive, but more a factor to be taken into account when making an informed decision to improve one's material worth. However, if a person's economic situation is so dire that she feels impelled to make a certain choice, then that choice is automatically characterised as coercive,[60] although perhaps insufficiently for the purposes of the trafficking definition. Repeated involvement in trafficking could also be taken as evidence of the prevalence of 'economic coercion' in the decision to be trafficked, or at least to enter a situation of exploitative facilitated migration. Deportation or repatriation into a destitute and hopeless situation may not be the most desirable option from the perspective of the trafficked person, who may still be making more money in exploitative conditions in the host state than he or she would in destitute conditions at home.

If 'coercion' is to be accepted to include severe economic coercion of circumstances, then this would considerably narrow the band of people who could be deemed to have given consent in a trafficking context. Economic coercion

*Women's Law Journal* 29, 49; J Bhabha 'Reforming immigration policy: start by protecting rights, not borders' (2005) *Boston Review*. http://bostonreview.net/bhabha-immigration-policy.

56 *People's Union for Democratic Rights and Others v Union of India and Others* [1983] 1 SCR 456.

57 Definition offered by the Report of the Special Rapporteur on Violence Against Women, its Causes and Consequences 'Further promotion and encouragement of human rights and fundamental freedoms, including the question of the programme and methods of work of the Commission: alternative approaches and ways and means within the United Nations system for improving the effective enjoyment of human rights and fundamental freedoms' (1997) UN Doc E/CN.4/1997/47/Add.4 at 19 http://www.unhchr.ch/Huridocda/Huridoca.nsf/0/043c76f98a706362802566b1005e9219?Opendocument (last accessed 14 February 2008).

58 J Spector *Prostitution and pornography: Philosophical debate about the sex industry* (Stanford University Press, 2006) 426.

59 The autonomy v paternalism debate as regards prostitution is discussed in ch 4.

60 See J Bhabha 'Trafficking, smuggling and human rights' (n 46).

arguably renders the nature of the consent damaged; that is, consent given in these circumstances cannot necessarily be equated to free will, or 'free agreement'.[61]

Munro notes that:

> … critics have identified a tendency in certain strands of liberal theory to analyse social problems by removing actors from their everyday environment, stripping them of the characteristics and relationships that influence their choices, and placing them in a sterile legal world where complex dilemmas are resolved by detached models of distributive justice and invocation of self-interested and conflict-oriented claims.[62]

As has been demonstrated earlier in this work, trafficking or facilitated migration for the purpose of sexual exploitation (or exploitation per se) is contextual and involves coercive factors including *inter alia* poverty and lack of opportunity for economic gain. These factors influence the choices and the 'consent' of those who opt to migrate or enlist the services of a trafficker/smuggler. Consequently, any consent given here should be viewed in its own context as opposed to being applied as an abstract conception or standard of consent.

'Coercion' as a 'means' element of human trafficking features to varying extents in the domestic legislation of CoE Member States who have ratified the CoE Trafficking Convention. The provisions contained within the Convention have been implemented into the domestic criminal codes, or similar, of the ratifying countries. Albania, for example, ratified the Convention on 6 February 2007, and Article 110/a of the Criminal Code defines 'trafficking in persons' as:

> The recruitment, transport, transfer, hiding or reception of persons through threat or the use of force or other forms of compulsion, kidnapping, fraud, abuse of office or taking advantage of social, physical or psychological condition or the giving or receipt of payments or benefits in order to get the consent of a person who controls another person, with the purpose of exploitation of prostitution of others or other forms of sexual exploitation, forced services or work, slavery or forms similar to slavery, putting to use or transplanting organs, as well as other forms of exploitation.[63]

The English translation of the Croatian Criminal Code, Article 178(2), envisages the following 'means':

> Whoever, by force or threat to use force or deceit, coerces or induces another person to go to the state in which he has no residence or of which he is not

61 See Law Commission *Consent in Sex Offences* (n 54); Scottish Law Commission *Report on Rape and Other Sexual Offences* (n 53), which endorsed the same definition of consent as 'free agreement'.

62 Munro 'Constructing consent' (n 41) 928.

63 Criminal Code of the Republic of Albania art 110/a, English translation provided by legislationline.org, a legislative database published and maintained by the OSCE Office for Democratic Institutions and Human Rights http://www.legislationline.org/ (last accessed 3 March 2009).

> a citizen, for the purpose of offering sexual services upon payment, shall be punished by imprisonment for six months to five years.[64]

The relevant legislation in Cyprus envisages the following 'means':

> Force, violence or threats … fraud … abuse of power or other kind of pressure to such an extent so that the particular person would have no substantial and reasonable choice but to succumb to pressure or ill-treatment.[65]

None of these excerpts seems clearly to envisage economic coercion as being included in the 'means' element of human trafficking; the 'means' elements most clearly include direct measures coming from the trafficker, as opposed to coming from external circumstances. On the other hand, none of the provisions is phrased so as explicitly to exclude economic coercion.

In considering the potential to argue in favour of the recognition of severe 'economic coercion of circumstances' in a migration and trafficking context, one might look to drawing parallels with other areas of the law; most notably that relating to 'duress of circumstances', such as can be seen in the domestic legal approach.[66] As Simester and Sullivan note, '… it would be unacceptably draconian to punish persons who have acted to avoid catastrophic harm to themselves, to those to whom they feel attached or feel responsible'.[67] However, the force of the terminology used – 'catastrophic harm' – indicates that this principle is not easily transferable into a situation that is not necessarily readily recognised as reaching that standard. In an 'economic coercion of circumstances' context, such as is being explored here, the 'harm' caused by severe economic circumstances may be more difficult to categorise as comparably catastrophic to a threat of imminent death or serious harm caused directly or indirectly by another human being.

The domestic case law relating to duress of circumstances still indicates that the motivating factor comes from another person, albeit somewhat indirectly.[68] That is to say, the commission of an offence by A can be linked to some form of threat made by B. The threat need not be to A;[69] neither need it be dependent upon the commission by B of any specific offence, or indeed any offence.[70] A threat made by a person that creates circumstances which lead A to commit an offence is still somewhat different to the situation where A commits an offence owing to

64 ibid art 178(2).

65 Law No 3(1) of 2000 (Cyprus) *Combating of Trafficking in Persons and Sexual Exploitation of Children* (English translation provided by legislationline.org).

66 See, for example, A P Simester, J R Spencer, G R Sullivan and G J Virgo *Simester and Sullivan's Criminal Law: Theory and Doctrine* (Hart Publishing, Oxford, 2010) 734.

67 ibid 725.

68 See *R v Willer* [1986] 83 Cr App R 225 (CA), *Conway* [1989] QB 290 (CA) and *Martin* [1989] 1 All ER 652 (CA).

69 *R v Martin* [1989] 1 All ER 652 (CA).

70 See *R v Willer* [1986] 83 Cr App R (CA), *Conway* [1989] QB 290 (CA).

pre-existing circumstances that are not attributable in any way to a person, such as severe economic pressure.

A problem with any acceptance of economic coercion of circumstances as sufficient to constitute 'coercion' as part of the 'means' element of trafficking is that what is to be included in or excluded from this category is a matter of degree. At what point is a person sufficiently poor to be deemed to have been economically coerced? Economic hardship may be suffered that does not go far enough to constitute economic coercion in this context. Is financial difficulty sufficient, or does a person have to be on the brink of starvation? The latter may constitute 'catastrophic harm' but not in the way intended by orthodox criminal law. Can it be assumed that a person has been economically coerced based upon her country or area of origin, or does determination of this matter merit enquiry into individual circumstances? We are presented here with a potentially broad spectrum, and the practicalities of determining such issues are likely to be arduous.

It is recognised here that inclusion of 'economic coercion of circumstances' as a form of 'coercion' for the purposes of human trafficking is a very ambitious argument – this form of coercion may considered to be too much 'at arm's length'. This is not to argue for states to accept the commission of 'legalised immigration offences', but simply to ask that trafficking and smuggling be seen in their proper economic and social context, as economic hardship at home will, as has been argued, frequently feature at the beginning of the smuggling/trafficking chain.

This issue has to be approached very tentatively, as Kennedy recognises: 'If we cut back the rules far enough, we would arrive at something like the state of nature – legalized theft'.[71] Beyleveld and Brownsword ask:

> ... what do we say about those all-too-familiar cases where agents who are in extreme or necessitous circumstances are tempted by financial inducements or other forms of incentive to enter into deals which they would not seriously contemplate were it not for their indigent or exiguous circumstances? Are we seriously suggesting that such agents – say, organ sellers in the Third World or surrogate mothers or plea-bargaining defendants in the First World – thereby make unforced choices and give valid consents to the bargains into which they enter? Of course, we are not suggesting any such thing. The most that we are saying is that such transactions cannot be impugned simply because the choice made by the needy agent was given in response to an external element having a positive bearing on the agent's interests.[72]

Consent in the face of 'economic coercion of circumstances' is morally, if not legally, suspect. However, this may not be enough to invalidate consent as a matter of law – the tenacity of this argument must be acknowledged – 'the mere

71 D Kennedy 'Distributive and paternalist motives in contract and tort law, with special reference to compulsory terms and unequal bargaining power' (1982) 41 *Maryland Law Review* 563, 582.

72 Beyleveld and Brownsword *Consent in the Law* (n 40) 135.

fact that the consent was induced by positive pressure does not equate to a forced choice'.[73]

To revisit the conditions for a valid consent that were analysed in Chapter 4, can consent given in the face of extreme economic coercion of circumstances be considered to be freely given? Arguably, it cannot. However, to recognise this as a factor comparable with direct coercion from a trafficker, capable of vitiating consent, is asking for an extension – although not a wholly unprincipled one – of the criminal law. Realistically, this would not be accepted by states, which have a legitimate interest in protecting their borders against those individuals whom the states will simply view as economic migrants. Inclusion of 'economic coercion of circumstances' as a type of 'coercion' seems, therefore, to be somewhat of a tenuous concept, although inclusion of this category would benefit potentially vulnerable people and would go toward supporting the notion of consent as completely 'free agreement'.[74]

It is submitted here that two counter-propositions on the duress of circumstances question may be made. First, it is clear that duress of this kind is not ordinarily a defence to the criminal law and so would not protect the 'trafficked' victim from criminal liability with respect to immigration offences in the absence of specific, trafficking-related exceptions. Further, distress of economic circumstances is precisely what border security is designed to protect against – the movement of economic refugees. There is no evidence in general that states regard such people as anything other than illegal immigrants, susceptible to peremptory removal.[75]

This section has attempted (although admittedly has not yet succeeded) in sketching out a prima facie case for the extension of 'coercion' to include 'economic coercion of circumstances' so that the broadest possible notion of 'coercion' is used, which would clearly be of the most benefit to putative victims. Nonetheless, economic factors may simply be considered a material factor that influences the decision-making process of the smuggled/trafficked person, and therefore this is insufficient to invalidate consent. Physical pressure or duress would probably be viewed more sympathetically than personal economic or financial pressure.[76]

### 7.4.2 Abuse of a position of vulnerability

The UN Trafficking Protocol requires signatory states to try to alleviate factors that make persons, especially women and children, vulnerable to trafficking, such as poverty, under-development and lack of equal opportunity.[77] This could be construed to mean that poverty, economic difficulty and gender discrimination

73 ibid 136.

74 The definition suggested by the Law Commission 'Consent in sex Offences: a Report to the Home Office Sex Offences Review' (1998) para 2.10.

75 States sometimes make exceptions to the removal policy with respect to specific individuals (not technically refugees) on humanitarian grounds, and that a case may be made for something similar for smuggled women or 'consensually trafficked', on a case-by-case basis.

76 Beyleveld, and Brownsword *Consent in the Law* (n 40) 143.

77 UN Trafficking Protocol art 9.

constitute positions of vulnerability, as used within the trafficking definition. Such circumstances leave the individual open to abuse by the trafficker, who may take advantage of such a situation when recruiting potential victims, and use the economic vulnerability of the victim as a tool of persuasion. Accordingly, the knowledge of the trafficker (as to the 'victim's' position of vulnerability) would be relevant here.

Although economic hardship may be a factor in many instances of trafficking, the wording of the Interpretative Notes for the Official Records (*travaux préparatoires*) of the negotiation of the United Nations Convention against Transnational Organized Crime and the Protocols thereto[78] imply abuse coming more directly from the trafficker, although broad interpretation could lead to an alternative reading. We know from the *travaux* to the Trafficking Protocol that the phrase 'abuse of a position of vulnerability' is, from the perspective of the victim, 'understood to refer to any situation in which the person involved has no real and acceptable alternative but to submit to the abuse involved'.[79] This elaboration provides little explanation or qualification of the meaning of the phrase in question, which is open ended. Is the trafficker to be held responsible for: (a) the economic situation of the would-be victim; or (b) the taking advantage thereof? As to the first point, indeed he cannot be. As to the second point, the trafficking definition potentially has scope to include this. 'Force' can be treated as 'power-play on the part of the intervening agent that is designed to elicit the consent of the target agent'.[80] This is what takes place when the trafficker abuses the position of (economic and social) vulnerability of the victim.

The CoE Trafficking Convention Explanatory Report provides further illumination on the terminology:

> By abuse of a position of vulnerability is meant abuse of any situation in which the person involved has no real and acceptable alternative to submitting to the abuse. The vulnerability may be of any kind, whether physical, psychological, emotional, family-related, *social or economic*. The situation might, for example, involve insecurity or illegality of the victim's administrative status, economic dependence or fragile health. In short, the situation can be any state of hardship in which a human being is impelled to accept being exploited.[81]

As made explicit in the excerpt above, the Explanatory Report to the CoE Trafficking Convention recognises that vulnerability may be, among other things,

78 United Nations General Assembly 'Report of the Ad Hoc Committee on the Elaboration of a Convention against Transnational Organized Crime on the work of its first to eleventh sessions, Addendum, Interpretative notes for the official records (*travaux préparatoires*) of the negotiation of the United Nations Convention against Transnational Organized Crime and the Protocols thereto' (2000) UN Doc A/55/383/Add.1.

79 ibid 63.

80 Beyleveld and Brownsword *Consent in the Law* (n 40) 131.

81 Explanatory Report to the CoE Trafficking Convention, 83 (emphasis added).

social or economic.[82] The report goes on to state that a wide range of means, coming directly from the trafficker, must be contemplated, including 'abusing the economic insecurity or poverty of an adult hoping to better their own and their family's lot'.[83] Similarly, as regards the national definitions of human trafficking considered above, reference to 'taking advantage of social ... condition' in the Albanian Criminal Code could indicate that the trafficker taking advantage of the victim's dire economic circumstances could suffice as a more direct 'means' or form of coercion. Indeed, '[t]he lack of viable economic alternatives that makes people stay in an exploitative work relationship does not in itself constitute forced labour though it may constitute a position of vulnerability as defined by the Palermo Protocol'.[84]

The phrase used in the *travaux* to the Trafficking Protocol[85] is replicated verbatim in the text proper of the EU 2011 Directive,[86] as opposed to in any preamble, *travaux* or explanatory reports. This sets the Directive apart from the other two main instruments considered throughout this book, and is significant in that it brings the issue of 'abuse of a position of vulnerability' more to the forefront of the discussion of the scope of the 'means' capable of invalidating consent here. The 2002 EU Framework Decision also included specific mention, in the main body of the text, of the meaning of 'abuse of a position of vulnerability', using largely the same terms.[87] The preamble to the EU 2011 Directive states that: 'factors that could be taken into account when assessing the vulnerability of a victim include, for example, gender ...', thereby expanding upon previous instruments that have largely concentrated on other criteria as to what constitutes 'vulnerability', such as social or economic vulnerability. However, such criteria (that is, lower social or economic status linked to gender) are frequently not mutually exclusive.

Accordingly, these explanations (as to the meaning of 'abuse of a position of vulnerability) imply that a person may be vulnerable as a result of lack of economic opportunity or financial difficulties, or being rejected by their community for one reason or another. Consequently, they may be particularly vulnerable to persuasion or veiled coercion from traffickers and smugglers, and therefore agree to be transported and exploited in some manner. This indicates abuse of a position of vulnerability at an early, almost pre-trafficking stage – the beginning of the chain.

The recent Project Acumen report, compiled by the Association of Chief Police

82 ibid.

83 ibid 84.

84 B Andrees (International Labour Organization) 'Forced labour and human trafficking: handbook for labour inspectors' (International Labour Office 2008) 13 http://www.ilo.org/wcmsp5/groups/public/---ed_norm/---declaration/documents/publication/wcms_097835.pdf (last accessed 11 April 2011).

85 That abuse of a position of vulnerability is 'understood to refer to any situation in which the person involved has no real and acceptable alternative but to submit to the abuse involved'. See UN Doc A/55/383/Add.1.

86 EU 2011 Directive art 2(2).

87 2002 EU Framework Decision art 1(c).

Officers (ACPO), recognised 'economic reasons' to be a prevalent 'operational indicator' as a form of 'recruitment by abuse of a position of vulnerability' in trafficking amongst the sample of migrants used, thereby indicating abuse of economic vulnerability right at the start of the trafficking chain.[88] In terms of abuse of a position of vulnerability in this context, the abuse or coercion would be based upon the lure of money to be made, rather than the threat of money to be withheld. For various reasons, including the fact that the abuse took place in the country of origin, it may be difficult to show objective proof of abuse of a position of vulnerability in this context. This category of 'means' may be meant to be reserved for more arguably clear-cut cases such as those outlined in the opening paragraph to this section – the exertion of abuse and/or control by a community leader, for example.

Although used as a case study example here, there may be other external factors that influence the decision to migrate besides economic coercion, which may also be insufficient to constitute a 'means' element of trafficking, thereby rendering the individual subject to such explotation. Outside the formal definition of trafficking, in any case, we are left with a body of persons whose consent is questionable, for economic reasons or otherwise. These persons may have still experienced exploitation, perhaps in severe conditions. When we couple these persons with those who have been trafficked but misidentified as 'not trafficked', we have justification for considering what concessions may be made for the ostensibly 'consenting' trafficked person.

The analysis of 'economic coercion of circumstances' recognises that it is indeed difficult to sustain an argument that these migrants who are subject to severe economic coercion of circumstances should be treated as trafficked victims. Such a paternalist stance is somewhat extreme and not particularly fashionable; neither is it likely to have a positive reception from states upon whom the anti-trafficking regime places obligations. However, owing to the contextual nature of migration and trafficking and the role that economic hardship clearly has to play in the continuance of the phenomenon, it may be possible to retain a stance that recognises the autonomy of the 'consensually trafficked' (who have been subjected to exploitation of some form), although simultaneously to recognise the potentially highly vulnerable position of such persons, and to sketch out a prima facie case for such persons to have access to more favourable treatment than if they were simply viewed as economic migrants, in appropriate cases.

## 7.5 Recommendations for dealing with the 'consensually trafficked'

Betts states that: 'Two analytically coherent groups face threats to their human rights that require that they are not immediately returned to their country of origin but that they are identified and receive access to the specific forms of

88 Project Acumen: ACPO Migration and Associated Matters 'Setting the record' (n 2) 27.

international protection that they require'.[89] These are, first, migrants whose protection needs stem from conditions in the origin county, and yet which are unrelated to political persecution or conflict. They may have fled dire economic and social situations, but may not conform to the requirements of the 1952 Refugee Convention. Betts refers to them as 'distress migrants'.[90] The second category identified by Betts are irregular migrants who have protection needs arising as a result of their movement.[91] Their circumstances can change for the worse in a variety of ways in transit:

> The range of barriers to movement created by states to control migration, and the increasing importance of smugglers and traffickers, has contributed to making irregular migration treacherous. Irrespective of the reasons why a person left her country of origin, she may face threats to her human rights that emerge during the process of movement.[92]

Betts recognises that formally trafficked persons are not the only ones who may be in need of help: (a) stranded migrants may face particular vulnerabilities as a result of being caught in transit without any means to move onwards with their journey or back to their country of origin; (b) trafficked persons may face vulnerabilities that stem from being forcibly moved for purposes of exploitation; (c) victims of trauma and violence in transit may have particular needs that make it inappropriate to simply return them to their country of origin; (d) forcibly expelled migrants may face violence and human rights abuses in their host states or upon return to the country of origin.[93]

Beyond the reach of ordinary human rights law, can we ask for more for the ostensibly 'consensually trafficked'? The fact that the trafficking definition states that 'consent will be irrelevant where … (the "means" are used)' still potentially leaves room for consideration of cases where there is consent or at least the appearance of consent owing to lack of objective proof of coercion, that is, where consent may in fact be 'relevant'. It may be possible to sketch out a prima facie case for the 'consensually trafficked' to have access to more favourable treatment than if they were simply categorised as economic migrants. The bases for making this argument are various, and will be discussed in the following section.

### *7.5.1 The consideration of concessions for the 'consensually trafficked': can such an approach be justified?*

There are various rationales for considering the potential for concessions to be made by states as regards the 'consensually trafficked', who constitute a body

89 A Betts 'Towards a "soft law" framework for the protection of vulnerable migrants' Research Paper No 162 (New Issues in Refugee Research, UNHCR, 2008) 8.

90 ibid 8.

91 ibid.

92 Betts 'Towards a "soft law" framework for the protection of vulnerable migrants' (n 89) 2.

93 ibid 2–3.

of persons that can be viewed as being in a 'special position': that of 'more than smuggled', but 'less than trafficked'. Primarily, it is necessary to recognise the role that economic hardship clearly plays in situations of migration and trafficking, and this therefore cannot be ignored. Many smuggled or trafficked persons may have been 'pushed' to search out migration channels through severe economic need, or because the position of vulnerability resulting from their economic need has been abused by the trafficker.

Secondly, the issue that – as was demonstrated in Chapter 5 – the realities of the coercion/consent spectrum in a trafficking context are that determinations of consent/lack thereof (and therefore status as 'trafficked' or not) as regards each putative victim can be difficult and may not always be correct. There will be genuine 'hard cases' and there will be instances where those charged with identifying victims simply get it wrong and incorrectly identify an individual as 'not trafficked' when, in reality, she has been. Misidentification may occur for various reasons[94] – ineffective procedures,[95] preconceptions about the amount of 'voluntary' women,[96] potential discrimination on the basis of nationality (particularly in terms of third country nationals),[97] and Immigration quotas that have to be met.

Finally, that the conditions of 'exploitation' experienced by those identified as 'consensually trafficked' individuals (that is, those who fall short (or appear to fall short) of the 'means' threshold provided within the trafficking definition) may in reality be comparable to those experienced by formally trafficked persons. As noted by the Anti-Trafficking Monitoring Group:

> … one of the key problems is the incorrect application of the trafficking definition when assessing a victim. Too often the authorities fail to apply the (CoE Trafficking) Convention and do not define as victims all those who were subject to the crime of trafficking. Instead, the system creates a narrow, legally dubious, interpretation of a victim, and attaches conditions that have been proven to impede identification, and have also been found to undermine prosecution in some cases. For example, in numerous cases reviewed by the research, the authorities concluded that as the person concerned agreed to come to the UK for work, they could not have been trafficked despite the fact that the deception and abuse should, according to the Convention, render such consent irrelevant.[98]

94 Discussed in ch 4.

95 As evidenced by the cases of *R v O* [2008] EWCA Crim 2835 and Re *LM* [2010] EWCA Crim 2327, [2011] 1 Cr App R 12, [2011] Crim LR 425, discussed in ch 6.

96 As appears to be the case following research conducted in Birmingham, which identified that police there have preconceptions as to the level of 'complicity' of the 'victims'. See Statement by Sarah Garrat (n 44).

97 See Anti-Trafficking Monitoring Group 'Wrong kind of victim? One year on: an analysis of UK measures to protect trafficked persons' (June 2010).

98 ibid 12.

This research indicates that application of the current domestic system is indeed deficient, despite broadly incorporating the standards laid down and obligations imposed by the CoE Trafficking Convention. It also compounds the possibility that there is a proportion of misidentified victims who will have needs as regards support and assistance yet will not have access to it.

Furthermore, there is the issue of those who fall below the standards of coercion required by the trafficking definition – either through misidentification, or through genuinely (or ostensibly) not having been subject to a comparable level of coercion as a formally identified trafficked person. Jordan notes that: '[e]ven if a person agrees to work in very bad conditions, for very little money, with very little freedom, he would still be a victim of trafficking if the trafficker intended to hold him in debt bondage, involuntary or forced conditions'.[99] But, what if the trafficker did not hold her in debt bondage, or similar? These 'very bad conditions' alluded to still exist. Should we really, on an international legal level, deem this acceptable? True autonomy in a sex work context is the ability 'to say that (a woman) alone can define the nature of her relationships with others – except to the extent that the state is prepared to exercise its coercive regulatory authority by forcing her into, or redefining, such relationships'.[100] The situation of consensual exploitation resulting from facilitated migration may constitute such a situation; there may be, in order to achieve full protection of the exploited and vulnerable, a need for the state to 'redefine' such relationships and deal with the exploited 'victim' accordingly.

The figures relating to the identification of individuals discovered in the UK and identified as 'trafficked' vary significantly, depending on where the individual originates from. The Anti-Trafficking Monitoring Group Report has proven this,[101] as it transpired through the report's findings that a much higher percentage of UK nationals were positively identified as trafficked (in the UK) when compared with, in particular, third country nationals discovered in the UK.[102] The report goes on to state that:

> This research suggests the UK is creating a 'hierarchy' of victims, and allows, intentionally or not, discrimination against certain categories of victims, such as those who were trafficked before the Convention came into force (but identified after), or those coming from particular countries or regions. The research indicates that the system fails to treat those who have been trafficked as victims of crime and places too much emphasis on judging them, rather than bringing traffickers to justice.[103]

99 A D Jordan 'Annotated Guide to the complete UN Trafficking Protocol' (May 2002, updated August 2002) Ann D Jordan Director, Initiative Against Trafficking in Persons, International Human Rights Law Group, 11.

100 P H Schuck 'Rethinking informed consent' (1994) *Yale Faculty Scholarship Series*, Paper 2765, 901.

101 See Jordan 'Annotated Guide to the complete UN Trafficking Protocol' (n 99) 9.

102 ibid.

103 ibid 13.

States that have no wish to tolerate the continued presence on their territory of those they perceive to be economic migrants, nor to have any restrictions placed on their power of peremptory removal, have no incentive to be generous in identifying as putative victims those not formally victims of trafficking. These kinds of policies, which are common, do not bode well for the protection of some of those women who are certainly in need of it.

In assessing the reasons not to opt into the EU 2011 Directive, Damian Green stated that:

> … the European Parliament might propose changes to the draft Directive which could affect UK interests, such as expanding … *the support to be provided to individuals not yet identified as victims of trafficking* (emphasis added).[104]

Clearly, supporting those who ostensibly do not merit bespoke assistance is a somewhat touchy subject with the UK Government. Nonetheless, the ostensibly 'consensually trafficked' individuals clearly exist – the consensually smuggled and exploited sex worker, or the unfortunate who displays insufficient 'indicators' to be identified as trafficked, even though she may have been severely coerced. In fact, it has been reported by NGOs in Europe that:

> … traffickers use the work permits to bring foreign women into the Dutch prostitution industry, masking the fact that women have been trafficked, by coaching them to describe themselves as independent 'migrant sex workers'.[105]

Bakirci notes that trafficked persons are, first and foremost, victims and witnesses[106] – victims of exploitation and witnesses of the criminal activity that comprises the trafficking process. There are 'workers', trafficked victims and the 'consensually trafficked' and exploited individuals, who come somewhere in between. Those who are exploited through the sheer awfulness of the conditions of work – albeit to which they may have ostensibly agreed – are still victims and witnesses. Unfortunately, but realistically, they may also be criminals, particularly in terms of the voluntary breach of immigration laws, although any prosecution here should be discretionary and examined as to whether it is in the 'public interest'.

The evidence considered throughout this section and indeed this book points toward deficiencies in the identification system and possible discriminatory

104 House of Commons European Scrutiny Committee, Twenty-fourth Report of Session 2010–2011 (ordered by the House of Commons to be printed on 30 March 2011) 3.7 (emphasis added) http://www.publications.parliament.uk/pa/cm201011/cmselect/cmeuleg/428-xxii/428xxii.pdf (last accessed 1 June 2011).

105 J Raymond '10 reasons for not legalising prostitution' (2003) 2 *Journal of Trauma Practice* 315.

106 K Bakirci 'Human trafficking and forced labour: a criticism of the International Labour Organization' (2009) *Journal of Financial Crime* 160–65, 165.

treatment of putative trafficked victims. Consequently, it seems justifiable to consider specifically what concessions may be considered for the 'consensually trafficked'.

### *7.5.2 What concessions can justifiably be considered?*

States have a clear right to criminalise and to deport those non-nationals who unlawfully enter their territories. However, as the CPS Protocols show,[107] the power to prosecute[108] may be exercised under discretion and some discretionary factors affect those who are the victims of trafficking. It is suggested here that those discretions ought to be extended from beyond 'trafficked' women – it is, after all, 'sound utilitarian theory to confine the imposition of sanctions to circumstances where they will secure some benefit'.[109] This is not to argue for a policy of non-prosecution, but for a policy for prosecutorial discretion with respect to the 'consensually trafficked', to be considered on a case-by-case basis. Any reason for doing so is in answer to the humanitarian need of those engaged in the sex industry and takes into account the considerable difficulties of the definition of 'trafficking' and the evidential problems with respect to certain of its elements. It is conceded, however, that governments might not be easily persuaded to give the benefit of any doubt to a group of women, some of whom almost certainly will be 'mere' economic migrants.

Domestic case law underpins this point. In *Kibunyi*,[110] the appellant had initially been sentenced to 12 months' imprisonment for possession of false identity documents. It was argued for the appellant that: 'even if she were outside the trafficking definition, the circumstances as described were so close to trafficking as to constitute mitigation, so substantial that it causes her case to fall outside the conventional sentencing structure'.[111] This ground of appeal was dismissed,[112] as the appellant's 'indicators' (as to trafficking for exploitation) fell short of the 'exploitation' threshold that forms part of the trafficking definition and, on that basis, that she had therefore effectively agreed to commission of the immigration offence.

107 See Crown Prosecution Service 'Prosecution of defendants charged with offences who might be trafficked victims' and 'Prosecution of young defendants charged with offences who might be trafficked victims' http://www.cps.gov.uk/legal/h_to_k/human_trafficking_and_smuggling/ (last accessed 1 January 2014).

108 For offences committed as a result of having been trafficked, such as immigration offences – for example – possession of a forged passport or documents under Forgery and Counterfeiting Act 1981 s 5. The CPS guidance states that: 'Where there is clear evidence that the suspect has a credible defence of duress, the case should be discontinued on evidential grounds' indicating that there should be a causal link between the victim's offence and the action (of, say, coercion) of the trafficker. See Crown Prosecution Service (n 107).

109 Simester, Spencer, Sullivan and Virgo *Simester and Sullivan's Criminal Law* (n 66) 725.

110 *R v Kibunyi (Jacinta)* [2009] EWCA Crim 9, (2009) 173 CL & J 94.

111 ibid para 14.

112 In making this decision the court applied *R v Kolawole (David Oladotun)* [2004] EWCA Crim 3047, [2005] 2 Cr App R (S) 14.

The recently released Project Acumen Report[113] includes an analytical section that focuses on 17,000 migrant women working in the UK off-street sex sector. Their findings clearly identify a three-tier diaspora.[114] Of the 17,000 subjects, the report identifies 2600 as trafficked. This body of persons is identified by the report as 'highly vulnerable', and states that: '[a]lthough most are not subject to violence themselves, many are debt-bonded and strictly controlled through threats of violence to family members'.[115] The second category – consisting of 9600 women – are considered to be 'vulnerable'. The report notes that:

> Although they have elements of vulnerability to trafficking, most are likely to fall short of the trafficking threshold. They tend to have day to day control over their activities, and although they may have large debts, they generally do not consider themselves to be debt-bonded.[116]

The final category consists of 5500 women who are considered to meet the 'trafficked' or 'vulnerable' thresholds.[117] The report notes that there is no 'single story' as regards those involved in sex work: '[s]ome are subject to kidnap, rape and imprisonment, some enter the sector independently and are effectively self-employed within it, and others fit somewhere between these extremes'.[118] It is those who 'fit somewhere between' who are the chief concern of this book.

It has been discussed throughout this chapter that not only are there bespoke provisions for formally identified trafficked victims resulting from obligations placed on states by the anti-trafficking regime, but there are also options for international protection that are available to any human being in need of protection. This is the basis of a humanitarian and human rights-orientated regime that respects the dignity of the human. As noted earlier, those who fall short of, say, the strict requirements of the Refugee Convention criteria have recourse to various discretionary remedial concessions on humanitarian grounds, including exceptional rights to remain in the territory. These concessions acknowledge the potential for genuine 'hard cases', which discretionary measures mitigate, to a degree, without undermining the integrity and aims of the refugee regime.

A comparable humanitarian response to marginal or questionable cases of trafficked women, even of women who have not formally been trafficked but who have been identified as 'exploited' and/or 'vulnerable' to trafficking might be appropriate, in light of the circumstances in which these women are recruited into

113 Project Acumen: ACPO Migration and Associated Matters 'Setting the record' (n 2).
114 ibid 5.
115 ibid.
116 ibid.
117 The report states that: '[t]hese women were aware before leaving their home country that they would likely become involved in prostitution, live and work largely independently of third-party influence, keep a significant proportion of the money they earn and are not subject to debt-bondage or threats of violence'. See Project Acumen: ACPO Migration and Associated Matters 'Setting the record' (n 2) 5.
118 ibid 5.

the trade in humans and the severity of the conditions in which they find themselves in the destination states. Consequently, it is submitted here that individual governments may be able to adopt a more encompassing approach. This could include, for example, a policy parallel to a humanitarian right to remain, which complements the international anti-trafficking legal regime, as this would indeed constitute a response to the trafficking phenomenon that must be seen within context and addressed from a perspective that not only aims to criminalise the traffickers, but also to protect their victims. This parallel policy should include access – assessed on a case-by-case basis – to the bespoke rights currently available to formally trafficked persons, including the granting of rest and recovery periods and residence permits owing to the 'personal situation' of the 'consensually trafficked' woman.

Smuggled, and trafficked human beings, and victims of exploitation and abuse, were specifically recognised in the report of the Global Commission on International Migration (GCIM) in 2005 as having specific protection needs. How to address these needs in a way that will be politically acceptable is where the difficulty lies. Betts considers the need for a 'soft law' framework for the protection of vulnerable migrants.[119] If states offer what could be perceived as generous subsidiary protection, and to too broad a group, the fear is that this may lead them to take on a 'disproportionate protection responsibility'. Therefore, we cannot ask for too much, particularly in terms of 'hard' law. This is off-putting to states: 'In the current political climate, however, most states appear reluctant to commit to new formal multilateral agreements in relation to migration'.[120] But if we propose a 'soft law' approach with guidelines that point to appropriate treatment then this may begin to bleed through into practice. When taking into account the more accommodating provisions for victims that are offered in, for example, Italy, then we can see that not all are averse to tackling the exploitative migration phenomenon with a closed mind and with border protection as first priority. However, the fact that the domestic regime is currently failing genuine victims[121] does not bode well in terms of asking for more for those who fall short of victimhood for trafficking purposes. Nonetheless, the protection gaps – both for formally trafficked persons and the 'consensually trafficked' vulnerable migrant, are evident.

Betts notes that:

> International migration law offers a compendium of international legal obligations that relate to migration. Within this overarching framework, international human rights law, in particular, highlights a range of obligations that states already have towards vulnerable migrants.[122]

There are normative standards as regards migrant protection in situations that are not clear-cut, that is, humanitarian and discretionary leave etc. Let us point

119 Betts 'Towards a "soft law" framework for the protection of vulnerable migrants' (n 89).
120 ibid 5.
121 As discussed in ch 6.
122 Betts 'Towards a "soft law" framework for the protection of vulnerable migrants' (n 89) 3.

to them. The international community would not need to create new binding norms but could base the approach upon existing states' commitments according to international protection as discussed in the previous chapter. This mirrors the suggestion made by Betts.[123] Soft law development could lead to protective guidance for those vulnerable migrants who fall below the formal trafficking threshold. Non-binding standards may be the best we can ask for. Betts gives example of those countries that may often see people leave in search of asylum but who rarely meet the persecution threshold (citing the example of Zimbabwe). The UNHCR refers to these as 'neither/nor' or 'mobile and vulnerable' – it seems that we are seeing a parallel with failed trafficked victims and/or 'consensually trafficked' exploited persons.

In context, this book has established that the definition of human trafficking is technical and may be mechanical in its application. The unclear (or basic lack of) implementing legislation in the UK further muddies the waters, as does the use of 'indicators' by those charged with identifying victims,[124] such as the requirements of ostensible signs of physical or psychological harm or debt bondage, fear or anxiety and, as regards the testimony of the potential victim, in terms of whether elements of coercion, deception or threat are reported.

It was discussed in Chapter 3 that an ostensible consent does not necessarily equate to a genuine valid consent, and also that a valid consent can be difficult to establish. This, coupled with the clandestine nature of trafficking and exploitative activity having the potential to mask the coercive realities of some cases, paves the way for genuine consideration of adoption of policy that deals with borderline cases or where the individual is identified as having been exploited, or as 'vulnerable' to trafficking, on a case-by-case basis and which assesses the needs of those involved.

At the 'strong' end, this may go so far as, in some cases, to protect against peremptory removal, particularly where there is, say, the potential for retrafficking, or where the individual is clearly vulnerable and in need of assistance, such as psychological or basic health assistance. Where the individual case is borderline or unsure, a preferable position to adopt is that of a presumption of 'trafficked' as opposed to 'not trafficked', and at least minimum concessions as regards health treatment or counselling be considered for the 'victim' prior to any consideration of peremptory removal. This should not be interpreted as an open-door policy to consensual economic migrant sex workers, but instead as something more than simply a nod to the notion that there is not a clean line to be drawn – evidentially or factually – between the formally trafficked and 'consensually trafficked' individual.

In its Tenth Report, the JCHR noted that: '[m]any asylum seekers and refused

123 ibid.

124 Such as evidence of physical or psychological harm or debt bondage, signs of fear or anxiety, and whether the testimony of the potential victim includes elements of coercion, deception or threat. See Home Office/UK Border Agency 'Enforcement instructions and Guidance, Chapter 9 – identifying victims of trafficking' http://www.ukba.homeoffice.gov.uk/sitecontent/documents/policyandlaw/enforcement/oemsectiona/chapter9?view=Binary (last accessed 3 April 2009).

asylum seekers are vulnerable individuals who are reliant on protection and support from others'.[125] In the way that the system dealing with refused applicants is deficient, similarly this may be the case with 'refused' trafficked victims unless positive state action is taken to make some concessions where necessary and appropriate. Those who are not formally identified as 'trafficked' yet who have been subjected to awful conditions of work or who are unable to leave the UK for some reason (such as fear of reprisals from traffickers or smugglers) are the ones who will suffer.

At the 'weak' end, it may be desirable to amend or add to the anti-trafficking regime or at least pursue a 'soft law' framework in the manner identified by Betts, at least to provide for states to consider offering more favourable treatment to those who are borderline cases or are not formally identified as trafficked, although who are still in need of some form of assistance or support, using tentative language such as that used within the Trafficking Protocol as regards actual trafficked victims.[126] At the 'hard' end, the relevant instruments could be amended to include an obligation to provide a system – potentially skeletal – which assesses the individual needs of any migrant sex worker who appears to be vulnerable and who may (ostensibly or genuinely) fall short of the scope of the trafficking definition.

Of course, there is an issue as regards measuring a standard of 'exploitation' against accepted labour standards while the UK continues not to recognise sex work as a 'legitimate' (that is, formally legalised and regulated) form of labour, although this does not have to be an absolute barrier to the application of these standards. Victim protection of the 'consenting' trafficked victims currently has to be drawn from human rights, labour rights or a new, bespoke system. Since in the UK sex work is not legally regulated and 'legitimised', a bespoke system for dealing with exploited yet ostensibly consenting sex trafficking victims seems the preferable way to proceed. According to such a system, the needs of the individual victim – who can legitimately be referred to as a 'victim' owing to the exploitation suffered – could be assessed on a case-by-case basis that realistically takes into account the fact that coercion and sexual exploitation are very real problems, nationally and globally, which may be masked by the appearance of consent or the incorrect application of victim identification and assistance procedures.

## 7.6 Conclusion

The CoE Trafficking Convention defines a 'victim' in a trafficking context as '… any natural person who is subject to trafficking in human beings as defined in

125 Joint Committee on Human Rights Tenth Report (Session 2006–2007) 'The treatment of asylum seekers' 5 http://www.publications.parliament.uk/pa/jt200607/jtselect/jtrights/81/81i.pdf (last accessed 30 January 2011).

126 In that the state may 'consider' implementing more favourable provisions. See Council of Europe Convention on Action against Trafficking in Human Beings and its Explanatory Report art 6(3) (adopted 3 May 2005, entered into force 1 February 2008) Warsaw, 16.V.2005, Council of Europe Treaty Series No 197.

this article'.[127] The *Oxford English Dictionary* offers a range of definitions as to what constitutes a 'victim', including that of 'One who perishes or suffers in health, etc., from some enterprise or pursuit voluntarily undertaken,'[128] thereby suggesting that in a general sense, harm – such as exploitation – which results from even a consensual situation, does not preclude an individual being attributed some form of victim status and catered for accordingly. A wider conception of 'victim' in the context of exploitative facilitated migration is without doubt desirable and is, this chapter has argued, justified.

Beyond the formally trafficked, it has been argued that concessions may be made for the 'consensually trafficked'. This is not entirely unprincipled in the face of serious sexual exploitation that takes place on a global scale on a daily basis, and the fact that the question of consent/lack thereof will continue negatively to affect not only those who have been consensually transported and exploited, but also those who have in fact been formally trafficked.

It is necessary to make an explicit acknowledgement that arguing for further protection of women who fall outside the present trafficking frameworks (which may include some women who are simply economic migrants) is not likely to be a politically favourable cause at a time when many governments are trying to impose limits on entry and residence of non-nationals. The question is political because either we need new agreements (or unilateral national legislation) or the exercise of administrative discretions in favour of women in the 'grey area', neither of which may be forthcoming. However, the courts may not be wholly without the means to help – a more relaxed approach to the meaning of consent might be possible, perhaps; human rights obligations might be interpreted strictly, and so on, and ultimately, the political tide might turn. If a particular individual, who has been exploited, falls short of the formal definition of 'human trafficking', there is still unquestionably inherent value in intervention to help break the cycle of exploitation.

127 CoE Trafficking Convention art 4.

128 *Oxford English Dictionary* http://www.oed.com/ (last accessed 27 June 2011).

# 8 Conclusion

> [T]he problem of consent is unlikely to vanish whatever means are adopted to deal with it.[1]

## 8.1 Introduction

This research set out to investigate the legal nature of human trafficking, and it rapidly recognised the centrality of consent in the trafficking of women for sexual exploitation. Coercion and lack of consent are the essential elements to distinguish the trafficking of people from people smuggling. Once trafficking is established, a great deal follows – the criminality of the trafficker, the obligation of states to cooperate in anti-trafficking measures and the identification of victims of trafficking and specific measures for their protection, as a necessary condition for determining who are the victims of trafficking and how they should be treated. 'Consent', however, turns out to be a far from simple notion. The problematic nature of the inclusion of a 'means' or 'lack of consent' element of the definition of human trafficking is analysed and criticised in this body of work, first on the basis that consent is an inherently mutable concept, the absence of which is difficult to determine, and secondly, because inclusion of this element renders identification of trafficked victims difficult and creates a loophole in the protections offered to those who are transported and exploited.

Following the Introduction to this book provided in Chapter 1, Chapter 2 provided the contextual and legal background to set the scene for the remaining substantive chapters of the book. As a necessary starting point, Chapter 2 opened with consideration of the factors underlying the continuance of the transnational trade in women for sexual exploitation. This involved recognition of the point that, since a proportion of trafficking at least begins on a voluntary footing, the 'push' factors are the same as regards economic migrants, victims of human trafficking and those who have entered a situation of 'facilitated migration for the purpose of exploitation', that is, the 'consensually trafficked'.

The 'push' factors identified highlight the fact that voluntary and involuntary

1 J Temkin *Rape and the Legal Process* (2nd edn, Oxford University Press, Oxford, 2002) 176.

transportation into working in the sex sector takes place against a complex backdrop of socio-economic factors that underpin and perpetuate the global sex trade. The inquiry conducted in Chapter 2 provided a snapshot of these 'push' factors and other relevant issues such as the involvement of organised crime, in order to illustrate the contextual nature of smuggling and trafficking. Poverty, lack of opportunity, unemployment and gender discrimination feature highly in discourse surrounding migration push factors, and therefore play a central role in the continuance of the migration and trafficking phenomenon. These factors work together to render women particularly vulnerable to the exploitative transnational sex trade market.

The transnational aspect of human trafficking and the need to combat the spectrum of exploitative activities that it involves requires a comprehensive regime that targets traffickers and provides for victims. This was outlined in Chapter 2, which identified the central transnational criminal law and human rights anti-trafficking regime at a UN, CoE and EU level, and the corresponding obligations imposed upon the state as regards the criminalisation of trafficking offences, provision for prosecution and punishment, monitoring mechanisms and preventative measures, such as demand sanctions.[2]

Furthermore, and central to the book, the provisions relating to providing support, assistance and protection to victims were outlined in Chapter 2. These include the ordinary human rights obligations addressed to states as regards any individual (as opposed solely to trafficked persons) and also a brief outline of the bespoke provisions of the anti-trafficking regime that are directly applicable and available solely to victims of human trafficking. As was further discussed in Chapter 6, there is some variation as regards state obligations between the three main instruments considered in this book, and as discussed throughout the book, the 'lack of consent' requirement of human trafficking can render problematic the identification (and therefore the subsequent treatment) of victims.

As noted in the Introduction to this book, as with all transnational criminal projects it is necessary to begin with a comprehensive definition of the activity to

2 As regards demand sanctions, the corresponding UK provision imposes an evidential burden comparable to that located in the trafficking definition thereby creating the same problem of identifying who is, and who is not, a 'victim' in this context. Neither criminalisation nor regulation are particularly likely to reduce the demand for sexual services, yet opting for regulation ought to reduce exploitative conditions and the coercion/lack of consent issue as regards trafficked women may also be reduced, although it seems realistic to conclude that coercion/lack of consent will continue to play a part in the trafficking of women for sexual exploitation, and in turn traffickers and migration facilitators will play a part in meeting this demand. See, for discussion of these issues: J Elliott 'Criminalising the purchase of sexual services: the use of strict liability as a form of risk management?' in K Doolin, J Child, A Beech and J Raine (eds) *Whose Criminal Justice: State or Community?* (Waterside 2011); Home Office 'Tackling the demand for prostitution: a review' (November 2008); G Ekberg 'The Swedish law that prohibits the purchase of sexual services: best practices for prevention of prostitution and trafficking in human beings' (October 2004) 10(10) *Violence against Women* 118–218; V Clausen 'An assessment of Gunilla Ekberg's account of Swedish prostitution policy' (January 2007) http://www.sexworkeurope.org/site/images/PDFs/ekberg_kritik.pdf (last accessed 3 July 2008, link no longer live).

be targeted. Chapter 3 analysed the elements of the trafficking definition provided within the instruments considered throughout the book,[3] in terms of it being a tripartite process comprising an 'action', a 'means' and a 'purpose'.

The 'action', of recruitment, transportation etc is the least problematic aspect of the definition and is sufficient to cover all methods of – for want of a better word – obtaining the putative victim. It is established that, although theoretically the international instruments considered could cover 'internal' trafficking,[4] this may frequently be dealt with according to national laws. Furthermore, it is established that border-crossing need not be illicit.[5]

The 'means' aspect is the more recent and most controversial element of the definition. A wide range is envisaged, from direct physical force to psychological coercion, and the scope of the 'means' elements – which are not always wholly separable – is analysed. This element, which was not present in the previous relevant anti-trafficking instrument,[6] is problematic on the basis that the many and varied 'means' envisaged are open to varying interpretations, and it may at times be difficult to tell at which point on a spectrum of consent or coercion (or some other 'means') a particular case may fall.[7]

As regards the third element of the trafficking definition, the discussion clearly highlights that the central 'purpose' aspect of this phenomenon is 'exploitation', with the definition envisaging a non-exhaustive range of possible activities that are included, at a minimum, within the scope of 'exploitation', such as slavery, forced labour and the exploitation of prostitution. A specific section on the interrelation of treaty obligations justifies the use of international human rights law instruments to elucidate the meanings of the terms used where possible.[8]

Sexual exploitation, prostitution in particular, is the central focus of this book, and the discussion in Chapter 3 recognised that these exploitative activities are frequently treated as – but are not necessarily – separable: sex work may be capable of being viewed through a labour paradigm[9] and therefore as a form of labour[10] and, further, that this 'purpose' element of human trafficking, that is, sexual exploitation, can amount to slavery if the relevant conditions of the 1926 Slavery Convention are met. Clearly, therefore, human trafficking according to current accepted international legal definition consists of transportation into an exploitative situation (or the intention to exploit) against a backdrop of coercion or some other 'means', and therefore lack of consent.

3 The UN Trafficking Protocol, the CoE Trafficking Convention, and the EU 2011 Directive.

4 Bearing in mind the requirement of the UN Trafficking Protocol that the offences must be 'transnational in nature'.

5 To have such a requirement in place would be to render the legal instruments considered inapplicable to, for example, those trafficked within the EU.

6 Including the 1949 Trafficking Convention.

7 Where no such objective proof (of, say, coercion) is evident, this renders correct victim identification inherently difficult.

8 See ch 2.

9 B E Hernandez-Truyol and J E Larson 'Sexual labour and human rights' (2006) 37 *Columbia Human Rights Law Review* 391–445, 391.

10 That of 'sexual labour'.

Chapter 4 commenced with consideration of the basic conditions for a valid consent: that consent must be freely given; that it must be informed; that the consenting agent must have the capacity to consent; and that the timing of consent is a relevant factor. This section of the chapter explored and drew upon the meaning, role and effect of consent in different areas of the law, and drew conclusions that there are differences as to the effect of the giving of consent in different situations, and that a higher standard of free and informed consent may be required where the act consented to concerns physical integrity and close personal relationships as opposed to more arm's length commercial transactions. This analysis served to introduce and define the notion of consent, which is central to this body of work, at a sufficiently early stage in order to lay the foundations for specific analysis of the role of consent in human trafficking in Chapter 5, and to draw upon the different sources of the law discussed in this section of Chapter 4 in order to establish and justify why some are more persuasive to the argument maintained throughout the remainder of the book.

Furthermore, the 'autonomy v paternalism' approaches to consent in the context of prostitution and sexual labour are discussed and, although the autonomy of the consenting sex worker is recognised, it is considered that in situations such as where exploitative sex work is undertaken, there are limits to the justificatory scope of consent.

The legal response (to trafficking) also leaves open the matter of consent to prostitution and sexual exploitation on the basis that different states view these matters differently and, therefore, attempts to adopt a single approach, whether hostile or sympathetic to the prostitution aspect would in some instances stand in the way of ratification of the anti-trafficking instruments. Although some view prostitution as inherently exploitative, or as an act of violence against women,[11] prostitution itself is decriminalised or legalised in various states.[12] The argument is made that prostitution can indeed constitute a legitimate form of labour, in a philosophical if not always in a legal sense. However, since the evidence considered throughout the chapter points to a proportion (potentially high) of prostitution being forced or appearing to be consensual when it is in fact anything but, it is argued that the highest standard of consent should be required here.

The legal framework renders human trafficking an activity that is characterised by lack of consent (on the part of the putative victim), the role of which was considered in depth in Chapter 5. The controversial consent element goes against the grain of early international anti-trafficking instruments and leaves one with the impression that a central focus of the inclusion of this element was recognition of the rise in voluntary illicit migration, facilitated by globalisation, that is, improved ease of movement and communication. Indeed, the rise in such migration may have altered the face of trafficking as previously understood, and the legal response reflects this. To see trafficking merely as an aspect of economic migration does not provide adequately for victims of trafficking and severe exploitation.

11 As is the position in Sweden.

12 Such as the Netherlands.

Consent is transformative but it is also an elastic notion, uniform application of which is difficult to achieve. Furthermore, uniform application of this concept, which is not a normative or empirical constant, would not necessarily be appropriate in all situations anyway. The conditions for a valid consent that were discussed in Chapter 4 were revisited, and discussed in the context of human trafficking. The distinction is reiterated as regards consent to arm's length agreements and those that involve bodily integrity and/or personal relationships. The 'dichotomy' approach taken by some commentators to consent/coercion is rejected, and instead a notion of a spectrum of consent/coercion is recognised.

The central argument is therefore that, in a trafficking and migration context, there may in some circumstances be consent (or at least the appearance of it) on the part of the putative victim to transportation for exploitation, which means that these individuals may fall outside the scope of the trafficking definition. It follows from this that some women who are transported for sexually exploitative purposes or for prostitution may not be accorded the status of a trafficked 'victim', and that those who facilitated their migration into a situation of exploitation (for gain, therefore taking them beyond the scope of 'smuggling', at least in a moral if not in a legal sense) may not be prosecuted for trafficking.

There is, therefore, a loophole between smuggling and trafficking, according to the current international legal definition. Smuggling constitutes an 'action'.[13] Trafficking constitutes an 'action', a 'means' and a 'purpose'. The existence of ostensible consent (or lack of 'indicators', such as objective evidence of force) leaves the putative trafficked victim somewhere between the two: 'more than smuggled', yet 'less than trafficked'. In response to this loophole created by the definitions of smuggling and trafficking, it is proposed that the 'gaps' identified in the anti-trafficking regime be supplemented by an approach that restricts the effect of 'consent' on the status of the putative 'victim' and the potential for a defence to criminality on the part of the trafficker, who has nonetheless engaged in exploitative conduct.

Chapter 6 primarily critiqued the lack of a victim-centred focus in the UK anti-trafficking legislative regime, and went on to consider a more all-encompassing approach. This was followed by a critical analysis of the current victim-specific provisions of the three main legal instruments considered throughout this book.

The 'means' or 'lack of consent' element of the trafficking definition has been clearly established to cause difficulty in identifying victims. Although the difference between trafficking and smuggling can be difficult to maintain, it is submitted that not only may the current international standards for assistance and protection for trafficked victims be deficient, but also that the requirements of the

13 '[O]f transporting an individual from one location to another for 'financial or other material benefit' in art 3 of the Protocol against the Smuggling of Migrants by Land, Sea and Air, Supplementing the United Nations Convention against Transnational Organised Crime (adopted November 2000 by United Nations General Assembly Resolution A/RES/55/25, entered into force 28 January 2004) (Smuggling Protocol).

anti-trafficking regime have not necessarily been implemented and used to the best possible effect (from the victims' perspective) in the UK.

On the basis that valid consent can be so difficult to determine, it was argued in Chapter 7 that women who seek out the services of traffickers or migration facilitators because of lack of opportunity in the origin state, or for whom there is no ostensible coercion/lack of consent, should, in some cases, be treated as 'victims' and therefore entitled to some favourable treatment and/or protections in the destination state. There can be little doubt that this proposal will not appeal to destination states, who see these women in the same light as ordinary illicit economic migrants, who are not entitled to any special rights or protections in the destination state and who can therefore be subject to deportation. This would place the women firmly back in the category of 'smuggled' rather than 'trafficked' persons. However, to return to the point made above, they may still have been subjected to severe exploitation, which cannot be rendered justifiable by ostensible consent. Liberalist perspectives as to autonomy in the context of exploitative migration are considered, and it is concluded that a quasi-paternalist stance may be appropriate here.

This chapter considered in some detail the role of economic 'push' factors, as were outlined in Chapter 1, in terms of their influence on the decision to migrate, and the potential for recognition of 'economic coercion of circumstances' as a 'means' element is discussed. Women leave because of the pressure of economic circumstances – either because of the opportunity to better themselves economically or because their home situation is sufficiently dire to leave them no effective choice. This therefore places them at various points on a spectrum of economic coercion. The degree of severity of their economic situation renders it something from influential to severely coercive. Ultimately, it is conceded that states would not respond positively to such a departure from the norm, the orthodox criminal law position being that any form of coercion would necessarily have to come directly from the trafficker. Nonetheless, the role of economic factors in the decision to enter a smuggling/trafficking situation cannot be underestimated and clearly has a role to play in the consent/coercion debate, and accordingly traffickers/migration facilitators taking advantage of the most economically marginalised section of society in the origin states – that of women – may be capable of constituting 'abuse of a position of vulnerability', as contained within the trafficking definition.

This chapter explored what concessions may justifiably be offered to the 'consensually trafficked'. In response to the anticipated responses of states to taking such an encompassing approach, one can look to the treatment of those discovered in the destination state. Certain persons are entitled to certain rights and protections, in terms of, for example, protection against removal to a destination where there is a real risk of serious ill-treatment,[14] or protection against removal to a state where they will be subjected to persecution as a result of falling within the certain categories of persons recognised by the Refugee Convention. Certain

14 ECHR art 3.

obligations are therefore placed upon the state as a result of the provisions of the relevant instruments, such as the ECHR and the Refugee Convention.

There have been indications that refugee applicants and failed asylum seekers have been exposed to conditions that constitute violations of their human rights during the periods while they are awaiting decision or awaiting removal. These conditions are clearly not restricted to putative victims of human trafficking; they may affect anyone. Certain categories of persons may have particular needs that require particular treatment and responses, such as trafficked and sexually exploited women, who it has been demonstrated constitute a particularly vulnerable[15] body of persons, and remain so throughout the trafficking/exploitative facilitated migration process, whether or not they can strictly be deemed to have been coerced or to have given consent.

Furthermore, it was argued that not only should the widest possible interpretation of the 'means' element and the highest standard of consent be adopted so that the highest possible number of exploited victims may have access to the bespoke rights attributed by the anti-trafficking regime, but also that there is room for consideration of concessions to be made by states, considered on a case-by-case basis, for those who have been subject to exploitation but who fall short of the requirements of the technical trafficking definition. The global sex trade is gendered, and takes place against a backdrop of exploitation, and on a spectrum of coercion and consent of those caught up in it. These themes were explored as part of an attempt to address the central enquiry of the book. Nonetheless, it was recognised that there may indeed be reluctance on the part of governments to concede too much for the 'consensually trafficked.'

## 8.2 Conclusions: the way forward

The question of 'means' or 'lack of valid consent' highlights a category of persons who will have been determined – sometimes incorrectly – not to have been trafficked. Furthermore, the international anti-trafficking regime does not provide for those who have consented to be transported into a situation of exploitative sex work, although who have been subjected to an unacceptable level of exploitation. The voluntary undertaking of conduct does not, of itself, render it harmless, and should not leave the putative 'victim' beyond the reach of specific aid. Interpreted too strictly, the consent question may mean that traffickers have a defence and that exploited persons do not have adequate remedy for their treatment. As

15 On the point of state responses to the vulnerable subject, Martha Fineman states that 'Vulnerability is posited as the characteristic that positions us in relation to each other as human beings and also suggest a relationship of responsibility between state and individual. The nature of human vulnerability forms the basis for a claim that the state must be more responsive to that vulnerability'. Women who have been trafficked, or smuggled and exploited constitute a body of vulnerable persons to which the state owes some responsibility, and this should be reflected in the transnational anti-trafficking, anti-exploitation regime. See M Fineman 'The vulnerable subject and the responsive state' (2010) 60(2) *Emory Law Journal*, Emory Public Law Research Paper No 10-130 9.

regards those who are, by definition, trafficked, and also those who are so similar to individuals who have been trafficked or who have been misidentified as 'not trafficked', such differential treatment as is envisaged by the fallacious coercion/consent dichotomy, which is far from a clear-cut divide, cannot be easily justified.

As has been established, there is a distinction, well understood by the law in theory if not in practice, between smuggling people and trafficking people. A substantial group of such people are smuggled in order to work in the destination state. Some of these will know full well the conditions in which they will be working but are content to do so, even if those conditions would not be lawful in the destination state, for example with respect to minimum wage legislation and health and safety conditions.

These people may be driven by the pressure of economic circumstances in their home state, but this is not enough to affect their consent to the cross-border transfer (and nor will it affect their criminal liability for any immigration offences which they may commit). In some cases, the exact conditions in which they will be working are not explained to the persons involved – very poor wages, very harsh working conditions, high fees to gang-masters, de facto no right to leave the employment. Here, although it will be a case-by-case inquiry, we might sometimes conclude that the worker did not consent to be moved to these (exploitative) conditions, so that we should say that she had been trafficked, rather than smuggled. But to maintain the distinction between smuggling and trafficking, we should have to concede that the conditions must be very bad, approaching or even attaining those of de facto servitude. Not to do so would not accord with the claims states make to be able to remove smuggled workers forthwith, including those smuggled to conditions not compliant with national law (quite apart from the formal unlawfulness of an illegal immigrant working at all).

This is a distinction that is accepted for women transferred to work in the sex trade. This book has argued that some women consent to doing so, the transaction for them being not so different from the worker smuggled to pick vegetables or build roads. Such women could not, by reason of their trade alone, claim access to the benefits that would apply to the treatment of trafficked women (for whatever purpose but including the sex trade). The categories of 'willing' sex workers included those who made the economic calculation that this was a viable work choice (the 'Belles de Jour') and those who were motivated to travel by reason of their desperate economic plight at home, who also exist on a spectrum of 'choice'.

Just as for the vegetable picker, any failure by his employer to meet local labour standards was a matter for local law enforcement authorities and the worker's removal was a simple application of immigration law, so it should be for the sex worker. A problem, of course, is that prostitution is not, in the UK, subject to a comparable regime of work place regulation as most other trades, although some might say that the regulation and its enforcement against pimps and madams are sometimes harsher than they are against farmers and road builders. However, the immigration consequence is the same: the sex worker is liable to peremptory removal to her national state and to face the consequences of willingly breaching immigration laws.

Empirical studies show that the conditions of workers in the sex trade are more likely to reach those of exploitation than simple, mere illegality for a large proportion of those involved.[16] These awful circumstances are relevant in two different contexts. The first goes to the responsibility of the destination state. It has positive obligations to respond to servitude under human rights treaties, whatever the nationality (including its own) of the women involved. But it also has obligations with respect to foreign women, the deportation of whom may cause a return to the unacceptable conditions or subject them to a real risk of other harsh treatment in their national state, factors which should influence any deportation decision (although not necessarily their prosecution for immigration offences, if they were smuggled into the country).

However, the exploitative nature of their work may be relevant to another matter. It is hardly likely that any 'smuggler' would reveal these conditions to any woman seeking to be transported to another state, so that there would be no consent to the transaction: the woman would have been trafficked, not smuggled, and would be entitled to the protection provided by trafficking law, in addition to the protection of her human rights (which might include the application of the criminal aspects of immigration law to her). The evidence[17] seems to be that a significant proportion of women transported and who work in the sex trade fall into this last category, although there is no justification for saying that they all do. Even if one went so far as to say that all prostitution was exploitative (which this book does not), we might find that some women were prepared to accept this, so bad were their own conditions at home and, if they did, they would not have been trafficked.

Nonetheless, as regards those identified as formally trafficked, it appears the international regime relevant to these women is deficient, particularly in terms of implementation of the victim-centred obligations into the UK legislative regime. It has been identified that there are deficiencies in the UK NRM,[18] particularly in terms of the identification of victims, which clearly undermines the object and

16 See J Raymond '10 reasons for not legalising prostitution' (2003) 2 *Journal of Trauma Practice* 315; C H Hauge 'Prostitution of women and international human rights law: transforming exploitation into equality' (1995) 8 *New York International Law Review* 23; Home Office 'Tackling the demand for prostitution: a review' (November 2008); Home Office 'Paying the price: a consultation paper on prostitution' (July 2004); Eaves 'Men who buy sex: who they buy and what they know' (2009) http://www.eaves4women.co.uk/Documents/Recent_Reports/Men%20Who%20Buy%20Sex.pdf (last accessed 14 January 2014); L Brussa 'Survey of prostitution, migration and traffic in women: history and current situation' (European Union, EG/PROST (91) 2); M Coy, M Horvath and L Kelly (Child and Women Abuse Studies Unit) 'It's just like going to the supermarket': men buying sex in East London (2007) http://www.cwasu.org/filedown.asp?file=17242_LMU_Demand_Report_Text_screen-1.pdf (last accessed 1 January 2014).

17 See, for example, L Brown *Sex Slaves: The Trafficking of Women in Asia* (Virago Press, 2001), which is based upon an empirical study conducted by Brown and includes numerous accounts and excerpts of the experiences of trafficked victims and the deception and exploitation that they have experienced.

18 The Anti-Trafficking Monitoring Group 'Wrong kind of victim? One year on: an analysis of UK measures to protect trafficked persons' (June 2010).

purpose of the anti-trafficking regime. Mistakes have also been made as regards returning formally trafficked victims to the origin state where they were at risk of ill-treatment, such as retrafficking, on their return.[19] Misidentification can have severe adverse consequences for those who actually have been trafficked.[20]

Furthermore, lack of access to assistance and support for those who fall short of the threshold of the trafficking definition, yet who have still been subject to severe exploitation, creates an unacceptable situation where tolerance of consent to exploitation is evident. There is a need for a paradigmatic shift in attitude (by those involved in the victim identification regime) toward the trafficked victim or exploited migrant. Indeed, investigation into whether an individual is a putative victim of trafficking should take precedence over concerns regarding the individual's immigration status.[21]

In practice, it might be that the proportion of transported women working in the sex trade whose circumstances are exploitative is so great that we should reasonably accept a presumption that they have been trafficked and should be protected accordingly (even though local women working in the same conditions would have no similar, mandatory protection). If the state were able to rebut the presumption in a particular case, we might want to make the argument that the effect of the conditions of her 'work' and the uncertainty of the risk to the woman if returned to her national state were so great that, as a matter of humanitarian concession, the state should allow the benefits (or at least a minimum level of similar benefits) afforded to trafficked women on a general basis (analogous to the humanitarian right to remain sometimes accorded to failed refugee applicants). However, this would not necessarily be a matter of obligation for the state, which might very well want to retain its power to remove at once any foreign 'Belles de Jour' who came to its attention.

Along the same vein, the consideration of a policy of prosecutorial discretion as regards offences committed by the 'consensually trafficked' as regards, say, immigration offences, as is available for the formally trafficked, is suggested. Furthermore, it is considered that the policy of prosecutorial discretion as regards offences committed by victims identified as formally trafficked (and having been committed as a result of having been trafficked) should be a more definite and less discretionary policy of non-prosecution – it is difficult to sustain a 'public interest' argument in favour of prosecuting such persons in many situations.[22] It is,

19 See, for example, Alan Travis 'Sex trafficking victim wins substantial damages from Home Office' *The Guardian* (April 2011).

20 Such as in the case of *R v O* [2008] EWCA Crim 2835. Although it was decided pre-ratification of the CoE Trafficking Convention, this case is illustrative of the consequences of misidentification. See J Elliott '(Mis)Identification of victims of human trafficking: the case of *R v O*' (2009) 21(4) *International Journal of Refugee Law* 727–41; J Elliott 'Victims or criminals: the example of human trafficking' in Maria João Guia (ed) *The Illegal Business of Human Trafficking* (Springer, forthcoming 2014); *OOO et al v Commissioner of Metropolitan Police* [2011] EWHC 1246 (QB).

21 Home Office/UK Border Agency 'Enforcement instructions and guidance, Chapter 9 – identifying victims of trafficking'.

22 To reiterate what was said in the UK Action Plan on tackling human trafficking: 'It is difficult to envisage circumstances where it would be in the public interest to prosecute genuine victims of

however, more difficult to sustain the same argument as regards the 'consensually trafficked', who may have ostensibly consented or willingly flouted domestic laws.

It must be recognised that asking for such concessions, particularly as regards the 'consensually trafficked', may not be popular with states. The UK, for example, stressed that, as regards the decision whether or not to opt in to the EU 2011 Directive, that it was of great importance that the UK could 'still maintain control over our criminal justice system'.[23] This can be related directly to the preceding paragraph – the UK is clearly keen to avoid interference with its interests in terms of criminal law offences and corresponding sanctions.

The arguments advanced throughout this book are not intended to be about removing, undermining or threatening autonomy, or indeed about doubting the validity of human agency to give genuine consent. This is about recognising the tensions caused by the need to determine consent – or the lack of it – in an incredibly sensitive and potentially coercive situation which is, by nature, clandestine. Accordingly, this is about providing a response that takes all of those things into account, and properly provides for not only victims of trafficking, but victims of transportation into exploitation.

It is recognised that the arguments advanced throughout this book ask for a great deal. However, it is argued that such a position is justified, owing to the 'special position' of 'consensually trafficked' persons, whose conditions of 'work' may be comparably as bad as those faced by the formally trafficked person, or who may be misidentified as a consequence of failings of the authorities charged with identifying them. The type of changes requested for consideration are not uncontroversial and would, if deemed acceptable, probably take a very long time to be brought into effect, owing to such concessions being somewhat of a departure from the norm. However, these concessions are asked for solely within the isolated situation of ostensibly consenting transported and severely exploited individuals: it does not ask for an 'open door' policy for all smuggled sex workers.

The central focus of the anti-trafficking (and therefore anti-exploitation) regime should be exploitation, rather than consent. This book has argued that either consent should be deemed irrelevant, or – as is the preferred argument here – the middle category of persons who can be referred to as 'less than trafficked, more than smuggled' should be provided for by a bespoke system, considered on a case-by-case basis, so that victims are not left without access to necessary and appropriate rights and protections, and so that traffickers cannot rely upon consent as a defence to their criminality as a trafficker.

The destination state must tread carefully. Showing proof of coercion, determining the timing of consent and/or exactly what has been consented to may

human trafficking for immigration offences'. Home Office and Scottish Executive 'UK Action Plan on tackling human trafficking' (March 2007) 57.

23 Malcolm Harbour (West Midlands Conservative MEP), quoted in *The Kidderminster Shuttle* 'UK Government's opt-in to trafficking directive welcomed' (3 April 2011) http://www.kidderminster-shuttle.co.uk/news/8946640.UK_Government_s_opt_in_to_trafficking_directive_welcomed/ (last accessed 15 June 2011).

at times serve to make an arbitrary distinction between 'consenting' and non-consenting trafficked persons, when the reality is that the cases may be so alike that little purpose beyond immigration control (although an important concern on the part of the affected state) is served by treating these individuals differently.

# Index